RECASTING ISLAMIC LAW

RECASTING ISLAMIC LAW

RELIGION AND THE NATION STATE IN EGYPTIAN CONSTITUTION MAKING

RACHEL M. SCOTT

CORNELL UNIVERSITY PRESS

Ithaca and London

First published 2021 by Cornell University Press

ISBN 978-1-5017-5397-8 (paperback)
ISBN 978-1-5017-5398-5 (PDF)
ISBN 978-1-5017-5399-2 (epub)

Library of Congress Control Number: 2020950257

For Michael and Clea

CONTENTS

ACKNOWLEDGMENTS

Many people, some of whom have paid a high price for their political commitments, have directly and indirectly helped me with this book manuscript. Some of them have helped me in small—but nevertheless influential—ways and some in much greater ones. I am grateful to them all: Munir Fakhri ʿAbd al-Nur, Gamal ʿAbd al-Sattar, Ananda Abeysekara, ʿAbd al-Munʿim Abu al-Futuh, Waleed al-Ansary, ʿIssam al-ʿAryan, Muhammad Salim al-ʿAwwa, ʿAbd al-Muʿti al-Bayyumi, Nathalie Bernard-Maugiron, Tariq al-Bishri, Kent Blaeser, al-Amir al-Boraei, Brian Britt, Vivian Fuʿad, ʿAbd al-Hamid al-Ghazali, Najib Ghibrial, Muhammad Shahat al-Gindi, Carmen Gitre, Muhammad Habib, Rafiq Habib, Madeleine Hall, Milad Hanna, Manzoor ul Haq, Tom Hardwick, Fahmi Huwaydi, Elizabeth Shakman Hurd, Cornelis Hulsman, Muhammad ʿImara, Hilary Kalmbach, Samer al-Karanshawy, Bettina Koch, Abu al-ʿIla Madi, Elizabeth Struthers Malbon, Andrew March, Samir Marcos, Roel Meijer, Michael Munir, Muhammad Munir, Bishop Murqus, Ibrahim Najm, Ronald Nettler, Nicole Ni, Mohammed Pervaiz, Muhammad ʿAbd al-Fadil al-Qusi, Mohamed Ragab, Muhammad Salah, Hasan al-Shafiʿi, Abd al-Khaliq al-Sharif, Nadine Sinno, ʿIssam Sultan, Youssef Sidhom, Ahmed al-Tayyib, Bishop Thomas, and al-Qasabi Mahmud Zalat.

I would also like to thank all the staff at the Arab-West Report in Cairo for the important work they do, the staff at Leila Books in Cairo, along with the Interlibrary Loan staff at Virginia Tech's University Libraries. I would particularly like to thank all those whose published work I have cited and used. Their rich explorations have enabled me to write this book.

I am indebted to all the conveners, organizers, and participants of conferences at which I have presented portions of this work and which often gave me considerable food for thought: "New Directions in Middle East and North African Studies 2 Symposium" at Northwestern University, 2012; "Egypt and the Struggle for Democracy" at Georgetown University, 2014; "Religious Heterodoxy and Modern States" at Yale University, 2014; "Arab Citizenship in the New Political Era," organized by the Norwegian Centre for

Human Rights and the Middle East and North Africa Research Group, Ghent University, held in Rabat, Morocco, 2014; the joint symposium on religion and politics between Virginia Tech and the University of St. Andrews, 2016; and "Status and Justice in Law, Religion, and Society" at Washington and Lee University, 2019. I also thank the participants and organizers of the panels at which I presented portions of this work over the years at the Middle East Studies Association and the American Academy of Religion. Additional thanks go to the organizers and participants of the ASPECT Working Papers Series at Virginia Tech.

Research for this project was enabled by the Dean's Faculty Fellowship, College of Liberal Arts and Human Sciences, Virginia Tech, the Virginia Tech Humanities Summer Stipend, and the National Endowment for the Humanities Summer Seminar, "The Study of Religion: Past and Present," University of Virginia, July 2011.

Brill publishers has allowed me to use a revised version of a book chapter: "Citizenship, Public Order, and State Sovereignty: Article 3 of the Egyptian Constitution and the 'Divinely Revealed Religions,'" in *The Crisis of Citizenship in the Arab World*, ed. Roel Meijer and Nils Butenschøn (Leiden: Brill, 2017), 375–405. I also thank Routledge for permission to include a revised version of a section (267–71) of a book chapter on "The Golden Age and the Contemporary Political Order: The Muslim Brotherhood and Early Islam," in *Routledge Handbook on Early Islam*, ed. Herbert Berg (Routledge, 2017), 258–73.

My gratitude goes to all the editors and staff at Cornell University Press, especially Karen Carroll and Susan Specter for their careful editing. I am particularly grateful for Jim Lance's continued support and faith in this project. The anonymous reviewers at Cornell University Press generously gave up their time to review this manuscript, and their comments and feedback have made this a better book.

I am especially grateful for the support of my father and parents-in-law, Tom and Brenda, without whom I would not have had the necessary time to begin, continue, and complete this work. Lastly, I thank my husband, Michael, and my daughter, Clea, for quite simply everything. I cannot sufficiently express how fortunate I am to have you both by my side supporting me with such loving willingness.

Note on Translation and Transliteration

I have used a modified version of the IJMES system of transliteration. The only diacritical marks used are those to denote the Arabic letters ʿayn (ʿ) and hamza (ʾ), although the initial hamza has been dropped. Ulama and sharia are treated as Anglicized words and have no markings. I have transliterated the names of individuals and places whose English name is not well known, but have used the English version for names and places that are well known in English, such as Nasser, Sadat, Shenouda, and Tawadros. I make a small number of concessions to Egyptian pronunciation of these names by using the "G" instead of "J" and sometimes modify the vowels. When the main source for a person's writings is an English source, or when the person is relatively well known in English according to particular transliteration, I have deferred to that source's transliteration of the name as opposed to using my own.

Readers might notice inconsistency in the transliteration (including capitalization) of names in the footnotes. I consult a range of Arabic and English texts. If the source is in English, I have used the spelling and capitalization of the name as it is found in that source. In the case of Arabic texts, I have transliterated the name according to the modified IJMES system above and have capitalized according to the Chicago Manual of Style. Where the citation or quotation includes another author's transliteration I have endeavored to be faithful to that author's transliteration.

I have cited the source in the language in which I consulted that source. Unless otherwise noted, all translations from sources listed in Arabic—including the constitutional articles—are my own.

RECASTING ISLAMIC LAW

Introduction

In the aftermath of the 2011 uprising against the three-decade-long rule of Egyptian President Hosni Mubarak, a striking mural appeared on the external wall of one of the former buildings of the American University in Cairo. In it, a figure in black, holding something that looks like a rosary, attached to which are the symbols for Judaism, Christianity, and Islam, appears to be bowing before a pharaonic figure. This pharaonic figure, which is accompanied by a leopard, is reminiscent of the paintings of men that appear on ancient Egyptian reliefs. To the left of the mural is the word "ta'addab" or "Be polite!" The mural is one of a large number of pieces of graffiti that appeared on walls and buildings around Tahrir Square following the ouster of President Mubarak. The graffiti was painted and drawn by multiple artists and included images of those killed in the uprising as well as pictures and slogans protesting the brutal actions of the Supreme Council of the Armed Forces. Such art formed a response to—and commentary on—the revolution of 2011 and the violence and power struggles that took place before the counterrevolutionary coup of 2013.

In this particular picture, a man, who appears to represent religion in Egypt in a generic sense, is bowing before a symbol of ancient Egypt that predates and transcends the three religions. Ancient Egypt is often invoked as something that binds Egyptians together and is therefore often used as a symbol for Egyptian nationalism and the Egyptian state. The picture suggests the artist's desire for religion to submit before Egyptian national identity. It seems to say that religion's submission to Egyptian nationalism and the Egyptian state is the appropriate basis on which Egypt should form its political future. Notwithstanding the complexity involved in reading artistic intention, the mural represents some kind of commentary on the question of the relationship between religion and politics in postrevolutionary Egypt. Such a question has always been deeply fraught. This was particularly the case during and after the stalled so-called Arab Spring.

Art was one way in which Egyptians tried to capture and define the relationship between religion and politics. Another way Egyptians attempted to delineate this relationship was through law, specifically through the writing and rewriting of constitutions. Constitutional debates, constitutional writing, and the annulment of constitutions featured consistently in the political discussions that took place after the ouster of President Mubarak. Constitutional debates became the main focus of different political constituencies—nationalist, Islamist, liberal, and secular—that jostled to shape the postrevolutionary order.

This book charts the relationship of the religious to the political as evidenced in Egypt's constitutions since the late nineteenth century, with particular attention paid to the most recent two (2012 and 2014). In postrevolutionary Egypt, key political players—including the Muslim Brotherhood and other Islamist groups; secular, socialist, and liberal parties; members of the former National Democratic Party; al-Azhar; the military; and the Coptic Orthodox Church—all presented their views on what the future of Egypt should be like. Views on the appropriate relationship between religion and politics involved debates about what the source of legislative and judicial authority should be; who has the authority to speak for the sharia (premodern Islamic law); and what aspects of the sharia should be applied in the modern Egyptian state. The relationship of the religious to the political also included answering questions about what role Egypt's Coptic Christian minority would have in the postrevolutionary order; how this role would affect other religious minorities, such as Baha'is; and the extent to which the Coptic Orthodox Church would continue to represent Coptic Egyptians as a community. Important also were the role of women and the family and the extent to which Egyptians should be treated as individual citizens or as part of familial structures and religious communities.

In these discussions, the question of what role the sharia should or should not have took central stage. Here, I am using the term the "sharia" as opposed to the broader English-language term "Islamic law," in order to distinguish the sharia from what I term modern Islamic state law. The sharia refers to the law that encompasses premodern jurists' law, rooted in the multivalent tradition of the four Sunni schools of law. The full scope of the sharia is impossible to capture. As Wael B. Hallaq has shown, the sharia is a colossal project: the sharia consists of "a hermeneutical, conceptual, theoretical, practical, educational, and institutional system."[1] In premodern Islam, the sharia, as jurists' law, was distinct from the law of the ruling polities. At the same time, it was connected to and informed by the needs of governance.

The status of the sharia in the modern Egyptian legal system is a complex question. The common narrative is that, in the nineteenth century, the sharia was relegated to the sphere of family law and the Egyptian legal system was based on Western, mainly French, law for its civil and criminal codes. The turn away from Ottoman and Islamic sources was in part due to the influence of colonialism, but was also due to the fact that Egyptians wanted to establish a judicial system that centralized state power. Egypt emerged from the nineteenth century with the sharia having become mostly limited to the sphere of personal status law, which encompasses marriage, divorce, inheritance, and guardianship. It was not until the Constitution of 1971 that the sharia was given a greater role in other aspects of Egyptian law. Since then, Egypt's Supreme Constitutional Court has taken a cautious and flexible approach regarding the extent to which it has allowed the sharia to influence other aspects of modern Egyptian law.

Discussions of the role of the sharia in postrevolutionary Egypt were based on an enduring binary that constantly pitted the secular and the Islamist as diametrically opposed entities. Islamist groups such as the Muslim Brotherhood and the Salafis desire to make the Egyptian legal system consistent with Islamic legal norms. Islamists are unified by their wish to see Islam expressed politically. Yet they differ over what kinds of political rights and duties such a political expression of Islam would entail. Such a vision of Egypt's political future is often set in opposition to the vision of what are termed secular parties, which are much less strident in their desire to see Islam influence Egyptian politics.

The binary between the Islamist and the secular was used by different parties in the constitutional debates to legitimize themselves and delegitimize others. The Constitution of 2012 was delegitimized within much of the Egyptian press—as well as within the Western media and academia—by claims that it was Islamist. The 2012 Constitution was decried as Islamist with reference to clauses that were seen as leading to the establishment of the sharia as state law. For example, there were many claims that the 2012

Constitution undermined the equality of women. Opponents of Article 10, which emphasized the importance of the Egyptian family, maintained that it consigned women to the domestic sphere. The 2012 Constitution was also criticized for being detrimental to the principle of legal equality because of Article 3, which stated that "the principles of the religious laws of Christian and Jewish Egyptians are the main source for the legal regulation of their personal status affairs, their religious affairs, and for the nomination of their religious leaders."[2] Part of Article 4, which stated that the Council of Senior Scholars should be consulted in matters pertaining to the sharia, was singled out as leading Egypt in the direction of a religious state, or a theocracy like that of Iran. Narratives that framed the Islamist nature of the constitution as troubling evoked a particular conception that posited a binary between the religious, often deemed as retrograde, antimodern, and unsupportive of human rights, and the secular, which is often defined as modern and democratic.

The delegitimization of the 2012 Constitution as Islamist laid the foundation for the removal of President Muhammad Mursi—a member of the Muslim Brotherhood—in 2013 and the establishment of a new constitution in 2014. The Constitution of 2014 was praised as secular, tolerant, rational, and civil. The Cairo Institute for Human Rights Studies praised the new constitution as a positive development in citizenship rights.[3] The International Bar Association stated that "Egypt is turning a corner in 2014, and the new constitution provides a solid basis for this fresh start."[4]

This is not to deny that there were important differences between the Constitution of 2012 and the Constitution of 2014. For example, Article 44 of the 2012 Constitution which stated that "insulting or opposing all messengers or prophets is forbidden" was removed from the Constitution of 2014.[5] Yet, while the 2014 Constitution was lauded for its secular—and therefore modern and democratic—nature, it had a number of important continuities with the Constitution of 2012. Zaid Al-Ali, the senior adviser on constitution building for the International Institute for Democracy and Electoral Assistance (IDEA), stated that the draft of the 2012 Constitution "is not as controversial as many people assumed it would be. For better or worse, it is generally in line with Egyptian constitutional tradition."[6] Al-Ali contends that many of the controversial articles in the constitution were "merely leftover provisions from the 1971 constitution."[7] In addition, a number of the controversial clauses that related to Egypt's minorities, women, and to the religious scholars, continued—either in full or in partial form—in the Constitution of 2014.

This book cuts across the polarity between the Islamist and the secular that characterized legal debates to analyze the complex effects of constitutional commitments to the sharia. In speaking of constitutional commitments to the sharia, I refer to articles in the constitution that specifically mention the sharia and those that are seen as implicitly related to the sharia. I maintain that constitutional commitments to the sharia have caused the sharia to be recast in modern Islamic state law. I use the metaphor of recasting to imply that, when articles relating to the sharia are inserted into the constitution, the result is that much of the material and substance of the sharia is reused, while that substance is molded into a new form. The new form that the norms of the sharia take is defined by the needs of the modern nation state.

Of course, the sharia is not in itself a fixed body of law. It is a multivalent tradition, central to which was "open-ended argumentation," as Brinkley Messick has shown.[8] When the sharia is applied as modern Islamic state law, some aspects of this multivalent Islamic legal tradition are brought to the fore, while other aspects are deemphasized. Modern Islamic state law is therefore characterized by a myriad of shifting continuities and discontinuities with the sharia. As a result, neither religion nor politics emerges as dominant, but each is consistently brought to bear upon the other.

In showing the particular forms that the sharia takes when it is applied as modern Islamic state law, I push back against an underlying assumption that introductions of the sharia into modern state law result in some kind of revival of medieval Islam. This assumption was popularly encapsulated by Graeme Wood, for example, in describing ISIS as "very Islamic," since, he claimed, the "religion preached by its most ardent followers derives from coherent and even learned interpretations of Islam."[9] In making a neat connection between learned interpretations of Islam and ISIS's application of those interpretations, Wood missed a consideration of the ways in which those interpretations of Islam are changed when they are applied by the modern state. Current academic scholarship on Islam is not immune from the view that the sharia is immutable and inflexible. Islamist movements also replicate this assumption. In calling for an ideal past to be retrieved, they underestimate the extent to which reviving the past irretrievably changes it. This book illustrates the unsustainability of such assumptions by explicating the complex and varied relationships that modern Islamic state law has with its premodern antecedents.

More importantly, however, the book's engagement with the question of the effects of constitutional commitments to the sharia also complicates some excellent scholarship from the last decade that has emphasized the ways in which modern secular power has transformed the sharia and drawn it far away from its premodern antecedents.[10] Modern Islamic state law, such a perspective holds, is primarily a product of the modern nation state or of secular power. From such a perspective, modern secular power is invested with a far-reaching determinism to impact the forms that modern Islamic state law takes. In emphasizing the ability of modern secular power to transform law, at times one is left wondering what it is precisely that the modern secular state is being contrasted to. For example, Andrew March critiques the binary that Hussein Ali Agrama draws between the understanding of *hisba* in the sharia and its incarnation in modern Egypt. Hisba refers to the individual or collective duty to intervene to command what is good and forbid what is wrong. Such a binary, he states, "feels heavily scripted" and strongly stated.[11] Khaled Fahmy has also critiqued Agrama for delineating a fundamental disparity between premodern hisba and hisba in modern Egypt by portraying hisba in the premodern context as disconnected from state power and violence.[12] Likewise, the late Saba Mahmood's emphasis on the secular state as being responsible for the intensification of interreligious conflict and for the increasingly precarious situation of minorities is in danger of leading to a binary by which the Ottoman or premodern legacy is pitted against the modern.[13] In a similar vein, Wael B. Hallaq contends that the Islamic state is an impossibility and a contradiction since the sharia is, he argues, incompatible with the positive law of the state and its sovereignty. In the modern period, he maintains, the sharia was effectively "dismantled" and "eviscerated" and then *"re-created* according to modern expediency" (Hallaq's italics).[14]

Considering modern Islamic state law's discontinuities *and* its continuities with premodern sharia, this book suggests that the sharia is not so much eviscerated by the modern state when it is applied as modern Islamic state law, but is rather recast in its service. More specifically, however, it explicates those discontinuities and continuities through definite empirical examples. An explicit engagement with the granular nature of such change is called for and provided by a close reading of four different case studies to illustrate the precise and subtle ways the sharia is recast through— and brought to bear upon—constitutional commitments. Change does not work in a unitary way, but often takes multivalent directions. Such change often carries the legacy of the past with it. Employing a broad historical scope and engaging deeply with premodern law and the Ottoman legal and political legacy illustrates the means by which the present inherits—and departs from—the past.

Thus, modern Islamic state law contains ideas and concepts derived from the sharia, but such ideas and concepts have been reshaped into a different form. The form that this takes is dictated by the needs of the modern Egyptian state. Just as Nimer Sultany has shown that revolutions maintain "varying levels of legal rupture and continuity with the pre-existing legal order," this book illustrates the specific ways in which the sharia, when attached to constitutional commitments, becomes modern Islamic state law.[15] Modern Islamic state law constitutes neither a break from nor a continuation of what went before, but is rather the result of a recalibration of legal norms derived from the sharia.

Constitutional commitments recast the sharia in a way that involves the recasting of premodern debates about religious and political authority and the role of the ulama of al-Azhar (chapter 4) and the formation of particular forms of inclusion and exclusion for Egypt's religious minorities (chapter 5). They also involve an altered conception of the relationship between the sharia and the concept of the public interest in relation to women's rights (chapter 6) and the reshaping of the nature and extent of personal status law for Egyptian Christians (chapter 7).

One of the striking things about Egypt's history, and about the revolution of 2011–13 in particular, was how constitution writing and debating featured so prominently. Constitution writing was invested with defining and answering fundamental questions about the identity of Egypt and about the will of the people and of the nation. In these events, the constitution was not seen dispassionately as a document for managing the internal workings of governance and of various institutions of the state. The amount of energy and political capital that was expended on constitutional articles was perhaps disproportionate given the extent to which constitutions are actually adhered to. The vitriol and misrepresentation of particular constitutional articles that occurred in Egypt in the aftermath of the Arab Spring suggests something about the power of constitutions. The most recent Egyptian constitutions were invested with a kind of power that transcended their particular articles. This occurrence indicates that constitutions mark important moments when society and the state look backward in terms of understanding how the present is the sum total of the past. They also look forward in the sense that they reflect how key figures who have captured the state at that moment envisage how it will develop in the future.

All constitutions—in shoring up the power of the modern nation state—undertake to manage the relationship between religion and politics. In thinking about constitutions in such a way, this book draws upon recent theorizations of secularism that see secularism not so much in terms of the absence of religion but in terms of a particular position toward religion itself.[16] Such theorizations have framed the secular as the way in which the state manages and intervenes in religious affairs, along with seeing the parameters for this management and intervention as subject to renegotiation.[17] As Hussein Ali Agrama maintains, defining the relationship between religion and politics is at the heart of the modern state and such a definition is a constant, ongoing process.[18] Both Islamic and secular constitutions function in this way.

Constitution debating, constitution writing, and laws and public attitudes informed by constitutional articles show how the state manages the relationship between religion and politics. Constitutions represent moments when the state manages and defines who is the minority and who is the majority and what the relationship between the two is.[19] Constitutions involve the state defining who has religious authority and what sphere religion should inhabit. They also represent the attempt to mold what citizenship and national culture are. The modern nation state needs to define a nation's particular cultural commitments and to speak in the name of the national will that it claims to represent. While the extent to which constitutions—and those interpreting them and applying them—manage religion varies, they are unified by this common project.

In looking at how constitutions delineate the relationship between religion and politics, I draw on constitutional articles, constitutional and political debates, party and governmental and nongovernmental manifestos, along with legal cases and documents, interviews, Islamist political tracts, and on Islamic political and legal theory. I examine not just constitutional articles, but also the idea of constitutions, their function, their role in contemporary Egyptian politics, and the charged discourse surrounding these constitutions. Tamir Moustafa has called for investigating the "radiating effects of law" in the sense of looking beyond the direct effect of legal decisions to examine the ways that courts provide a platform from which activists can assert broad claims about Islam and the role of the state.[20] I do this with constitutions in Egypt.

Discussions of constitutions in the Middle East have tended to focus on the extent to which constitutions advance democracy, the balance of powers, and human rights.[21] Some work on Islam and constitutions has investigated the concept of Islamic constitutionalism in Islamic political theory, in terms of Islamic understandings of human rights, equality, and the separation of powers.[22] Nimer Sultany has addressed the role that constitutions have played in revolutions and in legitimizing new regimes in the Arab Spring. He shows that constitutions worked to institutionalize and entrench the emerging political order and that "constitutions in particular exemplified both law's centrality and its contradictions."[23]

While questions of democracy, human rights, and political legitimacy are important, what we need to examine more closely is the role of constitutions in defining national culture and, following from the work of James C. Scott and Timothy Mitchell, making the state and the citizenry representable and readable.[24] Here, I ask the reader to think about the way constitutions embody an expression of the goals and aspirations of the nation. Hanna Lerner contends that such a "foundational aspect of the constitution has been generally neglected by studies in comparative politics."[25] Constitutions function to craft national culture and fashion citizenship in the service of the state. When Islamic legal norms derived from the sharia are attached to constitutional commitments, Islamic legal norms are utilized—and partly altered—by the constitution's role in fashioning citizenship and crafting national culture.

In the study of religion, law and constitutions have not figured prominently, in part because law is assumed to be separate from religion. However, Moustafa argues that "legal institutions play important roles in *constituting* struggle over religion" and in adjudicating debates over the role of religion.[26] He contends that "law and courts do not simply stand above religion and politics. Instead, they enable and catalyze ideological conflict."[27] Winnifred Fallers Sullivan has shown how law's entanglement with the question of religion is at the heart of the modern state. The US Constitution institutes freedom of religion through the First Amendment. Sullivan has shown that American courts must decide what counts as religion and what religion is.[28] Law in Egypt faces a similar challenge: under a constitutional commitment to the sharia, the Egyptian courts must decide what gets to count as the sharia and who gets to speak for it.

This book is divided into two parts. The first part, chapters 1 through 3, provides a theoretical and historical look at constitutions, national culture, secularism, and the sharia. The second part, chapters 4 through 7, looks at individual case studies that illustrate the broader claims made.

Chapter 1 calls for a closer look at the significance of constitutions for thinking about how national culture is crafted and the ways that citizenship is fashioned in the service of state formation. Engaging with recent theorizations of secularism that view the secular as the state's project of defining the relationship between religion and politics, the chapter calls for rethinking the way that the concept of Islamism is commonly framed. When constitutions—whether they appear secular or Islamist—undertake to manage the relationship between religion and politics, Islamic legal norms are recast in the service of the modern Egyptian state.

Chapter 2 investigates the history of the sharia and addresses the nature, scope, and underlying philosophy of premodern sharia and its presumed relationship with the state. While complicating the narrative that the sharia is incompatible with state law, it addresses the extent to which premodern sharia is conceptually different from modern state law and contends that contemporary Islamic states which seek to apply the sharia as state law encounter a number of challenges. The chapter then looks at aborted attempts to codify the sharia in the nineteenth century and attempts to reintroduce the sharia through constitutional commitments in the latter part of the twentieth century.

Chapter 3 surveys constitution making and writing in Egyptian history and shows how constitutions in Egypt have formed an inherent part of the ending of old political orders and the making of new ones. Constitution making has become inextricably bound up with the ongoing making and remaking of Egyptian nationalism. Constitutions are a means by which the state makes itself legible to its citizens and in so doing lays out the social and political expectations that the state has of its citizens, as well as the expectations those citizens have of the state. The chapter examines the commitments that Egypt's constitutions have made to religion, Islam, and the sharia.

Chapter 4 addresses contemporary debates about the locus of Islamic legal authority, about who gets to speak for the sharia, and about the relationship among Egypt's legislative bodies, the Supreme Constitutional Court, and the ulama of al-Azhar. The chapter argues that such debates, while echoing their premodern antecedents, reflect a recalibrated conceptualization of the relationship between the sharia and the state. While tensions over the role of al-Azhar vis-à-vis the state and legislative authority have a number of parallels in premodern political theory, one of the ways in which this tension manifests itself in contemporary Egypt is in struggles over the distinction between what is Islamic and what is non-Islamic. After the revolution of 2011 such a distinction was a mechanism by which al-Azhar and the Muslim Brotherhood tried to establish their own spheres of authority and limit those of others.

Chapter 5 examines how the principle of the "heavenly" or the "divinely revealed religions" has become a key component of Egyptian nationalism. As a result, Islam and Christianity have become more deeply intertwined through the utilization of the concept of "divinely revealed" in contemporary Egyptian nationalism. While the nationalization of the concept of the divinely revealed religions has formalized the difference between the heavenly and the nonheavenly religions, in this chapter I call for complicating the assumption that the modern secular state has necessarily intensified interreligious conflict. Rather, I contend that the concept of the divinely revealed religions has created new forms of inclusion and exclusion by connecting Judaism, Christianity, and Islam, and by excluding other religions in the process.

Chapter 6 illustrates the way in which the concept of the family has become entangled in modern constitutional debates about the religious or the secular nature of the constitution. Women's rights and the family came to be used as a delegitimizing or legitimizing tool in debates about the Constitutions of 2012 and 2014. The chapter shows how constitutional debates about the family and women's rights elucidate a particular conception of the relationship between state, society, and law. Those identified as Islamist have adopted a deep and pervasive understanding of the role of the state by supplementing and moving beyond the specific regulations of the sharia in order to represent the interests of the governed.

In chapter 7, I argue that the judicial autonomy of non-Muslims over personal status law has taken on a particular dynamic since the 1950s. While discussions of the so-called *millet* system have often assumed that this system meant that non-Muslims were left alone and had considerable autonomy, this chapter shows that the nature of this negotiation in contemporary Egypt is predicated on a new dynamic, in which non-Muslims are free to apply their own law only by way of exemption from national law. As a result of the promulgation of Article 3 of the 2014 Constitution, a number of Coptic Christians are seeking to negotiate an exemption from Islamic inheritance law. One of the consequences of the negotiation of this exemption is that Copts are articulating differences between Christianity and Islam—and therefore between Christians and Muslims in Egypt—on questions of gender.

All four of the chapters in Part II address the specific ways that Egyptian constitutions delineate the relationship between religion and politics. Just as the mural mentioned earlier represents one vision of what the relationship between religion and politics should be, this book examines the myriad ways in which this relationship plays out in the lives of contemporary Egyptians.

PART I

Constitutions and the Making and Unmaking of Egyptian Nationalism

CHAPTER 1

Constitutions, National Culture, and Rethinking Islamism

In 2013 the Egyptian economist and political commentator Galal Amin complained that the problem besetting Egypt was that some organizations, particularly the Muslim Brotherhood and the Salafis, wanted to subvert the "natural place of religion" and return Egypt to the "middle ages."[1] Religion, he declares, "is a part of life but it is not life in its entirety."[2] Bringing religion out from its natural place into the public sphere, Amin maintains, would lead to sorrow and distress, and would jeopardize the rights of Egypt's Coptic Christians. Political Islam, he continues, prevents Egypt from undergoing a national and cultural revival: for religion to be a means of such a revival, it must remain in its proper place.[3]

The conception that religion needs to be kept in its proper place, and that what that proper place is can be readily understood by reasonable members of the populace, underscores modern secularist assumptions about the nature of religion. Such assumptions about religion see any calls for politicized religion such as Islamism as a subversion of the modern natural order of things. In this chapter, however, I argue that Islamism should not be seen as an antimodern aberration that does not respect the proper place of religion. Islamism should rather be seen as a political movement that has been molded by the concerns of the modern state. Both Islamists and secularists have a shared concern with delineating the relationship between religion and politics. Both seek to renegotiate the relationship between religion and politics and impose their vision of such a relationship on modern state structures, even if Islamists see that relationship as more heavily colored by Islamic norms.

Seeing Islamists and secularists as engaged in a similar project draws upon more recent theorizations of secularism. Such theorizations view secularism as the state's project of promoting an abstract notion of religion and its ongoing involvement in managing religion. Both secular and Islamist constitutions share statist perspectives that hold that it is the right of the state to decide what place religion should occupy and the kinds of rights and obligations that should be given and expected accordingly. This is not, however, to deny that there are differences in how constitutions and states, commonly defined as secular or Islamic, determine such boundaries and the rights and duties they attach to these norms.

One of the ways in which the relationship between religion and politics is defined is through constitutional texts and laws that are promulgated based on those constitutional texts. Constitutions often demarcate the relationship between religion and politics and determine who gets to speak for—and represent—both. Constitutions also establish the relationship between religion and national culture and claim to represent the will of the nation.

Constitutions are most often analyzed through the lens of their capacity to guarantee democracy and human rights. However, they should also be understood in terms of their power as foundational ideological statements. Constitutions reflect how national culture and its relationship to religion and to particular religious traditions are crafted. They therefore can be seen as the way that citizenship and its relationship to religion are fashioned in the service of state formation. The modern nation state is predicated on certain homogenizing concepts, such as national culture and the idea of the national will. Through them, the state legitimizes its claim to represent its citizens. Drawing on the work of Timothy Mitchell and James C. Scott, this chapter demonstrates that constitutions are a means by which modern states represent themselves as objectlike, to be viewed, rendered legible, mapped out, and understood. This applies to how the state wishes to be understood by members of its population and by other nation states.

Constitutions, Ideology, and the Modern State

During the late nineteenth and twentieth centuries, promulgating a constitution was an accepted norm in modern politics. Earlier views of democracy in the eighteenth century emphasized the importance of the rule of the majority and constitutionalism was seen as less democratic since it placed limits on the government.[4] However, Hanna Lerner shows that, "today the idea of a fundamental transformation of a political regime or the creation of a new one, whether by revolutionary means or otherwise, that does not involve the drafting of a new constitution is unthinkable."[5] Almost two hundred countries have written or codified constitutions. A small number have not.[6]

Nathan Brown claims that "scholars stopped studying constitutions [more than a generation ago] because they increasingly seemed quixotic: if political authority was to be constrained, it would not be done with mere pieces of paper."[7] Constitutions, he argues, do not reflect political reality. This is certainly the case in contemporary Egypt, where Egyptians are frequently arrested without a warrant, interrogated without a lawyer present, tortured, and detained for indefinite periods without charge.[8]

The relationship between a constitutional text and the interpretation and application of that text in law is a complex one. For example, Catharine A. MacKinnon shows that constitutional commitments to gender equality do not relate to the equality of the sexes in reality. Norway and Australia have some of the highest international rankings regarding gender equality, yet the former has no commitment to equality between men and women in its constitution and Australia has no formal written constitution.[9] Furthermore, many countries with the lowest gender-equality rankings in the world—such as Malawi—have substantive provisions guaranteeing gender equality and equal rights for women and men.

Another reason for the contemporary popularity of constitutions is that constitutions are often seen as inherent to the concept of the rule of law, which is concerned with impeding the exercise of arbitrary power.[10] Constitutions are commonly created to limit the arbitrary use of power since they provide a supralegal framework. Constitutional rules are different from ordinary legislation because they are, Lerner points out, "accorded higher status since they regulate the rules of the game, and determine the procedures by which ordinary laws can be enacted."[11] Thus, constitutional rules are less vulnerable to the will of governments for the reason that the amendment of constitutional articles is more involved than the writing of new legislation.

Rule *by* law does not itself guarantee the rule *of* law.[12] In many states, law can actually facilitate the exercise of authoritarian power. An example of this relates to the amendments that were made to the Egyptian Constitution of 1971 in 2007. While these constitutional amendments were presented by the Egyptian state as leading to the strengthening of the rule of law, in fact they further entrenched authoritarian practices in the Egyptian order. Thus, while the Egyptian state ruled through the law, it was not a democratic state that protected civil liberties.[13]

Nathan J. Brown maintains that constitutional rules do not simply restrict power but enable it. Constitution writing of the late eighteenth century, he argues, empowered governments. Indeed, there is no causal relationship between either constitutions or constitutionalism and democracy. Brown contends that constitutions in the Arab world have generally been written in such a way as to increase the power of political authority as opposed to limiting it. In addition, while constitutions and constitutionalism are often platforms for the establishment of human rights, it is not inevitable that such provisions be included.[14]

The possibility of guaranteeing human rights and for providing the rule of law cannot therefore alone account for the important role that constitutions play in modern political systems. Constitutions must also be seen in terms of their power in the foundation of a new political order. For the Romans, Hannah Arendt asserts, the source of authority lay in the foundation of Rome and in its ancestors. Central to Roman politics was "the conviction of the sacredness of foundation, in the sense that once something has been founded it remains binding for all future generations."[15] She contends that the act of revolution remains, in Western political history, the type of event for which the notion of a foundation is imperative. Like the Romans, Arendt argues, "Machiavelli and Robespierre felt founding was the central political action, the one great deed that established the public-political realm and made politics possible."[16] Revolutions, she claims, are attempts to repair foundations and "to renew the broken thread of tradition."[17] In the American Revolution, the founding fathers established a new polity, and the constitution confirmed and legalized this act of foundation.[18] Reverence for the US Constitution has transformed the document into a "sacred symbol of nationhood."[19] It founded the state and embodied the aspirations of a particular sector of society.

Ulrich Preuss claims that constitution making is the power to create a political order ex nihilo. Constitution making is a revolutionary act that both consolidates the achievements of the revolution and puts an end to the revolution that made the constitution possible. The relationship between the revolution and the constitution is therefore "ambivalent," since "the constitution is the final act of the revolution."[20] Yet constitutions continue to be important beyond the time when they are formed. While the moment of foundation remains the source of the constitution's legitimacy, the constitution also serves to provide a map of the relationship that the state is to have with its citizens. The new constitutional order depends on articulating who constitutes the nation and what its political values are.

Timothy Mitchell argues that, "in the metaphysics of capitalist modernity, the world is experienced in terms of an ontological distinction between physical reality and its representation."[21] This distinction between reality and the modes by which reality is represented involves envisioning society as a political and conceptual structure that is separate from people themselves. Nineteenth-century Europeans were concerned with the representation of things, with guides, signs, maps, or sets of instructions.[22] Mitchell shows that, when Egyptians visited Europe in the nineteenth century, everywhere they went, "everything seemed to be set up before one as though it were the model of the picture of something."[23] Everything was arranged before an observing subject into a system of signification. In the colonial process, Mitchell argues, colonial powers would try and reorder Egypt as something "picture-like, legible, rendered available to political and economic calculation."[24]

Constitutions can be seen as important examples of the process that Mitchell refers to. Constitutions have come to operate as signifiers. They have become a means by which the state and national culture are represented. A constitution is representative of a political and conceptual structure that exists apart from the people themselves. Countries use constitutions to exhibit themselves to other countries and establish their legitimacy in the international system and render themselves amenable to political calculation. Via the constitution, those who control the state can signal to the rest of the populace what it stands for, and thus the constitution serves as a mechanism for disciplinary control. Constitutional texts can condition the populace by creating certain expectations about what being a citizen means.

James C. Scott illustrates that central to the power of the modern nation state was the project of making a society legible. The premodern state, he argues, "was, in many crucial aspects, partially blind; it knew precious little about its subjects."[25] The modern state, Scott shows, is based on "the concept of a uniform, homogeneous citizenship."[26] It aims to make the populace readable and therefore more governable. Part of the project of creating this legibility involved creating a uniformity of customs, viewpoints, laws, forms of taxation, and measures. Such uniformity gave the state a synoptic view of its citizens. State officials advocated uniformly laid out and navigable cities, standardized surnames, and a "uniform homogeneous, national administrative code."[27] This move toward standardization and legibility coincided with a new conception of the state's role, which was aimed at the improvement of all members of society. These attempts by the state to make its populace readable involve, Scott contends, simplification since the representation of an existing social community can only be done through a "schematized process of abstraction and simplification."[28] It involved the "discovery of a society as a reified object that was separate from the state and that could be scientifically described."[29]

Constitutions can be seen as a way modern states strive to create this legibility. Thus, constitutions represent a means by which the state—or those stakeholders whom the process empowers—portrays and projects an image of itself and the way that it wishes to be understood. This process of creating legibility does not however simply describe but also shapes the people to fit the state's categories.[30]

Understanding constitutions as expositions of state ideology sometimes assumes that there is some kind of consensus before the constitution is made, "understood in 'thick' terms of cultural, national or religious homogeneity, or in 'thin' terms of shared liberal political culture."[31] Yet such a consensus does not exist in deeply divided societies such as Egypt, which are struggling over the question of what the nation is and what it believes in. In some cases, delay in writing a constitution happens because the parties involved want to avoid difficult decisions about the nature of the nation state. By putting off the decision about precise constitutional commitments, overt conflict is avoided. For example, one of the reasons why the Israeli Knesset decided in 1950 to refrain from writing a constitution was the conflict between secular and religious definitions of the Jewish state. Fearing that establishing a constitution would exacerbate tensions, it was indefinitely delayed.[32] However, while delaying the writing of a constitution can put off conflict, constitution writing can also be used as a tool by which different actors use the constitution to limit the actions of the opposition. It can also operate as a means by which political actors define—and limit—the boundaries within which their political antagonists can operate.

The lack of preconstitutional consensus does not mean that constitutions in deeply divided societies cannot be read as ideological statements. In fact, constitutional texts can be read as declarations that provide insight into the concerns that dominate the political scene at a particular moment. In addition, they can be read as attempts to channel the formation of values in a particular direction and silence dissent. Seeing constitutions as representative of ideological commitments does not also assume that ideology is neatly applied in the constitutional process. Brown suggests that we should understand constitutions not so much as a product of design but rather as a product of a fraught process of bargaining.[33]

Brown points out that constitution writers have become increasingly verbose over the twentieth century. Among the chief reasons for the extension in the lengths of constitutions is because long sections describing the ideology of the state are included. Often, he shows, such proclamations carry little legal weight due to the wording. Yet, he argues, "they are not designed to limit the government. Instead, they serve notice that an ideological orientation represents not a transient policy direction but a defining feature of the state."[34] Saïd Arjomand writes that constitutions are "important as transcendental justifications of political order."[35] In the wake of the Soviet Constitution of 1918, he asserts, "we witness the advent of a new genre, the ideological constitution, whose central goal is not the limitation of government but the transformation of society according to a revolutionary ideology."[36] The ideological constitution, has lengthy preambles or ideological statements.[37]

Religion, Culture, and Citizenship in State Formation

One of the underlying assumptions of our current political order is that citizenship forms the normative basis for the direct relationship between individuals and the modern nation state. The legitimacy of the modern nation state depends on the participation of the citizenry and a relatively strong commitment on the part of citizens. It is also assumed that this relationship gives rights to the citizen. Yet citizenship as bestowed upon the citizen by the state also makes certain demands and conveys both rights and obligations.

For Wael B. Hallaq, the state asserts its sovereign will, which "knows only itself, deferring to nothing but itself," over the citizen.[38] Thus, to be a citizen means acknowledging that one lives under a sovereign will and that the state is supreme. The citizen, Hallaq contends, is a "subjectivity fashioned in the service of a state."[39] Fashioning the citizen involves fashioning the question of religious identity, what religion is, which religious identities are to be given a status in the nation, and which religious identities are not accorded a status. This is critical to the project of modern states regardless of whether such states are defined as secular or Islamic.

Citizenship is often contingent on the concept of a national culture that binds citizens of a nation together and forges their relationship to the state. David Lloyd and Paul Thomas argue that culture "occupies the space between the individual and the state" so that the state can lay claim to universality and representation.[40] The state, they maintain, "is an exemplary institution of the people, ideally moving them towards the realization of their own essence."[41] Cultural formation ends up "forming citizens for the modern state."[42] The articulation of a national culture has aided the formation of new states such that Matthew Arnold in 1867 stated that "culture suggests the idea of the State."[43] Wael B. Hallaq asserts that law, in representing the state's will, must use the concept of culture and that "through the sovereign will's legal manifestation the state does not stand independently of culture. In other words, the state produces and thus possesses its own community."[44]

Raymond Williams argues that the idea of culture in the sense that we use it today in terms of "a whole way of life" or as an "abstraction and an absolute" came into English thinking during the Industrial Revolution, which produced new cultural relationships and changes in thought and feeling.[45] The articulation of culture as a way of life in an abstract sense has facilitated the development of the concept of a national culture that binds a national community. This is an intrinsic part of state formation. Tomoko Masuzawa shows that the idea of culture that was tied to the destiny of the whole nation developed in the German-speaking world in the nineteenth century. The construction of such a thing as German culture aided the formation of the unified German state in 1871.[46]

Even in seemingly secular societies, the position that society takes toward religion forms a key component in how the culture of that society is defined. Secular societies are not neutral toward religion, but make particular institutional decisions to place it in particular places. Thus, religion—in terms of the variety of ways religion is managed, theorized, and mythologized even if that involves the supposed absence of religion from the public sphere—is a key part of culture.

If the concept of a national culture legitimizes the state's claim to represent its citizens, the concept of a national will is also central to that legitimacy. The assertion that the national will is central to the legitimacy of the political process has become ubiquitous in contemporary political events. During President Erdogan's crackdown on the attempted military coup by a faction of the Turkish Armed Forces in 2016, he stated that those people who turned out to protest the attempted coup represented the "national will" and represented "the people."[47] Likewise, in discussions about the 2016 referendum over Britain's withdrawal from the European Union, the concept of the national will was frequently invoked. The commentator David Dimbleby stated that the "British people have spoken and the answer is 'we're out!'" In postreferendum Britain, references to "the will of the people" became a means of trying to silence dissent and disagreement.[48]

After the ouster of the Egyptian president Hosni Mubarak in 2011, a statement from the Faculty of Law at Cairo University called on Mubarak to "comply with the will of the nation," and, among other actions, draft a new constitution.[49] Similarly, during the military coup against the government of President Muhammad Mursi in 2013, Mursi was criticized for having ignored the calls of "the people." The assertion that there is such a thing as a collective will has become important for the modern state. Talal Asad argues that the modern politics of nation states are predicated on the belief that there is "such a thing as a homogeneous nation, that a homogeneous nation has the right to absolute independence represented by a state, and that the state must reflect the nation's singular personality."[50]

In Egypt, during the coup against Mursi, a common complaint was that he did not represent and act for all Egyptians. Asad points out that the idea that an elected president could be the leader of all Egyptians was never questioned. He asserts that an elected president "responds to the conflicting interests of fellow citizens by yielding to those who exert effective pressure on his government."[51] Elections, however, cannot express the common will since elections take place because such a common will does not exist. It is precisely because of diversity that democracy has emerged, Asad argues, "for addressing the ineradicable presence of difference, disagreement, and mutual hostility within the modern state with minimum damage."[52]

The expectation that the national will should and could be represented was expressed in common conceptions about the function of the constitution in Egypt. The constitution was not only seen as something that could establish the boundaries within which sectors of the state and its various institutions could operate to facilitate the workings of the political system. Rather, the constitution was expected to be a kind of embodiment of the national will and an expression of what being Egyptian means. This explains the heightened emotion with which the constitution was treated and why clauses relating to identity and to religion were subject to so much more debate. This is in part why the subject of the constitution emerged as so contentious and why such importance was attached to clauses that seemed to speak to the idea of a national character and identity. This helps explain why the constitution was abolished, written, abolished, and written again in the space of three years.

Constitutions can be seen as key moments whereby this notion of a totalizing national culture is asserted. Earlier Egyptian constitutions served similar purposes, but they were less developed in this respect. It was not until 1956 that the Egyptian constitution was drafted in the name of "We, the Egyptian people." Since then, Egypt's constitutions have become more and more detailed and verbose in articulating what Egyptian culture is and which understanding of Egypt's past it purports to uphold.

This concern with using the constitution as a form of representation of the Egyptian body politic can be seen in the texts of the preambles to the Constitutions of 2012 and 2014. Both, particularly the latter, are grandiloquent in their claims to represent the people of Egypt and to speak for the nation's history. The preamble to the 2012 Constitution implied that, through the revolution of 2011, the people of Egypt had "recovered the spirit of our great civilization and the fragrance of our radiant history."[53]

The preamble of the 2014 Constitution, however, outdid that of the 2012 Constitution in the extent of its claims to represent Egyptian society. The preamble to the Constitution of 2014 states: "We are now writing a constitution that represents the dream of generations for a thriving and cohesive society and a just state that realizes the present and future ambitions for the individual and the community."[54] It would, the constitution declared, "treat the wounds of the past," and "protect the homeland from everything that might threaten it or threaten its national unity."[55] In January 2014, the newspaper *al-Ahram* referred to the constitution as a constitution "for all Egyptians" and linked the constitution to Egypt's contribution to human kind and the world.[56]

While the universalizing language claiming to represent all Egyptians is evidenced by the word "our" in both the 2012 and 2014 Constitutions, the 2014 preamble is more assertive in its claim to represent the will of the people. It states: "We, the citizens, women and men, we the Egyptian people, sovereigns in a sovereign homeland, this is our will (*hadha iradatna*). This is the constitution of our revolution. This is our constitution."[57] The writers of the constitution sought to appropriate the legitimacy of the 2011 revolution and state that the January 25 revolution, which ousted Mubarak, and the June 30 revolution, which ousted Mursi, together allowed Egypt to regain its "independent will." The preamble also says that "the Revolution of January 25–June 30 is unique among the great revolutions in the history of humankind on account of the extent to which the people participated, estimated to be tens of millions. It is also unique on account of the prominent role played by the youth who are striving for a rising future."[58] It also says that "the popular will was protected by the people's army and with the blessing of al-Azhar al-Sharif and the national church."[59] In so doing, it asserts a continuity between the ouster of Mubarak and the ouster of Muhammad Mursi.

Managing Religion

Much academic literature about Egypt and its constitutions has charted a process of increasing Islamization over the twentieth century. The Constitutions of 1923 and 1956 were praised for their secular nature. This was done on account of the absence of any reference to the sharia and because both constitutions made a commitment to religious freedom. This is despite the fact that both constitutions stated that Islam was the religion of the state. The description of both constitutions as secular was based on Peter Berger's more commonplace definition of secularism, which defines secularism as involving aspects of society being separated from the domination of religious institutions and symbols.[60] Gamal ʿAbd al-Nasser, under whose presidency the Constitution of 1956 was promulgated, has been described as a man of the future, an "apostle" of "nationalism, socialism, and modernization," whereas mullahs, monks, and priests, "with their dogmas, rites, and hierarchies, were creatures of an increasingly irrelevant past."[61] The secular nature of the 1923 and 1956 Constitutions was, it was argued, undermined by the Constitution of 1971, which made a formal commitment to the sharia and marked what has been referred to as religion's political ascendancy.[62] This reversal of the secular nature of Egypt's constitution was seen as catastrophic for women and the Copts. Similarly, the Constitution of 2012 was portrayed as threatening to the secular nature of Egypt, a threat that abated with the suspension of the Constitution of 2012 and the promulgation of the Constitution of 2014.

Such discourse about Egypt's constitutions assumed that the project of directly defining the religious and the secular is possible. Claims about the relative secular or religious nature of a constitution assume that religion can be empirically measured and that the boundaries between what religion is and what it is not can be easily drawn. They also assume a specific relationship between past and present. The assumption is that the constitution is modern because it is secular and that any attempt to insert Islamic law reverses the modern nature of the constitution. The insertion of premodern legal norms into a statement on the sharia is seen as detracting from—or undermining—the constitution's modernity.

Hussein Ali Agrama has pointed out that the question of whether Egypt is a secular or religious state has dominated discussions about modern Egypt. He argues that one of the problems with the question is that it does not tell us about the criteria we use to define a secular state. He maintains that, ultimately, it is not possible to say whether Egypt is a secular or religious state. The question of Egypt's secular or Islamic nature "is rather a question whose persistence, force, and irresolvability expresses the peculiar *intractability* of our contemporary secularity" (Agrama's italics).[63] Thus, for Agrama, the very query into whether something is religious or secular lies at the heart of modern secularism.

Agrama's discussion of secularism builds on the thought of Talal Asad who maintains that it is only possible to approach the secular indirectly. Differentiating the concept of the secular from the political project of secularism, he argues that the "secular" and the "religious" are not essentially fixed categories and that the "secular . . . is neither continuous with the religious that supposedly preceded it . . . nor a simple break from it."[64] The secular is "a concept that brings together certain behaviors, knowledges, and sensibilities in modern life."[65] What is distinctive about secularism, he contends, is "that it presupposes new concepts of 'religion,' 'ethics,' and 'politics,' and new imperatives associated with them."[66]

The idea that the secular brings together certain sensibilities and that concepts such as religion and politics become associated with new imperatives allows for the jettisoning of the idea that secularism is the absence of religion and Islamism is its presence. This circumvents the problems that are involved in narrating Egypt's constitutions in terms of the number of references they do or do not make to religion. Viewing secularism in terms of a collection of different sensibilities and assumptions means that, even when religion is present, the way that religion works, is seen, and is invoked by political actors is filtered through those very assumptions.

Agrama questions whether there has been an Islamization of the law in Egypt since the promulgation of Article 2 of the 1971 Constitution, which made a commitment to the sharia. In fact, he contends, the law has come to conform to secular liberal expectations of religion in different ways. He uses the case in which a hisba (which refers to the right of an individual to bring a case against someone if that person sees the other person neglecting what is commanded and practicing what is forbidden within Islam) was brought against Nasr Abu Zayd in 1995.[67] This case resulted in Nasr Abu Zayd being declared an apostate, which meant that he was forced to divorce his wife. Much literature on the case of Nasr Abu Zayd portrays his indictment as an example of a creeping Islamization of Egyptian law and society.[68] However, Agrama argues that the use of hisba here was not a sign of the Islamization of law but rather a sign that the sharia has come to conform to liberal law since it represented a moment that reflected—and perhaps reinscribed—the power of the state to decide what was religious and what religion's role should be. This was further enhanced when the state limited the right of hisba to state officials.[69]

Khaled Fahmy has critiqued Agrama's discussion of hisba, showing that it was an integral part of the functioning of Islamic empires before modernity and maintained through violence.[70] Indeed, 'Abd al-Hamid al-Ghazali (d. 1111) and Ahmad ibn Naqib al-Misri (d. 1368) discussed the question of whether hisba should be limited to officials of the ruling polity.[71] While both agreed that this was not the case, al-Misri did state that intimidation and threatening to strike someone "requires the caliph because it may lead to civil disorder."[72] This raises the question of whether limiting the right of hisba to state officials is entirely the product of what Agrama terms "modern secular power."

Yet Agrama's illustration of what the modern state does is particularly compelling. He sees secularism less in terms of the absence or presence of religion and argues that "one way to think about the active principle [of secularism] is to see the state as promoting an abstract notion of 'religion,' defining the spaces it should inhabit, authorizing the sensibilities proper to it, and then working to discipline actual religious traditions so as to conform to this abstract notion, to fit into those spaces, and to express those sensibilities."[73] However, this does not result in any finite resolution since the process of drawing the line between religion and politics is continuous and indeterminable so that what best characterizes secularism is "an *ongoing, deepening, entanglement in the* **question** *of religion and politics*" (Agrama's italics and bold).[74] Thus, for Agrama, it is more a question of *how* the secular is renegotiated and *how* the state manages, disciplines, and defines religion and determines the institutional mechanisms through which this is done.[75]

Understanding secularism as the way in which the state defines what constitutes the religious and the civil, along with seeing the parameters for this definition as subject to ongoing renegotiation, allows us to think less in terms of secularism as a particular model for state and society and more in terms of the variety of religion-state relationships that can be continuously reformulated. This is useful for thinking about Egypt's constitutions which continually draw the line between the civil and the religious in different ways.

Yet understanding secularism in such a way is in danger of making the term "secularism" lose all its explanatory purchase since it implies that all states or political actors who hanker after state power are somehow secular. While Andrew March finds much that is productive in Agrama's description of the ways in which religion is a means by which the state expands its power, he criticizes Agrama for reifying secularism and for portraying secular power as an agent that itself acts directly on the world rather than something deployed by agents or institutions.[76] In addition, he criticizes Agrama for not limiting himself to saying that secularism is *one* way in which religion becomes politicized, but instead saying that "it is secularism itself that makes religion into an object of politics."[77]

Gregory Starrett points out that defining the secular as a means by which the state exerts control over religion actually creates conceptual problems. If, he asks, "the government of Iran exercises more control over religion than the government of the United States, does that mean that Iran is a more secular place than the United States?"[78] He contends that "the secular's usefulness as an analytical concept is deeply suspect" since the secular is precisely characterized by the fact that it cannot be pinned down.[79] Thus, he argues, the significance of the secular lies in the way that it functions rather than what it describes. Starrett therefore advocates that one should treat the secular as a normative category rather than as a descriptive one.[80] Malika Zeghal has pursued this approach in her discussion of debates about religion and state in Tunisia during the Arab Spring. She points out that discourse about secularism and Islamism shows how each camp in the debate reified the other. She argues that a look at Islamic narratives on secularism helps "anchor 'Islamism' and 'secularism' as political identities and constituencies."[81] An examination of such narratives about secularism shows the ways in which the differences between parties in Tunisia focused on political procedures and competing ways of life more than they did on "blueprints for a social and political order."[82]

Starrett is correct to emphasize the importance of looking at the secular from the perspective of the user of the adjective. Such an approach can manifest the various and complex ways it is used and defy common expectations. Yet answering Starrett's question of how one addresses countries that exercise "more" control over religion than others, would involve defining the religion that one is exercising more or less control over. In addition, saying that the secular cannot be used descriptively, but can only be understood normatively, is the same as saying that similarly contested concepts such as religion, culture, modernity, or the West cannot be used descriptively and can only be understood normatively. Yet Asad says the idea of the "West" is not simply a "Hegelian myth," but something that "informs innumerable intentions, practices, and discourses in systematic ways."[83]

It seems that Starrett's disentanglement of the descriptive and normative senses of the secular, while important, might not easily be done. This is also because those who use secularism in the normative sense actually need to do what Agrama points out is so central to "secular power," that is, draw the line between religion and politics. Even according to the common definition of secularism—that it is the process by which state and society become liberated from the influence of religion—before state and society can be liberated from religion, it is necessary to determine what it is that state and society are going to be liberated from. Thus, a decision must be made about what constitutes religion.

Yet March's critique that Agrama's "secular power" appears to be everywhere as an operative agent rather than something deployed by particular agents or institutions raises an important question about secular power's implied ubiquity and about its lack of analytical purchase. The question of whether it is secularism itself that makes religion into an object of politics or whether secularism is merely one way of making religion an object of politics is best addressed in further scholarship. Here, I would like to posit that constitution making is one way that religion is made into an object of politics or, to use Tamir Moustafa's term, the means by which religion is "constituted." Thus, constitutions can be seen as one institution through which what Agrama terms "secular power" is deployed. This resists the potential overreach of "secular power" while taking one of its central definitions, the very question of drawing the line between religion and politics and of demarcating different boundaries, seriously.

Rethinking Islamism

Here, I focus on an examination of the modern state's project—be it secular or religious in the more common sense of the word—of making religion into an object of politics. Whether this is what Agrama terms "secular power" or simply what modern states do is a matter of debate. In any case, rather than identifying the differences between secularism and Islamism, it is useful to think in terms of what secularism and Islamism—and secular and Islamist constitutions—have in common, specifically that both involve the state's management of religion. This involves deciding what acts, rights, and freedoms count as religious. Islamism takes a specific stand on religion. So does secularism. Contrary to common assumptions, secularism is not neutral with regard to religion: positively endorsing a political space that is absent of religion is not showing neutrality toward religion, but is rather adopting a particular position toward it. Thus, one of the things that secular and Islamic states do in regulating religious tolerance or religious freedom—and its limitations—is to define what religion is, which manifestations of religion are orthodox, which are heterodox, and what the relationship between religion and culture is. Constitutional texts are key to establishing the parameters within which particular understandings of religious identity, religious authority, and national culture are applied.

Such an approach casts the phenomenon that we call "Islamism" in a very different light. Many contend that political Islam should be understood as an attempt to establish an Islamic state and to implement the sharia. In this respect, an Islamist is someone who thinks that Islamic ideas, concepts, and legal norms should be referred to and applied in contemporary Muslim states. Likewise, Islamism, as others have argued, refers to thinkers and activists who claim that Islam is an all-embracing ideology for state and society and that Islam needs to be expressed politically. The contemporary

Islamic thinker Yusuf al-Qaradawi (b. 1926), for example, states that "Islam cannot be anything except political," and that the "character of Muslims" also "cannot be anything except political."[84]

Understanding Islamism in terms of a movement that advocates the political expression of Islam allows for the inclusion of a wide range of thinkers who have differing attitudes about what kind of political system this would entail. While Islamists are preoccupied with state power, this does not mean they have a particular—or the same—image of the state in mind or that it should be a model of the Islamic caliphate. Islamists encompass a wide range of thinkers and activists with varied ideas about democracy, the Islamic state, gender, citizenship, and religious authority.

In calling for Islam to be expressed politically, it is often assumed that the particular relationship between religion and politics that is being called for simply has to be retrieved from premodern history and reapplied in the modern period. Many Islamists are concerned that the modern Islamic world has been disconnected from the premodern Islamic order. This premodern Islamic order constitutes a time in the past, most often the period of the Prophet and the rightly guided caliphs (610–661), in which Islam's political nature is deemed to have been perfectly realized. Such a perspective holds that this disconnection from Islam's past culminated in the importation of Western civil and criminal law. Political Islam calls for the reversal of this secularization and for the application of Islamic law assuming that it is the past that has to be retrieved, although what aspect of the past is to be revived and how is contested among Islamists themselves. It is this relationship with the past that has often been taken at face value by critiques of Islamism, which also assume that Islamists simply want to retrieve the past and that in being retrieved, this past will be imposed upon the present.

Such definitions of Islamism imply that Islamism constitutes an aberration or a departure from modernity. Such definitions assume that when something like an Islamic legal norm or principle is reintroduced, the norm or principle is simply the agent of change for those who are subject to it, but that the norm or principle itself remains unaltered. Yet a reintroduction of something alters both the receiver and the giver. Islamism is a modern project that has in many ways been constituted by the modern nation state's project to delineate the relationship between religion and politics even if a not dissimilar delineation was important for classical jurists. Islamism should therefore be conceptualized with reference to the means by which it has absorbed particularly contemporary concerns and the ways that Islamic norms and laws have been reworked in light of those concerns.

Thinking about Islamism and the contemporary Egyptian state in this way breaks down the binary between the Islamic and the secular. This is the binary through which much of Egyptian politics has—and continues to be—framed. The idea that there is an ongoing conflict between secular and Islamic forces is central to Egypt's coverage of itself and to international coverage of the country. Yet, as will be shown in this book, the agendas and the motivations of many of the key players and groups cannot be understood as Islamic or as secular. Dispensing with the binary will allow us to see what really is at stake in the constitutional debates about religion and the relationship between religion and the state in contemporary Egypt.

A demand for Islam and for the sharia is also a demand for the state's intervention in the relationship between religion and politics. A call for secularism is also a call for states to intervene and assign a particular place to religion. A request by the populace for Islamism and for secularism constitutes a request for the state to determine who gets to speak for the religion that is being managed and defined and what the relationship between identity and difference is.

Thinking about Islamism in this way is not to deny that there are important distinctions between the kind of state envisaged by, for example, Islamists like members of the Muslim Brotherhood and the kind envisaged by groups that identify themselves as secular—at least in the traditional sense. Nor is it to dismiss the political threat that radical groups like ISIS and al-Qaeda pose. However, it is to say that Islamism itself is varied and that many Islamists are not so much concerned with the concept of jihad and who the enemy is, but with questions of modern governance. Clearly, the ways in which particular secular and Islamist groups draw the line between religion and politics will differ not only from each other but also among themselves. However, all states or state actors are involved in the modern imperative to manage religion and manage what counts as religious, even if they do so in distinct ways.

The distinction between religion and politics occurred in premodern Islamic governance. Abdullahi An-Na'im points out that, in Islamic history, religious and political authorities were differentiated and separated. Most regimes, he argues, could be characterized as a mixture between separation and convergence. There was, he claims, no single Islamic model for state and religious institutions.[85] Agrama acknowledges that there are a number of instances in medieval Christian Europe and premodern Islamic history in which various writers and political actors delineated some kind of separation of spheres of authority. Yet Agrama states that there are different issues at stake in the modern distinction between religion and politics and that such concerns with the separation of temporal and spiritual authority arose under very different presuppositions and "elicited and mobilized very different desires and anxieties."[86] Agrama contends that defining the boundary between religion and politics in the context of the modern state acquires a "distinctive salience," and is particularly bound up with modern secular power. Defining the boundary between religion and politics in the contemporary context has "inescapable consequences for how essential freedoms are identified, selves and their motives defined, and ways of life can be lived."[87]

Yet, while Agrama powerfully illustrates what such anxieties are in contemporary Egypt, he does not discuss the ways in which those particular stakes are new or what those stakes were in different contexts in premodern Islamic history. Indeed, such a delineation did have its own particular—albeit different—salience for classical jurists, as chapter 2 will show. It is this distinction between past and present, between modern secular power and what went before, that is in danger of effacing the subtle differences and similarities between premodern sharia and its application in the contemporary context.

Thinking about modernity as a different set of stakes and sensibilities is a useful way of discerning what is modern about the project of Islamism. However, it is also important to address the ways in which those stakes and sensibilities inherit premodern concerns. I maintain that, when the sharia is applied as modern Islamic state law through constitutional commitments, the sharia becomes embedded in the aspirations of the modern nation state in ways that constitute both continuity and change.

In this chapter, I have called for seeing constitutions in terms of their role as ideological statements through which the state claims to represent its citizens. Constitutions play an important role in the foundation of new political orders. They constitute a revolutionary act which both consolidates and puts an end to the revolution that made the constitution possible. Constitutions also provide a map of the relationship that the state is to have with its citizens. Thus, utilizing the work of James C. Scott and Timothy Mitchell, I have argued that constitutions have come to operate as signifiers that announce what national identity and national culture are and declare the nature of the relationship between citizens and the state. They are used by those who control the state to exhibit to the rest of the populace what it stands for. They thus serve as means of control by creating certain expectations about what being a citizen entails.

The concept of citizenship forms the normative basis for the direct relationship between individuals and the modern nation state. Citizenship is often contingent on the concept of a national culture in terms of a whole way of life that binds citizens of a nation together and forges their relationship to the state. The expectation that the national will should and could be represented was expressed in common conceptions about the function of the constitution in Egypt. This is why Egypt's constitutions were framed, in what Malika Zeghal, building upon Foucault, refers to as a "discursive explosion," in terms of how they spoke to the religious or the secular nature of the Egyptian state.[88]

However, secularism and Islamism cannot be understood in terms of the greater or lesser presence of religion, since this implies that such terms are self-evident. Here, recent theorizations of secularism that emphasize secularism is the process by which the relationship between religion and politics is constituted are useful. Looking at constitutions in terms of how they define the relationship between religion and politics allows us to think in terms of what secularism and Islamism—and secular and Islamist constitutions—have in common, specifically that both involve the state's management of religion. Dispensing with the Islamist/secular binary will allow us to see what issues are at stake in the constitutional debates about religion and the relationship between religion and the state in contemporary Egypt.

CHAPTER 2

The Sharia as State Law

Contemporary Muslim majority states make a number of commitments to the sharia. Some states, including Egypt, Saudi Arabia, Syria, Yemen, and Sudan define the sharia as the—or a—source of legislation. Other states, such as Iraq and Afghanistan, maintain that any enacted law cannot be contrary to Islamic tenets. Still others, like Jordan, constitutionally acknowledge the partial impact of the sharia within the realm of personal status law. Any state that has the task of making state law compatible with the sharia or enforcing the sharia must confront challenges and grapple with conceptual differences between the sharia, rooted in the premodern discursive practices of the four schools of law, and modern state law. Wael B. Hallaq argues that the structures of the modern state have never been compatible with Islamic governance and that applying the sharia as state law is an impossibility since, "as a paradigm of governance, [the modern state] evolved in Europe . . . [and] is uncomfortably seated in many parts of the world."[1] Likewise, as Sherman Jackson argues, there is "a particular ideological difficulty that results from a fundamental conflict between the theory underlying the nation-state and that of the Islamic legal tradition."[2]

Jackson and Hallaq raise important questions about the relationship of modern state law to the sharia. However, the argument that this incommensurability is inherent emphasizes the normative expectations that were made of the sharia at the expense of considering the historical and institutional contexts in which the sharia was elaborated. According to Mohammed Fadel, framing the "displacement of the traditional law-finding methods of the ulamā in favor of centralised legislation" as catastrophic effaces developments in governance and the role of the law in the Arab provinces of the Ottoman Empire.[3] In fact, in many cases, the sharia and state law existed alongside one another and were mutually supportive. At a number of points, particularly in the Ottoman Empire, there were moments when state law and the sharia were much closer.

This chapter charts some of the key features of premodern sharia and delineates the conceptual differences and similarities between the sharia and modern state law. It focuses on two main areas. First, it examines the ways in which the sharia was developed, interpreted, and applied by private scholars who often had a suspicious view of the Islamic polity and who endeavored to protect the sharia from too much intervention by the state. Thus, the sharia was developed by individuals and in institutions that were connected to—but still separate from—state institutions. Second, it considers the fact that Islamic jurists organized themselves into four schools of law. These four schools recognized the concept of mutual orthodoxy, the idea that there were multiple possible answers to a legal problem or issue. This meant that, in many respects, the sharia had an uneasy relationship with codified state law, which is based on the predictability and uniformity of state law.

However, while delineating the conceptual differences between the sharia and modern state law, the chapter also addresses the ways in which the premodern polity appropriated the right to make legislation and how the sharia itself established the possibility of state law existing alongside it. The concept of *siyasa shar'iyya* laid the groundwork for a closer relationship between the sharia and the law-making capacities of the ruling polity.

In nineteenth-century Egypt, the sharia was, to some extent, marginalized and underwent important transformations. The sharia was relegated to the sphere of family law while European law was introduced for civil and criminal codes. Even in the area of family law, the sharia was subject to codification which, in many respects, marked a shift away from premodern sharia. This marginalization of the sharia had three important consequences. First, in consigning the sharia to the sphere of the family, the family took on an increased role and became more representative of religion, tradition, and cultural authenticity. The second consequence was that the sharia came to play an increasingly important role in political discourse that opposed the postcolonial Egyptian state. The demand for Islam became, as

Iza R. Hussin shows, a demand for state intervention in the sharia. The state in turn was increasingly seen as the appropriate vehicle for the establishment of the sharia.

Drawing on the work of Armando Salvatore, I argue that the third consequence of the marginalization of the sharia was that it led to the emergence of the idea of the sharia as a concept, which meant that the sharia, for the most part, was not seen as a body of laws and texts rooted in particular institutional methodologies. Rather, it became a rallying cry and was presented as a solution to cultural and political problems. Islamist thinkers increasingly came to refer to the sharia not in connection with its particular complex laws and methodologies, or the multivalence that had existed in premodern contexts, but in terms of a concept, the application of which would lead to national regeneration. It is this idea of the sharia that enabled a commitment to it to be inserted in the Egyptian constitution in the 1970s.

The Ruling Polity and the Sharia

One of the features often mentioned in discussions about the incompatibility between the sharia and modern state law is the fact that premodern sharia was jurists' law. The sharia was formulated by scholars, who had expertise in the Qur'an, Hadith, and the sources of jurisprudence. These scholars were not affiliated with the ruling polity and believed that the polity should not interpret the sharia, but only provide the circumstances for its application. Often suspicious of the ruling polity's ability to be just, these scholars worked to insulate the sharia from manipulation by the ruling authority.

In the contemporary context, the appropriate venue for the making of laws is often considered to be the centralized sovereign state. Such a state issues decrees or legislation defining the law for a geopolitical entity that has a monopoly on the legitimate use of violence. On this basis, law derives from the state and serves state power. The state retains the exclusive authority to determine what is and what is not legally binding within its territorial boundaries. The ability to restrict legal authority is central to the sovereignty of the state. Thus, modern states have an interest in precluding the existence of other legal authorities to which citizens can turn. Such an assumption was voiced by Sir John Scott (1841–1904), the British judge for the new International Courts of Appeal in Egypt, who stated in 1899 that "there are, as everyone is aware, various systems of justice in Egypt. The ordinary right of a state to impose upon all those who dwell within its limits the authority of its own laws, administered by its own courts of justice, does not yet prevail."[4]

Sherman Jackson argues that the idea that state sovereignty alone has the right to decide what is and what is not law did not exist in classical Islam.[5] In premodern Islamic thinking, Hallaq contends, the state served the law and not the other way around. Political institutions, including the executive and the judiciary, were subordinate to the sharia. Hallaq argues that paradigmatic sharia was a moral system in which law was part of the moral structure and not the director of it. In contrast, the modern state regulates religious institutions, thus "rendering them subservient to its legal will."[6]

An important aspect of this conception of law in premodern sharia was what might be described as a form of pessimism about the state's ability to serve as a moral entity.[7] Lawrence Rosen contends that there was little expectation that justice would be an integral feature of the state. Rather, it was particular persons, including laymen or jurists, who were seen as embodying the features of the just. Many commentators of the classical and medieval periods had doubts that a ruler could be truly just. The ruling polity was seen as regulating reciprocity but was not seen as possessed of justice in itself.[8] This was why the ideal role of the religious scholars, it was maintained, was to keep at some considerable distance from the ruling polity. The historian 'Abd al-Rahman al-Jabarti (1753–1825), for example, drew upon expectations inherited from the Islamic tradition and criticized the scholars of his time by describing the ideal scholar as someone who "refused to serve the rulers as judges and in other religious posts out of piety because authority leads to tyranny, oppression and corruption."[9]

Private scholars, who were drawn from the merchant and artisan classes, interpreted and devised the sharia, sometimes in opposition to the state. From the end of the eighth century, such scholars tried to develop jurisprudence that was consistent with their understanding of divine commands. The Abbasids (750–1258) were keen to show their piety and therefore supported these scholars, allowing them to develop the law outside the structure of the ruling polity. By the end of the eighth century, a body of positive legal rulings on a whole range of issues covered by the sharia, along with a number of judicial institutions, had developed.

There were early attempts to exert more control over the ulama and centralize legal authority in the caliphate. For example, Ibn al-Muqaffa' (d. 759) argued that it was the caliph's right to promulgate and enact the legal decisions of a uniform, binding code. Muhammad Qasim Zaman illustrates that al-Muqaffa' saw the ulama "essentially as functionaries of the caliph, co-opted into the state apparatus."[10]

Yet, even though the caliph was required to be able to employ independent legal reasoning, or *ijtihad*, from the mid-ninth century on, it was the jurists and not the caliphate who, for the most part, possessed the author-ity to interpret the law. The influential treatise of the Islamic jurist of the Shafi'i school of law, Abu Hasan al-Mawardi (d. 1058), provides us with an example. Al-Mawardi argued that the caliph was obliged to enforce—not promulgate—the law. It was his duty to provide the circumstances under which the sharia could be applied. Al-Mawardi wrote that the caliph "must guard the faith, upholding its established sources," and administer the legal penalties "so that the faith should remain pristine and the nation free from error."[11] The Shafi'i jurist Ahmad Ibn Naqib al-Misri (d. 1368) also empha-sized that the caliph's role was to apply the law, protect it, and preserve it from alteration.[12]

Asifa Quraishi argues that this system formed a kind of balance of powers between the state and nonstate actors. This was not, she argues, the balance of power that we see in modern systems, between state institutions—that is, between the executive, judicial, and legislative branches of government. She characterizes the classical Islamic balance of power as one between the government as a whole and the Islamic scholars—between the state and nonstate powers. Neither had complete authority over the law. These state and nonstate actors recognized each other's role in the premodern Islamic system.[13]

Sami Zubaida argues that, for the most part, the institutions and practices of the sharia were dominated by the ulama, with the idea that the sharia had divine origins and could not be subject to the legislation of the state.[14] This enabled Islamic jurisprudence to develop in such a way as to have a legal scale of evaluation that included two categories, recommended and reprehensible, which were ethical evaluations that dealt with individual con-science and were not legally enforceable.[15] Thus, Islamic jurists made a dis-tinction between the legal status of an act and its desirability from a religious perspective.[16]

The jurists sought to protect Islamic law from the state by limiting the area over which the state had jurisdiction. One of the ways they did this, Rosen shows, was by limiting the range of *hudud* punishments (punishments that are believed to have been fixed by God).[17] Baber Johansen points out that Hanafi jurists made a distinction between the "claims of God" and the "claims of men," narrowing the former and thus minimizing the area that was subject to state interference. Hanafi jurists thus tried "to protect the rights of the individual against all possible infringements by the authorities."[18]

Sherman Jackson shows how, in Mamluk Egypt, the Maliki jurist Shihab al-Din al-Qarafi (1228–85) tried to limit the government's authority. For al-Qarafi, the state enjoys only executive authority and needs to impose order upon society. The state, he argued, does not have the right to organize and control the law. Al-Qarafi sought to restrict the government's authority over the content of the law by "limit[ing] the range of matters over which government could legally claim the authority to resolve disputes."[19]

Mohammed Fadel, however, has emphasized the ways in which the premodern polity appropriated the right to make legislation. Fadel argues that jurists in the later Mamluk and Ottoman eras contended that, while an administrative act could not order the commission of something that was forbidden in jurists' law, or order the omission of an act that was obligatory in jurists' law, administrative acts "could legitimately compel an individual to perform, or refrain from performing, an act that, from the perspective of the jurists' law, was either disfavoured, permitted or merely supererogatory."[20] Fadel thus shows the ways in which *fiqh* (Islamic jurisprudence) acted as a negative restriction or a limit on state law while also enabling the polity to move beyond that law and supplement it.

The premodern Islamic state therefore appropriated the right to make legislation and referred to—and used—the sharia. In addition, while the state and the sharia were theoretically separate, the sharia also coexisted with a wide variety of institutions and state-society relations. Sami Zubaida illustrates that many other legal rules, institutions, and practices interacted with the sharia and its institutions. The sharia courts were only one of a number of judicial tribunals, most of which, such as those for criminal prosecution and punishment, were directed by the rulers outside the framework of the sharia. The qadi's (judge of a sharia court) court illustrated the point at which state law and the sharia coexisted. While the qadi's authority was given to him by the ruler, he was obliged to rule according to the sharia. The qadi judged with reference to—and not in contradiction to—the sharia.[21]

The qadi's court reflected the requirements of an increasingly complex legal system. The Islamic ruling polity's production of its own law as a means by which to govern sometimes led to tension between state law and the law of the jurists. To resolve this tension, from the eleventh century, jurisprudence employed the concept of siyasa shar'iyya, or administration in accordance with the sharia, to adapt the sharia to the requirements of the Muslim community.[22] Ibn Taymiyya (1263–1328) and Ibn Qayyim al-Jawziyya (1292–1350) developed a theorization of siyasa shar'iyya. Ibn Taymiyya argued that a ruler's law was to be deemed legitimate if it was consistent with the sharia and if the ruler had cooperated with the jurists to ensure that the law did not command people to sin and advanced public welfare.[23] Ibn Taymiyya emphasized that the ruler should follow the Qur'an and the Sunna when counseled to do so. In the case of a dispute the opinion that is more in conformity with the Qur'an and the Sunna should be followed.[24] He thus opened up a space for rule with reference to the sharia. Siyasa shar'iyya was implemented in what Clark B. Lombardi calls "qadi's fiqh" where a ruler could require the courts to "find their rules of decision in a body of *fiqh*."[25] Such a judgment would be legally binding, even if there were alternative interpretations within fiqh. Thus, Lombardi argues, while fiqh would "no longer be the sole source of positive legal norms in an Islamic state, it remained a crucial source of negative restrictions on the state's legislative power."[26]

The mutual relationship between fiqh and siyasa was important for Islamic governance. Siyasa and fiqh were different types of law and both of them made up the rule of law. Siyasa came from the ruler's assessment of public need and dealt with areas about which Islamic literature gave little direction. Quraishi points out that rulers were not able to form new fiqh or change the content of existing fiqh and that their power was limited to the realm of siyasa. However, the existence of siyasa enabled fiqh scholars to oppose forcing a particular fiqh doctrine upon the population. This enabled the multivalent nature of fiqh to be protected. Thus, Muslim rulers often applied siyasa rules to everyone, while appointing "a variety of *fiqh* scholars as judges so that laypeople seeking to resolve their *fiqh*-based legal conflicts could do so according to their chosen school of law."[27]

Quraishi argues that the possibility of creating siyasa law means that siyasa should not be seen as opposed to fiqh, but rather as part of it. Quraishi contends that "it could be said that when a state makes a *siyāsah* rule for the public good, then the state is acting consistently with its Islamic obligation to uphold the Sharī'ah."[28] In fact, classical fiqh scholars were deferential to rulers, and for the most part did not oppose siyasa power.[29]

Sherman Jackson shows that the sharia itself enabled law to go beyond the sharia. He contends that the sharia imposed limits on its own jurisdiction.[30] Fadel also argues that, rather than representing an immutable set of prepolitical rights and obligations, fiqh included the entitlement "to promulgate morally binding positive law which goes beyond the pre-political rights and duties of the jurists' law."[31] Fadel concludes, therefore, that rather than representing the failure of fiqh or a product of necessity and arbitrary power, siyasa actually represents a conception of public law that was the "result of the deliberations of an idealized agent acting to further the national good of his principal, the Muslim community."[32]

The doctrine of siyasa shar'iyya helped facilitate and legitimate governance in the Ottoman Empire.[33] Ottomans consistently maintained respect for the sharia even though the Sultan's *qanun*, or law, originated independently of it. Suleiman the Lawgiver (1494–1566) classified existing practice in sharia

terms. Ebussuud Efendi, who was the shaykh al-Islam—the highest religious office—under Suleiman, tried to bring the law of the empire, the
qanun, and the sharia, much closer together. Qanun frequently referenced
the sharia and qanun and fatwas often declared the qanun's compatibility
with the sharia.[34] Yet the Ottomans also went further and brought religion
and law into their own institutions, ultimately making both religion and law
subject to imperial authority. The Ottomans integrated the ulama into the
bureaucracy with religious offices existing in all levels of the government in
what Ahmet Kuru has referred to as an "ulama-state alliance."[35] Jurists were
appointed to serve as legislative advisers and judges. Qadis who based their
decisions on the sharia, as well as qanun and customary law, were treated
by the Ottoman Empire as state functionaries administering state law, and
"not as purely religious judges following the books of *fiqh*."[36] Haim Gerber
shows that the Ottomans attempted to include qanun legislation within the
sharia, which was something that the Ottoman state had never done before.
A collection of fatwas authored by Ebussuud Efendi (1490–1574) reveal that
the Ottoman state aimed to innovate, possibly to legislate, within the sharia
by using the authority of the sultanate.[37]

Premodern Islamic history was characterized by a relationship of some
distance between the sharia and state law, but this distance was not complete or consistently maintained. The extent of the distance between the
ruling polity and the sharia varied and was subject to negotiation. While the
sharia and siyasa existed as separate realms of law, they also often mutually
reinforced one another. State law enabled the sharia to maintain its status as
jurists' law, and the sharia enabled state law to function if it ruled in conformity with the sharia. The Ottoman Empire made attempts to close this gap
by using the sultan's authority to legislate within the sharia.[38]

The Schools of Law

One of the other central features of premodern sharia that is often mentioned in arguments about the incommensurability of the sharia and state
law is that the sharia was formulated, interpreted, and often applied through
a system of multiple schools of law. Contrary to common assumptions made
by contemporary groups wishing to apply the sharia, the sharia is not a specific body of legal rules. Rather, it is a set of institutions and various interpretive methodologies, which flourished within the system of multiple schools
of law.

While the sharia can be found in the extant texts of Islamic jurisprudence, premodern sharia was also rooted in certain premodern institutions.

These institutions had particular methods for assessing evidence and discovering facts that were reflective of different personal relationships. Lawrence Rosen emphasizes that justice in premodern Islam was not an abstract ideal. Justice, he argues, was not rooted in manuals and texts, but was personalized and contextualized. Rosen argues that the qadi did not aim to implement a consistent body of legal doctrine, but rather aimed to put "people back in the position of being able to negotiate their own permissible relationships."[39]

These judicial processes were rooted in the different methodologies of the schools of law. A school of law was similar to an independent association or guild of jurists, characterized by a particular interpretive methodology. Initially, there were numerous schools of law, all of which employed independent legal reasoning, or ijtihad, to determine questions of *fiqh* (Islamic jurisprudence) using the various sources. Up to about the ninth century, ijtihad referred to a freer type of direct scriptural interpretation whereas later forms of ijtihad more strictly adhered to laws relating to the different sources of Islamic jurisprudence, with each school emphasizing different sources.[40]

By the end of the eleventh century, the number of permanent Sunni schools was reduced to four, known as the schools of law. This coincided, Jackson argues, with increasing emphasis on *taqlid*, or following in the footsteps of previous legal reasoning, as opposed to ijtihad, using independent legal reasoning. Jackson refutes Hallaq's argument that the gate of ijtihad did not close, and contends that taqlid did indeed come to be dominant, and ijtihad increasingly restricted. The emphasis on taqlid increased the authority of the school of law thereby taking authority away from the individual jurist. The schools of law relied on taqlid to sustain and perpetuate their authority. The Maliki jurist Shihab al-Din al-Qarafi (1228–85) posited that a view acquired orthodox status not because it came from someone exercising ijtihad, "but because its advocate represented one of the orthodox" schools of law.[41]

All four schools were equally orthodox and mutually recognized. The system of schools of law inherently recognized a plurality of perspectives. The Shafi'i jurist Ahmad Ibn Naqib al-Misri (d. 1368) asserted that "scholarly differences are thus something natural, even logically necessary."[42] The doctrine of mutual orthodoxy stems from the fact that the process of legal interpretation was viewed as a fallible human activity, and thus legal decisions could only be accepted as probable interpretations of divine will, not certain ones. The standing of legal reasoning was based on the intention of the jurist undertaking the legal reasoning and not on the result of such reasoning.[43]

The doctrine of mutual orthodoxy meant that caliphs, sultans, and rulers would frequently appoint judges from multiple schools of law. The Mamluks (1250–1517), for example, appointed a separate judge for each of the schools of law.[44] Until the mid-nineteenth century, the sharia courts applied the doctrines of all four schools of law. While the Hanafi school of law was the official school of the Ottoman Empire, before the nineteenth century the sharia court system accepted the doctrines of the other three schools of law. The doctrine of mutual orthodoxy allowed individuals to apply to the school of law that best aligned with their interests.[45]

However, the doctrine of mutual orthodoxy was challenging for rulers who wanted to apply a single, predictable body of law. While in theory the authority of all four schools of law was equal, in practice some schools were closer to sources of power. This proximity conferred added legitimacy to the particular school of law, often at the cost of the other schools.[46] In thirteenth-century Mamluk Egypt, for example, the Shafi'i school emerged as dominant. The Mamluk chief justice refused to implement rulings handed down by judges from other schools when these contradicted the Shafi'i school. The jurist Shihab al-Din al-Qarafi (1228–85) was a member of the Maliki school, which was the second largest school in Cairo at the time. Jackson shows that al-Qarafi protested these exclusivist policies and developed "a theory designed to preserve the integrity of his and, by extension," all the schools of law.[47] Al-Qarafi attributed what Jackson refers to as "corporate status" to the schools of law "by virtue of which the views of all the schools are protected as constituents of the larger edifice of orthodox Sunni law."[48] The school of law emerged as the sole repository of legal authority. This allowed the members of a certain school of law to act according to its jurisprudence while also being exempt from the rules of another school of law.[49]

Jackson maintains that there was little concern with the problem of the relationship between schools of law and sources of power in the formative and medieval periods. However, this relationship became an important issue in the postclassical period.[50] This was particularly so in the Ottoman Empire, which supported the Hanafi school of law. All appointments made from Istanbul were of Hanafi qadis. The chief mufti was a Hanafi. Muftis and qadis of the other schools of law were appointed locally based on the needs of the population.[51] The Hanafization of law was pursued more rigorously in the nineteenth century when Sultan Mahmud II (r. 1808–39) enforced the Hanafi school of law in all the courts. The Hanafization of the sharia courts ended the flexibility that the subjects of the Ottoman Empire had enjoyed. In Egypt, which had been part of the Ottoman Empire from the early sixteenth century, the Hanafi school became the official school of law in 1856.

By this time, the grand mufti of Egypt—a position that had been created by Muhammad ʿAli (1769–1849) in 1835—was invalidating court decisions that were not based on Hanafi rules.[52] The head of al-Azhar had always been a Shafiʿi from 1725 to 1870, but from 1870 until 1969 more than half were Hanafis.[53] Kenneth Cuno argues that the process of Hanafization had such an impact in Egypt that, by 1897, the Hanafi school of law was known as the "established doctrine" when referenced in legal documents.[54]

Hanafization precipitated the decline of the schools of law and the authority of the ulama. Muhammad ʿAli sought advice on reforming Egypt not from the ulama of the schools of law but from "progressive Sunni jurists," such as the writer and intellectual Rifaʿa al-Tahtawi (1801–73). Muhammad ʿAli's government established national schools with a European-style curriculum unaffiliated with the schools of law. Nineteenth-century courts increasingly applied official law codes as opposed to qadi's jurisprudence. There was no requirement that judges be classically trained. By the twentieth century, the institutions of the schools of law had weakened and their domination of educational and judicial training institutions had ended. The schools of law no longer controlled law in Egypt.[55]

Modern Islamic reformist thought mirrored this movement away from the schools of law. The Islamic jurist and founder of Islamic modernism, Muhammad ʿAbduh (1849–1905), called for reviving Islam by breaking the power of taqlid over men's minds and eradicating its deep-seated influence.[56] Muslims, he argued, had distorted Islam's perfection by closing the door to ijtihad and blindly following taqlid. The Qurʾan and Sunna were to be the true guides by which men possessing intellect could deduce legal stipulations. He called "the attitude that always wants to know what the precedents say" stupid and foolish and wrote that "mere priority in time, it [Islam] insisted, is not one of the signs of perceptive knowledge, nor yet of superior intelligence and capacity."[57] While there is clear antipathy in ʿAbduh's thought toward an overreliance on Islamic jurisprudence of the four schools of law, he did not call for bypassing the schools of law and the writings contained in Islamic jurisprudence entirely. At times, he praised certain jurists, particularly those of the early Islamic period.[58] Nevertheless, one of the implications of such an approach—and not necessarily one that was advocated by ʿAbduh—was a rejection of too much reliance on the schools of law and their various methodologies.

Later thinkers would take this antipathy toward Islamic jurisprudence of the four schools of law much further. For example, the Islamic reformer Rashid Rida (1865–1935) emphasized returning to the Qurʾan and the Sunna, and rejected the authority of many rules of the classical tradition. For Rida, only those points of law on which the companions of the Prophet had reached a consensus were binding. Rida wrote that a ruler's law did not need to conform to the ijtihad of the jurists. Ijtihad, he stated, is a matter of opinion and is not infallible. As long as laws did not contravene explicit texts, they should be followed.[59] Rida was critical of the factions that sided with a special imam and with particular ulama. He stated that "the multiplicity of schools in the religion contradicts the religion's purpose" and has contributed to divisions in Muslim society.[60] The decline in the authority of the schools of law contributed to a situation in which reformers would select from different doctrinal schools (a process known as *takhayyur* and *talfiq*, harmonization) to reach what they felt was the best outcome. This process of selection also enabled reformers to develop a version of the sharia that was closer in form to European law. Yet, in doing so, the sharia was transferred into a set of positive legal norms that had been separated from their institutional context. Such an institutional context, Anver M. Emon argues, had formed a vital component of the meaning and sense of the sharia.[61]

Such an approach to the schools of law can be seen in the thought of the contemporary judge and writer, Tariq al-Bishri (b. 1933), who served on the committee to review the Egyptian Constitution of 1971 that was set up by the Supreme Council of Armed Forces after the revolution. In calling for Egypt to establish its own judicial independence, al-Bishri advocates "taking from Islamic *fiqh* within the scope of a renewal (*nahda 'ilmiyya*) of this *fiqh*, without being tied to a particular school of law, while also respecting harmony with the general legal structure" of Egypt.[62] Law, he argues, should be made in the national interest, and broader principles, such as the idea that rights are not absolute but are restrained by the public interest, should be taken from fiqh. He calls for opening the gate of ijtihad in Islamic legislation and for this ijithad to take into account the reality of daily life in Egypt.[63]

The decline of the schools of law facilitated the move toward state centralization and the codification of the sharia. It also led to changing sensibilities about the nature of religious authority. This meant that more Egyptians without classical legal training began to serve as judges and began to conceive of ideas about a much closer relationship between the sharia and the state. Those, like Rashid Rida, who wanted greater proximity between the sharia and state law, found that their ideas and writings gained traction.

Codification

In the contemporary context, lawmaking is considered to be vested in the centralized sovereign government, which issues decrees and legislation that define the laws of the territory under its control. A single legal code assumes a level of uniformity and predictability that is considered to be important for political control and stability.

Codification is a process of forming statutory law in which a broad range of interconnected subjects are treated systematically and simultaneously in one document, as opposed to the episodic treatment of isolated issues. Codification is designed to make law more transparent, consistent and accessible. Codified law is different from common law, which is derived from custom and judicial precedent. Codification refers to the laying down of laws from the beginning to be applied to a number different future situations rather than the giving of a verdict in the context of a specific case.[64] Modern law making often—at least in civil law systems and less so in common law systems—assumes codification and codification presupposes that only the state determines what law is. In turn, the codification of law facilitates the state's increasing involvement in everyday affairs.

In the nineteenth century, the Ottoman Empire, which laid many of the foundations of modern Egyptian law, pursued a policy of state centralization, legal consolidation, codification, and Islamization. This process was driven by the idea that legal authority resides in the impersonal institutions of the state and not in the sultan or in God. Such ideas began to take shape with the reforms of the Ottoman Sultan Mahmud II (r. 1808–39). Mahmud II established the Council for Juridical Enactments, thereby locating legislative authority in an institution that was distinct from the sharia and from the will of the sovereign.[65]

This project of centralization and increased state control continued under the government of Sultan 'Abd al-Hamid II (r. 1876–1909). Ottoman officials wanted to centralize power over legal institutions and practices and centralize and consolidate state control. The codification of the sharia formed part of these reforms. The sharia was used in this project to enhance the empire's legitimacy.[66] Sultan 'Abd al-Hamid II had an absolutist vision of state control that was Islamic and emphasized one united identity. Karen Barkey argues that it was a modernist plan intended to unify the Ottoman people under a common ideology.[67]

The first attempt in the Ottoman Empire to codify the sharia was known as the *majalla* which was published from 1870 to 1877. It was intended to be accessible and comprehensible to all.[68] The majalla was based on the opinions of the Hanafi school of law and dealt with a variety of subjects. However, the majalla resembled European codes much more than it did the sharia. While the majalla was based on the Hanafi school of law, it did not always incorporate the dominant opinions of the Hanafi school, and sometimes incorporated legal norms from other schools of law.[69] Samy Ayoub cautions against seeing the majalla as representative of a fundamental break with premodern sharia and argues that the majalla both continued and changed the Hanafi legal tradition. The majalla, he argues, came out of Hanafi legal norms, was faithful to those norms and doctrines, and was justified by its drafters by reference to Hanafi norms.[70]

However, Ayoub also points out that the majalla fostered the role and authority of the Ottoman state. Ayoub emphasizes that the main function of the majalla was to cover the judicial aspect of fiqh. The codifiers of the majalla were much less concerned with the ethical dimensions of fiqh as shown by the fact that the categories that qualify human actions in Hanafi fiqh were not maintained in the majalla.[71] Messick argues that the majalla "for the first time brought closure to the 'open text' of shari'a jurisprudence."[72] The central feature of the sharia was that it did not give the ruler legislative authority. However, with the majalla, public officials and not the jurists, were given the authority to produce the sharia, which was then to be approved by the sultan.[73]

Officially, the majalla had jurisdiction throughout the empire, but it was not applied in Egypt. Initially, there were attempts to establish an independent Egyptian legal system with codified sharia. Muhammad 'Abduh (1849–1905) recommended codifying the sharia by compiling a compendium of the positions of all the schools of law from which qadis could choose, hoping that this would facilitate consistency in jurisprudence.[74] Muhammad Qadri Pasha (1821–88), a secular lawyer trained by Azharis in comparative law, wrote a codification of the sharia in the style of European legal codes, modeled on the Ottoman majalla.[75] Qadri Pasha also wrote a compilation of the Islamic rules on endowments and a book on Islamic personal status law. While both of Qadri Pasha's books were based on Hanafi law, they reconstructed Hanafi law in the form of positive law by selecting a single rule from among the multiple opinions within the Hanafi school of law.[76]

However, in 1883 the Egyptian government abandoned Qadri Pasha's draft Islamic code, deciding instead to adopt European secular codes of law based largely on French law. The Mixed Courts had been established based on French codes in 1875 to adjudicate cases between Egyptians and foreigners. This led to the adoption of French codes for civil law, civil procedure, criminal law, criminal procedure, commercial law, and maritime commercial law in the National Courts. This was not the first time European law had been introduced. Leonard Wood points out that, in the mid-nineteenth century, the Ottoman-Egyptian ruling elite applied criminal laws, constitutional laws, and land laws of mainly French and Swiss origin. The investigative procedures followed were also of European origin. The

Ottomans had established Nizamiyya courts, based on French law, as part of the Tanzimat reform process.[77]

The adoption of Western codified law is often framed as resulting from colonialism, in which Egyptians are accorded little agency. Rudolph Peters argues that, until 1883, the government was "keen on creating a legal system that would ensure the correct application of Ḥanafī law" and that the "wholesale reception of foreign law in Egypt beginning in 1883 must therefore be attributed to strong foreign pressure."[78] While codification predated the direct colonial encounter in Egypt, it was done, Hussin argues, "in the shadow of colonial power."[79] Kenneth Cuno contends that the Ottoman Empire—including Egypt—defensively adopted European-style and European-derived codes and courts hoping to bring an end to the unequal treaties that had been imposed on it by Western powers.[80]

Nathan J. Brown, however, asserts that legal reform should not be understood solely in terms of colonial pressure and cautions against removing "the initiative from the subject population."[81] He argues that the Egyptian elite consciously turned away from Islamic and Ottoman sources toward Europe to establish an independent judicial system that centralized state power. The Egyptian government, Brown argues, used the construction of the National Courts to keep the courts out of the control of the British. Legal reform, Brown argues, was initiated before the peak of European control and "what attracted such elites was not the Western nature of the legal systems they constructed but the increased control, centralization and penetration they offered."[82]

Leonard Wood concedes that many who worked in the Islamic courts and who were experts in Islamic law "interpreted Egypt's European law as an affront to Egypt's religious, cultural, national, and transnational Muslim identity."[83] However, he contends, the new Franco-Egyptian law was not stridently opposed. Most Egyptian law professionals, he writes, "believed that they were living in an age in which the old legal order no longer mattered—and they conducted their work accordingly."[84] Egyptian Muslims in the 1870s and 1880s revered the sharia, but it had been marginalized by the growth of secular courts since the middle of the century.[85]

In addition, the adoption of Western codified law was supported by some ulama who feared that the codification of the sharia would result in them losing their authority over the interpretation of the sharia.[86] Many ulama disapproved of the majalla project, seeing acts of codification as the state taking over the sharia.[87] When Khedive Ismail (1830–95) approached the scholars of al-Azhar with a request to write a compendium on sharia laws and penalties organized like European laws, he was refused. The Egyptian intellectual

Rifaʿa al-Tahtawi (1801–73) excused himself from this process "saying that he did not wish to be denounced as an infidel."[88] Rashid Rida criticized Islamic jurists who opposed the codification of the sharia on the grounds that it contradicted Hanafi doctrine. He advocated selecting from the sharia rulings that would accord with the sultan's needs as a defense against the introduction of foreign law.[89]

Islamic traditionalists thus aligned with many elite and secular Egyptians in their opposition to the codification of the sharia. Leading Egyptians, Brown writes, "shared a common belief with many colonial officials that the *shariʿa* in its present form was unsuitable for a modern state."[90] Husayn Fakhry Pasha (1843–1920), the new minister of justice, argued that a code based on the sharia "would not be consistent with the arrangements to which Egyptians were accustomed" and urged that the laws that were being applied in the Mixed Courts be adopted in the National Courts.[91] Brown shows that, while this did foment discussion in Egypt, and there were proponents of a greater use of the sharia in the National Court codes, such discussion was relatively limited.[92]

The legal scholar ʿAbd al-Razzaq al-Sanhuri (1895–1971) wrote the first version of the Egyptian Civil Code in 1949. Malcolm Kerr shows that, in drafting the civil code, al-Sanhuri relegated the sharia to a third and therefore minor place by selecting some concepts from the sharia on a piecemeal basis.[93] However, Mohammed Fadel argues that al-Sanhuri acknowledged a role for the premodern Islamic legal tradition within state law and thus "assured the continued relevance of that tradition precisely at a time when its continued legal relevance was increasingly in doubt."[94] In so doing, Fadel contends, al-Sanhuri reinforced "the notion that the law was an artifact of sovereign will rather than the product of the religious and discursive practices that constituted Pre-Modern Islamic Law."[95]

Personal Status Law

In modern Egypt, civil and criminal codes have been based for the most part on European law. In the nineteenth century, the sharia was marginalized and consigned to the sphere of the family. The codification of other areas of the sharia outside of the family occurred in other areas of the Ottoman Empire and did not take effect in Egypt. In relegating the sharia to the domain of the family, the family became increasingly associated with morality, and in turn with notions of cultural authenticity and tradition. The religious and the private realms were, Hussin argues, "co-constituted over the Muslim family."[96]

Yet, while the family gained a particular resonance for its association with the sharia in the colonial period, its role as an identifier is not solely the product of nineteenth-century colonial intervention. Lev E. Weitz shows how family law was central for medieval Middle Eastern Christians in their articulation of difference from their Muslim counterparts. Weitz argues that Christian bishops in early medieval Syria, Iraq, and Iran responded to the development of Islamic jurisprudence from the seventh to the ninth centuries by forming new traditions of communal law.[97] East Syrians, in particular, he argues, "developed the most extensive tradition of Christian law in the medieval caliphate."[98] The distance of Egypt's Coptic community from the center of Islamic legal thought—and its relatively large size—meant that it was not until the eleventh century that Coptic elites produced law that regulated Christian households.[99]

Weitz argues that marriage and the family became central to the creation of an area of communal law for Christians. In the seventh century, marriage was brought under the "purview of religious law" and became "constitutive of the religious community as a social body."[100] Weitz points out that "it would take several centuries for the Latin and Greek churches to develop a systematic theology of marriage as a sacrament."[101] Safi Ibn al-'Assal (c. 1205–65), whose compilation of church writings helped form the basis of Coptic ecclesiastical law, discusses family law—such as marriage, divorce, and inheritance—in considerable detail.[102] These areas were a source of competition between the jurisdiction of non-Muslim communal courts and the sharia courts, as will be seen in chapter 7.

The construction of family law or what came to be known in the late nineteenth century as personal status law is intertwined with the history of non-Muslims in premodern Islamic law. It also stems from the Ottoman Empire and what had emerged by the nineteenth century to be called the millet system. The millet system gave non-Muslims of the Ottoman Empire considerable judicial autonomy over what came to be described as "religious" laws, which were laws relating to the family and other civil issues such as education. Niyazi Berkes argues that, in the early nineteenth century, Sultan Mahmud II (1785–1839) wanted to abolish the millet divisions and establish equality for non-Muslims. However, he was prevented by the colonial powers which lobbied for the continuation of the privileges of the Empire's non-Muslim communities.[103] Colonial powers lobbied for such privileges based on existing areas of law over which non-Muslim communities had autonomy.

Niyazi Berkes argues that it is the failure to abolish the millet system that led Mahmud to make a distinction between worldly and religious affairs and to exclude an area defined as religious from reform. Mahmud pushed the office of the shaykh al-Islam outside the area of the government that was to be reformed. He then equated the office of the shaykh al-Islam with the millet system. In so doing, Mahmud placed matters that were of concern to the millets in what was defined as the religious realm. While the office of the shaykh al-Islam had initially been intended for the interpretation of and consultation about religious-legal matters related to temporal affairs, after Mahmud's reforms, it became the highest office regarded as religious and was seen as having jurisdiction over Muslims only. It was also seen as remaining beyond the scope of reform. Thus, separate religious courts emerged that were not part of the reform process, thereby separating the sphere of government, legislation, and law from the domain of religion. From Mahmud's time, Berkes shows that the word "religious" acquired a new meaning and came to be identified with that which is unchanging. Reform was limited to the creation of a body of public law separate from the sharia. The Reform Charter of 1839 opened the "first formal breach between the 'temporal' and the 'religious.'"[104]

It is often assumed that personal status law or family law was simply left unchanged as a result of the British abstaining from interfering in religion.[105] Conversely, in pushing back against this argument, others have argued that in restricting the sharia to the area of personal status law, this category of law was effectively constructed or invented.[106] Yet it is also important to note the ways in which the construction of a new category of family law was based on existing areas over which non-Muslims had judicial autonomy. Thus, family law was not so much invented, but the boundaries between what it stood for and what it did not stand for became more heavily inscribed.

During the late Ottoman Empire, the codification of the sharia in the form of the majalla did not include family law. The commission drafting the majalla had intended to produce a body of laws to govern the family, but the shaykh al-Islam opposed continued codification and the committee dissolved without having codified marriage, family, and inheritance laws.[107] In 1886 a statement was issued by the Ministry of Justice that matters relating to marriage, divorce, alimony, retaliation, wills, and inheritance would come under the jurisdiction of the sharia courts. Berkes maintains that, by opposing further codification, the ulama made sure that the sharia would continue to operate within aspects of private religious law and that the sharia provisions with regard to constitutional, criminal, and commercial law would be removed.[108]

As a result, the sharia no longer had jurisdiction over commercial and criminal cases. The sharia courts were confined to what came to be known as family law, which evolved to be limited to marriage, divorce, inheritance, and the custody of children and was eventually referred to as personal status law. The term personal status was first used in 1875 by Muhammad Qadri Pasha, who had written a codification of the sharia in the style of European legal codes. Even as late as 1880, the term "matters of the sharia" was often used to denote personal status. The first definition of personal status was given by the Egyptian Court of Cassation, Egypt's highest civil and criminal appellate court, in 1934.[109] The concept of personal status was derived from "statut personnel" in the French Napoleonic Code, which was a reference to laws related to one's person vis-à-vis the law.[110]

While the jurisdiction of the sharia courts narrowed, the courts were also changed. The sharia courts were bureaucratized: an appellate system was introduced, new emphasis was put on documentation in judicial proce- dure, and written codes were authorized.[111] A code for the sharia courts was promulgated in 1880 and amended in 1887; it restricted the jurisdiction of the sharia to the family. While the sharia was retained for family law, Cuno argues that it was changed through the process of codification and was influ- enced by the Napoleonic Code of 1804.[112]

Before 1920, the Egyptian courts applied Muslim family law. This law was uncodified, although it accorded official status to the Hanafi school. The codification of family law began in the 1920s and the very act of sub- jecting Hanafi law to statutory provisions represented "the subordination of the Sharīʿa to legislative power."[113] Tarek A. Elgawhary argues that the concept of codifying personal status law was theoretically and operationally problematic for some ulama who saw it as un-Islamic. However, he shows that for others it was a way to preserve the Islamic legal heritage. Muham- mad ʿAbduh (1849–1905), for example, defended and advocated the codifi- cation of personal status law.[114] He called for the establishment of articles of law that would "indicate rulings in a straightforward manner, apply to all possible cases, be set forth in logical categories, and use simple linguis- tic constructions."[115] For ʿAbduh, the purpose of codifying the law was to ensure public welfare and the order and cohesion of society.[116] Elgawhary argues that the majority of the ulama accepted codification of the sharia in theory, "but often critiqued the result of the actual codification process."[117] In fact, he contends, the ulama were more concerned that they had not been included in the codification process than they were with the product of such codification.[118]

The codification of family law in Egypt occurred in 1920, 1923, 1929, and then in 1943 and 1946. Hanafi law formed the basis of family law, and the main opinion of the Hanafi school—while sometimes selecting from other schools of law—was applied to any questions that had not been addressed directly in the codes.[119]

Nationalists were aware that the maintenance of different personal status courts for matters of family law for Muslims and non-Muslims could undermine the nationalist project. Criticisms of the existence of separate sharia and non-Muslim communal courts date to as early as the 1890s, but became more important from the 1930s on.[120] For this reason, during the 1930s and 1940s, the Egyptian government proposed to transfer the jurisdiction of the sharia and communal courts to a unified system. Other proposals aimed to further restrict the jurisdiction of the sharia and communal courts and reform their procedures. However, the leaders of the non-Muslim communities—supported by the British authorities—resisted these proposals, assuming that such reforms would end up imposing the sharia. As a result, all the proposals were dropped.[121]

However, in 1955 Nasser abolished the sharia and the communal courts. The law that abolished the courts aimed at consolidating the state's legal sovereignty. The memorandum that accompanied the law stated that *"the rules of public law require that the sovereignty of the state be complete and absolute in the interior, and that all those who live in it, without distinction or nationality, be submitted to the laws of the country, to its courts and to a single juridical jurisdiction"* (italics in the cited source).[122] The authors of the memorandum argued that Egyptian law, in which Egyptians submit themselves to numerous jurisdictions, undermined the sovereignty of the state. The law for the reorganization of the courts stated that judgments in matters of personal status would be issued "according to the most approved opinion of the school of Abū Ḥanīfa except where specific legislation has been issued."[123] For non-Muslim Egyptians who had organized communal jurisdiction at the time of the promulgation of the law, judgment was to be issued "according to their own legislation." However, notably it included a caveat: such legislation was to pay "due regard to public order."[124]

The Sharia as State Law and the Idea of the Sharia

Today, the great majority of countries of the Islamic world base their legal systems on the understanding that the state should monopolize legal authority. Yet, Hallaq shows, to assume that the state should exercise legal authority is "neither obvious nor normative" for the Islamic world.[125] But Islamic revivalists who call for the application of the sharia advocate that it is the role of the state to deliver the sharia. Wood argues that, for much of the nineteenth century, sharia was understood as a flexible source of law that could exist alongside state law.[126] Khaled Fahmy shows that, in the 1840s and 1850s in criminal law, the Egyptian state utilized the sharia alongside the siyasa councils.[127]

Wood argues that in the nineteenth century, the political elite had mixed feelings about the marginalization of the sharia. The idea that the sharia should be revived to replace Franco-Egyptian law only became a fully developed theory in the twentieth century. It was from the 1920s on, in particular, that the sharia "was increasingly identified and advertised as a singularly complete and valid source for the development of a comprehensive system of positive laws that was created, managed, and enforced by the state."[128] Proponents of this view felt that the sharia should supersede all other law "and could not exist comfortably parallel, let alone in a state of subjugation, to 'man-made' laws that were considered morally inferior."[129]

Wood contends that, from the 1930s, there was a much more explicit opposition to European law.[130] Advocates of the revival of the sharia increasingly saw sharia in terms of positive law. Rashid Rida (1865–1935) called for the centralization of Islamic legal authority within the state. After the demise of the caliphate in 1924, Rida advocated the revival of the caliphate and emphasized the continued importance of its temporal and religious role. He also asserted that the ulama should make decisions of public law and policy acting in consultation with the caliph. Thus, "the 'ulamā' no longer need to consider themselves the sole guardians of the law against governmental corruptions."[131] Rather, political authority should lie in the hands of the ulama. Rida proposed one single body that would be legislative and judicial. The consensus (ijmaʿ) of the jurists who are qualified had binding authority and was to become a kind of formal institution for the first time in Sunni Islam.[132]

Hussin illustrates that the marginalization of the sharia "was accompanied by its symbolic centralization."[133] The sharia provided a platform for challenging the authority of the colonial state. Thus, the delivery of the sharia—or lack thereof—became "central to the legitimacy of the state."[134] This shift tied "the individual Muslim to the state through the delivery of Islamic law."[135] The understanding that it is the role of the state to deliver the sharia has become ubiquitous in Islamist thought.

Islamic theorists no longer saw the state as something to be kept at arms' length, but as something to be captured and utilized in the Islamic renewal project. Islamic reformers wanted to revive Islamic traditions and the sharia, but they also emphasized the importance of modern courts and legal codes. Such an approach to the sharia as state law undermined the distinction between the sharia and siyasa. Yet those who called for a revival of the sharia advocated something akin to the removal of such a separation.

It was with the postcolonial state—from the 1970s on in particular—that the impetus to collapse the separation between the sharia and siyasa and locate Islamic legal authority in the state became a dominant demand. Hassan al-Banna (1906–49), the founder of the Muslim Brotherhood, emphasized the importance of establishing Islam from the grassroots up and his thought was therefore less developed with respect to the state. However, many later Islamists associated with the moderate branch of the Muslim Brotherhood sought to locate Islamic legal authority in the state. The Muslim Brotherhood has been committed to the concept of the Islamic state as central to the Islamist vision. Yusuf al-Qaradawi (b. 1926), an Egyptian Islamic scholar and chairman of the International Union of Islamic Scholars, contends that the idea that Islam is a religion and not a state is a malicious idea implanted by Western imperialism. The comprehensive nature of the sharia means that it "must become immersed in all aspects of life."[136] He writes that "the Islamic state is an ideological and an intellectual one. It is a state that is based on a doctrine ('aqida) and on a method (manhaj). It is not a mere 'security apparatus' that would preserve the umma from internal assault or from external invasion. Rather, its function is deeper and greater than that. Its function is to educate the umma and instruct it in the teachings and the principles of Islam and prepare a positive atmosphere and suitable climate for making Islam's doctrines, its ideas and teachings into a practical and palpable reality."[137] For al-Qaradawi, the notion in premodern writings that it was the state's role to provide the circumstances under which Muslims could live according to the sharia has given way to a much deeper conception of the state's role. It is the role of the state to help every Muslim perform his duty of commanding good and forbidding wrong.[138] The Islamic state, he asserts, believes "in a single morality, a morality for all people, a morality that cannot be divided up or be made variegated."[139]

The idea of the state as something to be captured and utilized in the Islamic renewal project has featured prominently in the way that the sharia is used in contemporary discourse on the relationship between Islam and the modern state. The sharia became a rallying cry for social justice. It became the focal point for the ideal of a utopian future. The sharia was a way that the ulama sought to establish their authority and a means by which Islamists sought to undermine the authority of the ulama. Perhaps more importantly, the sharia increasingly became an idea to challenge the postcolonial state. What various political and religious actors meant when they invoked the sharia varied. For its advocates, the sharia is seen as a repository of culture, tradition, and authenticity. Conversely, for its detractors, it is reactionary.

The concept of a transcendental unrooted sharia has figured prominently in contemporary discussions about the sharia and the modern
state. In such discussions, the idea of the sharia as an entity that one either
chooses to have or not to have, that one opts in or out of, has become
normalized. Armando Salvatore argues that the idea of the sharia "laying
a monopolistic claim to regulating public life and society" only emerged in
the last quarter of the nineteenth century.[140] During this time, he writes,
sharia was reformulated as a contribution to the normative structure of the
public sphere and was seen as a "norm-ideal mediating between the project
of reform of selves and society and the legitimacy of a reformed legal system."[141] While debates on the sharia were not highly visible, sharia "was an
issue, and indeed a central and inescapable one for the reform project."[142]
Sharia discourse portrayed the sharia as an idea that connected the project
of reform for individual Muslims and society with the legitimacy of the
legal system. This new conception of the sharia was presented as something
that would order and civilize, an abstract entity disconnected from its multivalent history.[143]

The idea of the sharia as a civilizing concept also gained traction through
the religious / secular binary. Salvatore maintains that, prior to the 1920s, it
is anachronistic to refer to an opposition between secular and Islamic intellectuals. He argues that, before the turn of the century and even later, a
clear awareness of the distinction between the secular and the Islamic did
not yet exist. The need for the distinction between the Islamic and the non-
Islamic in discourse in the Egyptian public sphere arose in the 1920s and
1930s.[144] By the 1930s, the idea of an Islamist opposition to the secularization
of Egyptian law had developed. Such opposition tended to emphasize modern approaches and attitudes to Islamic law. Clark B. Lombardi shows that
many of the Islamists of the time reimagined the classical doctrine of siyasa
shar'iyya, "arguing that the state must apply a code of law that was drafted
in accordance with some re-imagined modern vision of *siyāsa shar'iyya*."[145]
Islamists emphasize interpreting the sharia and drafting Islamic legal codes
with a view toward creating positive law. Salvatore argues that, from the
1960s to the 1980s, sharia became highly visible, "laying a monopolistic claim
to regulating public life and society."[146]

Abullahi An-Na'im argues that the concept of an Islamic state is postcolonial and is "based on a European model of the state and a totalitarian view
of law and public policy as instruments of social engineering by the ruling
elites."[147] He maintains that those who advocate "a so-called Islamic state
in the modern context seek to use the institutions and powers of the state,

as constituted by European colonialism and continued after independence, to regulate individual behavior and social relations."[148] But, An-Na'im points out, sharia principles cannot be enacted and enforced by the state as public law since "if such enactment and enforcement is attempted, the outcome will necessarily be the political will of the state and not the religious law of Islam."[149] He argues that an Islamic state results in a narrow part of Islam being taken to represent Islam itself, since the process of codifying the sharia requires that state officials select from among differing legal interpretations rooted in the schools of law.[150]

The idea of the sharia—disconnected from the varied methods of the schools of law—has led, to use An-Na'im's term, to a "narrowness" in the way that the sharia is referred to by Islamists. This narrowness has often been described as vagueness. The Muslim Brotherhood, for example, has been criticized for its political slogan "Islam is the solution" and for being vague on what aspects of the sharia they wish to be implemented. Bruce Rutherford argues that calls to implement the sharia are more about identity than they are about specific legal rulings. He argues that, in the works of contemporary Islamic thinkers, it is the moral and cultural importance of the sharia that is dominant. Thus, according to Rutherford, Islamic theorists do not aim to implement a particular legal code but rather to "re-ground Egyptian society in its Islamic history, culture, and tradition."[151]

We can see the idea of the sharia in the thought of the contemporary jurist Tariq al-Bishri (b. 1933). For al-Bishri, the sharia represents an ideological heritage "al-turath al-fikri." This heritage, he argues, is shared by all people including people from other religions and denominations.[152] Thus, al-Bishri contends, the sharia is a unifying force for all Arabs as well as for Muslim non-Arabs and "expresses an authentic sphere (majal) in which the religious and the nationalist trend can meet."[153] For al-Bishri, the sharia will help create an Egyptian national consciousness that emphasizes national unity between Muslims and Egypt's Coptic Christians but is also rooted in the Islamic tradition. Thus, through the sharia—subject to new interpretations and independent research—contemporary Muslims can reconcile the split that Egyptian society is afflicted by, the split between what is new and what has been inherited. Such reconciliation would, he argues, give greater weight to "the legal system that is more continuous with the environment, and more connected to the people and their heritage" than to a legal system that is foreign and newly arrived.[154] For al-Bishri, Islamic jurisprudence on the question of the state, law, and the constitutional system is relatively undeveloped.[155] Thus, he maintains, Islamic thinking needs to distance itself from the approaches of Islamic jurists and come up with new ways of addressing Islamic sharia and the state. He himself does this in his thinking regarding the principle of equal citizenship for non-Muslims.[156] For al-Bishri, the sharia is less a body of law and more of what he refers to as "a referential authority" or a *marji'iyya*. Al-Bishri's concept of the frame of reference reflects an understanding of the sharia as an idea or a concept as opposed to a body of processes and rules. Secularism, he argues, is also a marji'iyya that produced socialism, Nazism, liberalism, and capitalism. Likewise, the Islamic frame of reference is capable of producing different approaches, ideas, and opinions.[157] It also allows for thinking in terms of the various possible norms that the sharia can yield through ongoing reinterpretation.

The idea that the sharia provides guidance or a number of possibilities within a frame rather than mandating specific instructions is reflected in the argument, frequently made by Islamist actors, that they do not want a religious state, but rather a civil state with an Islamic frame of reference. A November 2011 Muslim Brotherhood party platform declares that the state envisaged by the Freedom and Justice Party is "a modern Islamic, national, constitutional and modern state which has the Islamic sharia as a frame of reference."[158] The Muslim Brotherhood was emphasizing that, while on some issues the sharia is more definitive in its guidance, on most others it establishes general rules and principles "leaving the details to be worked out through interpretation and legislation according to what suits the period of time or environment."[159] The concept of the sharia as a frame of reference has emerged as the dominant way of thinking about the sharia. It has taken over conceptions of the sharia as a body of complex laws, treatises, and writings rooted in particular institutional methodologies.

In this chapter, I have undertaken a historical analysis of the sharia. I have shown that, contrary to the argument that the sharia is inherently incompatible with modern state law, premodern rulers gave themselves the right to legislate. The concept of siyasa shar'iyya enabled the premodern Islamic polity to legislate without the need to positively enforce Islamic jurisprudence. However, this was based on the assumption that the sharia would provide a negative restriction on the polity's legislative capacity. Premodern Islamic systems remained obligated not to contravene the sharia. Thus, while premodern Islamic systems appropriated the right to make legislation, it was bounded by a higher law. It is for this reason that premodern sharia is somewhat conceptually different from modern state law. Premodern sharia was formulated as jurists' law by individuals with scholarly expertise in the Islamic texts. These individuals were private scholars who felt that it was important for them to retain a level of distance from the ruling polity. Doubting that a ruler could be truly just, these scholars endeavored to protect the sharia from too much state intervention. While this distance from the ruling polity was in part compromised by what Ahmet Kuru refers to as the "ulama-state alliance" from the eleventh century on, such distance remained a powerful ideal.[160] Maintaining the distinction between the sharia and state law also enabled the schools of law to flourish and maintain the concept of mutual orthodoxy. This multivalence of the sharia was increasingly threatened by the state's legal capacities, particularly in the Ottoman period, when the sponsorship of one school of law became a means by which the empire sought to gain control over legislation.

In the nineteenth century, the sharia was marginalized and relegated to the sphere of family law while European codes were introduced for civil and criminal codes. Family law, which eluded the kind of reform that other areas of law were subject to, became tied to the idea of religious difference and to communal identity. While colonial powers lobbied for family law, family law is not just a product of colonial interventions but is, in some respects, also a continuation on from the history of non-Muslim communal law. However, as a result of those interventions, the family became more specifically demarcated and gained a new resonance. Family law remained the one area that was not fully subject to the state's efforts to consolidate legal control through the unification of law in Egypt.

The marginalization of the sharia had three important consequences. The first consequence was that, in consigning the sharia to the sphere of the family, the family became more associated with religion, tradition, and cultural authenticity. The second consequence was that the sharia became central in discourses that opposed colonial, and, more specifically, postcolonial rule. Thus, rule by the sharia became central to new Islamist discourses that called for a return to Egypt's culturally authentic past. It became vitally important for Islamist oppositional politics from the 1970s on. However, the sharia that became central was tied to the state and to state power. So calls for a return to the sharia were manifested in terms of the enforcement of the sharia as state law.

The third consequence of the marginalization of the sharia was that it led to the emergence of the sharia as a concept, an idea, or a frame of reference. This meant that the sharia, for the most part, was seen not in terms of a specific body of laws, but as an idea, divorced from its institutional methodologies. Islamist thinkers increasingly came to refer to the sharia not in terms of its particular complex laws or the multivalence that had existed in premodern contexts, but as an ahistorical concept, the application of which would lead to national regeneration. Invocations of the Islamic frame of reference as opposed to a specific body of law reflects how Islamist thinking became attached to the sharia as an abstract concept, disconnected from premodern sharia. The emergence of the sharia as an idea then made it possible for commitments to the sharia to be inserted in the Egyptian constitution at a later date.

CHAPTER 3

Constitution Making in Egypt

The lyrics from a popular Egyptian colloquial song, which was widely sung in the streets during the 1919 revolution against the British, include the following words: "The Egyptian is resilient; and now he is willing and able and can do anything. His achievements are worthy of praise and he will do this all to gain a constitution. We are the sons of the Pharaohs, which no one can dispute."[1] The lyrics of this song show how the idea of a constitution contained the promise of an undefined but better political future. In this song, the promise of a constitution is inextricably linked to independence and the establishment of a new political order. The song sung by protestors reflected something abstract about the power of a constitution. The constitution, it implied, could lay the foundations of a new political order and speak for the nation as a whole.

In Egypt, constitution making has formed an inherent part of the ending of political orders and the making of new ones. Constitutions—particularly the most recent—have played an essential role in articulating the essence of the nation or the national will through which the state claims the right to represent its citizens. Constitution making has become bound up with the ongoing making and remaking of Egyptian nationalism.

Constitution drafting and constitutional annulment have played an important role in Egypt's history since the promulgation of its first constitution in 1923 and the establishment of the 1956 Constitution shortly after Egypt's full independence in 1952. In 1971 a new constitution was promulgated under Sadat's neoliberal order when concerns about the Islamic nature of the state became increasingly vocal. Yet constitution writing played a particularly important role in the events after the Egyptian revolution of 2011. The Constitutions of 2012 and 2014 took on a rhetorical power that transcended the specifics of the constitutional clauses themselves. The 2012 Constitution, which became known as the "Brotherhood's constitution," was maligned, and was directly associated with the organization's brief period in power. Conversely, the 2014 Constitution was framed as a way of healing the divisions in Egyptian society. Critiquing one constitution and praising the other became a key tool in the polarized politics that characterized Egypt. The fact that constitutions were able to be used as weapons in political maneuvering speaks to the role of constitutions in Egyptian identity politics. In the debates about the 2012 and 2014 Constitutions, the very nature of the Egyptian state and society was, it was argued, at stake.

The central role of constitution making in the articulation of Egyptian national identity forms the first part of this chapter. The second part of the chapter focuses on the introduction of Article 2 to the 1971 Constitution, which made a formal commitment to the closer entanglement of the sharia and state law. The fact that constitutions were not seen simply as a means for directing political processes, but increasingly as a reflection of the very core of the Egyptian nation itself, explains why, starting in the 1970s, Islamists were so interested in establishing a commitment to the sharia in the constitution. Since its introduction in 1971 and amendment in 1980, this article has continued to form the cornerstone for the relationship between religion and the state in Egypt. The introduction of Article 2 in 1971 linked the sharia to state law in a new way. In tying the sharia to state law, the sharia was seen as an expression of the essence of the nation.

The Making of the Egyptian State

In the Arab and broader Islamic world over the past century and a half, there has been a rich history of constitution writing. There is a clear link between the act of independence and the founding of a new political order through a constitution. Constitutions in the Arab and Islamic world have also played an important role in articulating the political and social ideologies that form the basis of these new political orders. The first Ottoman Constitution was promulgated by Sultan ʿAbd al-Hamid II in 1876. It was done under pressure from a small group of reformist bureaucrats.[2] The constitution provided a means by which ʿAbd al-Hamid II assured European powers that the Ottoman

Empire was reforming and would not fragment.[3] The Ottoman Constitution is reflective of the state of transition that the empire was going through. It contained a number of reformist measures to check the power of the sultan and contained references to national identity and homogeneity. It promoted Ottomanism, which advocated that citizenship was based on a geographical area without regard for religion (Article 8), and Article 17 established equality before the law "without prejudice to religion."[4] The Ottoman Constitution established Islam as the official religion and declared that "the state protects the free exercise of all the religions recognized in the Empire and accords the religious privileges granted to the different communities on condition that no offense is committed against public order and good morals" (Article 11).[5]

Egypt's first constitution appeared in 1882, shortly after the promulgation of the Ottoman Constitution. It only had fifty-three articles, many of which were short and focused on the role of the ruling council, and on questions of electoral procedure.[6] Nathan Brown argues that the constitution was designed to support a state more able to resist foreign occupation.[7] It did little to proclaim a new ideological orientation. This lack of ideological orientation must be partly understood by the fact that Egypt was still technically part of the Ottoman Empire and did not separate from it until 1914. Up until then, Egyptians had been Ottoman citizens. The nationalist narrative emphasizes that Egypt was only nominally part of the Ottoman Empire throughout the nineteenth century.[8] Khaled Fahmy, however, contends that Muhammad 'Ali should be understood as an Ottoman reformer, who did not aim for Egyptian independence from the Ottoman Empire, but rather had ambitions to establish hereditary rule over this Ottoman province.[9]

The Egyptian nationalist perspective also emphasizes that Egyptians saw themselves as Egyptians and not as Ottomans by the latter part of the nineteenth century. Will Hanley, however, questions the idea that Egypt was independent of the Ottoman Empire before the turn of the century. He maintains that Egyptians saw themselves as Ottoman subjects with Ottoman nationality until as late as 1905.[10]

It is perhaps for this reason that the Egyptian Constitution of 1882 did not contain ideological statements. Neither did it contain any statement of basic principles about Islam. According to Brown, at the time, "Islam was simply not an issue. . . . Egypt's first constitution did not dabble in transcendental truths."[11] Brown argues that the Constitution of 1882 and other nineteenth-century Arab constitutions did not proclaim new principles. They often reiterated Ottoman norms, referring to the will of the ruler rather than to the people or the nation. Brown argues that the fundamental purpose of nineteenth-century constitutions was to reform state authority and enhance its efficacy.[12]

By the 1919 revolution against the British occupation in Egypt, many called themselves Egyptians.[13] The second Egyptian constitution was promulgated in 1923 and followed Egypt's formal separation from the Ottoman Empire in 1914 and the 1919 revolution after which it gained partial independence from the British. The 1923 Constitution laid the foundation for the emerging Egyptian nation state. A number of the concepts that were to feature prominently later on, such as the concept of the Egyptian people and the nation, were present. The constitution "discussed the relationship that men and women had to the 'nation' (*al-umma*) as the source of power/authority (*masdr al-sulutat*)."[14]

The 1923 Constitution declared Egypt a sovereign, free, and independent state, with Islam as its religion and Arabic its official language. The Egyptian Constitution of 1923 was seen by royalists as maintaining the position of the monarchy in Egypt, whereas the nationalists saw the constitution as establishing the nation as the source of all power and representing a contract among members of the nation.[15] Private property was protected and the sanctity of the home affirmed (Articles 8 and 9). The constitution guaranteed freedom of thought and gave freedom of expression "according to the limits of the law" (Article 14). It gave freedom of assembly, also subject to the law (Articles 20 and 21). It asserted the equality of all citizens before the law regardless of origin (*asl*), language, or religion (Article 3).

The constitution received little opposition from Islamic reformers. At the Muslim Brotherhood's Fifth General Conference in 1939, Hasan al-Banna, who founded the Muslim Brotherhood in 1928, expressed his support for the constitution, seeing its potential to guarantee personal freedom, preserve the principle of consultation (*shura*), and necessitate the ruling powers' procurement of popular support. Constitutions, he asserted, help ensure the responsibility and accountability of the rulers before the people. Al-Banna claimed that "the Muslim Brotherhood considers the system of constitutional rule the closest existing system of governance in the world to Islam."[16] He did, however, state that the constitution was in need of clarification and certain parts were vague and subject to a variety of interpretations. He also argued that the constitution is one thing and laws another, and called for greater compatibility between the laws of Egypt and the teachings of Islam.[17] He felt that the constitutional stipulation that Islam is the religion of the state was sufficient to require that the laws of Egypt not contradict Islam, mentioning the Islamic laws on adultery, usury, drinking, and gambling in particular.[18]

The Constitution of 1923 declared Islam as the religion of the state (Article 149). According to B. L. Carter, the Constituent Assembly agreed to the inclusion of this article without discussion or opposition including from its Coptic members. Carter also reports that there was little opposition from Copts among the broader Egyptian populace, although the newspaper *al-Watan* clearly preferred that a state religion not be established. Carter argues that "many Copts seemed to feel that the constitution adequately protected their interests, and they counted on the continuance of Muslim good will."[19]

During discussions about the 1923 Constitution, the British supported a parliamentary quota for the Copts, while both Muslims and Copts were divided on the issue of quotas. The Constitution of 1923, however, did not mention quotas for Christians. It stipulated the equality of all Egyptians before the law regardless of religion (Article 3), and gave absolute freedom of belief (Article 12). It stipulated that "the state protects freedom to practice religious rites and creeds according to prevailing customs in Egypt within the bounds of public order (*al-nizam al-ʿamm*) and decency (*adab*)" (Article 13).[20]

While the constitution declared that Islam was the religion of the state, no commitment was made to the sharia. Brown argues that the absence of any constitutional reference to the sharia was not publicly criticized.[21] Issues related to Islam and the relationship between the sharia and positive law, he contends, attracted little public debate, and after the promulgation of the constitution, "debates about religion were rarely phrased in constitutional terms."[22] Hasan al-Banna, for example, did not lament the absence of a constitutional statement on the sharia. While he argued that the Muslim Brotherhood considers the principles of constitutional rule "agreeable with, or rather derived from the system of Islam," he mentions that some laws need clarifying, tightening, and limiting so that they are not so subject to manipulation. While he was concerned that Egyptian law should be more consistent with religion, he was more concerned with cultivating an allegiance to Islam within the next generation.[23]

The Constitution of 1923 has been praised for having provided opportunities to realize a state free from religious bias and from state interference. For Samir Marcos, this was a time that emphasized citizenship for Copts that transcended religious identity.[24] According to Carter, the constitution laid the foundation for Copts' legal equality with Muslims.[25] Paul Sedra contends that, from the late nineteenth century on, elite Copts possessed "disproportionate influence and wealth" and played a prominent role in negotiating the nature of Egyptian nationalism.[26] The constitution—along with the 1919 revolution against the British in which Muslims and Copts participated—has been credited with the onset of a kind of golden age for Egyptian Copts in which lay Copts were active in the political arena.

However, for Carter, the expectations created by the 1923 Constitution were not fulfilled. He contends that the use of ethnicity and religion in the struggle for power that characterized the 1930s stymied the constitution's potential. Copts, he writes, felt that the rules of the constitution had not been followed. Secularism, "had failed, and in its place kinship, communal networks and the church became increasingly important to those trying to escape the effects of discrimination."[27] Carter maintains that it was only when the constitution's promise of equality failed to materialize that Copts began to voice their concern about Islam being the religion of the state.[28]

We, the Egyptian People

The Constitution of 1923 remained in force (albeit interrupted from 1930 to 1935) until the revolution of 1952 which brought an end to the British occupation and the Egyptian monarchy. A new constitution was issued by Gamal 'Abd al-Nasser in 1956. Unlike the 1923 Constitution, the 1956 Constitution made repeated references to "We, the Egyptian people." This reflected the growing need for the constitution to invoke the national will as the source of its legitimacy. The constitution declared the right to liberty, freedom from fear, dignity, and justice and reflected a more inclusive national discourse. Article 3 of the 1956 Constitution declared Islam to be the religion of the state.[29]

The constitution's emphasis on the Arab identity of Egypt was a key feature. The preamble stated that "We the Egyptian people feel our reciprocal existence in the greater Arab entity."[30] This was, according to Mervat Hatem, quite new and "partly designed to stress the homogeneity of the new nation."[31] The Constitution of 1956 made the president stronger than the Egyptian monarch had been by weakening the legislative authority and enhancing the president's ability to issue decrees with the force of law.[32] According to Brown, this ensured that "Egypt's judicial institutions would now operate within an authoritarian context."[33]

The Constitution of 1956 has similarly been singled out for its secular nature. According to Hatem, the emphasis in the 1956 Constitution on Islam as the religion of the state "did not seek to subordinate the Copts to Muslims in the new national society."[34] Article 31 stipulated that "Egyptians are the same (sawa') before the law. They are equal in rights and in public duties. There is to be no distinction between them on account of sex, origin (asl), language, religion, or creed."[35] In addition, Article no. 43 stipulated that freedom of belief was absolute. However, it contained an important caveat, which was similar to one in the 1923 Constitution: the right to religious worship and beliefs would have to be in "in accordance with the customs prevailing in Egypt within the bounds of public order (al-nizam al-'amm) and decency (adab)."³⁶ Reflecting common narratives about the constitution's secularity, Hatem argues that such articles about freedom of belief and religious discrimination "fostered a legal belief in the horizontal comradeship between Muslims and Copts and men and women."³⁷ Not only that, Hatem writes, but the constitution actually forbade the formal use of religion to discriminate and create divisions. In this way, she argues, it helped secure equal citizenship for everyone.³⁸

After Anwar Sadat became president in 1970, he issued a new constitution in 1971 which remained in effect (with some important amendments in 1980 and 2007) until the removal of Hosni Mubarak from office in 2011. Sadat suggested that the new constitution would express "the true Egyptian way of life and tradition."³⁹ By this time, the Egyptian public sphere had come to be dominated by conceptions about the relationship between the secular and the Islamic. It reflected a growing concern with the question of what role religion should have. This was increasingly expressed in constitutional terms. According to Brown, members of the 1971 drafting committee had many debates about the relationship between socialism and democracy, the role of Islam, and women's rights.⁴⁰

The 1971 Egyptian Constitution contained a number of measures that have been described as liberal. It stated that the government would be based on the rule of law. Article 46 guaranteed "freedom of belief ('aqida) and freedom to practice religious rites."⁴¹ It guaranteed freedom of thought and gave freedom of expression within the limits of the law (Article 47). It strengthened parliamentary autonomy and the independence of the judiciary. It also prohibited unauthorized searches and torture.⁴² However, these liberal measures were counteracted by the increasing power that the constitution gave to the presidency.

The 1971 Constitution also established the importance of judicial review. Article 68 prohibited any legal provision for removing an administrative act or decision from judicial review. This, according to Brown, represented an initial step toward a more liberal order, while laying the foundation for a state of law and institutions. While Nasser had undermined the independence of the judiciary by "establishing new judicial structures that operated under thinly disguised executive domination," the constitution made a clear commitment to developing state institutions, particularly Egypt's judicial institutions.⁴³ The constitution stated that "the rule of law (siyadat al-qanun) is the basis of rule in the state" (Article 64).⁴⁴

However, the most significant part of the 1971 Constitution was that it formally introduced an explicit statement on the sharia. In so doing, it translated the idea of the sharia as a civilizing order and a symbol of Islamic cultural authenticity and projected it onto the constitution. Article 2 of the 1971 Constitution stated that "Islam is the religion of the state, Arabic is the official language, the principles of the Islamic sharia are *a* main source of legislation." In 1980 Article 2 was amended to read, "The principles of the Islamic sharia are *the* main source of legislation."[45]

The Arab Spring and the Heart and Soul of Egypt

In February 2011, President Hosni Mubarak was deposed in a revolution that ended his thirty-year presidency. At the time, it was assumed that the revolution would usher in a new era of democratic accountability. The aims of the revolution were simple: the protesters called for Mubarak to relinquish the presidency and demanded bread, freedom, and social justice. The revolution was characterized by a broad range of participants, and included Egyptians from all classes, political affiliations, and religions. The revolutionary atmosphere of Tahrir, the square in which the protesters assembled, was celebrated for its inclusive and ecumenical nature: constant references were made to Christians and Muslims praying alongside one another. According to Brown, in March 2011, when asked if the judiciary was divided over the revolution, a senior judge who was connected with the part of the judiciary that did not want confrontation with President Mubarak, said, "Everyone is with the revolution now!"[46]

The description of Mubarak's ouster as constituting a revolution or an Arab Spring was premature. In 2013 what was called a "popular-backed" coup took place in which Egypt's first democratically elected president, Muhammad Mursi, was removed from office. This resulted in the reestablishment of military rule by Mursi's minister of defense, 'Abd al-Fattah al-Sisi, who was supported by the army. Brown points out that most state institutions survived and remained relatively unchanged.[47] In fact, since 2011, the army has succeeded in augmenting its power, its control of the Egyptian economy, and its visual presence in Egyptian public life. Despite the aims of the revolution, Egypt's torture epidemic continues unabated.[48]

What was notable about the revolution of 2011 and the counterrevolution of 2013 was the prominent role that the abolition of constitutions, the writing of constitutions, and the promulgation of constitutions played in the unfolding events. This says something about the intrinsic role and function of constitutions in revolutions as recording the founding moment of politics. The conflict that occurred over the constitution, its drafting, and its role in the transition raises questions about the relationship between sovereignty, democracy, constitutionalism, and the judiciary. The following questions have been raised, but not answered: Does the collectivity of the people exist prior to the constitution or is it the very act of constitution making which creates that collectivity and, consequently, its constituent power? Whenever a constitution is created, what is the source of the constituent power? Who gets to decide what voices get to count in the forming of a constitution? How is what Ulrich Preuss describes as the "pre-political commonness of a group of people" to be represented in constitution drafting?[49]

Postrevolutionary environments are mostly unstable and often there are no existing procedures for answering these questions. Groups tend to take the position of supporting the strategy that will maximize their interests. The history of the events that took place after the revolution of 2011 is complex and fraught. There are two features, however, that are particularly important with regard to the constitutional writing process that took place. One is the importance that was attached to constitution writing. Constitutions were seen as having to reflect the will of the people, although whether the will of the people could—or should—be captured was generally unquestioned. The other feature of the constitutional writing that took place was the moral outrage that accompanied the drafting and promulgation of the 2012 Constitution. This outrage illustrates that the importance of constitutions transcends their ability to provide mechanisms for the workings of government and various procedures. The uproar was symbolic of how constitutions had become the focus for the political struggles over the essence of the Egyptian nation.

Following the ouster of Mubarak, the Constitution of 1971 was suspended on February 13, 2011.[50] In the months following Mubarak's removal, debate focused on the procedure for writing a new constitution. There was considerable debate about how a new Constituent Assembly to draft a new constitution would be formed. The road map established by the Supreme Council of Armed Forces (SCAF) scheduled the election for the People's Assembly and the Shura Council before the formation of a Constituent Assembly, which was the body that was to be responsible for drafting the constitution. It would thus allow the electoral process to determine the Constituent Assembly's makeup. This came to be a deeply acrimonious issue that colored the whole process. Liberals, intellectuals, and the youth were concerned that this road map favored preexisting political groups and organizations, such as the former National Democratic Party and the Muslim Brotherhood, and would therefore prejudice the constitution writing process. Thus, liberal and secular forces pushed to draft a new constitution ahead of parliamentary elections. They wanted to focus on a new constitution first, with a broad committee representing all sectors of Egyptian society taking the time to draft the document that would then guide Egypt through the first elections. Such groups, Kristen Stilt argues, were willing to put up with a long military rule in order to prepare the constitution before holding elections.[51] They criticized the Muslim Brotherhood for wanting to have elections before the writing of the constitution. Amina Shafiq of *al-Ahram* complained that, for the Brotherhood, democracy "is little more than having ballot boxes that are not tampered with."[52] She called for "a full-fledged and liberal democracy, not one that is reduced to having multiple parties or free elections."[53]

During the summer of 2011, SCAF granted some concessions to liberal secular groups who had opposed elections before the writing of a constitution. A number of parties that formed the Democratic Coalition for Egypt were asked to draft a set of supraconstitutional principles, which would serve as guidelines for the drafting of the new constitution. Yet Islamist parties objected to the idea of supraconstitutional guiding principles, claiming that they "would circumvent or expropriate the will of the people."[54] Muhammad Sa'd al-Katatni, secretary-general of the Muslim Brotherhood's Freedom and Justice Party, warned that "the people will protect the gains of their revolution and defend their right to a constitution that expresses their opinions and is the sole document governing them, drawn up without any prior restrictions."[55]

In November 2011, a document containing principles intended to guide the drafting of a new constitution was issued. While it stated that these principles were not supraconstitutional and they were not unchangeable, and while it affirmed that "the people are the source of sovereign power," the document laid down a number of fundamental principles and gave SCAF power to veto any provision of the forthcoming constitution that "contradicts the fundamentals of Egyptian state and society and the general rights and freedoms that have become consolidated through successive Egyptian constitutions."[56] It also stated that "the Arab Republic of Egypt is a democratic state based on the principle of citizenship and upon the rule of law. It respects pluralism and ensures freedom, justice, equality and equal opportunity for all citizens without bias or discrimination. The Egyptian people are a part of the Arab nation and will work to bring about its comprehensive unity."[57] It reiterated a commitment to Article 2 of the 1971 Constitution declaring that "Islam is the religion of the state, Arabic is its official language, and the principles of the Islamic sharia are the main source of legislation." It also affirmed that non-Muslims are able to have control over their own personal status laws and religious affairs.[58]

The elections for the Shura Council and the People's Assembly in the period November 2011–January 2012 returned an Islamist victory. The Salafi al-Nur party became the second largest party in the People's Assembly after the Freedom and Justice Party. The Freedom and Justice Party decided to translate their electoral success into domination of the Constituent Assembly. The People's Assembly and the Shura Council selected a Constituent Assembly in March 2012. However, opponents stressed that, because parliamentary majorities are transitory, the assembly's makeup should reflect all aspects of Egyptian society. This Constituent Assembly was dominated by Islamists, although several Copts were placed on it.[59] According to Zaid Al-Ali, despite the concerns of liberals, "one of the more remarkable aspects of Egypt's constitution-drafting process is that it is the country's first by an elected body," since Egypt's past constitutions were drafted in secret by unrepresentative and unelected political elites.[60]

In April 2012, the Supreme Administrative Court declared this first Constituent Assembly to be unconstitutional on the grounds that its membership included fifty members of the People's Assembly. In addition, on June 14, 2012, the Supreme Constitutional Court announced that the elections held six months earlier for the People's Assembly were invalid because of a misapplication of rules for independent candidates. Barely noticed by the Western media, SCAF followed with an administrative decree to dissolve the People's Assembly. Nimer Sultany calls the intervention by the Supreme Constitutional Court "juristocratic" and argues that it effectively subordinated constituent power to judicial power and thus collapsed the "distinction between legislation and adjudication."[61]

During this time, Mursi was elected president in June 2012 after two rounds of elections. In early June, a new Constituent Assembly somewhat less dominated by Islamists was established. The drafting of the constitution, however, continued to be acrimonious both in terms of process and content. Those deemed secularists walked out and boycotted the drafting process, repeatedly citing the failure of the dominant Islamist factions to compromise on key issues, including the place of religion in the affairs of the state.[62] The Constituent Assembly and the constitution itself were criticized for being unrepresentative and noninclusive.[63] The constitution was criticized for being "more Islamic" than any previous constitution.[64]

In November 2012, it looked like the Supreme Constitutional Court was set to dissolve the Shura Council. Mursi abandoned the Muslim Brotherhood's policy of "risk aversion and gradualism" and, in November 2012, issued a Constitutional Declaration in which he immunized the Constituent Assembly and the Shura Council from dissolution by the Supreme

Constitutional Court.[65] The step allowed the president to issue decrees and draft laws with no oversight from parliament or the judiciary. Mursi had told the Muslim Brotherhood leadership that the declaration would remain in effect until mid-2013, by which time the new constitution would have been drafted and the next national elections held.[66] The Muslim Brotherhood claimed that the Supreme Constitutional Court was poised to dissolve the Constituent Assembly and the Shura Council and said that if they did not do something now, the Muslim Brotherhood headquarters—and possibly the organization itself—were in danger of being dissolved.[67]

The decree enraged the secular opposition, members of the judiciary, and the revolutionary and leftist youth movements. The Western media emphasized that this was an Islamist president showing his true Islamist colors. Representatives of the three Coptic denominations withdrew from the Constituent Assembly "protesting what they believed was a plan by the Freedom and Justice party to ensure that Islamists would be able to control the wording of the new constitution."[68] It was claimed that the draft constitution was "unrepresentative of Egypt's diverse identity."[69] The military also stepped in, arguing, somewhat disingenuously, that while the army had wanted to remain out of politics, "we are citizens with families who are not immune to the effects of what's going on," advising that "the ruling party should learn the way people ought to be governed" and the Islamists cannot alone write the constitution.[70]

While the events were used to criticize the Muslim Brotherhood and undermine its legitimacy, they raised the complex problem of the very source of national sovereignty itself. It is arguable that the origin of the Supreme Constitutional Court was the—as yet—unratified constitution. It is therefore a question whether the Supreme Constitutional Court could claim to have jurisdiction over the process of drafting the very document that would give it its powers.

The declaration of immunity resulted in getting the Constitution of 2012 passed. In December 2012, the Constitution of 2012 was ratified by referendum. Sixty-four percent voted in favor although only 33 percent of eligible voters turned out to vote. In the spring of 2013, a grassroots organization called Tamarod was founded to register opposition to Muhammad Mursi and to force him to call early elections. Tamarod created a surge in opposition to Mursi, and in July 2013, the army and the old regime used this opposition to remove Mursi from power. Both the recently appointed Coptic Orthodox pope, Tawadros II, and the shaykh of al-Azhar were at the side of 'Abd al-Fattah al-Sisi when he announced the end of the Mursi government. It was deemed to be a popular revolution, with Tamarod led by the "people's will."

Muslim Brotherhood accounts see the institutions of the state, such as the judiciary and the police, as having deliberately undermined Mursi's ability to get anything done.[71] The Muslim Brotherhood has argued that the reason for its failure was that the deep state was set against it. Mursi was elected with no political support from the institutions of the state. He did not have the backing of the police, the army, the judiciary, or the press. This meant that, while the Muslim Brotherhood was officially in power, it did not have effective control.[72] There are suggestions that Tamarod was aided by the army, which was supported by the Gulf monarchies.[73] Yasser El-Shimy argues that "no single institution has been as effective in undermining Morsi's presidency, and the Brotherhood's rise to power in general, as the judiciary."[74]

Much has been said and written about the reasons for Mursi's swift removal from power. The majority of accounts lay the blame with the Muslim Brotherhood itself. Yet promoting factional interests, political miscalculations, and overstepping one's mark fail to account for the vitriol and moral outrage that accompanied the crushing of the Muslim Brotherhood. In fact, despite claims that the Muslim Brotherhood was trying to bring about the "Brotherhoodization" of the state, Brown argues that "the extent of personnel changes was not that large." For Brown, Mursi attempted "to placate the state rather than reform it."[75] For example, the Muslim Brotherhood attempted to appease the military through establishing a National Defense Council which would take control of the military's budget (Article 197). In addition, Sultany argues that judges in Egypt "generally maintained institutional continuity that hampered judicial reform, legal continuity that thwarted holding former regime officials accountable, and constitutional continuity that obstructed political re-constitution."[76] This allowed the status quo to reassert itself.

One mistake was that the Constituent Assembly used the 1971 Constitution as a starting point for its discussions. This was partly because the Constituent Assembly was limited by a six-month time frame. The draft of the 2012 Constitution had considerable continuity in terms of style, tone, and organization with the 1971 Constitution. Thus, Zaid Al-Ali argues, "while the new constitution claims to be a product of the people's will, it is heavily influenced by the preceding decades of autocratic rule."[77]

The political incompetency of the Muslim Brotherhood also fails to explain why protests in favor of Mursi were violently suppressed with the dispersal and massacre of pro-Mursi protesters at sit-ins in al-Nahda Square and Rabiʿa al-ʿAdawiyya Square in Cairo in August 2013. Amid the unrest, journalists and several hundred to a thousand protestors were killed by police and military forces. The shaykh of al-Azhar has not spoken out against the subsequent atrocities against the Muslim Brotherhood and ʿAli Gumaʿa, the former grand mufti of Egypt, legitimized the violence. This, Masooda Bano argues, has exposed al-Azhar's "moral authority to unprecedented risks."[78]

After the coup, the Constitution of 2012 was suspended. A new constitutional declaration was issued by ʿAdly Mansour, head of the Supreme Constitutional Court. It stated that the redrafting process would be overseen by a Constitution Committee of ten jurists and law experts—chosen by judicial bodies—who would then refer their draft of the constitution to a Constitution Committee made up of fifty individuals, later known respectively as the Committee of 10 and the Committee of 50. The Committee of 50 was dominated by state institutions and syndicates.[79] Only six of its members came from political parties and therefore reflected a very different perception of how Egyptian society should be represented. Sultany argues that each side ended up doing what it accused the other of doing—that is, excluding the other side from the process. He contends that the "drafting committee's product, like the previous Islamist-dominated committee, reflected the drafters' attempts to promote their factional and institutional interests."[80]

As had happened with the Constitution of 2012, little debate was offered about Article 2 of the 1971 Constitution. Negotiations continued on the basis that Article 2 should remain, with some suggestions that explanatory clauses be added. The 2014 Constitution continued the privileges for the military that had appeared in the 2012 Constitution.[81] In addition, judges obtained guarantees of their independence.[82] The drafting of the new constitution was not without complaint, although this was far more muted. The vitriol and moral outrage were no longer present and coverage in the Western press was considerably reduced.

The Constitution of 2014, like its predecessors, has failed to accomplish what many of its drafters claimed it would—establish a stable, democratic state in which human rights are respected. The consistent failure of Egypt's constitutions to deliver on their promises does not fully account for the continued importance attached to them. I suggest that constitutions should also be seen in terms of their foundational character, and their ability to construct new orders and mark the end of old ones. They must also be seen in terms of their ability to make the state legible on both the international and national levels. Constitutions function as maps by which members of society navigate and by which the state itself projects on its citizens the expectations it has of them. They should be seen in terms of how the citizen is fashioned and how the relationship between religion and politics is defined. In Egypt, constitutions were not seen simply as tools for political processes, but as a reflection of the very essence of the Egyptian nation. This explains why, starting in the

1970s, Islamists were so interested in establishing a commitment to the sharia in the constitution, and why this clause was retained in subsequent constitutions. For them, and for many other Egyptians, the centrality of the sharia in the constitution helped define the core of Egypt itself.

Article 2

Constitutions often serve as a means by which the state lays out the social and political expectations it has of its citizens as well as the expectations those citizens may have of the state. This is why the increasing concern with the Islamic or secular nature of the state was translated into particular constitutional statements. The Constitutions of 1923 and 1956 only made nominal and symbolic references to Islam by stating that Islam was the religion of the state. However, no commitment was made to the sharia. In the 1930s, the Egyptian public sphere became increasingly concerned with the legitimacy of Western law and with whether Egypt was a secular or an Islamic state. This helps explain the appearance of Article 2 of the 1971 Constitution, which had enormous symbolic importance and represented the culmination of the idea that the state was the appropriate vehicle for the application of the sharia. It read that "the principles of the Islamic sharia are *a* main source of legislation." This was amended in 1980 to read, "the principles of the Islamic sharia are *the* main source of legislation."[83]

The introduction of Article 2 was seen by many as a retrograde move. Yet, in many respects, it constituted a departure from the premodern idea that the sharia was jurists' law. While the premodern ruling polity could supplement the sharia, it could not supersede or control it. Thus, a constitutional commitment to the sharia was predicated on a modern conception of the relationship between the state and law, whereby the state monopolizes legal authority. Central to the development of this way of thinking was the political ideology of the Islamist thinker Sayyid Qutb (1906–66). During the 1960s, Qutb developed a more fully fledged theory of the state that was to play a prominent role in Islamist thinking. Qutb articulated the modern concept of sovereignty (*hakimiyya*), the belief that the right to make judgments and issue laws belongs only to God. Giving the right to make judgments and issue laws to anyone other than God rendered one an unbeliever.[84] Islam, he asserted, does not simply "involve words and slogans or religious rites and prayers. Indeed, it is next to this and that and before this and that a system (*nizam*) that judges and a method (*manhaj*) that passes judgment and a leadership that is obeyed and a creation that leans towards a specific system and a specific method."[85] Sayyid Qutb argued that legislation made by an individual or governing class cannot be free of self-interest and puts people in a state of "servitude" (*'ubudiyya*) to someone other than God. Only by adhering to the system—which he also referred to as a "manhaj"—that God had revealed for the life of people, could people be freed from such servitude. Only when the manhaj of God rules the life of human beings does the dominion of one individual, family, class, community, or sex disappear "and true and complete justice [become] realized."[86] It is only the manhaj of God that is not subject to the vagaries of human weaknesses.[87]

Qutb's concept of hakimiyya, while having roots in the thought of the Pakistani thinker Abu al-'Ala Maududi (1903–79), was quite new. In calling for God's right to legislate through the concept of hakimiyya, Qutb firmly tied the sharia to the sovereignty of the state. In so doing, it could be argued that Qutb ironically made the sharia more—rather than less subject—to the hakimiyya of someone or something other than God by more specifically intertwining the sharia with the sovereignty of the modern state. Qutb's thought had a profound influence on Islamic thinking during the 1970s and became central to the oppositional politics that led to the assassination of Anwar Sadat in 1981.

Dawood I. Ahmed and Tom Ginsburg refer to Article 2 as a type of Islamic supremacy clause. The idea of the supremacy clause may have come from colonial India where the British could constrain "the application of domestic and customary laws which they may deem to be repugnant to British law and moral sentiment."[88] Almost half of the constitutions of Muslim countries contain these supremacy clauses with the majority having been put into effect between the 1990s and 2002. Ahmed and Ginsburg argue that Sadat included an Islamic supremacy clause in order to legitimate the extensive presidential authority given by the 1971 Constitution since, in spite of its more liberal provisions, the constitution substantially increased the president's powers. As such, the Islamic supremacy clause was a concession to secure the regime and its constitution's legitimacy.[89]

Yet Article 2 was not specific. No definition was given about the way the principles of the Islamic sharia would be interpreted and applied. The constitution did not mention the role of various state and state-related institutions that deal with religious matters: the state mufti, the Ministry of Endowments, mosques, al-Azhar, or the courts.[90] Article 2 was promulgated because the sharia as an abstract idea had taken root among the Egyptian public. Article 2 reflected the idea that the sharia could speak to the cultural commitments of the state and its populace.

The introduction of Article 2 represented a much more explicit attempt to amalgamate the sharia and state law to produce a new modern Islamic state law. Adel Omar Sherif, deputy chief justice of the Supreme Constitutional

Court, argues that a juristic paradox was created by the adoption of Article 2. The constitution presents itself as the fundamental law of the state and the expression of the will of a sovereign people. Yet the implication that the sharia should guide interpretation and that it supersedes other legal rules implies that the sharia constitutes a presupposed body of substantive rules from which state-enacted legislation should be developed. This would invalidate any state positive legislation—along with, potentially, the law contained in the constitution itself—unless such legislation conformed to the sharia. At the same time, Sherif argues, "Islamic law does not acquire validity unless it is incorporated into the state-enacted legislation."[91] This, he contends, "suggests that Islamic law on the one hand and state-enacted legislation or secular law on the other, reflect two different autonomous legal orders."[92]

Sherif is clearly uneasy with allowing the sharia to constitute a presupposed body of substantive rules, or supralegislative norms, from which state-enacted legislation should be developed.[93] This reflects a general attitude in the judiciary that supports the supremacy of state-enacted positive legislation. According to Brown, "one of the most senior judges in the country claimed in a personal interview in 1991 that judges who insist on the superiority of the Islamic *shari'a* to positive legislation will find their careers stalled."[94] The Supreme Constitutional Court, according to Brown, has upheld state-legislated positive law and has confirmed that the source of law is the state.[95]

The other aspect that is new about the application of Article 2 is that a Supreme Court ended up taking over judicial review of the sharia. Prior to 1969, all Egyptian courts were authorized to consider the constitutionality of legislation. From 1969 on, the right to exercise the constitutional review of legislation was vested in the Supreme Court, which was renamed as the Supreme Constitutional Court in the 1971 Constitution and reformed into a more independent entity in 1979.[96] Thus, by 1980, the Supreme Constitutional Court of Egypt had been established as the highest authority on questions of constitutional interpretation. While the Constitution of 1971 had not stated who would interpret the sharia, the Supreme Constitutional Court emerged as the main institution for dealing with Article 2 cases.

Giving constitutional review in sharia-related matters to the Supreme Constitutional Court affirms the authority of the state to speak for the sharia. This marks a shift from premodern notions of the relationship between law and the state which assumed that the jurists and the four schools of law would put limits on the polity's legislative capacities even if that limit was in the form of a negative restriction. The Supreme Constitutional Court judges are civil law judges with little training in Islamic law. Clark B. Lombardi has shown that it has been the Supreme Constitutional Court and not the ulama of al-Azhar, which, since the court's founding in 1979, has assessed whether legislation conforms to the principles of the sharia. The Supreme Constitutional Court judges, when adjudicating Article 2 cases, do not generally consult with al-Azhar. The court clearly does not wish to look to the ulama for guidance and does not agree with the idea that only those judges who have Azhari training can interpret the sharia. In the first six Article 2 cases from 1989 to 1992, the court did not refer to the ulama or even cite the ulama to support its conclusions.[97]

Despite the lack of strong parallels between the role of the Supreme Constitutional Court and premodern sharia, Islamists have used Article 2 cases as a judicial avenue to push for the implementation of the sharia. For Islamists, Tamir Moustafa argues, "litigation was one of the few available avenues to challenge the status quo from within the formal legal/political system."[98] It is common for lawyers to challenge laws and the actions of government claiming their opposition to the sharia. This is one possible strategy that a litigant can pursue.[99]

In adjudicating on Article 2, the Supreme Constitutional Court was faced with the challenge of defining what counts as the "principles of the Islamic sharia." In defining what the sharia is and what religion is, the court itself has an important role that, according to Lombardi, it has handled carefully. When the court was first confronted with Article 2 cases, it was a young and fairly weak institution.[100] For this reason, it was initially reluctant to adjudicate on Article 2 cases. In 1985, however, the court was faced with a case that was initially brought by the shaykh of al-Azhar at the time, 'Abd al-Halim Mahmud (1910–78), but was continued by his successor, Shaykh Jadd al-Haqq 'Ali Jadd al-Haqq (1917–96). The case was connected to interest on overdue payments. The court held that constitutional change was not retroactive and that Article 2 was addressed solely to parliament as a guide for its legislative authority. With this ruling, the Supreme Constitutional Court hampered attempts to make Egypt's European-based civil and criminal codes comply with the sharia. Nevertheless, the ruling stipulated that Article 2 requires all Egyptian legislation enacted after the amendment to be consistent with the principles of the sharia.[101]

For some time after this, the court did not establish any clear method of interpreting and applying Article 2. Lombardi argues that in the 1990s, however, the court began to publicly express a more systematic methodology for deciding on the principles of the sharia. The methodology has been articulated in a way that relates to a number of methods of Islamic legal reasoning, while giving judges the freedom to interpret the sharia themselves so as to "develop a jurisprudence of Islamic law that preserves (and even reinforces) the Court's existing jurisprudence—including its progressive property rights and women's rights jurisprudence."[102]

Lombardi illustrates that the Supreme Constitutional Court's interpretation of the sharia has been in line with liberal constitutionalism and the liberal rule of law. He argues that the court has used a range of modernist methods for interpreting Islamic law.[103] It has referred widely and directly to the Islamic tradition, "drawing vocabulary and concepts from a range of classical and modernist Islamic legal theories, but leaving unclear its position on some particularly controversial matters."[104] This method has given the court considerable latitude in its interpretation of the principles of the sharia. The court emphasized that rulings unambiguously recorded in Islamic legal literature and known to be authentic must be respected. However, the court considers the number of such cases to be small. In a case over custody law in 1993, the Supreme Constitutional Court rejected the ruling that Egyptian legislation had to be consistent with Hanafi law and declared that modern Muslims were not bound by the classical juristic tradition. The court has also emphasized that any ruling must further the broader goals of the sharia. These goals have been interpreted in a manner that reinforces the court's liberal constitutional values and liberal jurisprudence.[105] Brown and Lombardi show how such an approach was continued in a 2013 case relating to Egypt's personal status law and grandparental visitation rights.[106]

The Supreme Constitutional Court has therefore taken a flexible approach to the application of the sharia. Mohammed Fadel argues that the Supreme Constitutional Court has not felt the need to systematically connect modern Islamic state law to premodern Islamic legal norms. He argues that the court has treated Article 2 as just one of numerous constitutional principles rather than as a body of supraconstitutional norms. He has argued that all these constitutional principles must be read together as a whole to reconcile premodern sharia with modern notions of democracy and human rights.[107]

According to Lombardi, the move to insert the sharia into the constitution and therefore to constitutionalize the sharia in late twentieth-century Egypt "represents a commitment to the idea that state law must be a modern analogue of *siyāsa shar'iyya*," or administration in accordance with the sharia.[108] Yet the relationship between siyasa and the sharia in premodern jurisprudence was based on the assumption that the two systems would remain distinct and would work parallel to one another. The obligation was that the former should not contradict the latter. However, Article 2 cases represent a greater amalgamation of siyasa and the sharia than was envisaged by those who had theorized about this relationship. Article 2 has in some respects confirmed the authority of the state over the sharia itself. This is distinct from allowing the sharia to limit siyasa. In this sense, the sharia is integrated into state law in a way that takes the concept of siyasa shar'iyya further and results in modern Islamic state law. In amalgamating the sharia and siyasa, the Supreme Constitutional Court is carving out a considerable space for positive legislation. This is enabled by the fact that the sharia is being interpreted by the Supreme Constitutional Court as a set of principles or as a cultural ideal. The court is interpreting Article 2 in narrow terms as applying to only those norms and principles specifically stated—as mandatory or prohibited—in the text. According to Adel Omar Sherif, deputy chief justice of Egypt's Supreme Constitutional Court, "when the Egyptian constitution upholds the primacy of Islamic law in its Article 2, it is upholding the primacy of these clearly known core values that lie at the center of Egyptian society. If those values are violated, a breach of the Constitution has occurred. Anything less than a violation of these clear, core values does not constitute a violation of Islamic law under the Egyptian Constitution. Rather, anything else is viewed as a realm within which the legislature has space to govern accordingly."[109] Thus, what has emerged is a strong statist approach to the regulation of the sharia. A minimalist understanding of the extent to which the sharia can limit state legislation has also emerged. The court is effectively asserting the primacy of the state as the locus of law and has declared that the sharia does not constitute a presupposed body of substantive rules from which state-enacted legislation should be developed, but rather a body of principles which can be referenced and serve as a guiding point in the development of state-enacted legislation. Giving a court judicial review of the sharia constitutes a new form of centralization of legal power.

In this chapter, I have addressed the popularity and importance of constitution making in the modern Egyptian nation state. Constitution writing has been a key part of the remaking of the Egyptian political order. The nature of the evolving Egyptian state has been mirrored in the priorities expressed by Egypt's various constitutions. The constitution writing process of 2012–14 symbolized the prominent position that constitution writing has come to hold not only in Egypt, but also in the Arab world and beyond. Considerable energy and anxiety were expended on constitution writing, such that it became central and vital to the legitimacy—or lack thereof—of the political process after the revolution of 2011. The heart and soul of the polity, and the relationship between the state, Egyptian citizens, and the law, were being determined. Likewise, the very origins of the polity itself—where it comes from and who gets to speak for it—were being decided.

Constitutions were not seen simply as establishing mechanisms for political processes, but as a reflection of the spirit of the Egyptian nation. This partly explains why, starting in the 1970s, Islamists, armed with notions of the concept of Islamic state sovereignty, were so interested in establishing a commitment to the sharia in the constitution. While Article 2 was initially controversial, it has evolved to form a largely unquestioned cornerstone of the relationship between religion and the state in Egypt. There was relatively little discussion of removing Article 2 during the 2012–14 constitutional debates.

Article 2 has been seen as a violation of Egypt's secular nature, which was embodied in the Constitutions of 1923 and 1956. Yet it shows the way in which the relationship between the religious and the secular is being renegotiated. The article does not constitute the insertion of premodern sharia but is the product of the changes that occurred to the sharia in the nineteenth and twentieth centuries. Those changes included seeing the state as the appropriate vehicle for the sharia along with seeing the sharia as an idea or concept divorced from its institutions and methodologies. In fact, it was the emergence of the idea of the sharia itself in the early nineteenth century that then made the introduction of a statement on it possible in the Constitution of 1971. Article 2 represented the sharia as a concept, detached from its institutional props and premodern methodologies. It also, however, represented the subordination of the sharia to state positive legislation. It has been the Supreme Constitutional Court that has adjudicated Article 2 cases thus establishing the state as the locus of legal authority. At the same time, questions have been raised over the extent to which the decision making process of the Supreme Constitutional Court should be restrained by the sharia.

PART II

Recasting Islamic Law: Case Studies

CHAPTER 4

The Ulama, Religious
Authority, and the State

In the years shortly before and after Egypt's independence from Britain in 1952, the Islamic thinker and preacher Muhammad al-Ghazali (1917–96) launched a scathing attack on the ulama (the religious scholars) of al-Azhar, the most important Sunni religious establishment for Egypt and the broader Sunni Islamic world. For al-Ghazali, the ulama had failed to institute social justice in Egypt. The ulama, he argued, had distorted the texts in order to "serve trivial objectives, avoid clashing with those in power," and "choose prevailing customs or traditions."[1] He railed against the failure of the ulama to be politically engaged, being satisfied "with the performance of personal worship."[2] He claimed that the ulama had served the interests of those in power by facilitating the spread of poverty. By misinterpreting texts, he argued, they had encouraged people to forget their rights and be satisfied with their poverty.[3]

Al-Ghazali's critique of the ulama of al-Azhar, an institution from which he graduated, reflected the assumption that the religious scholars had an important role to play in Egyptian politics and society. It also showed that many Egyptians felt that the ulama had reneged on their duty to protect Islam and ensure that Islamic legal norms—and the broader principle of socioeconomic justice—were applied in the Egyptian public sphere. Yet the question of what precisely it was that the ulama should do to ensure that Egyptians and the Egyptian state adhered to Islamic legal norms remained elusive. Premodern texts contain many references to the need for the ulama to keep their distance from the ruling authorities, and, in so doing, protect Islam. However, those texts tend to be less specific about what institutional mechanisms are necessary for ensuring that the ulama fulfill their duty to apply the sharia. For example, Ibn Taymiyya says that people who have authority are of two kinds: rulers and scholars. However, he is not specific about the relationship between the two.[4]

In Egypt in the 1950s, there was no constitutional statement on the sharia. The Constitutions of 1923 and 1956 also made no mention of the ulama of al-Azhar. The first constitutional statement on the sharia occurred with Article 2 of the 1971 Constitution, which, when amended in 1980, stated that "principles of the Islamic sharia are the major source of legislation." While the Constitution of 1971 established a Supreme Constitutional Court as the body that was to interpret the constitutionality of laws (Article 175), it did not specifically define who would make a decision about the constitutionality of legislation in cases that related to Article 2. It did not address who had the authority to speak for and represent the sharia. In the 1980s, the Supreme Constitutional Court—not the ulama of al-Azhar—emerged as the institution that adjudicated on the constitutionality of legislation in Article 2 cases. However, there was considerable tension in the Egyptian public sphere about whether judges on the Supreme Constitutional Court were the most appropriate individuals to decide what is and what is not the sharia, since they, unlike the ulama al-Azhar, were not trained in Islamic jurisprudence.

Such tension increased when the Supreme Constitutional Court decided to interpret the "principles of the Islamic sharia" in a way that minimized the number of Islamic texts—and therefore the number of Islamic legal norms—that are binding on the court. As a result, some felt that the ulama of al-Azhar should have a formal role in speaking for the sharia and should therefore be involved in determining the constitutionality of legislation as it pertained to the sharia.

The revolution of 2011 and the constitutional debates that ensued provided the opportunity to address what role al-Azhar would have in adjudicating Article 2 cases. It also provided the opportunity to address what role al-Azhar would have in the Egyptian state and governance more generally. The 2012 Constitution gave al-Azhar a more formal role by declaring that the ulama of al-Azhar should be consulted on matters relating to the sharia (Article 4). Yet Article 4 was ambiguous because it did not specify whether the decision that resulted from such a consultation was legally binding. In the spring of 2012, during the brief period of the Muslim Brotherhood's control, a conflict ensued in the Egyptian parliament about Islamic financial bonds and how Article 4 should be interpreted. However, before the law relating to Islamic bonds could be brought into effect, the Egyptian president Muhammad Mursi was removed from power. In the Constitution of 2014, the part of Article 4 that had been at the heart of the conflict over Islamic bonds was removed. The Constitution of 2014 ended up establishing the Supreme Constitutional Court as the ultimate arbiter on questions regarding the compatibility of legislation with the sharia. However, while it no longer stated that al-Azhar should be consulted on matters relating to the sharia, it did establish al-Azhar's right to represent Islam. The outcome therefore was that, while al-Azhar was not given the right to decide on Article 2 cases, the constitution more formally inscribed al-Azhar as the main reference for Islamic affairs. In so doing, it gave al-Azhar an undefined leverage in the legislative process when issues related to Islam were involved.

This chapter addresses three important outcomes of these protracted debates and describes how the sharia has been recast into modern Islamic state law through constitutional commitments to the sharia. It illustrates the ways in which the presumed locus of Islamic legal authority—that is, who gets to speak for and represent the sharia—has shifted from its premodern antecedents. It shows that understanding constitutional articles about who is to represent the sharia cannot be understood either as a simple continuation of premodern commitments to Islamic authority, nor as a complete break from them. The complex ways in which the relationship between the sharia and the ruling polity were understood by premodern jurists were brought to bear on these constitutional debates.

The first outcome of the debates was that the role of al-Azhar and its ulama was—and continues to be—a source of intense concern in the Egyptian sociopolitical order. As Muhammad al-Ghazali's writing shows, the relationship between the ulama and the ruling polity has long been a source of tension in contemporary Egypt. This has particularly been the case since the 1960s. The debates about al-Azhar and its role in the constitution in the postrevolutionary context did not resolve this tension. While unease about the appropriate role of the ulama of al-Azhar and their relationship to the ruling polity also existed in premodern sharia, this unease in postrevolutionary Egypt was filtered through constitutional commitments to produce different outcomes.

The second outcome of the debate was that the role of the Supreme Constitutional Court in deciding on the constitutionality of legislation was confirmed and strengthened. While locating Islamic legal authority in the Supreme Constitutional Court had in effect been the legal reality since 1979, the Constitution of 2014 solidified—and further legitimized—the state's right to adjudicate on Islamic legal matters. In so doing, the idea that the sharia should be subordinate to modern Islamic state law was consolidated. Locating the authority to speak for the sharia in the Supreme Constitutional Court therefore marked a departure from premodern understandings of the sharia which emphasized the limited nature of the polity's right to legislate.

The third outcome of the debate was that the role of the scholars of al-Azhar was defined by modern conceptions of religion. The separation between the Islamic and the non-Islamic became central to how the role of al-Azhar in contemporary Egypt is understood by al-Azhar itself and by other political actors. All parties distinguished the Islamic from the non-Islamic as a way of establishing their own authority and limiting that of others. Separating religion from nonreligion is central to how the modern state regulates religion. In Egypt, establishing al-Azhar's right to speak for the Islamic has tied the institution itself to the problem of differentiating what Islam is from what it is not.

This chapter addresses the three outcomes of the debates to show how the sharia has been recast by the modern nation state. It first traces the events and debates about the question of who has the authority to speak for the sharia in the decades leading up to the Egyptian revolution of 2011, then focuses on the aftermath of the revolution and the key debates that took place during the interconstitutional period. It then proceeds to discuss the significance of these events and illustrates the way in which the debates about al-Azhar, the Supreme Constitutional Court, and who gets to speak for the sharia, represent how the presumed role of the sharia has been filtered through modern assumptions about the role of religion.

The Egyptian Revolution and the Constitution of 2012

The Egyptian revolution of 2011 gave al-Azhar the opportunity to renegotiate its relationship with the state. Premodern sharia had been developed by private scholars, who emphasized the importance of maintaining distance between the Islamic scholars and the state. From the eleventh century on, this separation had been weakened, Ahmet T. Kuru argues, as the ulama became increasingly allied to the state. This alliance began under the Seljuks (1037–1194), then spread to other Sunni states, particularly the Mamluks.[5] This separation was also undermined under the Ottomans, but particularly so from the nineteenth century, when the state, as opposed to the ulama, emerged as the carrier of legal authority. This shift in legal power enabled the state to appropriate al-Azhar, which was founded in 972 and gained its status as the preeminent institution of Sunni Islam at the end of the eighteenth century. The appropriation of al-Azhar by the state from the early nineteenth century on challenged the separation of powers between the jurists and the state that had been so frequently held up as the ideal. This appropriation by the state partly began during the time of Muhammad 'Ali (1769–1849), who established courts independent of Islamic law and nationalized much of the land of religious endowments (awqaf). Daniel Crecelius argues that Muhammad 'Ali "showed an open disdain for the ulama. He no longer consulted them on matters of government and policy and if they opposed him he simply found a way around their opposition."[6] However, it was not until Egyptian independence and the presidency of Gamal 'Abd al-Nasser (1918–70) that the state's control over al-Azhar reached its peak. In 1956 the sharia courts, previously controlled by the ulama, were incorporated into the civil system. In Law no. 103 of 1961, al-Azhar became attached to the presidency with a special minister responsible for it, and the shaykh of al-Azhar was appointed by the president from among al-Azhar's scholars (Article 5).[7] The same law placed family and public endowment lands under the supervision of the Ministry of Endowments.[8] Al-Azhar thus became a state-supported rather than a privately endowed institution.

The theme of al-Azhar's subordination to the state has dominated the historiography of al-Azhar since the 1960s. There is no shortage of polemics against al-Azhar itself and against its capture by the state. Such censure argues that the nationalization of al-Azhar has hindered it from playing its role as the guardian of Islam and that it has been used as a political tool. These criticisms draw on premodern assumptions that it is best for religious scholars to maintain distance from the ruling polity.[9] Polemics against al-Azhar have served to justify the claims of Islamist groups like the Muslim Brotherhood that they can return the state to Islamic morality. In 2008 'Abd al-Mun'im Abu al-Futuh complained: "We are not satisfied by al-Azhar and it is a government organization . . . it is used politically and while sometimes al-Azhar voices a political opinion, if it is afraid of the government, it does not talk about politics."[10] According to the Islamist writer and thinker Fahmi Huwaydi, "the people do not trust al-Azhar" and it is a historical institution that came after Islam. As long as it "belongs to the government," he argues, it will be discredited.[11] Unease about al-Azhar's role is also felt from within the institution. One member of al-Azhar's Islamic Research Academy, Muhammad Shahat al-Gindi, complained prior to the revolution in 2011 that al-Azhar lacked the power to enforce its decisions. He called for a constitutional stipulation stating that al-Azhar has the authority to implement its opinion according to the sharia.[12]

However, a number of authors have questioned this narrative of subordination and have emphasized that al-Azhar and the ulama in general have become increasingly independent and assertive.[13] Malika Zeghal argues that most of the ulama resented their submission to the regime in the 1960s. The Islamist violence of the 1980s, she argues, meant many independent ulama, followed by more official ulama, acted as political negotiators.[14] As a result, the ulama "regained a new public, national, and transnational centrality in the second half of the twentieth century."[15] Tamir Moustafa argues that the Islamist violence of the 1990s increased al-Azhar's leverage over the government and that the government "became increasingly dependent on al-Azhar for religious legitimation."[16] During this time, the Islamic Research Academy, created in 1961, emerged as a group of prominent scholars with Islamist sympathies and issued a number of fatwas that were not conciliatory toward the regime. In addition, a group of scholars calling themselves the al-Azhar Ulama Front were often critical of official policies. The Front clashed repeatedly with the shaykh of al-Azhar and the regime banned the Front in 1998.[17] During the Arab Spring, the Front attacked the head of al-Azhar and the state mufti for being too close to the Mubarak regime.

Additionally, official representatives of al-Azhar and the Ministry of Fatwas have emphasized that al-Azhar has a central role in the Egyptian political system and point to the fact that in the People's Assembly—which has now been replaced by a House of Representatives (supplemented in 2019 with a Senate)—there is a permanent religious committee and a member of al-Azhar who attends every session.[18]

The Constitutions of 1923 and 1956 made no mention of al-Azhar. Neither did the Constitution of 1971. This was despite the fact that Article 2 of the 1971 Constitution stated, from 1980 on, that the principles of the Islamic sharia are the main source of legislation. While the 1971 Constitution was not specific about what the principles of the sharia were and made no reference to who was going to interpret them, it did state that the Supreme Constitutional Court would judge the constitutionality of legislation (Article 175). After the amendment of Article 2 in 1980, the Supreme Constitutional Court emerged as the entity that decided on the constitutionality of legislation in Article 2 cases. The Supreme Constitutional Court, however, took a liberal and utilitarian approach to the principles of the sharia. As a result, some Islamists were unhappy with the way the Supreme Constitutional Court adjudicated on these matters. Questions emerged about whether the Supreme Constitutional

Court judges were qualified to decide on the constitutionality of legislation since they had not been trained in Islamic jurisprudence. For example, the Salafis were "dismayed by the court's refusal" to consider a number of hadith as legally binding.[19] Some argued that only al-Azhar had the authority to speak for the principles of the sharia.

In 2007 the Muslim Brotherhood issued a Draft Party Program which tried to address this question. The platform contained a number of clauses that had been inserted by conservative members of the organization. It stated that the Egyptian legislative authority must consult with a body of ulama over the sharia. However, it also limited the authority of the Islamic jurists, charged with speaking for Islam, to aspects of the Qur'an and the Sunna upon which there is juristic consensus. The platform stated that there are certain clear texts in the Qur'an and the Sunna that have been agreed upon by all jurists and which are not subject to debate. However, the other texts of the Qur'an and the Sunna are open to the interpretations of the ulama, based on the methods of the Islamic jurisprudence of the schools of law. Such interpretations are human endeavors and can be rejected.[20] The Muslim Brotherhood was accused of laying the groundwork for the establishment of an Iranian-style clerical state.[21] Such critiques, however, did not take account of the fact that the Twelver Shi'ite tradition is more legally homogeneous and hierarchical than the Sunni tradition. They also did not take into account the fact that the Muslim Brotherhood did not intend to bind state legislation to the jurisprudence of the four schools of law.

In addition, many members of the Muslim Brotherhood criticized the platform by stating that al-Azhar should only be a consultant on issues relating to the sharia. Figures such as 'Issam al-'Aryan, a prominent member of the Muslim Brotherhood affiliated with the Freedom and Justice Party, and 'Abd al-Hamid al-Ghazali, a professor of economics at the University of Cairo, emphasized that al-Azhar should not monopolize religious authority. They argued that the People's Assembly, in seeking the advice of al-Azhar, would have the right to decide on the compatibility of legislation with the sharia.[22] 'Abd al-Mun'im Abu al-Futuh, who broke with the Muslim Brotherhood and ran for the Egyptian presidency in 2012, emphasizes that the People's Assembly has the right to consult with numerous parties including Yusuf al-Qaradawi, scholars in Tunisia, as well as al-Azhar.[23]

After the revolution of 2011, the question of how the roles of al-Azhar and the Supreme Constitutional Court would be defined in the constitution reemerged. Various parties within al-Azhar successfully used the opportunity afforded by the revolution of 2011 to assert greater independence for al-Azhar. In March 2011, a group of religious scholars demanded that the

Supreme Council of Armed Forces (SCAF) restore al-Azhar's independence. The current shaykh of al-Azhar, Ahmed al-Tayyib, was appointed by Hosni Mubarak in 2010. In 2011 he seized upon the postrevolutionary environment and convened meetings between Egypt's intellectual elite and religious leaders to discuss al-Azhar's position.

The result of these meetings was the publication, which was broadcast on live television, of "The Document of al-Azhar on the Future of Egypt" in June 2011.[24] The document stressed al-Azhar's role as a representative of moderate Islamic thought. It stated that al-Azhar's function was to "determine the relationship between the state and religion and clarify what the correct foundations of siyasa shar'iyya are."[25] The document called for the establishment of a national constitutional modern democratic state in which the authority to legislate lies with the people's representatives as long as it agrees with what the document defined as the "true Islamic concept."[26] Islam, it stated, has left individual societies to choose the structures and institutions that are most appropriate for them, "on the condition that the comprehensive principles of the Islamic sharia are the principal source of legislation."[27] The document calls for the independence of the institution of al-Azhar and for reviving the Senior Scholars' Council (hay'at kibar al-'ulama'), which would have the power to elect the shaykh of al-Azhar.[28]

The document clearly reflects a desire on the part of al-Azhar for it to be more independent from the state. To some extent, the document supports the status quo, ensuring that commitment to the sharia is maintained but that the political system be relatively self-determining. Assem Hefny has argued that the document represents a "remarkable development in Al-Azhar's thinking" since 1979 toward identifying "itself with the state's political orientation" and "keep[ing] pace with political developments."[29] Importantly, the al-Azhar document shows that al-Azhar does not seem to see itself as having a direct involvement in the legislative process. The document does not attempt to assert any kind of direct legislative or constitutional role for al-Azhar and implies that the legislative process lies with the People's Assembly.

Yet it would be a mistake to read the document as a mere reinforcement of the status quo. The document affirms al-Azhar's right to determine the relationship between religion and state and its right to clarify siyasa shar'iyya. It ends by claiming that al-Azhar has the right to speak about and represent Islam, stating that "al-Azhar considers itself the specialist body that is to be referred to in Islamic affairs, Islamic sciences, Islamic heritage, and Islamic thought without withdrawing the right of the people to express their opinions once they have fulfilled the necessary learned requirements, conformed to the etiquette of dialogue and respected what the ulama of the umma have agreed upon."[30] Al-Azhar was clearly staking its right to speak for what constitutes Islam and to speak on Islamic issues due to its knowledge of Islamic texts and interpretive methodologies. The document showed that al-Azhar intended to carve out its own sphere of authority by delineating a particular sphere that is Islamic—as opposed to the un-Islamic.

Perhaps surprisingly, the al-Azhar document won support from key political parties, such as the al-Wafd and al-Tagammu, which are often defined as secular. The support of such parties indicated that there was a general acceptance that al-Azhar should be independent from the government, yet have an increased role in speaking for Islam. According to Nathan J. Brown, such groups were interested "in buttressing al-Azhar not for its own sake but as a means of strengthening a religious counterweight to Islamist movements."[31] He argues that al-Azhar had allayed fears that it intended to make a firmer commitment to the application of the sharia and establish an Islamic state. In so doing, al-Azhar received a clear statement of support from secular parties for the institution's independence.

In early 2012, the Supreme Council of Armed Forces issued a decree amending Law No. 103 of 1961, in which the state supports what it refers to as the "independence of al-Azhar" and its financial needs.[32] While the law did not get much coverage, it was extremely significant since it partly addressed the problems that resulted from the restructuring that had occurred in the 1960s, which had effectively absorbed al-Azhar into the state and bound it tightly to the executive. The SCAF decree of 2012 revived the Senior Scholars' Council and made it responsible for electing the shaykh of al-Azhar and for nominating Egypt's mufti. The law states that one of the Senior Scholars' Council's responsibilities was to "decide—on a legitimate basis—on religious and legal affairs, and on contentious social issues that the world and Egyptian society face."[33] The decree affirmed that al-Azhar represented Islam, stating that "al-Azhar represents the final frame of reference in everything that relates to the affairs of Islam, its sciences, its heritage, and its juridical ijtihad and its new thought related ijtihad."[34] The decree thus stated that al-Azhar spoke for Islam and helped establish al-Azhar's partial independence, although it was still linked to the state and subject to governmental oversight.[35] The decree was followed up in 2013, when the prime minister issued a decree enabling the shaykh of al-Azhar to issue and amend stipulations from the 1961 law regarding the internal administration of al-Azhar.[36]

During the months leading up to the promulgation of the 2012 Egyptian Constitution in December 2012, discussions focused on whether Article 2 of the 1971 Constitution, amended in 1980 to state that "the principles of the Islamic sharia are the main source of legislation," should itself be amended. A few arguments were made to remove Article 2 from the constitution altogether. However, this position did not have influential advocates. Michael Hanna argues that the existing clauses on the sharia were, for the most part, accepted as an unalterable starting point for the debate. Thus, he maintains, "even avowedly secular parties have bowed to the current realities of Egyptian society and ceded the fight over the inclusion of Islamic law."[37]

Most members of the Constituent Assembly wanted to elaborate Article 2 or keep it the same. Initially, the Salafis pushed for Article 2 to include a reference to the *marji'iyyat al-Azhar* which would make al-Azhar the frame of reference for questions involving the sharia. The Salafis then demanded that the reference to the principles of the sharia in Article 2 be changed to rulings, although this did not get the support of others and the article ended up remaining unchanged.[38] However, a new article, Article 219, was added to define the principles of the Islamic sharia as stated in Article 2 as "*including* its entire body of guidelines, its fundamental and jurisprudential rules, and its valuable sources with respect to the doctrines of the Sunni schools of law and the community" (my italics).[39] Article 219 connected the principles of the sharia to premodern Islamic jurisprudence, but did not limit those principles to premodern Islamic jurisprudence. David Kirkpatrick argues that Article 219 was a compromise between the Salafis, the liberal intellectuals, representatives of the church, al-Azhar, and the secular parties. He states that liberals and Christians on the committee believed they had done well since this was the loosest possible definition of the sharia. He argues that the Salafi leaders also believed they had won "a secret victory," since Shaykh Borhani argued that Article 219 mandated a strict and literal approach to the sharia.[40] There is a possibility that Article 219 could have resulted in curtailing the parameters within which the sharia could be interpreted. While it is true that some conservative Muslims may have hoped that Article 219 could overturn previous Supreme Constitutional Court rulings, Mohammad Fadel argues that, because the article simply includes such rules and does not exclude other sources, this "hope seems textually unjustified."[41]

In addition to Article 219, an entirely new article on al-Azhar was added to the 2012 Constitution. While the 1971 Constitution made no mention of al-Azhar, the preamble to the 2012 Constitution states that al-Azhar has "throughout history been the guardian of the identity of the homeland, has taken care of the eternal Arabic language and the respected Islamic sharia, and has been a lighthouse for moderate, enlightened thought."[42] More importantly, an article that constitutionally enshrined al-Azhar's independence and established its role in the legislative process of the state was added. Article 4 of the 2012 Constitution states:

> The eminent al-Azhar is a comprehensive independent Islamic institution that alone has jurisdiction over all of its affairs. It is responsible for spreading the Islamic message, for the religious sciences, and for the Arabic language in Egypt and the world. *The opinion of the Senior Scholars' Council of the eminent al-Azhar is taken in matters connected with the Islamic sharia.* The state ensures complete financial support for the realization of al-Azhar's objectives. The shaykh of al-Azhar is independent and cannot be dismissed. The law determines the method by which he will be chosen from among the members of the Senior Scholars' Council. All the above is determined by the law (my italics).[43]

The most significant and contentious part of Article 4 implies that the legislature and the Supreme Constitutional Court have a duty to consult with the Senior Scholars' Council of al-Azhar before rendering their decisions. However, it raised—but did not answer—a very important question. It did not state that the opinion of al-Azhar's scholars is binding upon the legislature or on the court. There was therefore some question about whether either branch had the discretion either to accept or reject the advice of the Senior Scholars' Council.

Hasan al-Shafiʻi was one of al-Azhar's representatives on the 2011 Constituent Assembly, which drafted the 2012 Constitution. Al-Shafiʻi is a member of al-Azhar's Senior Scholars' Council and former director of the Arabic Language Institute in Cairo. While he was a graduate from al-Azhar, he was connected to the Muslim Brotherhood when he was young and went to prison in the 1960s. He spoke out against the coup against Muhammad Mursi. Al-Shafiʻi stated that the representatives of al-Azhar were clear that they did not want al-Azhar to take charge of the interpretation of constitutional texts. He argues that the representatives of al-Azhar wanted what he refers to as "a modern state" based on a distinction between the judicial, executive, and legislative bodies and based on the interpretation of constitutional texts by a Supreme Constitutional Court.[44] Al-Shafiʻi stated that the Salafi parties wanted the constitution to state that the Senior Scholars' Council should actually take charge of the interpretation of the constitutional texts. However, he argues that he and the other two representatives of al-Azhar (the former mufti, Nasr Farid Wasil, and a member of the Senior Scholars' Council, Muhammad ʻImara), were clear that they did not want this to happen. He argues that al-Azhar does not want to get entangled in the balance of powers, in the relationship between the judiciary, the executive branch, and the legislature.[45]

The position of the Muslim Brotherhood on Article 4 similarly emphasized the importance of the Supreme Constitutional Court, although initially the organization was conflicted. Carrie Wickham writes that, "in the assembly's heated debates on these issues, Brotherhood figures . . . found themselves between a rock and a hard place, seeking to placate their secular counterparts while protecting themselves from the charge that, in a bow to public pressure, they have diluted their commitment to Shari'a rule."[46] In November 2011, the newly established political wing of the Muslim Brotherhood, the Freedom and Justice Party, issued a party platform stating that the state envisaged by the Freedom and Justice Party is "an Islamic, national, constitutional, and modern state which is based on the Islamic sharia as a frame of reference."[47] It is a state, it argued, which is a civil state in the sense that it is not a military state nor is it a police state. Neither, it stated, is it "a theocratic state (dawla theoqratiyya) which is ruled over by a class of men of religion—let alone one ruled over in the name of divine right. For there are no infallible people who can monopolize the interpretation of the Qur'an. Rather, legislation is entrusted to the people which possesses holiness (qadasa). Rather the rulers in the Islamic state are citizens elected according to the will of the people. The people are the source of authority (sulta)."[48] The platform also states that "the Supreme Constitutional Court should supervise the constitutionality of . . . legislation."[49]

Both Article 4 and Article 219 strengthened the role of al-Azhar in the legislative process. At the same time, however, Article 175 of the 2012 Constitution stated that "the Supreme Constitutional Court is an independent judicial entity, which is based in Cairo, and which alone decides on the constitutionality of laws and statues."[50] The Supreme Constitutional Court had been established as the ultimate arbiter on the constitutionality of legislation according to Article 175 of the 1971 Constitution. Yet, in stating that the Supreme Constitutional Court "alone" decides on the constitutionality of laws and statutes, Article 175 of the 2012 Constitution further established that it was the Supreme Constitutional Court and not the ulama of al-Azhar that would decide on Article 2 cases. Thus, while Articles 4 and 219 established more authority for al-Azhar, this authority was restricted by Article 175. The preamble to the 2012 Constitution also states that "the judiciary is proudly independent and is entrusted with the noble task of protecting the constitution, establishing the scales of justice, and preserving rights and freedoms."[51]

Articles 2, 4, 175, and 219 of the 2012 Constitution raised a number of questions relating to the issue of the relationship between law, the state, and sovereignty. What was the process for deciding on the constitutionality of laws and statutes when they pertain to the sharia? If al-Azhar was to be consulted, what was to be done with its decision? Was it enforceable? If al-Azhar determined that a piece of legislation was against the sharia, could the Supreme Constitutional Court overrule such a determination?

Such questions illustrate the ongoing tension regarding the source of legislative authority in the state and the relationship between the sharia and state law. Such tension—as has been seen—has its premodern antecedents in the debates about the relationship between fiqh and siyasa. Yet these tensions were now operating in the context of a constitution that represents the state's monopoly over legal authority. In seeking to answer questions raised by Article 2 of the 1971 Constitution, the Constitution of 2012 generated new ones. Thus, in trying to settle questions posed by Article 2 of the 1971 Constitution, the Constitution of 2012 simply continued tensions among Egyptians over what role al-Azhar should have.

A Parliamentary Battle and the Constitution of 2014

While Article 219 was not tested prior to its removal from the 2014 Constitution, Article 4 was. Article 4 served as an important reference point during a political argument that emerged in the short period of Muslim Brotherhood rule. The argument that took place involved al-Azhar and the Salafis, the Muslim Brotherhood–dominated Shura Council and Muhammad Mursi, and the liberal and secular opposition parties. It emerged over a bill in the Shura Council that related to Islamic legal bonds, or *sukuk*.

Sukuk refer to the Islamic equivalent of bonds. Whereas interest-bearing bonds do not comply with Islamic law, sukuk do because they are based on the concept of asset monetization, which involves releasing cash from an asset. The bond owner has a tangible interest in the investment and is thus able to collect profit as a rent, which is allowed in Islamic finance law.

The sukuk project aimed at reducing the budget deficit by increasing foreign currency reserves. It was spearheaded by the Freedom and Justice Party and the Salafi al-Nur party, and was initially presented to the People's Assembly in early 2012. The debate pitted al-Azhar against the Muslim Brotherhood. In late 2012, the financial committee of the Shura Council submitted a project for the sukuk to al-Azhar entitled "qanun al-sukuk al-islamiyya al-siyadiyya" (the law of sovereign Islamic sukuk).[52]

In December 2012, al-Azhar rejected the project on the grounds that it was not compliant with the sharia and endangered the state's sovereignty.[53] Al-Azhar objected to the sukuk program because, among other things, it gave foreigners the right to own sukuk. Al-Azhar proposed that only Egyptians be allowed to own them.[54] In February 2013, a revised draft of the sukuk law, in which the objections of al-Azhar had been considered, was presented to the Shura Council. A provision for not allowing the mortgaging of state-owned assets had been included along with a provision that a sharia committee would oversee its implementation. It also stipulated that foreigners had no right to possess sukuk. In addition, a change that had not been requested by al-Azhar was made: the term "Islamic" was removed from the title of the law.

The Shura Council then refused to submit the revised bill to al-Azhar. Debate erupted in the Shura Council between the Muslim Brotherhood and the Freedom and Justice Party on one side and the Salafi al-Nur party and al-Azhar representatives, particularly Hasan al-Shafi'i, on the other. Hasan al-Shafi'i threatened to resign if the Shura Council did not submit the bill for al-Azhar's approval. 'Abd Allah Badran, head of the Salafi al-Nur party in the Shura Council, said that to be compliant with the constitution, the law should be submitted to al-Azhar. In a dramatic speech, 'Issam al-'Aryan of the Freedom and Justice Party responded to these demands by saying that al-Azhar is appreciated and respected, but he objects to its intervention and its transgression on the institutions of the state.[55]

The Shura Council refused to submit the law to al-Azhar, approved the law in late March, and then submitted it to President Mursi. During that time, those opposed to the Muslim Brotherhood formed a somewhat unlikely alliance with al-Azhar and defended it from the Muslim Brotherhood. A number of activist parties and independents formed an organization called the Front to Defend al-Azhar. Such groups claimed that al-Azhar was their shelter, their fortress and referred to al-Azhar as the House of the People.[56] They supported the "role of al-Azhar al-Sharif as a religious frame of reference (marji'iyya)" for Egypt and were afraid that extremist trends were usurping this frame of reference.[57] They argued that this was a way to save Egypt from the rule of the Muslim Brotherhood.[58] Such groups wanted al-Azhar to become a buffer against Islamic forces, to neutralize what was viewed as the growing influence of the Islamic movement.[59]

Succumbing to mounting pressure from al-Azhar's Senior Scholars' Council and from the media and the Salafi al-Nur party, President Mursi referred the law to the Senior Scholars' Council in early April.[60] On April 11, 2013, al-Azhar finally approved a law that would allow the country to issue sukuk but said that some articles, which had been passed by the Shura Council, should be amended. Al-Azhar argued that the time frame for the sukuk needed to be defined, and objected to issuing bonds for religious endowments for more than twenty-five years. Al-Azhar also complained about Article 20 of the sukuk law, which stipulated that the president and the minister of finance have the last say on whether sukuk conform to the sharia. In April 2013, Rafiq Habib, a Coptic intellectual and former deputy chairman of the Freedom and Justice Party, issued a paper in which he argued that al-Azhar had overstepped its role in the sukuk law controversy by going beyond the question of whether it is compliant with the sharia.[61] Habib argued that Article 4 gives the Senior Scholars' Council the right to be consulted, but that it does not have a right to oversee and approve legislation.[62] Al-Azhar's complaints were incorporated and then the law was approved by the Shura Council in early May. On May 8, 2013, the Egyptian president approved the law allowing the government to issue sukuk.[63] The law, however, was abolished after the removal of President Mursi in July 2013.

After the coup of July 3, 2013 and the suspension of the Constitution of 2012, Article 219, which had defined the principles of the Islamic sharia as including the jurisprudence of the four Sunni schools of law, was not immediately removed. In the interim constitutional declaration, made by 'Adly Mansour, the content of Article 4 did not appear, while Article 219, which had defined the principles of Islamic sharia as including the jurisprudence of the four schools of law, was retained as part of Article 1.[64] It is interesting that 'Adly Mansour, head of the Supreme Constitutional Court, included something for which the Muslim Brotherhood had been criticized. During the constitutional deliberations in 2013, Article 219 was discussed. The Salafis hoped to keep the article or insert something equivalent to it, while the three representatives of the Egyptian Christian denominations threatened to withdraw from the process if it was not removed. After intense debate, al-Azhar ended up supporting the removal of Article 219 from the 2014 Constitution.[65]

In the final draft that appeared in 2014, the whole of Article 219 and part of Article 4 were removed from the amended constitution and the remainder of Article 4 was moved to Article 7. Article 7 now reads:

> The eminent al-Azhar is an independent Islamic institution that alone has jurisdiction over all of its affairs. It is the principal reference (*marji'*) for the religious sciences (*'ulum diniyya*) and for Islamic affairs. It is responsible for *al-da'wa*, as well as for disseminating the religious sciences and the Arabic language in Egypt and the world. The state

undertakes to allocate enough financial support so that it can achieve its goals. The shaykh of al-Azhar is independent and cannot be dismissed. The law determines the method by which he will be chosen from among the members of the Senior Scholars' Council.[66]

Article 7 therefore removes the 2012 stipulation that al-Azhar is to be consulted on matters pertaining to the sharia. The rest of the article relating to al-Azhar—which helped establish al-Azhar's independence as an organization and al-Azhar as the representative of Islam, both of which marked an important change with previous constitutions—is largely intact. Importantly, it still stipulates that al-Azhar is the main reference for religious sciences and Islamic affairs.

In addition, the 2014 Constitution strengthened the role of the Supreme Constitutional Court by removing the ambiguity concerning its role over the sharia. The Supreme Constitutional Court's role as arbiter on the constitutionality of legislation that relates to the sharia was placed in the preamble. The preamble to the 2014 Constitution affirms that "the principles of the Islamic sharia are the main source of legislation and the frame of reference for the interpretation of these principles lies in the body of the Supreme Constitutional Court rulings on that matter."[67] The 2014 Constitution also gives the Supreme Constitutional Court the authority to select its members with no oversight. Thus, as a consequence of this protracted debate, the authority of the Supreme Constitutional Court over the interpretation of the sharia was established. This, in turn, asserted the authority of state-centered positive law over the sharia.

Old and New Tensions

Making sense of the ideological and political motivations of the parties concerned in the constitutional debates about the role of al-Azhar is a challenge. The particular machinations of the different parties are difficult to follow and account for. Positions taken both reflected long-term ideological commitments and short-term political maneuvering. What is clear is that any reference to Islamist versus secular positions is insufficient in both describing and understanding what was at stake in the debates. This is shown by the fact that the secularists allied with al-Azhar against the Muslim Brotherhood's insistence that the sukuk law not be referred to al-Azhar.

It is perhaps particularly challenging to account for the fact that Ahmed al-Tayyib, the shaykh of al-Azhar, was so concerned with implementing Article 4 and with interpreting it in a way that enhanced al-Azhar's role, only to then oversee its removal from the 2014 Constitution. What might account for his initial support for Article 4 and his willingness to drop it is his intense opposition to the Muslim Brotherhood. Al-Tayyib emphasizes that al-Azhar is the "first and last authority" in the Sunni Islamic world and sees the Muslim Brotherhood as an organization that is trying to "take over the role of al-Azhar and its place in the hearts of Muslims."[68] Overseeing the introduction of Article 4 and his insistence on interpreting it so as to maximize the authority of al-Azhar might well have been a means by which he strengthened the role of al-Azhar vis-à-vis the Muslim Brotherhood. Similarly, understanding the fact that Ahmed al-Tayyib was willing to let part of Article 4 be removed could also be understood in light of the fact that al-Tayyib had less to fear from the Muslim Brotherhood at that time.

However, assessing motivations is an extremely difficult—if not impossible—task. It is more useful to focus on the broader significance of the protracted debates and their outcomes. This can highlight the extent to which premodern Islamic understandings of religious authority are brought to bear on debates about religious authority in the modern state.

The first outcome is that the debates and the constitutional articles simply prolonged, rather than resolved, the tension over what al-Azhar's role vis-à-vis the state should be. This tension had historical antecedents rooted in the concern voiced by religious scholars that they should not get too close to the ruler. Yet such concerns took on new dynamics in this context. While the Supreme Constitutional Court was established as the ultimate arbiter on the constitutionality of legislation, the Constitution of 2014 more firmly entrenched al-Azhar's right to speak for the sharia. Thus, the fraught relationship between al-Azhar, the Supreme Constitutional Court, and the question of the sharia and state legislation was not solved, but simply recalibrated. Now that al-Azhar's role has been inscribed into the constitution as speaking for Islam, there are likely to be more debates over the extent and nature of al-Azhar's role.

Hussein Ali Agrama argues that the structures that compose the rule of law open into a domain that is fraught with suspicion, anxiety, and incessant legislation. He argues that persistent vigilance against the potential abuses of power is a characteristic of liberal traditions, and that this vigilance is a response to—and results in—suspicion. In modern law, he argues, more and more forms of social and political relations become regulated and legalized, while also becoming subject to the suspicion and distrust that makes those regulations necessary. As legislation and regulation increase, the possibility opens up for more manipulation and circumvention through legal loopholes resulting in the need for more legislation. With modern law, he argues, anxiety and suspicion are manifested in the increasing concern with fact find-ing.[69] Claims, he argues, are received with skepticism and verifications and explanations are constantly demanded. The assumption is that "exceptions are to be overcome" and gaps "need to be filled."[70] Thus, Agrama argues, the law becomes more widely entrenched through the suspicion and distrust that accompanies it. However, increasingly complex legislation opens up more of the same potential for continued manipulation, "thereby fostering ongoing suspicion and distrust."[71]

Agrama illustrates this by comparing the Egyptian personal status law courts with the Egyptian Fatwa Council. The former are state courts—based on codified Hanafi law—and their rulings on family matters are subject to legal enforcement. Agrama illustrates that Egyptians view the rulings of the personal status courts with suspicion and often do not com-ply with them. The rulings of the Fatwa Council, however, are also based on the sharia but are not associated with any institutionalized mechanisms of enforcement. However, despite this, Agrama argues, one finds little noncompliance and "people take the fatwas they ask for very seriously."[72] Agrama uses this point to make an argument about the very nature of mod-ern law. He contends that, when the authority of the sharia comes under the rule of law, it partakes of the suspicion and distrust that characterizes the modern rule of law.[73]

The argument that suspicion of the law is a particular feature of mod-ern law is a compelling one. Yet, here, it is important to note that suspi-cion toward political authority also existed in premodern Islamic thinking. Such suspicion was reflected in the assumption that any political authority had to commit itself to the sharia, but that those who determined what the sharia was were, for the most part, not state functionaries. It was precisely because of suspicion toward the ruling polity that "Islamic law and its legal system tried—and largely succeeded—to keep largely (though not entirely) aloof from the circles of politics."[74] This is why jurists who were too close to the ruling power were seen to have compromised their ability to speak for Islamic law. Muhammad al-Ghazali (d. 1996) cites both the early jurist Sa'id ibn al-Musayyib (643–715) and the philosopher Abu Hamid al-Ghazali (1058–1111) who warn that it was better for the scholar to remain distant from the ruler so he would not be corrupted by him and to view those who get too close to rulers with extreme distrust. In so doing, Muhammad al-Ghazali was drawing on a long tradition of concern about the scholar's proximity to those in power. Such proximity would disable the ulama from playing its proper role as the voice of opposition to the ruling polity.[75] The ideal that was advocated was that "the provision of justice and legal advice was best done from a position that governing authorities could not directly undermine if they disapproved of the justice or advice offered."[76] This was a difficult balance to strike since too much distance could lead to the ulama being accused of reneging on their role. Ibn Taymiyya (1263–1328) denounced his fellow ulama who "faced with all these abuses, turn away from political involvement, arguing that the only way to stop them would entail rebellion and violence."[77] Even the concept of siyasa shar'iyya retained the idea that the sharia, and therefore the ulama, should act as a negative restriction—in the sense that no one should be forced to act against the sharia—on the ruling polity's legislative role. This level of suspicion toward the state is precisely why the authority of al-Azhar's ulama has been undermined, especially since the 1960s.[78]

The case of the ulama and al-Azhar shows that there was greater suspicion toward the law-making polity in the premodern context than Agrama allows for when he connects such suspicion in modern Egypt specifically to the modern rule of law. However, Agrama provides something very useful to consider in relation to the particular way in which this suspicion manifests itself in contemporary Egypt. Agrama argues that one of the consequences of suspicion of the law—by legal personnel and by members of the public toward legal personnel—is the demand for verification and explanation. This can also be seen in the evolution toward greater constitutional specificity. Nineteenth-century constitutions were relatively brief; in the twentieth century, they became more verbose. As has been seen, one of the explanations for this lies in the fact that constitutions are used more and more as ideological documents. Constitutions are longer because there is more and more demand for explanations and forms of verification. Constitutions require more rather than less explanation. Modern constitutions are like contracts and the greater suspicion that various parties have of one other, the more elaborations are required. The more suspicion that different parties have of one other, the more those parties anticipate the potential for texts to be interpreted in different ways. So, when each constitutional statement is explained by the addition of a new one that qualifies it, this opens up the door for another one that helps forestall some of the implications raised by the previous one.

This move toward greater levels of clarification is a useful way of thinking about al-Azhar and the constitution. Mistrust and the need for further clarification formed an important component of the writing of both constitutions in 2012 and 2014 and the testing of the Constitution of 2012 in the spring of 2013. While the Constitution of 2012, for example, partly settled the ambiguity about al-Azhar's role by stipulating that al-Azhar needed to be consulted on matters of legislation that pertained to the sharia, there were fears that al-Azhar would overstep its mark and impose its own legislative interpretation. Conversely, those who supported a greater legislative role for al-Azhar had been suspicious about the extent to which the Supreme Constitutional Court was committed to the application of the sharia. The Constitution of 2014 removed the part of Article 4 that had been so contentious, and established al-Azhar's right to speak for Islam. However, this did not quell suspicion about al-Azhar's role or about the capacity of the Supreme Constitutional Court to decide on Article 2 cases. While the Egyptian Constitution, has, for the first time, specified the role of the Supreme Constitutional Court and al-Azhar, this has, however, only served to generate more questions. The case of al-Azhar shows this anxiety and suspicion taking on new forms that need further clarification.

The Sharia as State Law

One of the most important outcomes of the debate about Articles 4 and 219 and al-Azhar and the Supreme Constitutional Court was that the authority of the Supreme Constitutional Court was formalized and enhanced. This reinforced the principle of state sovereignty over the sharia. Many Egyptians felt uneasy at giving legal authority to scholars who were not fully part of state institutions and the Constitution of 2014 showed this. However, there is something paradoxical in this. On the one hand, al-Azhar is not trusted because it is seen as being too close to the state; on the other, it is not trusted precisely because it is made up of religious scholars who are not elected state officials.

The normative relationship proposed by premodern Islamic theorists between the state and the sharia was one in which the role of the state was to facilitate—not interpret—the application of the sharia. In this sense, the law preceded the state. This was key to the distinction between fiqh, which contained ethical dimensions and recognized different scholarly approaches to legal questions as equally valid, and siyasa, the role of which was to facilitate the operations of the state in a way that advanced the public good and broader principles of fiqh. While such a normative ideal was often compromised in practice, which, as Ahmed Kuru illustrates, took place from the eleventh century on, the ulama retained the right to speak for and represent the sharia.[79] The concept that the state should be the vehicle for the interpretation and application of all law, including law that is Islamically informed, was in some respects novel when it was established in the nineteenth century. Islamic reformers increasingly adopted this position.

The Muslim Brotherhood has also inherited this perspective. This is why it was broadly supportive of the idea that the Supreme Constitutional Court should decide on the constitutionality of legislation. Thus, despite claims that the Muslim Brotherhood wanted to establish an Islamic state run by religious scholars, it was largely committed to the sharia as state law and to state officials speaking for the sharia. The Muslim Brotherhood's commitment to the role of the Supreme Constitutional Court in deciding on the constitutionality of legislation can be seen in the documents of their 2005 campaign, in which the organization "placed considerable emphasis on strengthening the autonomy of the judiciary. In its view, the judiciary is a 'safety valve' that allows for the resolution of disputes before they lead to violence or social disorder."[80]

'Abd al-Khaliq al-Sharif, a representative of the missionary section of the Muslim Brotherhood in 2013, voices such a position. According to his understanding of the implications of Article 4 of the 2012 Constitution, al-Azhar has an important role in the legislative process. However, he emphasizes that al-Azhar's role is only to help Muslims understand the Qur'an and the Sunna, which are the authoritative frame of reference for Muslims. He argues that al-Azhar or a Muslim scholar (*'alim*) cannot be the authoritative frame of reference. Thus, the Senior Scholars' Council can give its opinion according to its understanding of the Qur'an and the Sunna. The members of the council are due respect, he says, but that does not mean they are immune from criticism or that their opinion has to be taken. "If they are mistaken [in their opinion]," he says, "we will refute it."[81] For him, this is based on Islamic historical practice since early Muslims dealt with numerous legal questions for centuries before al-Azhar existed. Does it mean, he contends, that people such as Abu Hanifa (d. 767) and al-Shafi'i (d. 820) did not understand religion because al-Azhar did not exist?[82]

Similarly, Rafiq Habib, a Coptic writer who was a founding member of the moderate Islamist al-Wasat party in the 1990s, wrote a critique of al-Azhar's actions over the sukuk controversy. Habib had been involved in the Freedom and Justice Party but announced his intention to leave politics in December 2012.[83] Habib uses the concept of "frame of reference," or the authority to which one refers (marji'iyya) in his thinking. He maintains that the frame of reference for the constitution is not al-Azhar but rather the sharia. Habib states that only the community can claim authority in the name of the Islamic frame of reference. He acknowledges that al-Azhar should make its opinion known on general issues, national issues, and issues relating to the Islamic framework.[84] Yet this role is only consultative: if it were mandatory to take the opinion of al-Azhar into consideration, this would detract from the role of the legislative assembly. Rather, he contends, al-Azhar is an institution of knowledge and learning and it "should not be in competition with the other institutions of the state."[85] If its opinion were mandatory, that would give it "religious power (*sulta diniyya*) which would give al-Azhar power over the state itself."[86] Islam does not recognize sulta diniyya. In Islam, he argues, there are multiple Islamic entities and institutions and they all have "a role to the extent that they are trusted so that they can influence the umma."[87]

Likewise, a number of public intellectuals who have been associated with moderate members of the Muslim Brotherhood have asserted the importance of the Supreme Constitutional Court in deciding on the constitutionality of legislation. For the lawyer, Islamist intellectual, and former presidential candidate Muhammad Salim al-ʿAwwa, the ulama of al-Azhar have played an effective political role as a source of advice and guidance in Islamic history.[88] Yet for al-ʿAwwa the opinions of muftis and al-Azhar cannot be forced; this is grounded in Islamic history and in the views of the four schools of law. Fatwas, he contends, are by their very nature noncompulsory and courts are not obliged to enforce them. If such fatwas were compulsory, this would violate the principle of consensus, which holds that an important source of the sharia itself is the agreement of members of the community.[89] The implication here is that the opinion of al-Azhar has not only to be given, but also received for it to constitute a form of consensus.

Thus, for Muhammad Salim al-ʿAwwa, the Supreme Constitutional Court is the institution best suited to fulfill the role of constraining the power of the legislative branch.[90] He asserts that the Supreme Constitutional Court in Egypt is an independent body and that the judges themselves are "independent, and there is no dominion over them that forces them to judge contrary to the law."[91] He also argues that no one should interfere in such cases and criticizes those who denigrate the Egyptian judges or the courts. Agitation against a judicial decision is "a mistake and to appeal to the executive for assistance against it is a crime."[92]

The Muslim Brotherhood was not the only group to take this position. While the Salafi parties were clear that they wanted a stronger legislative role for al-Azhar, and while some members of al-Azhar also sought this, there are indications that Ahmed al-Tayyib, the shaykh of al-Azhar, did not want a direct legislative role for al-Azhar. In discussing the significance of Article 4 before its removal from the 2014 Constitution, Hasan al-Shafiʿi, one of al-Azhar's representatives in the Constituent Assembly, maintained that Article 4 made it necessary that al-Azhar be consulted, but did not establish a direct legislative role for al-Azhar. He stated that, "when the judges disagree with themselves or the people as a whole disagree about whether [a piece of legislation] conforms to the sharia or not, then it is to be referred to the Senior Scholars' Council."[93] Thus, for al-Shafi'i, the Senior Scholars' Council should only resolve differences over interpretation—that is, supplement the interpretation of the sharia by the legislative body and the Supreme Constitutional Court. Al-Shafi'i's perception of the ideal role of al-Azhar is that it "does not take part in politics in the sense of party politics connected with day-to-day governance and the issuance of judgments."[94] Rather it should enter into politics when the concerns are national.[95]

In addition, Muhammad 'Abd al-Fadil al-Qusi, who was a member of al-Azhar's Senior Scholars' Council and a supporter of Ahmed al-Tayyib, and al-Qasabi Mahmud Zalat, professor of *usul al-fiqh* (the foundations of jurisprudence), stated that the opinion of al-Azhar should be sought, although ultimately it is not an obligation that it be accepted or acted upon.[96] If there is a contradiction between the opinion of the Supreme Constitutional Court and that of al-Azhar, then the opinion of the Supreme Constitutional Court has greater weight. Al-Azhar should state its opinion, but ultimately it is up to the Supreme Constitutional Court to issue a determination. Al-Qusi calls for the law to be in accordance with both the Supreme Constitutional Court and al-Azhar. Yet 'Issam al-'Aryan's position that al-Azhar had no right to enforce its opinion was described by al-Qusi as "against the constitution, against Article 4," implying that the opinion of the Senior Scholars' Council is more than simply consultative. In fact, they contend, the president did end up referring the law to the Senior Scholars' Council, which is exactly what should have happened. Yet they are keen to contend, al-Azhar is a nongovernmental organization.[97] This aligns with al-Qusi's emphasis on the importance of the *marji'iyyat al-Azhar* for the civil Islamic state, which he positions between a civil state without a religion and a state that is based on rulers claiming to speak in the name of God.[98] Making al-Azhar the central frame of reference is necessary, he asserts, for "shaking off from the pure face of Islam the stains of extremism and crudeness and the misfortunes of violence and disunity that have overcome it."[99] Using al-Azhar as the frame of reference is vital, he maintains, for "faith in the essential truths of Islam." The method of al-Azhar is essential for harmonizing the relationship "between legislation, the goals of legislation, and the outcomes of legislation." It is also, he argues, essential for harmonizing the relationship between "reason and tradition."[100]

Brown asserts that al-Azhar emerged victorious from these events since it never wanted a constitutional responsibility. Its authority, he states, "was already established in law. Al-Azhar's current leadership seeks supreme moral authority and autonomy," and this is what the 2014 Constitution gives it.[101] Yet it is important not to underestimate the significance of the fact that these clauses have affirmed al-Azhar's right to speak for Islam. There are a number of reasons to account for why al-Azhar would not want direct legislative responsibility. One of them is that the concept of multiple mutually orthodox schools of law is central to al-Azhar's identity. Al-Azhar was structured around respect for the doctrine of mutual orthodoxy. Teachers and students are divided among the codes of jurisprudence.[102] Ahmed al-Tayyib, the current shaykh of al-Azhar, argues that learning about the differences of opinion of the four schools of law is central to the mission of al-Azhar. The fact that you can be a Maliki or a Hanafi is drilled into children from the age of ten, he says. This, he asserts, is particular to al-Azhar, and cannot be found in Iran, where there is only imami fiqh, he says, or in Turkey where there is only Hanafi fiqh. It is on account of al-Azhar, he says, that the four schools continue to exist.[103]

Historically, al-Azhar has been influenced by the process of Hanafization that occurred in the nineteenth century.[104] It has also been influenced by the decline of the four schools of law and the emphasis on studies that span the four schools of law.[105] However, at al-Azhar today, all four schools are represented as they are in the Ministry of Fatwas. In the recently established Senior Scholars' Council, there are ulama from all four schools of law. Members of the Senior Scholars' Council must be committed to the methodology of al-Azhar, which emphasizes training in the jurisprudence of the four schools of law.[106] The fact that al-Azhar's approach to the sharia is based on the four schools of law and the concept of mutual orthodoxy means that it would potentially be compromised if it embedded itself more deeply in the judicial legislative process. This is because the legislative process aspires to the consistency—and not the plurality—of law. The Constitution of 2014 confirmed that the Supreme Constitutional Court had the authority to speak for the constitutionality of legislation and to decide on Article 2 cases. Thereby, the precedence of modern Islamic state law over the sharia was confirmed.

For Habib, the establishment of al-Azhar as a consultant, rather than as a legislator, returned al-Azhar to its "historical role," which was an institution of learning that "would announce its opinion to society and define rights and oppose tyranny."[107] Ibrahim al-Hudaybi, grandson of the former supreme guide (2002–4) of the Muslim Brotherhood, Ma'mun al-Hudaybi, and a Muslim Brotherhood younger generation reformer makes a similar argument. He says that giving al-Azhar the final say in defining what the sharia is "limits

Islamic knowledge to al-Azhar," and gives the institution itself, rather than the historical methods that made it famous, a level of authority that does not accord with the kind of authority it had historically. He writes that "assigning an institution with the task of interpreting Sharia is unusual in Islam, where, traditionally, knowledge was not seen to be associated with any specific institution or religious hierarchy but to scholastic aptitude that the nation has accepted throughout its history."[108] The institution of al-Azhar became important because of the rigorous teaching methods that created balanced identities and produced capable students. Al-Azhar therefore became distinguished because of the methodology followed by the individuals who went there, and not as an institution in and of itself.[109] He argues that Islamists in the legislative process bring different understandings of the sharia "propagated through their different institutions" and this is a positive thing. However, this would not be possible if al-Azhar was made the referential authority for legislation since this would mean that competing groups would vie to take control of the institution and use it for their own political gains. It would mean that, in order for the Islamists "to make their doctrinal ambitions successful, their only option [would be] to take control of al-Azhar."[110]

Al-Hudaybi is correct in saying that establishing al-Azhar's role as that of a consultant rather than giving it a direct role in the legislation of the state is more in line with the role it had historically. Yet al-Hudaybi does not account for the Supreme Constitutional Court's role in deciding whether legislation is compatible with Article 2. Giving the Supreme Constitutional Court, a state institution, the role of deciding on the constitutionality of legislation vis-à-vis Article 2 effectively gives the ruling polity the right to decide and interpret the sharia, thereby centralizing legal authority in state institutions and detracting from the role of the ulama to operate in the way that he describes. Lawrence Rosen contends that "in classical Islamic thought no court could be higher than another because such a hierarchy would imply that the highest court actually knew the truth when in fact no such claim for absolute moral judgment is properly supportable."[111] Thus, giving a court supreme authority in the sense of having the last say on whether something is compatible with the sharia goes against the doctrine of mutual orthodoxy which holds that all interpretations are human and therefore imperfect. A Supreme Constitutional Court that has the final say on the sharia as far as it pertains to state legislation does not have premodern antecedents. Given the newness of the Supreme Constitutional Court's role, this also means that al-Azhar—be it as a consultant or as a spokesperson for the Islamic sphere—is put in a different situation, precisely because it has to be a consultant alongside a Supreme Constitutional Court that monopolizes Islamic legal authority for the state.

This is not to say that premodern sharia did not make way for state positive law. It did and had to. In some cases, premodern states appropriated the right to make legislation and the concept of siyasa shar'iyya allowed for that. Yet, for the most part, the sharia and siyasa existed alongside one another and remained distinct. Siyasa was bounded by the sharia. Premodern Islamic scholars retained authority over the sharia and that authority limited the ruling polity's right to legislate. It was maintaining the close but distinct relationship between the sharia and siyasa that allowed for the emergence of state law while not compromising the multivalent and infallible nature of the sharia. Yet giving the Supreme Constitutional Court the right to decide on Article 2 cases, thereby melding state law with the principles of the sharia into modern Islamic state law, moves the sharia further away from its premodern antecedents.

Islam and Non-Islam

The third outcome of these protracted debates about al-Azhar's role in the constitution was that al-Azhar's role as representative of the Islamic sphere was formalized. Modern conceptions about religion involve the belief that it can, should, and—in many cases—does occupy a separate and distinct sphere of activity, separate from the political. This is illustrated in conceptual language that distinguishes between the sacred and the profane, this world and the next, and the worldly and the otherworldly. Managing and constructing the relationship between religion and politics involves defining what religion and politics are and what sphere each should inhabit. Even for those—such as the Islamists—who advocate unifying religion and politics, what religion and politics are must be defined before such a unification can be achieved. In addition, while Islamists claim that they want the unification of religion and politics, they still maintain that the religious and the political should occupy different spheres of authority. A key part of determining the boundary between religion and politics involves determining who has the authority to speak for religion and for politics.

It is often argued that Islam does not recognize the distinction between the religious and the political spheres. It is true that transposing modern distinctions like religion and politics or the religious and the secular onto premodern Islamic history cannot easily be done. Yet the sharia is—and always has been—deeply involved in the drawing of boundaries that might be deemed comparable to the religious and the secular. Distinctions between the legal and the ethical and between legal and nonenforceable legal norms have featured prominently in the sharia. Distinctions between religion (al-din) and the world (al-dunya) also existed. Sherman Jackson has argued that the sharia itself imposed limits and distinguished between the sharia realm and the nonsharia realm with the latter opening up the possibility of assessing human acts about which the revelation did not speak.[112] In addition, the sharia and state law existed alongside one another legitimized by the relationship between fiqh and siyasa. While such distinctions do not neatly translate to a distinction between the religious and the secular, they do suggest possible antecedents. The role of the ulama in dealing with, interpreting, representing, and speaking for the sharia from a contemporary and a historical perspective has been deeply intertwined with the drawing of boundaries and the demarcation of spheres of influence.

One of the areas in which suspicion and the consequent demands for clarification in modern law manifests itself is in the distinction between the civil and the religious spheres. Such a distinction is central to our concept of modern governance. John Locke (1632–1704) argued that the duty of the magistrate was to procure, preserve, and advance civil interests. Locke distinguished civil concernments from the business of "true religion," which he saw as the regulation of men's lives "according to the rules of virtue and piety."[113] There was much at stake in attempting to distinguish "exactly the business of civil government from that of religion and to settle the just bounds that lie between the one and the other."[114] If such a distinction were not made, he argued, there would be no end to disputes between those who purport to care for men's souls and those who purport to care for the commonwealth.[115]

Locke was perhaps too confident about the possibility of drawing a line between the civil and the religious, although in arguing that everyone was orthodox to himself, Locke was perhaps aware that the line between the two would be understood differently. Distinguishing between the religious and the civil—or between what is religious and what is not—is a fraught legal exercise. Winnifred Fallers Sullivan narrates the case of *Warner v. Boca Raton*, which, in the 1990s, was brought on behalf of a group of residents of the state of Florida who sought to prevent city officials from removing numerous statues, paintings, Stars of David, and other formations that they had placed on the graves of their deceased relatives. The case centered on making a determination as to whether the religious practice in question was really religious in the eyes of the court. Addressing what constituted the "religious" involved addressing questions of religious authority, and the relationship between the religion that is lived and experienced by people and the religion that is stated in the scriptures. Ultimately, the problem of distinguishing religion from nonreligion for the purposes of protecting the freedom of the former, Sullivan shows, is an impossible one, and, she argues, ultimately "the law probably cannot get it right."[116]

Separating the civil from the religious or the religious from the nonreligious is thus central to how the modern state negotiates the relationship between religion and politics. In contemporary Egypt, suspicion over the role of al-Azhar and the locus of legal authority was accompanied by—or expressed through—the distinction between the religious sphere and the nonreligious sphere. Such a differentiation became central to how different political parties responded to the demands for further clarification about al-Azhar's role. It was used to carve out areas over which the Muslim Brotherhood and al-Azhar had control.

While Islamic legal authority came to be monopolized by the Supreme Constitutional Court and the state in 2014, al-Azhar did not lose out. One of the most important consequences of the debates and deliberations about Articles 4 and 219 is that al-Azhar emerged in a relatively strong position as the representative of Islam. Al-Azhar successfully established itself as the representative of a particular sphere of authority. The events showed that distinguishing the Islamic from the non-Islamic and the sharia from the non-sharia formed a key component not only in how al-Azhar understands itself, but in how other political actors understand its role. In determining that it represented Islam, al-Azhar more formally inscribed the fact that the distinction between Islam and non-Islam will become a prominent feature of Egyptian law making.

In the case of Article 4 and the sukuk law, the differentiation between the civil and the religious spheres represented an important moment. The Muslim Brotherhood removed the term "Islamic" from the law as a way of bringing it out of al-Azhar's purview. The move was a shrewd one. The removal of the term "Islamic" reinforced the right of the legislature to draw the line between the Islamic and the non-Islamic and the religious and the civil and in so doing curtail the right of al-Azhar to intervene in the question. It thus enabled parties to claim the bill was not Islamic, did not relate to the sharia, and therefore did not lie within al-Azhar's purview. In April 2013, Yousri Ezdawy, a political researcher at al-Ahram Center for Political and Strategic Studies, argued that the Shura Council had the right to bypass the scholars of al-Azhar since the term "Islamic" had been removed from the description: *"sukuk* are no longer considered a religious matter and so it is not obligatory constitutionally to refer the law to Al-Azhar."[117] Ahmed al-Najjar, a member of the economic committee of the Freedom and Justice Party, stated that the new law was entirely different from the previous one. He said that "it will not be called an 'Islamic sovereign sukuk law'; just 'sukuk law,'" but that it was still sharia compliant and would have a sharia committee to oversee its implementation.[118] While the attempt to stop al-Azhar from being involved in the sukuk law actually failed—since Mursi did in fact refer the bill back to al-Azhar—it reaffirmed al-Azhar's right to speak for Islam. It also ensured that in future legislation the parties involved will be more circumspect about how and in what ways the term "Islamic" is used.

The drawing of the line between the Islamic and the non-Islamic is the way in which a number of figures conceptualize al-Azhar's role. Gamal 'Abd al-Sattar was vice minister of endowments in 2013, a professor at al-Azhar University, and a member of the Muslim Brotherhood. 'Abd al-Sattar stated that, with regard to sukuk, "part of it was connected with the Islamic perspective because they were called—up to a certain point in time—*al-sukuk al-islamiyya*."[119] Demarcating the sphere of influence that pertains to the sharia as distinct from a sphere of influence that pertains to the nonsharia is key to al-Sattar's conception of al-Azhar's role. In this, al-Sattar contends that al-Azhar has a role in issues that are related to *al-hukm al-shar'i* (i.e., a verdict or judgment based on the sharia). He argues that there is no contradiction or conflict between the role of al-Azhar and that of the Supreme Constitutional Court. The distinction between the sharia and the nonsharia explains this. The implication is that, because al-Azhar deals with a "particular part" of the law, the al-hukm al-shar'i, this area of jurisdiction does not infringe upon that of the Supreme Constitutional Court, which has jurisdiction over an area of the law that does not relate to the sharia. He asserts that al-Azhar's opinion on religious issues that are connected with sharia must be taken.[120]

'Abd al-Hamid al-Ghazali, a professor of economics at Cairo University, argued that if an issue or a piece of legislation is "related to religion, the final say should be with al-Azhar's Islamic Research Academy, but if there is something connected to managing the economy, the final say should be with the People's Assembly."[121] There is, he maintains, an obvious difference between the "affairs of life" and "religious affairs." The People's Assembly has authority over the affairs of life and al-Azhar has authority over religious affairs. Yet he acknowledges the problem in drawing a line between the two, stating that, when something relates to managing the economy, the People's Assembly has the final say, but it is unfortunate that the Egyptian economic system charges interest because this is regulated by Islamic finance law.[122]

'Abd al-Mu'ti al-Bayyumi (1940–2012), the late Egyptian professor on the *usul al-din* (fundamentals of religion) faculty at al-Azhar University and former member of al-Azhar's Islamic Research Academy, stated that the legislative authority takes the opinion of al-Azhar in issues that are connected to religion. In addressing the question of where to draw the line, he states, "Islam rules legislation in general terms, but in religious issues it deals with details. Islam distinguishes between religious and worldly affairs. So there is no opposition between Islam and politics and economics. There is cooperation."[123]

In addressing the question of the extent to which members of al-Azhar should sit in the state's legislative bodies, Ibrahim Najm of the *Dar al-ifta'* and assistant to the former (2003–13) mufti, 'Ali Guma'a, states that this is appropriate "whenever the need arises," but that they will not just interfere in any issue. Al-Azhar can only interfere if the issue is connected with religion. There is no need, he argues, for a specialist in religion to attend every legislative session, although there is a permanent religious committee that ensures the overall objectives of Islam are being met and there are no violations of the sharia, such as in court cases that deal with capital punishment. He asserts that politics in Islam has two meanings: one in the sense of undertaking care of the Islamic community as a whole and the other in the sense of entering into the party process.[124]

In removing the term "Islamic" from the sukuk law, the Muslim Brotherhood tried to limit al-Azhar's authority to a particular sphere and, in so doing, protect the legislative body from any encroachment upon it. Yet, in limiting al-Azhar's role to speaking for Islam, it also reinforced and strengthened al-Azhar's right to speak for it. While the 2014 Constitution no longer states that al-Azhar should be consulted on matters of legislation, al-Azhar has firmly claimed its right—which is now constitutionally enshrined in Article 7—to speak for the religious sphere and thereby lay claim to it. It establishes al-Azhar as the main reference for religious sciences and Islamic affairs and establishes its authority to define the relationship between religion and state.

Yet, while reinforcing al-Azhar's role as the representative of Islam, the Constitution of 2014 did not resolve the question of the extent and nature of this authority. Nor did it resolve how the line between the Islamic and the non-Islamic would be drawn. In fact, when al-Azhar sought to amend the sukuk law, many of the grounds upon which it opposed the law did not strictly relate to clear principles of the sharia. Al-Tayyib argued that the law endangered the state's sovereignty and that sukuk should not be sold to foreigners. This points to the fact that al-Azhar's role to speak for Islam will only result in further struggle about how to draw the line between what is Islam and what is not. Further legal questions and debates that involve al-Azhar's role in the legislative process are likely to pivot around the distinction between Islamic and non-Islamic issues. Distinguishing the one from the other, however, is irresolvable and will, in turn, generate more questions.

The revolution of 2011 and the ensuing constitutional debates provided the opportunity to address the question of al-Azhar's role in Egyptian legislation. The question of what role the ulama should have has been a source of tension for centuries, but has been particularly the case ever since the state appropriated al-Azhar in the 1960s. The promulgation of Article 2 of the 1971 Constitution raised the question of who gets to speak for the sharia. In 2011 Egyptians sought to address the question of al-Azhar's role by constitutionally defining that role. While the Constitution of 2012 made various proclamations about the role of al-Azhar and the Supreme Constitutional Court, it generated more questions about the import of these constitutional commitments. Thus, while the Constitution of 2012 gave al-Azhar some kind of legislative role, the ensuing sukuk law controversy showed that those articles had simply given rise to further questions about the nature and extent of al-Azhar's role and about the locus of Islamic legal authority. Article 219 was not tested prior to its removal, but similarly had the potential to create more legal conundrums about the relative weight of the rules of the schools of law and the broader principles of the sharia.

One of the important outcomes of these debates was that the priority of modern Islamic state law over the sharia was established. There was considerable reluctance at giving authority to an unelected body of Islamic legal scholars. This illustrates that, despite Islamic legal history's tradition of suspicion of state authority, Egyptian lawmakers have consolidated the modern idea that the locus of legal authority lies with the state. Yet one should not go so far as to assume that this question is somehow settled. Despite the fact that the state asserted its authority over the sharia and despite the fact that there was considerable reluctance to give authority to an unelected body of Islamic legal scholars, vestiges of the premodern suspicion of the state and of state law remain.

The continued legacy of such suspicion was one of the reasons why al-Azhar was able to establish its right to speak for the Islamic sphere in future legislative negotiations. This shows that contemporary Egyptians have inherited a sense that the ulama should play some role in the legislation of the state. The Constitution of 2014 did so by stipulating that al-Azhar should speak for Islam. Yet, in doing so, the distinction between the Islamic and the non-Islamic became more firmly entrenched as a means by which al-Azhar's role would be understood by itself and others. However, the distinction between what is Islamic and what is not Islamic is far from self-evident. Giving al-Azhar the right to speak for Islam has simply increased the possibility of tension arising regarding how that role will be defined by itself and by others. The difficult nature of this question is likely to lead to further disputes between various parties as they use this distinction to limit the authority of others and augment their own.

Such outcomes illustrate the complex discontinuities and continuities that exist in debates about the role of al-Azhar in the modern Egyptian state. While drawing on the legacy of the relationship between the sharia and the law-making capacities of the premodern polity, the debate about who gets to speak for the sharia and what the relationship between the sharia and the state is, operates through distinctly charged questions about the relationship between the religious and the nonreligious spheres. They also operate with reference to new understandings about the role of the state and its monopoly on legal authority. A constitutional commitment to al-Azhar's role has reflected an increased need for constitutions to articulate what Egypt stands for. Yet inscribing al-Azhar's role through a constitutional commitment more formally establishes the constant need to distinguish between Islam and non-Islam.

CHAPTER 5

The "Divinely Revealed Religions"

The preamble to the 2014 Constitution contains the following grandiloquent passage:

> Egypt is the cradle of religion and the banner of the magnificence of the divinely revealed religions. On its land, Moses grew up (peace be upon him), the light of God was revealed to him, and the message descended to him on Mount Sinai. On its land, Egyptians embraced the Virgin Mary and her son and presented thousands of martyrs in defense of the church of Jesus (peace be upon him). When the seal of the messengers, Muhammed (peace and blessings be upon him), was sent to all people to complete noble characteristics, our hearts and minds were opened to the light of Islam. We were the best soldiers of the earth to fight on behalf of God, and we spread the message of truth and religious sciences throughout the world. This is Egypt: a homeland in which we live and which lives in us.[1]

This lofty passage illustrates that the drafters of the 2014 Constitution saw the concept of the divinely revealed religions (al-adyan al-samawiyya) as central to Egyptian nationalism. The divinely revealed religions, also translated as the heavenly religions, is a notion that emphasizes the mutually intertwined histories and theologies of Judaism, Christianity, and Islam. Thus, while Islam is presented as the religion that perfects religious sensibilities in Egypt and represents who Egyptians are, it is framed as historically and theologically linked with Judaism and Christianity. These three monotheistic religions are deeply rooted in the land of Egypt. Egypt's identity is permeated by this religious history. The constitution claims to speak for Egyptians as a whole—all Egyptians, it assumes, feel this connection to the divinely revealed religions. While sentiments about national unity between Copts and Muslims had been present in the preamble to the 2012 Constitution, the Constitution of 2014 outdid its predecessor in articulating a commitment to the heavenly religions.

Among the many new articles that appeared in the Egyptian Constitution of 2012 was Article 3. The article stated that "the principles of the religious laws of Christian and Jewish Egyptians are the main source for the legal regulation of their personal status affairs, their religious affairs, and for the nomination of their religious leaders."[2] The article thus gave Jews—although their population in Egypt is too small now for this to have much effect—and Christians, about 6–8 percent of the population, a level of judicial autonomy. This judicial autonomy was granted to Jews and Christians on account of their status as members of the heavenly religions.

While the statement on the judicial autonomy of the divinely revealed religions formalized what had been in effect in Egyptian case law since the country's independence from the Ottoman Empire in 1914, such a commitment went further and made a national proclamation about the special status of the divinely revealed religions. In so doing, it formalized the state's view that believers in non–divinely revealed religions, specifically the Baha'is, estimated to number around 2,000, are heterodox and therefore contrary to what being Egyptian means.

In criticisms in the Egyptian press and the Western media, Article 3 of the 2012 Constitution was accused of contributing to the "Islamist" nature of the constitution, and of detracting from the principle of legal equality. Such a strident identification with Jews and Christians and antipathy toward the Baha'is was seen as the result of the greater role of Islam and the sharia in the Egyptian public sphere. While this chapter demonstrates that this antipathy toward Baha'is is partly the result of a particular form of Islamization—in which multiple legal possibilities were jettisoned in favor of one—and is not discontinuous from Ottoman norms, it also shows that this antipathy became particularly resonant under the socialist, statist, and secular rule of Gamal 'Abd al-Nasser in the 1960s. This particular level of hostility in the Nasserist period indicates that the concept of the divinely revealed religions has become a national cultural concept that transcends the secular-religious divide. This was further illustrated when Article 3 was retained in the seemingly more secular Constitution of 2014. While Article 3 of the 2014 Constitution was opposed by some secular groups, it had a broad constituency of support that encompassed a diverse range of groups, including the Coptic Church, the military, and parts of the secular and judicial elite.

In looking at Egyptian Copts and Baha'is, the late Saba Mahmood argues that modern secular governance has contributed to the exacerbation of religious tensions, and that this has polarized differences between religions. Secularism, she argues, "promises to demolish religious hierarchies in order to create a body politic in which all its members are equal before the law."[3] Yet, she argues, modern secularism has resulted in a rise in inequality between religions and caused more interreligious conflict. It has thus led to the "increasingly precarious position of religious minorities in the polity."[4] This is in part because "modern governmentality involves the state's intervention and regulation of many aspects of socioreligious life."[5] The modern secular state, she contends, "is not simply a neutral arbiter of religious differences; it also produces and creates them."[6]

Mahmood's argument that modern secularism has resulted in the intensification of religious inequality and conflict is a vitally important intervention in pointing out the disparity between what secular states claim to do (consign religious differences to the private sphere) and what she claims they actually do (politicize such differences, leading to sectarian conflict). However, in emphasizing that interreligious relations have been transformed by the modern secular state, she overlooks how the management of religion in its current form in Egypt has closed off opportunities for some but opened up opportunities for others. Without a sufficient analysis of the premodern and Ottoman periods, a discussion of interreligious relations in Egypt can miss the ways in which religious tension and inequality have both continuity and discontinuity with the past.

In this chapter, I employ a broad historical scope to look at how the nature of religious belonging has become recast through constitutional commitments to the national will. I start by exploring premodern Ottoman history to discuss the *dhimmi* system of governance, the extent to which this system constituted a form of state recognition for non-Muslims, and how the Ottoman Empire dealt with the question of religious heterodoxy. I then return to modern Egypt to look at how the concept of the heavenly religions has become nationalized, leading to an intensification of some forms of difference but also to the emergence of new alliances. Briefly digressing to look at how and when the Baha'is were excluded from the Egyptian public sphere, I then return to the post-2011 context to show the ways in which the commitment to the concept of the divinely revealed religions has become nationalized to form an important cultural concept. While the concept of the heavenly religions has resulted in the exclusion of Baha'is, it has also resulted in more specific inclusion for Coptic Christianity centered on the church. This church-centric type of Christianity has become more specifically intertwined with Islam through such a constitutional statement.

This chapter argues that the commitment to the concept of the divinely revealed religions does not constitute a simple revival of premodern sharia even though it has origins in it. Rather, the application of Article 3 results in different dynamics between the state, members of the divinely revealed religions, and those who do not belong to those religions. Article 3 effectively gave constitutional recognition to the right of Jews and Christians to apply their own personal status law by virtue of their status as members of the heavenly religions. This system of judicial autonomy has origins in premodern sharia and the Ottoman Empire. However, in the context of the modern nation state, the process of giving an exemption from state law requires positive state recognition of the community being given the exemption. Giving positive state recognition to a religious community involves accepting that this religious community forms part of the cultural makeup of the broader national community. Article 3 makes a more formal commitment to the idea that some religious commitments are publicly acceptable while others are not. This new dynamic of positive inclusion and positive exclusion is not a simple incarnation of the sharia nor is it a break with it, but is born out of the nation state's demand to articulate a totalizing and unitary culture.

People of the Book and State Recognition

Article 3 gave Jews and Christians judicial autonomy over an undefined area of personal status law. The idea of giving judicial autonomy to the divinely revealed religions has origins in the premodern Islamic order. The dhimmi system was one in which Jews and Christians, and, in some cases, other non-Muslims were given legal protection and a level of religious and judicial autonomy in return for their submission to the Islamic ruling polity and their payment of the *jizya* (a poll tax). The specific legal rights and duties inherent in the dhimma contract were complex and not always clearly defined. The contract offered non-Muslims security of life and property, defense against enemies who attack, communal self-government, and freedom of religious practice. Most accounts of the role of non-Muslims in premodern Islamic societies assume that the dhimmis had considerable autonomy: they were allowed to retain their own religious organizations and places of worship and were entitled to their own religious trusts, law courts, and law codes, which covered an area of law that was broader than—although in some respects corresponded with—what is now denoted by the term "personal status." The nature and extent of this autonomy were subject to negotiation. Some non-Muslims were able to enforce their communal laws exclusively, while others—including the Copts—only had the right to concurrent communal autonomy (see chapter 7). In addition, while the dhimmi system gave protection and freedoms to Jews and Christians, the status of other non-Muslims remained ambiguous.

The dhimmi system is rooted in the sharia and Islamic theological principles. It was broadly based on the theological concept of the People of the Book (Jews, Christians, and Sabians), which implied that freedom of religion was to be accorded to fellow monotheists whose religion was based on some form—albeit a distorted or misinterpreted one—of revelation from God. However, Anver Emon argues that, rather than reflecting a particular Islamic ethos, "the Islamic legal treatment of non-Muslims is symptomatic of the more general challenge of governing a diverse polity."[7] Emon contends that, in the sharia, there was a mutually constitutive relationship between law and governance, so that the sharia should be understood as the rule of law embedded in the logic of empire and governance. He maintains that a particular legal doctrine was a direct product of the environment in which that rule was applied.[8]

The concept of the millet has often been used to refer to the system of governance, based on the dhimmi system, which developed between non-Muslims and the Ottoman Empire, although the term "millet" only dates to the nineteenth century.[9] The extent to which the dhimmi system of governance was formalized, organized, and systematized has been disputed. Benjamin Braude argues that there was "no overall administrative system, structure, or set of institutions for dealing with non-Muslims."[10] Karen Barkey, however, disputes this, pointing to the extent to which the Ottoman Empire organized the communities it conquered.[11] What is clear is that the level of formality of the relationship between the Ottoman Empire and its non-Muslim subjects varied. There was often a lack of clarity about what the rights and obligations of the dhimmi system of governance were. The system gradually emerged to provide a degree of religious, cultural, and ethnic continuity within the communities conquered by the Ottomans while also incorporating them into the Ottoman administrative, economic, and political systems.[12]

Yet the level of autonomy granted to these non-Muslim communities depended on what kind of state recognition—if any—they received. The most formal relationship that the Ottoman Empire had with non-Muslim communities, which came to be officially named as millets in the nineteenth century, applied to three main groups: Greek Orthodox Christians, Armenians, and, eventually, Jews. Each was managed differently.[13] The Greek Orthodox community was recognized in 1454 by a berat between Mehmed the Conqueror and the patriarch of the Greek Orthodox Church by which the latter had the power to administer many of the affairs of the empire's Orthodox community.[14] The Ottoman Empire preferred the Greek Orthodox model for dealing with non-Muslim communities due to its highly centralized nature. The Armenians and particularly the Jews, however, did not have such a developed ecclesiastical hierarchy. Yet, over time, the Jews and especially the Armenians developed simpler and more hierarchical patterns of organization. The Armenian community was officially recognized in 1461 and Christian groups that could not be fitted into the Greek Orthodox community were added into the Armenian Gregorian Church.[15] While such recognition was given due to the sharia concept of People of the Book, it was—perhaps even more so—given as a method of governance.

Jews, for example, were not officially recognized by the Sublime Porte, the government of the Ottoman Empire, until the nineteenth century in part because they were not so centrally organized. Bernard Lewis points out that, from the sixteenth century through the eighteenth century, there is little evidence that a chief rabbi who had jurisdiction over Jews throughout Ottoman lands existed. For the most part, Jews lived in separate communities, grouped around their own synagogue and led by their own rabbi.[16] It was not until 1835 that the Jews were recognized by an imperial decree as a millet under the authority of the *hahambashi*, the chief rabbi, with roughly the same status, rights, and duties over the entire Jewish community of the Ottoman Empire as the ecclesiastical leaders of the Greek and Armenian churches.[17]

British diplomacy was a driving force in the appointment of the hahambashi. In the 1830s, the British fashioned themselves as the protectors of Jewish interests in the Ottoman Empire, as did Russia with the Greek Orthodox and France with the Catholics.[18] In response to French pressure, Sultan Mahmud II (1785–1839) recognized the Armenian Catholic millet in 1831.[19] The sultan also responded to British and American pressure by recognizing Protestants as a separate millet in 1850.[20]

One of the most important components of the millet system was that it required official sanction by the state. Heads of the millets were chosen by the community, but the sultan had to approve their appointment. Upon official sanction, the heads of the millets had a position in the official hierarchy of the state.[21] This gave them a level of judicial autonomy, which sometimes involved the right to exclusive jurisdiction. However, the opportunity to exercise levels of communal autonomy was not limited to the more official form of the millets, although such autonomy often involved non-Muslims being able to have recourse to the sharia courts. Local Ottoman rulers entered into agreements with numerous groups without this level of formality. The word "ta'ifa" was used to define a number of social or economic groups, which included—but were not limited to—religious communities. Each ta'ifa was able to have its own leadership and its own rules and regulations, which were then affirmed and registered before the chief qadi.[22] Magdi Guirguis reports that the term "ta'ifa" was commonly used by the Ottoman administration for the Copts, and that Egypt's Copts used the term when they appealed to the state. She argues that the Ottoman administration dealt with them as if they were one group.[23] The Coptic pope was given a different mandate from the one given to the Greek Orthodox patriarch. The Coptic pope was appointed upon the approval of the Ottoman governor in Egypt, and due to the Coptic's community's distance from Istanbul and its localized nature in Egypt, the pope did not have the same level of contact with the Sublime Porte or the same official recognition from it.[24]

Such systems of judicial autonomy have often been looked at through the lens of the concept of toleration, which has been projected back onto Islamic history. Yet toleration should not be taken to assume positive endorsement of religious difference. Karen Barkey argues that toleration of non-Muslims was a strategy to organize the diverse communities of the Ottoman Empire, keep order, and maintain their loyalty. It was therefore "a means of rule, of extending, consolidating, and enforcing state power."[25] It is important to note here that Amnon Cohen argues that such tolerance and communal legal systems did not extend to notions of religious brotherhood. He argues that the Ottoman state regarded Christianity and Judaism with disdain, although this did not preclude their inclusion in Ottoman society.[26] There was no concept of some kind of unified Abrahamic identity. Aaron Hughes has linked the adjective "Abrahamic" to a modern interfaith agenda. He argues that the term is a "modern creation, largely a theological neologism" to promote ecumenism.[27] Hughes highlights the problems involved in translating the diversity and tolerance of the Ottoman Empire into positive endorsement.

Under the period of Ottoman reforms known as the Tanzimat (1839–76), equality for non-Muslims was established. In 1850 a decree opened up the army to non-Muslims. The Khatti Humayun Decree of 1856 emphasized the equality of all Ottoman subjects before the law, including the right to serve in the government.[28] It promised that "no one shall be compelled to change their religion" and undertook to ensure freedom of religious exercise, guaranteeing it for sects in localities where "there are no other religious denominations."[29] The decree also provided for greater non-Muslim participation in provincial councils, and, for the first time, for non-Muslim representation on Ottoman governing councils.[30] However, it reduced the control that religious leaders could exercise, since, for the first time, laymen were given a major voice in the governance of the millets.[31] The Khatti Humayun Decree also decreased the areas over which the millets had control. Education, for example, now came under government administration.[32] The decree assigned jurisdiction for criminal, civil, and commercial matters to the newly established Nizamiyya courts based on French codes. This restricted the jurisdiction of both the sharia and the non-Muslim communal courts.[33]

Niyazi Berkes argues that Mahmud II (1785–1839) wished to abolish the millet system to establish equality for non-Muslims. Yet Mahmud was hindered by the fact that the millet system had emerged as an important tool for international diplomacy by which the Christian powers of Europe exerted influence in the region.[34] Thus, the millet system was not abolished but retained and reformed. The Khatti Humayun Decree of 1856 granted legislative autonomy to non-Muslims with regard to "special civil proceedings, such as those relating to successions."[35]

In restricting the jurisdiction of the millets, the Khatti Humayun Decree also reaffirmed the immunities granted to them.[36] The decree affirmed that the rights and freedoms granted to the millets were given and controlled by the government.[37] However, it established greater state control over the millets, stating that each community should discuss its immunities and privileges—and reforms required—with the Sublime Porte.[38] The decree therefore recognized the dependency of non-Muslim communities on the state, requiring religious leaders to take an oath of loyalty to the Sublime Porte upon their entrance into office.[39]

In 1869 the Ottoman government imposed upon Ottoman subjects an Ottoman citizenship that was modeled on Western conceptions of citizenship: every person born of an Ottoman father was an Ottoman subject and was equal regardless of faith or language. Ottoman nationality established a more direct relationship between the individual and the state. Yet, in doing so, the relationship between non-Muslims and the state was altered by the fact that the Sunni Muslim character of the Ottoman government had acquired a new political significance. This is because the idea of the nation state needs the national community in order to justify its claim to represent its citizens, thereby making it necessary for the political system and the religious-national culture to be more intricately intertwined.[40]

After Egypt became officially independent from the Ottoman Empire in 1914, Egyptian Law No. 8 of 1915 gave formal recognition to the Khatti Humayun Decree.[41] The law recognized all already established judicial authorities and empowered those authorities to continue to exercise their rights and privileges based on Ottoman decrees. The reorganized Coptic Orthodox community had been officially recognized by the Sublime Porte in 1883.[42] The Rabbanite Jews were recognized in 1891.[43] Law No. 8 of 1915 also granted each non-Muslim community a communal council (*majlis milli*) to deal with questions of personal status and its own communal laws, customary or codified.[44] By the mid-twentieth century, there were some fourteen non-Muslim *majalis milliyya*, or communal councils. Some of these religious communities, such as the Coptic Orthodox Church, the Coptic Evangelical Church, and the Coptic Catholic Church, were formally recognized by the government, whereas others were simply tolerated.[45] The question of state recognition was to become more important.[46] While the new national Egyptian courts assumed jurisdiction over criminal and commercial matters, matters relating to marriage, divorce, custody, guardianship, and inheritance remained the province of the sharia courts for Muslims and the communal courts for non-Muslims.

Thus, while the system of dhimmi governance that emerged in the Ottoman Empire, later inherited by Egypt, was based on the sharia and theological notions of respect for the heavenly religions, it must also be seen in the context of what Emon refers to as the relationship between law and governance. Emon calls for eschewing the frame of tolerance through which the rules regulating the dhimmi system have been understood, arguing that tolerance "often hides the underlying regulatory features of governance that spark the need to discuss tolerance in the first place."[47] The dhimmi system of governance varied and included models that involved state recognition by the Ottoman Empire and less formal systems that involved acknowledgment of the judicial autonomy of non-Muslims on a more localized level. For the Ottomans, this was a method of governance and a mechanism of control. The Copts did not have the same official recognition and judicial autonomy as the Greek Orthodox or the Armenians until 1883. With the reform of the millets, this area of judicial autonomy was truncated and while judicial authority was maintained, it became more formally connected with—and dependent on—official recognition of the state. As the Ottoman state's Islamic character became more important, the dynamic between religious minorities and the state was altered. The idea of official recognition was to become more important upon Egypt's independence from the Ottoman Empire.

Islamic Heterodoxy

While the religious freedom of Jews and Christians has—with some important exceptions—been unquestioned by those advocating for the revival of
the sharia, the proposed treatment of religions that do not fall into the category of People of the Book has been much more ambiguous. The Sunni
schools of law have differing opinions on the question. The Hanafi school,
which was the dominant school of the Ottoman Empire, and the Maliki
school, which was second in importance in Mamluk Egypt (1250–1517),
argues that the jizya may be collected from any polytheist. Thus, all non-
Muslims received protection from the state on the basis that anyone who
submits to the political authority of the Muslim government can become
a non-Muslim subject of that government. However, the Shafi'i school
(dominant in Mamluk Egypt) and the Hanbali (dominant in Saudi Arabia)
schools argue that jizya may only be accepted from People of the Book and
Zoroastrians.

In her discussion of religious conflict in contemporary Egypt, Saba
Mahmood briefly mentions that the distinction between the heavenly and
nonheavenly religions "has no historical justification because there is no consensus in the shari'a on how to treat followers of non-Abrahamic religions."[48]
Such a distinction, she argues, is a product of modern secular governance.
She maintains that, in premodern Islamic empires, non-Muslims were subject to a variety of different institutional and legal arrangements and that,
while Ottomans did not generally have to deal with communities that were
not Muslim, Christian, or Jewish—such as Hindus or Buddhists—in other
parts of the Islamic world, this was not the case. The Islamic empires, she
argues, "could not afford to treat these religious communities as juridical
nonentities, heretics, or simply infidels, but had to integrate them into the
state's economic and governing structure."[49] She also inscribes a stark contrast between the premodern and the modern Egyptian state by saying that,
"under various premodern Islamic empires, followers of non-Abrahamic
religions were also granted state protection. The Egyptian government,
however, refuses to extend similar recognition to Bahais."[50]

However, there was no consensus among the four schools of law about
whether non-Muslims who were not Jews or Christians could be allowed to
maintain their own religion and therefore have a level of judicial autonomy.
The distinction between divinely revealed religions and others clearly has
theological roots in the sharia, although it is the social and legal implications of such a distinction that are more difficult to ascertain. Yet to say
that the distinction between the heavenly and nonheavenly religions had no

historical justification is to assume that what we consider to be religions were thought of as separate religions then. Those who did not identify as Jews or Christians were not necessarily seen as belonging to a different religion. In many cases, such followers were classified as heterodox and the Islamic legal classification apostate was sometimes applied to them. The writings of Ibn Taymiyya (1263–1328) attest to a level of antipathy to groups such as the Druze, the Alawites, the Qaramita, and the Batiniyya.[51] The Ottoman Empire frequently did not legally recognize groups it deemed heretical. Yet the consequences of the lack of state recognition were less pernicious at the time as there were more spaces for communities—under the rubric of ta'ifa, which were autonomous yet sometimes not recognized—to organize themselves. This premodern context was marked by a relative lack of state intrusion, meaning that there were many areas in which communities had considerable autonomy on account of their distance from the state. As such, this meant that the Ottoman Empire did not necessarily have to integrate groups it did not wish to legally recognize. It is for this reason that some heterodox Islamic sects—while not recognized—ended up possessing local judicial autonomy. This was particularly true of the Druze in Lebanon and the Alawites in the Levant.[52]

With the consolidation and centralization of the Ottoman Empire in the sixteenth century, the empire's identity as a representative of Sunni Islam became more important. In the sixteenth century, the empire had recently conquered many lands with Muslim majorities, such as Egypt and the Levant. In addition, the proximity of the powerful Safavid Shi'i Empire to the east caused the Ottoman authorities to question long-extant policies of religious tolerance and to place greater emphasis on the Ottoman Empire's Sunni identity. Barkey argues that, by the sixteenth century, the Ottoman Empire had developed from a multireligious syncretic empire to a more orthodox Sunni Islamic or scripturalist one. Under Selim II (1566–74), the construction of outsiders took on religious terms. Barkey argues that Ottomans would often persecute heterodox Sufi groups rather than non-Muslims, since heterodox groups did not fit easily into their model of organization and the boundaries between them and Sunni orthodox communities were not so clearly defined.[53] The scholar Ibn-i Kemal (d. 1534) classified communal acts of rebellion as signs of nonbelief and defined segments of the population as apostates. Ibn-i Kemal's scholarship reflected the way in which religious practice and sharia norms were utilized for state interests.[54]

Thus, while the Ottoman Empire officially recognized a number of non-Muslim religious communities, there were many groups that were not officially recognized. Non-Sunni religious minorities were not regarded as non-Muslims or as belonging to another religion. This included Shi'is, Druze, Yezidis, and Alawites. These were creeds seen by the Ottoman Empire as deviant and therefore, Necati Alkan contends, had no official status as autonomous religious communities and were increasingly defined as deviant during the reign of 'Abd al-Hamid II (1876–1909).[55] The Druze, for example, were not a recognized religion. The Druze often resorted to the sharia courts although, in some cases, matters of personal status were settled within the community.[56] The Ottomans refused to acknowledge the Shi'is as a separate millet that was to be protected, and they were seen, Alkan argues, as "sinning Muslims."[57] In addition, the Alawites of northern Syria were generally not "mentioned in official Ottoman documentation until after the second half of the 19th century."[58] In some cases, the Alawites were allowed by the authorities to make use of the sharia courts but, as apostates, their legal status was questionable.[59]

The understanding that these communities were heterodox intensified in the nineteenth century. During the period of the Tanzimat reforms, the Ottomans pursued a policy of "Sunnitization" of heterodox communities. This policy intensified in later years.[60] Religious conformity, Sami Zubaida argues, was increasingly emphasized and religious dissent was seen as rebellion.[61] 'Abd al-Hamid II feared that Protestant missionaries would try to convert heterodox Muslims, so he tried to convert Alawites to the official Hanafi-Sunni school. Muslim schools and mosques were established in non-Sunni areas.[62]

It is debatable whether the discrimination against those who were seen as heterodox Muslims marks a break with a more tolerant Hanafi jurisprudence. Hanafi norms could yield a number of possibilities and how these possibilities were translated into law varied and were subject to the form of governance that existed in a particular Islamic empire. Hanafism argues that polytheists— that is, those that were not identified as People of the Book—could be tolerated. Yet the category of polytheist does not necessarily include the category of apostate, which was often applied to include heterodox Muslims. Thus, heterodoxy and exclusion existed within premodern sharia and thus laid the foundation for its manifestation in modern Egypt. Islamic law, however, was malleable and responded to the needs of Islamic governance and the distinction between polytheist and apostate was not always upheld. It is at particular moments and junctures that these forms of inclusion and exclusion become operative, something which Emon's argument about the mutually constitutive relationship between sharia law and governance helps explain.[63]

What is clear is that the Ottoman Empire's development into a more centralized and modern state required increased legibility for its religious minorities in the sense of how these minorities related to the whole. This in turn necessitated clarification of the state's responsibility to them and their responsibility to the state. This process of formalization also demanded that the state fix its own identity and articulate more firmly which religious minorities formed part of the national culture. This need for the formalization of the state's identity meant that the classification of heterodox had different implications. Just as the Ottoman Empire was formalizing its relationship with non-Muslim communities in the form of the millet system, it was also formalizing its Islamic identity and thus its conception that non-orthodox Muslims were heterodox. The formation of the civil code of laws in the Ottoman Empire alleviated some of the consequences of the designation of non-orthodox Muslims as heterodox and partly secured their legal status. However, at the same time, it brought their status as different and potentially politically deviant into much sharper focus.

The Divinely Revealed Religions and Egyptian Nationalism

Michel Rosenfeld has argued that identity and difference—and the interplay between the two concepts—are an important part of constitutions. In the nation, he asserts, accommodating differences must be limited by the need to preserve the dominant identity. Accordingly, he contends, determining how and in what way individual and group differences gain constitutional protection involves consideration of the interaction between identity and diversity.[64] Modern constitutions express certain ideological commitments, including articulating a balance between identity and difference. Proclaiming such commitments may communicate—either internationally or domestically—their importance within a society.

The interplay between identity and difference has taken various forms in Egypt's constitutional history. The Egyptian Constitutions of 1923 and 1956 were praised for their secular nature and for the absence of any reference to religious difference. For example, in writing about the 1923 Constitution, Mervat Hatem maintains that the absence of any reference to religious distinctions in the constitution meant that religion did not make a difference in the exercise of the new rights of citizenship. Sameness, not difference, Hatem argues, "was to be a central concept in the discussion of the unity of the nation."[65] According to Hatem, "this suggested that religious matters were to be treated as spiritual matters that had no impact on the definition of the political rights in the homeland."[66] For S. S. Hasan, the constitution did not specifically mention the Copts because Egyptian nationalists had wanted to apply the French homogenizing model of national integration.[67]

Hatem's interpretation reflects the narrative that this historical period was a secular one that facilitated the integration of Copts and Muslims into the Egyptian state. However, the absence of language focused on religion and Islam does not mean that religion was necessarily relegated to the private sphere. It simply points to the fact that no need was felt to make a constitutional commitment to religion. Armando Salvatore argues that the idea of an opposition between the secular and the Islamic was only just developing at this time. It was only in the 1920s and 1930s that public discourse reflected an increasing need to distinguish the Islamic from the non-Islamic.[68]

Mervat Hatem points out that, despite the secular nature of the Wafd party's discourse, it still assumed that Islam would form an intrinsic part of Egyptian culture and encouraged the Copts to adopt this legacy as part of their national identity.[69] In addition, Sebastian Elsässer illustrates that the Egyptian nation at this time consisted of a conception of two—possibly three—religious communities living alongside one another. He argues that the mantra "Long live [the unity of] crescent and cross" served as the tenet of Egyptian nationalism and was expressed in a discourse of national unity. He maintains that religious symbols, references, and networks remained highly significant and that popular support "was often mobilized through religious or communal networks and expressed in a religious idiom."[70] This religious patriotism emphasized that national identity should remain connected to religious identity.[71]

Article 2 of the 1971 Constitution, which states that "the principles of Islamic jurisprudence are the main source of legislation," made a much more explicit commitment to the Egyptian state's Islamic character. Many argued that Article 2 symbolized the end of the secular democratic state in Egypt, the end of national bonds, and linked this with a rapid increase in sectarian conflict. Yet the promulgation of Article 2 in the 1971 Constitution is also reflective of the point at which the question of the state's secular or Islamic nature had become much more dominant in political discourse. Nevertheless, Article 2 introduced a specific commitment to the idea that state law could not contravene the sharia. What that commitment would mean in practice was—as we have seen—unclear.

When Article 2 was first promulgated, the Coptic pope Shenouda III (1921–2012) objected. Despite protests against Article 2 in the 1970s, many Copts have tempered their views as Article 2 has become more and more entrenched as a defining feature of the relationship between state and society. While there are common assumptions that the Copts would want a secular state and would therefore be opposed to Article 2, a constitutional commitment to the sharia has strengthened the claim that Copts should have their own personal status law. A number of Coptic writers have taken this position. Dr. Milak Tamir Mikha'il, a lawyer and writer on Egyptian law, contends that the church's ability to exercise its judicial competence in personal status law derives from Article 2 of the constitution.[72] Likewise, Dr. Nabil Luqa Bibawi, a Coptic author and vice-chairman of the Shura Council Information and Culture Committee, maintains that it is the sharia that gives non-Muslims the right to follow their own personal status law.[73]

That attitudes towards Islamic law among Copts are more ambiguous than is commonly assumed was manifest during the debate about the amendment of Article 2 of the 1971 Constitution that took place in 2005–7. While a number of secular Copts—and some secular Muslims—opposed Article 2, others called for amending Article 2 and giving Christianity a firmer platform in statements about the cultural identity of the state. Some suggested that such an amendment should take into account the fact that Egypt is a multireligious country, for example, by inserting a reference to Christians and Christianity as partners in the Egyptian homeland.[74] Amin Iskandar, a Coptic intellectual and political analyst, argues that Article 2 is logical since the majority of the Egyptian people are Muslim.[75] Pope Shenouda III, despite having opposed the introduction of Article 2 in 1980, took the position that "if rightly applied, all laws and articles are for the good of the people."[76] In early 2007, he rejected calls by Coptic expatriates for Article 2 to be removed and pointed to the danger of amending it.[77] While such a position can be partly explained by a reluctance to offend Muslims, the Coptic Orthodox Church has taken an ambiguous position on Article 2 precisely because the principle of legal pluralism within Islamic sharia supports the right for Christians to have autonomy over their own personal status law.[78]

Article 3 of the 2012 Constitution did make a constitutional commitment to a level of judicial autonomy for Jews and Christians. However, this only applied to the divinely revealed religions and not to non-Muslims as a whole. Article 3 stated that "the principles of the religious laws of Christian and Jewish Egyptians are the main source for the legal regulation of their personal status affairs, their religious affairs, and for the nomination of their religious leaders."[79] Another article, Article 43 of the 2012 Constitution, stated that "freedom of belief is protected. The state ensures the freedom to practice religious rites and to establish places of worship for the divinely revealed religions, as regulated by law."[80]

Articles 3 and 43 constitutionally enshrined the rights of Jews and Christians to follow their own personal status law. While it was the first time for such a constitutional declaration, it had long been established in law and practice. Article 46 of the 1971 Constitution had stated that "the state shall guarantee the freedom of belief and the freedom of practice of religious rites," but was limited in law and practice to the divinely revealed religions.[81] For example, in December 2006, the Supreme Administrative Court argued that the interpretation of Article 46 of the 1971 Constitution on the freedom to practice religious rites applies to the three divine religions only. While it affirmed freedom of belief, it distinguished belief from practice and denied freedom of practice to those religions that were seen as "a violation of public order and contrary to morality."[82]

While establishing the right of Jews and Christians to have their own personal status law, Articles 3 and 43 also constitutionally enshrined the principle of the divinely revealed religions as forming a key part of the relationship between religion and the state in Egypt. Such judicial autonomy was granted because Jews and Christians belonged to religions that were deemed legitimate based on the concept of the People of the Book. The relationship between these two clauses and Article 2 is particularly interesting, since these articles removed the question of the divinely revealed religions from the status of potential Islamic law provisions which the Supreme Constitutional Court might or might not apply to future legislation, and made religious freedom for divinely revealed religions a positive, state centered law. Article 3 removed the question of the divinely revealed religions within the sharia from the area of law over which the Supreme Constitutional Court had latitude of interpretation. Article 3 effectively established the concept of the divinely revealed religions—and the link between this concept and judicial autonomy—as part of constitutional law and thus made it difficult to alter.

Article 3, according to Paul Sedra, was presented by members of the Constituent Assembly as a concession "to the sensibilities of the Coptic community."[83] The three main Christian denominations in Egypt (the Coptic Orthodox Church, the Coptic Catholic Church, and the Coptic Evangelical Church) welcomed the article.[84] It represented the first time that the Egyptian Constitution had recognized the existence of other religions in Egypt. Article 3 gave Jews and Christians the formal recognition of the state. It also helped to alleviate fears that Islamists wished to impose the sharia upon them, since the article facilitated the control of the Coptic Orthodox Church over the Coptic community.

However, a number of Coptic groups and activists have opposed the fact that Article 3 increased the authority of the church over Copts. Such an increase in the church's authority at the expense of the laity can be traced back to Nasser, who weakened the Coptic laity by removing the religious endowments from the authority of the Coptic Orthodox Council and assigning them to the Coptic Orthodox Church. The nationalization of the courts in 1955 also removed one of the council's sources of power.[85] Sedra has criticized "the disproportionate attention afforded to the Coptic Orthodox Church as the purported representative of the community," which, he argues, has obscured "the vitally important intra-communal dynamics of the Copts."[86]

The Coptic intellectual Samir Marcos, for example, has long been a critic of the authority of the church over the Coptic people. Marcos argues that it is the very social conservatism focused around personal status law that is impeding the development of citizenship for Copts. The church's approach, he argues, is part of the problem. Marcos argues that you cannot behave as citizens while behaving as a religious community. The concept of citizenship transcends the notions of sect or religious community.[87] Samir Marcos and Vivian Fouad argue that the concept of citizenship "means surpassing the ideas of sect, denomination or *dhema*, where the nation absorbs all this." Citizenship, they contend, "also surpasses the idea of minorities."[88] They assert that those "who try to defend the rights of Copts on the basis of minority rights . . . and who see Copts as one homogenous block" are going against the concept of citizenship.[89]

These intracommunal fractures can be seen in the fact that many Copts participated in the uprisings of January 2011, despite the fact that the Coptic Orthodox Church had voiced its opposition to the involvement of Copts in the revolution. Such Copts participated in the revolution "first and foremost as Egyptians," Mariz Tadros argues, in spite of the opposition of the church.[90] The Maspero Youth Union, formed during the Arab Spring, challenged the church as the political representative of the Copts. It came out in opposition to Article 3 since it wanted to have a constitution based on citizenship that downplayed religious identity. Copts who have opposed the authority of the church do not simply constitute the secular laity. Angie Heo has pointed to the development of pious insiders who were raised and educated from "within the Coptic Church itself—as priests, deacons, and lay servants"—and have emerged as critics against the intervention of the church in politics.[91]

Organizations such as Right to Life (*al-Haqq fi al-hayat*) and Copts 38 have been campaigning against the Coptic Orthodox Church's control of personal status law. Since 2008 the Coptic Orthodox Church has limited the grounds upon which Copts can divorce and remarry.[92] Article 3 has served to formalize and enable such limitations. Such restrictions on divorce are likely to be further entrenched when the new unified Christian personal status law, which seems imminent at the time of writing, is passed. Such groups question the hold that the church has over the Christian community. They have appealed to the law of the centralized state to allow them to divorce and remarry. These networks of Christians have protested in front of the Ministry of Justice as well as in the Coptic Orthodox Cathedral. They have also petitioned to the courts for their rights.[93]

Paul Rowe has argued that "the neo-millet partnership between church and state is gradually eroding in the face of Coptic participation in the broader scope of Egyptian politics."[94] However, secular Copts did not emerge as prominent in either drafting the Constitution of 2012 or the Constitution of 2014. Indeed, the level of support the church has among the Coptic populace for its approach to personal status law can be shown by Youssef Sidhom, who is the editor of the Coptic newspaper *Watani* and son of the newspaper's founder, Anton Sidhom. He mentions Article 3—along with Article 63—as one of the inalienable articles that secure a modern, civil Egypt of tomorrow.[95]

Article 3 was frequently portrayed as pointing to the Islamization of the state. There are clearly parallels between limiting religious tolerance to People of the Book in some schools of premodern jurisprudence and a current constitutional article that only gives formal recognition to Judaism and Christianity. Certainly, the religious autonomy of religious communities— as opposed to religious individuals—and the fact that autonomy is given to the divinely revealed religions indicates that the article is theologically and judicially informed by the sharia. Modern Islamist literature is infused with the bond between Muslims and People of the Book. There are calls for the "freedom of establishing religious rites for all the known heavenly religions" and it is emphasized that Muslims are religiously compelled to have close relations with People of the Book.[96] Such views have had considerable influence over certain factions of the Muslim Brotherhood. One of the mechanisms by which the Muslim Brotherhood distanced itself from radical groups in the decade or so leading up to the revolution was through its rhetoric about Egypt's Copts, which included its advocacy of the concept of citizenship and its emphasis on the concept of the divinely revealed religions.[97]

The Muslim Brotherhood continued to see unity between Muslims and People of the Book as integral to the Egyptian state and to nation building during the revolution. For example, in 2011, the Freedom and Justice Party Platform stated that "we believe that it is necessary to support the role of the Egyptian church to safeguard the morals and values of our society and thus to confront the surge in moral and intellectual invasion, which is directed at Egyptian, Arabic and Islamic society. We should also support the values of social and familial cohesion and of national unity."[98] One of the means by which this should be done is through dialogue between the Egyptian church and al-Azhar. It also states that the Muslim Brotherhood would support the role of the church as a leader for Christians in the East.[99]

Yet a commitment to the divinely revealed religions cannot simply be seen in terms of a revival of the sharia. Such an approach would efface the precise implications that the concept of the divinely revealed religions has when it is applied as the positive law of the state. While the concept of the People of the Book had legal and social ramifications in the premodern Islamic order, such ramifications existed within a context in which the relationship between the sharia and state law was much more fluid. In premodern Islamic jurisprudence, the four schools of law took different positions on whether members of communities that were not of the divinely revealed religions could be tolerated. The exclusion of Baha'is as a group from being publicly recognized represents the fact that one among a number of options for addressing this question has been chosen and now has the backing of state law.

In addition, according religious tolerance to the People of the Book in premodern jurisprudence did not equate with a positive endorsement of a particular minority by the modern nation state. Copts themselves were not officially recognized by the Ottoman sultan with a millet partnership until the late nineteenth century. Article 3, however, does not simply establish the principle of religious tolerance for Jews and Christians but rather positively endorses this identity, while positively marginalizing others. In making a constitutional commitment to the concept of the divinely revealed religions, it has turned it into a national cultural concept. The nationalization of the divinely revealed religions is connected to the sharia but it is also connected to the state's need to articulate a national culture.

The Baha'is

Article 3 of the 2012 Constitution was criticized for explicitly excluding religions other than Islam, Judaism, and Christianity. The article does indeed do this, although the specific limitations on the rights of religions that are not seen as divinely revealed would only come into effect with the passing of particular laws limiting those rights. The implications for the Baha'i religion in Egypt illustrate how the concept of the divinely revealed religions works in contemporary Egypt. While Baha'is are relatively small in number, the question of their legal status speaks to broader questions about legal status and religion in contemporary Egypt. By looking at the history of Baha'is in Egypt, this section shows how the concept of the heavenly religions has become integral to how Egyptian citizenship is experienced.

The presence of Baha'is in Egypt dates from the late nineteenth century, possibly as early as the 1860s when Iranian Baha'is began establishing themselves in Alexandria and Cairo. The Baha'is gained their first Egyptian converts by 1896, when the Baha'i al-Gulpayagani (1844–1914) took up a post at al-Azhar, and, by concealing his faith, established himself as an important scholar there while converting a number of teachers and students to Baha'ism.[100] The legal status of Baha'is in Egypt is complex, and as Johanna Pink illustrates, is a product of the interaction between the sharia and state jurisdiction. Pink points out that because the Baha'i faith is post-Qur'anic, the sharia has no precedents for how to address it as a religion.[101]

The Baha'i faith—with its emphasis on the notion of continuing prophecy and a continuing revelation—constitutes a denial that the Qur'an is the final revelation and Muhammad is the seal of the prophets. For many, it poses a theological challenge to Islam. This was clearly expressed in the Egyptian fatwas on the Baha'is that date from about 1910, which is when Baha'is in Egypt gained widespread publicity. Egyptian fatwas on the Baha'is argued that the faith of the Baha'is constitutes unbelief (kufr) so that Muslims who embrace it are apostates.[102] However, Juan Cole illustrates that Muhammad 'Abduh (1849–1905) and Rashid Rida (1865–1935) disagreed about the Baha'i faith. 'Abduh viewed Baha'is as a creative minority which was striving to modernize Shi'ite Islam and whose ideas were relevant to Islamic reform in general. However, Rida saw Baha'ism as a pernicious threat to Sunni Islam.[103]

The fatwas that declared the Baha'i faith to be unbelief mostly focused on the status of Baha'is as individuals from the perspective of the sharia. They tended to concentrate on the sharia rules for apostasy and the implications that their state of apostasy would have for personal status law.[104] One example is the fatwa of Jadd al-Haqq 'Ali Jadd al-Haqq, the former shaykh of al-Azhar (from 1982 to 1996) on the question of whether a Baha'i's marriage to a Muslim woman is valid or not. Jadd al-Haqq states that Baha'is are not Muslims, "the Baha'i faith is not an Islamic faith," and "whoever joins the faith is no longer a Muslim and becomes an apostate from the religion of Islam."[105] He also argues that many jurists agree on the necessity of killing the apostate if he insists upon his apostasy. He affirms that the apostate's marriage is no longer valid (batilan) and if he was married to a Muslim woman or a non-Muslim woman then the sexual relations between them would be considered unlawful (zina).[106] Jadd al-Haqq focused on the fact that Baha'ism has altered a number of the key articles of the Islamic faith—such as the concept that Muhammad is the seal of the prophets—and changed a number of its laws. He did not address the question of Baha'is of non-Muslim descent who cannot be considered apostates other than stating that Baha'ism is a "faith that is made of a mixture of the following religions: Buddhism, Brahmanism, Paganism, Zoroastrianism, Judaism, Christianity, and Islam, and esoteric beliefs."[107]

Jadd al-Haqq's fatwa is typical of such Egyptian fatwas on the Baha'i question, which, according to Johanna Pink, have focused on the status of the individual as opposed to that of the religious group as a whole.[108] This reluctance to address the status of the group as a whole was also due to the fact that muftis were confronted with new questions relating to the relationship between the sharia and state jurisdiction and how certain more ethical or theological sensibilities, such as the concept of the People of the Book, could be translated into state jurisdiction. It appears to be the case to this day that muftis and jurists—and some Muslim Brotherhood members—tend to avoid this question. For example, Muhammad Habib, who was deputy supreme guide of the Muslim Brotherhood in 2007, argues that Baha'is clash with the public order and that the ulama consider them to be apostates. However, he argues that there is no actual law in the sharia that needs to be put into effect in this regard.[109]

Egyptian state law initially used the designation of apostasy as grounds for allowing Baha'ism to be a different—and possibly officially recognized—faith. Before 1952, Egyptian law provided a greater level of religious freedom and the ability to organize communally for Baha'is. An important event enabled this. In 1923 civil unrest broke out in Beni Suef in Upper Egypt, when village inhabitants demanded that the wives of three Baha'i residents be divorced from them on the grounds that their husbands had abandoned Islam. In 1925 the Appellate Religious Court of Beba, a province of Beni Suef, contended that "the Bahá'í Faith is a new religion, entirely independent, with beliefs, principles and laws of its own, which differ from, and are utterly in conflict with, the beliefs, principles and laws of Islám."[110] The court ordered the dissolution of the marriage contracts of the parties on trial.[111] It thus ruled that the Baha'i faith was a distinct religion, which implied that the Baha'is concerned had apostatized from Islam.

Shoghi Effendi (1897–1957), the great grandson of Baha'u'llah, the founder of Baha'ism, saw the ruling as a positive one, and a move away from stigmatizing the faith as an offshoot of Islam. For Effendi, the ruling meant that Baha'is could seek recognition from the government for the independence of Baha'ism. For him, it facilitated negotiations between the representatives of the Baha'i community and the Egyptian civil authorities regarding obtaining such official recognition.[112] The Baha'i News, a monthly magazine that started in 1924 to give updates on news and events in the worldwide Baha'i community, provides insight into the possibilities that lay before the Egyptian Baha'i community during the interwar period. The *Baha'i News* reports that the first Baha'i National Spiritual Assembly (NAS) was legally recognized by the government in 1936.[113] In the mid-1920s the Baha'is in Egypt established a printing house.[114] In the mid-1940s, Baha'is were also able to build their own meeting place, the Hazirat al-Quds in 'Abbasiyya, which included an assembly hall, library, and meeting rooms.[115]

In 1939, at the request of the Ministry of Justice, the mufti of Egypt issued a fatwa that Shoghi Effendi felt strengthened the claim that the faith was an independent one. In its inquiry, the Ministry of Justice asked for a pronouncement regarding a petition put forth by the Egyptian Baha'i community to the Egyptian government for the allocation of four plots to serve as cemeteries for the Baha'i communities of Cairo, Alexandria, Port Said, and Ismailiyya. In his reply, the mufti stated that the community is not to be regarded as Muslim and whoever "among its members had formerly been a Muslim has, by virtue of his belief in the pretensions of this community, renounced Islám, and is regarded as beyond its pale, and is subject to the laws governing apostasy." Since this community is not Muslim, he argued, "it would be unlawful to bury its dead in Muslim cemeteries."[116] As a result of this fatwa, two Baha'i cemeteries, one in Cairo and the other in Ismailiyya, were established.[117]

Baha'is also formulated their own personal status law covering marriage, divorce, inheritance, and burial and presented these laws to the Egyptian Cabinet. These personal status laws were included in the Ministry of Justice's request for the fatwa from the mufti about Baha'ism. The mufti declared that the Baha'i laws relating to personal status were evidence that Baha'ism should be considered a separate religion. During the 1940s, the Baha'i Egyptian National Spiritual Assembly was able to assume most of the duties and responsibilities connected with the conduct of Baha'i marriages and divorces, as well as burial of the dead.[118] Efforts were also made to have Baha'i marriage contracts legally recognized.[119] During that time, Baha'is were able to register themselves as Baha'is in state documents.

In the 1940s, Baha'is presented a petition to the Egyptian government requesting that they be recognized as a separate milla, "as a body qualified to exercise the functions of an independent court and empowered to apply, in all matters affecting their personal status, the laws and ordinances revealed by the Author of their Faith."[120] In 1944 Effendi wrote that he believed it would "eventually lead to the establishment of that Faith on a basis of absolute equality with its sister religions in that land."[121]

In 1945 the *Baha'i News* reported that regular meetings had "the official sanction and approval of the local authorities who have become convinced, as a result of attending some Bahá'í meetings, and reading Bahá'í literature that the followers of Bahá'u'lláh do not meddle in politics and are faithful and obedient subjects of their government wherever they live."[122] In June 1945, the *Baha'i News* reported that they are "very happy that . . . their Faith stands recognized as an independent religion with its own laws and institutions."[123]

This, of course, is not to deny that there were intermittent periods in which Baha'is experienced repression and persecution.[124] Yet, even in 1952, the climate was such that Shoghi Effendi reported that members of the Egyptian Baha'i community were engaged in missionary work.[125] In the same year, the Egyptian State Council argued that every citizen has the right to adhere to the Baha'i faith or even to be an apostate. It stated that the application of the sharia laws for apostasy were not applicable and "thus the registration offices are required to examine all marriage contracts submitted to them, even if they concern Baha'is" although it left the question of the validity of such marriages open.[126] While the petition for recognition as a milla was ultimately unsuccessful, the very act of petitioning for such recognition illustrated that Baha'is were not seen as antithetical to Egyptian nationalism in the same way that they are now.

It is with the independence of the Egyptian nation state and the further consolidation of the state and nation building process that one can identify increased restrictions on Baha'is and, notably, the increased use of the idea that the Baha'is are apostates to frame Baha'is as heterodox. This is often seen as the result of the increasing influence of Islam. However, it must also be viewed as a consequence of the state's centralization of personal status law courts. The nationalization of the personal status courts, which came out of the state's desire to consolidate its legal sovereignty, meant that the concern with what religions the state recognizes and what religions it does not recognize became more important. In 1955 the sharia and communal courts were nationalized under Law No. 462. The personal status law of all Egyptians was to be governed by the sharia, while the exception allowed for non-Muslims to be governed by their own personal status laws with the condition that such laws should fall within the limits of public order ("al-nizam al-'amm").[127] In 1979, the Court of Cassation confirmed that personal status law was governed by national law, which was informed by Islamic law, and Coptic Christian family law was only granted as an exemption.[128] The granting of an exemption had to conform with conceptions of public order, so that tolerance was not granted in the sense of simply being allowed to happen, but a level of positive endorsement had to be given to the group being granted the exemption. The state's centralization of personal status law courts therefore made the question of state recognition of Baha'ism more pressing. The idea of being exempt from national law became much more inextricably linked with the notion of national identity and national recognition. There must, it implied, be compelling enough reasons to exempt a community from national law.

Starting in the late 1950s, the concept of public order was increasingly invoked to argue for the lack of public representation and state recognition of Baha'ism as a separate religion. This was facilitated by Islamic writings that stated Baha'ism was a form of apostasy, but the implications of such apostasy took on a new form. This was because treating Baha'ism collectively as an aberration departed from the sharia provisions which relate to the question of apostasy of the individual of Muslim descent.

The move to restrict the presence of Baha'is in the public sphere came in the context of the newly independent Egypt and was brought about by the seemingly secular nationalist politics of President Gamal 'Abd al-Nasser (r. 1956–70). In 1957 Baha'i marriage contracts were declared invalid, as marriage contracts are valid only if both parties belong to a religious community recognized by the state.[129] Most notably, in 1959, in relation to a case of immigration, the administrative court in the State Council argued that the Baha'i faith constitutes apostasy and that an apostate, significantly, "may not become part of the Egyptian people."[130]

This trend toward the exclusion of Baha'is from the Egyptian public sphere culminated in Law No. 263 in 1960. It was preceded in 1959 by Nasser's issuance of a presidential decree that banned Jehovah's Witnesses because they were seen as supporters of Zionism. The Baha'is were also viewed as being agents of Israel and other foreign powers.[131] In 1960 Nasser issued Law No. 263 banning Baha'ism, and consequently, the communal properties of Baha'is were confiscated, including their libraries and cemeteries. Their temples were shut down and their historical records were destroyed. Since then, Baha'is have met in houses and have organized themselves informally.[132] The Baha'i cemetery in Cairo is the only collective property that was not confiscated in 1960 and, to this day, Baha'is are allowed to bury their dead there.[133]

Nasser's reasons for turning against Baha'ism seem to have been related to anti-Zionist sentiment. They were also due to the particular structure of personal status laws and the fact that the question of which religions were deemed legitimate and which were not became more important. Yet such moves were enabled in many respects since they resonated with Islamic theological sensibilities and could draw on Ottoman conceptions of hetero-doxy. This can be seen in further legal cases that upheld Law No. 263. In 1971 the Egyptian constitution specified that "the state shall guarantee freedom of belief and the freedom to practice religious rites" (Article 46), but in 1975 the Supreme Court upheld protections only for the three divinely revealed religions.[134] In 2006 the Supreme Administrative Court affirmed previous rulings and confirmed that Baha'ism goes against the heavenly revealed reli-gions, followers of it are apostates, and any recognition of it would be a "violation of the established order of the state."[135]

However, the version of the sharia enabling this legislation to be consoli-dated was a distilled one that was utilized to make a firm distinction between divinely revealed and non-divinely revealed religions. Such a distinction had not been made explicit by the Ottomans even though it had antecedents in the concept of apostasy.[136] The turn against Baha'ism thus also occurred in part because the state recognition of legitimate and illegitimate religions became more pressing during the project of state centralization and consoli-dation. This in many respects was distinct from periods of Islamic history in which certain religious communities were tolerated without being officially recognized. Yet such a dynamic between minorities and the state had pre-cursors in the Ottoman Empire, although at that time official recognition did not include the same official endorsement in the sense that those being officially recognized constituted a part of national culture. In this new con-text, toleration, in the sense of judicial autonomy, could only be granted to those who were officially recognized, and official recognition had to support Egyptian nationalism.

A National Project

In this final section, I show the ways in which the sharia-based commit-ment to religious freedom and judicial autonomy for Jews and Christians has become nationalized and embraced by a wide array of political actors in Egypt. In some respects, Articles 3 and 64 of the 2012 Constitution, which gave Jews and Christians the right to apply their own personal status law, can be seen as the result of the increasing influence of the sharia. Yet one must also accept that, in translating Islamic legal norms into judicial autonomy for Jews and Christians in contemporary Egypt, the sharia has been recast in the process. Such recasting has resulted in new and more explicit forms of inclusion and exclusion. While the Baha'is have been excluded and have been designated as heterodox, this has been accompanied by greater inclusion for Christians and—theoretically—for Jews.

When I speak of the inclusion of Christians in contemporary Egypt, this is not to deny the vulnerability of Copts. Copts have been subject to confessional violence particularly since the 1970s. The upheaval of the revolutionary events has only led to more violence and more reminders of the fragility of Muslim-Christian relations. In January 2011, for example, a bombing in Alexandria killed twenty-three Copts. The state's failure to protect them resulted in a significant "rupture in relations between Copts and the Mubarak regime."[137] Under the interim rule of the Supreme Council of Armed Forces, Copts who engaged in a sit-in in front of the Maspero Television building, the headquarters of the Egyptian state television, in October 2011 were attacked by the security forces and the army resulting in twenty-four deaths. Sectarian clashes and brutal crackdowns continued under the rule of Muhammad Mursi, and after the coup against Muhammad Mursi in 2013, over forty churches were torched in August 2013 in retaliation for Copts having supported the coup.

Indeed, it is precisely the fragility of Muslim-Christian relations in Egypt that explains the investment in the concept of the divinely revealed religions since the revolution of 2011. The concept is viewed as way of reinforcing this unity in the face of sectarian strife. That the concept of the divinely revealed religions has become a key component of Egyptian nationalism is even clearer when one recognizes that singling out Jews and Christians for recognition and a level of communal autonomy resonated with a broader constituency beyond that of the Islamists. The concept of the divinely revealed religions has come to form a national cultural concept. While this dates back in many ways to the revolution of 1919, as Sebastian Elsässer has shown, it has become particularly emphasized in the post–Arab Spring era.

This can be seen, for example, in a manifesto issued by the Democratic Front, which was a coalition of thirty-four parties including the Labor Party and the Egyptian Arab Socialist Party. The manifesto, issued in the summer of 2011, detailed fundamental guiding principles for the forthcoming constitution. One of these principles was a commitment to the ability of non-Muslims who belong to the divinely revealed religions to apply their own personal status law and oversee their own religious affairs.[138] A similar commitment also appeared in a document issued by al-Azhar after the revolution entitled "Document of al-Azhar on the Future of Egypt."[139]

Such support can be seen in the responses of the Orthodox, Catholic, and Evangelical churches in Egypt to the Constitution of 2012. These denominations jointly issued a document expressing their particular concern with the 2012 Constitution, and presented it to Judge Mahmoud Mekki, who was the vice president of Egypt at the time. However, the Coptic churches did not express any concern with Article 3. Rather, they expressed some concern with Article 43, which read as follows: "Freedom of belief is *protected*. The state provides for the freedom to practice religious rites and to establish places of worship for the divine religions, as regulated by law." The authors of the document complained that there was "a serious flaw," which, they argued, constituted a "trap" for Egyptians. The trap, they argued, was the clause stating "as regulated by law." This flaw, they argued, "gives rise to suspicions of intentions to pass legislation that would restrict or manipulate the freedom of belief and practice of religious rites."[140] The authors then proposed that Article 43 should be amended to read: "Freedom of belief is *absolute* and freedom to practice religious rites is ensured. The state guarantees the freedom to build places of worship for the heavenly religions as regulated by the law." While the clause "as regulated by law" would be maintained, freedom of belief would be strengthened from being "protected" to "absolute," and freedom to practice religious rites would be "ensured" as opposed to "regulated by law."[141]

In addition, a commitment to the judicial autonomy of the divinely revealed religions appeared in public discourse after the coup against Muhammad Mursi in July 2013. After the Constitution of 2012 was abolished, 'Adly Mansour, who was head of the Supreme Constitutional Court, issued an Interim Constitutional Declaration, which stated that "the state ensures . . . the freedom to practice the religious rites for the divinely revealed religions (Article 7)."[142] Including a commitment to the heavenly religions represents a strategic move by the judiciary and the military to gain support from the church and assert its support for national unity, while bolstering its Islamic credentials to move against the Muslim Brotherhood.

In the new constitution that was passed in January 2014, Articles 3 and 43 were retained by the differently configured Constituent Assembly. A slightly amended version of Article 43 became Article 64 and states: "Freedom of belief is *absolute*. The freedom to practice religious rites and establish places of worship for the divinely revealed religions is a right as regulated by law." Thus, the Coptic religious leaders' demand for "absolute" instead of "protected" religious freedom was applied although the freedom to practice religious rites remained to be "regulated by law." According to Mona Zulficar, who was in the Constituent Assembly for the 2014 Constitution, the commitment to freedom of belief as absolute "is wonderful, because what we had in the previous constitutions, in the Brotherhood [constitution], we had nothing."[143]

In a partial concession to the problem that the lack of recognition of the nondivinely revealed religions has caused, Article 6 of the 2014 Constitution did establish the right for everyone to have identity documents. This was in part a way of making up for the bureaucratic quandary that many Baha'is have been in for decades. According to Mona Zulficar, it was her suggestion as a solution to Articles 3 and 64 and "I got it through."[144]

While maintaining Article 3 in the constitution was supported by the Salafis and representatives of al-Azhar, it was also supported by the Coptic churches. In its memorandum released in late July 2013 about the Constitution of 2012, the Coptic Orthodox Church did not seek to abolish Article 3, and Bishop Bola, who was the bishop of Tanta and the church's representative on the Committee of 50, which drafted the 2014 Constitution, requested that it remain as it was.[145] There were some questions as to whether the article should be amended to include the category "non-Muslims." Safwat al-Bayadi, the representative of the Protestant churches in the Constituent Assembly of 2014, stated that initially he supported the insertion of non-Muslims. The Catholic Church also supported this. Yet Bishop Bola affirmed the importance of the article remaining as it was.[146] Al-Bayadi maintains that, in the end, it was wise to keep it as it is "as it would not be good to upset the religious elements in society who look to the Azhar and Salafi scholars."[147] Bishop Bola stated that "we have written a constitution that takes into account all Egyptians" and that was completed by consensus. The problems facing Baha'is, he argues, can "only be dealt with through better public awareness, education, and acceptance of the other."[148] Indeed, there were some reports that suggested some Christians, along with al-Azhar and Salafis, responded with anger to the suggestion that it be amended to read non-Muslims.[149] Mona Zulficar stated that al-Azhar and the Coptic denominations opposed amending the article and said that those who do not believe in the three divinely revealed religions "can pray in their homes or their hotel rooms."[150]

While the Constitution of 2012 had mentioned the Coptic Church as the national church in its preamble and noted its pharaonic heritage, Article 50 of the 2014 Constitution made a firmer recognition of the diversity of Egypt's cultural heritage, stating that Egypt's national heritage is based on the ancient Egyptian, Coptic, Islamic, and modern periods and that the state commits to protect and maintain this heritage. Any attack upon such heritage is a crime punishable by law.[151] In this sense, it outdid the Constitution of 2012 in fostering respect for the divinely revealed religions.

In addition, the 2014 Egyptian Constitution also went further in recognizing the communal rights of Copts in a way that reaffirms the concept of the divinely revealed religions. Under a section entitled "transitional provisions," Article 235 made a commitment to a new law to regulate the construction and renovation of churches "in a manner that ensures that Christians are able to freely practice their religious rites."[152] The opening of a new Coptic cathedral outside of Cairo in January 2019 is a direct result of this, and marks a break with the 1915 declaration that the Ottoman Khatti Humayun Decree of 1856, which included restrictions on building churches. Also under transitional provisions, Article 244, marking a reversal of the 1923 decision not to include quotas for Christians, states that "the state shall work to ensure appropriate representation for Christians, people with disabilities, and Egyptians residing abroad in the first House of Representatives that is elected after the confirmation of this constitution. This is as regulated by the law."[153] Positive discrimination for Copts, women, and youth was one of the conditions that the Coptic Orthodox Church set for its participation in the Constituent Assembly.[154] Thus, the Constitution of 2014 has taken the concept of the divinely revealed religions further and has entrenched the idea that Copts are a community with communal rights—in some areas—superseding individual rights.

The church's position on Article 3 is perhaps difficult to understand if the concept of the divinely revealed religions is understood as resulting from the implementation of the sharia and the Islamization of the state. It could be argued that Copts, feeling hemmed in by the continued existence of Article 2, saw Article 3 as a way of strengthening their rights. However, the explanation for the church's support for Article 3 also lies in the fact that the church had a great deal to gain in retaining these articles. The Coptic Church's political and social roles, had, since the time of Nasser, been strengthened so that the church emerged from Sadat's period as the effective political representative of the Copts. Article 3 reinforces the idea that Egypt is made up of religious communities as opposed to self-governing religiously unaffiliated individuals. It also indirectly leads to the restriction of Christian citizens' right to marry and divorce, since it reinforces the church's stance that it should be allowed to control the divorce and remarriage of Coptic Christians. The maintenance of separate personal status law for Copts ties individual Copts to Christianity and to the church since the church will be the institution that will make fundamental decisions about marriage and divorce. It reinforces the control of the church over the Coptic community and thus reinforces religious differences. Paul Sedra argues that Article 3 will have an important impact on the balance of power within the Coptic community and upon its political development.[155] Here, the reason Bishop Jeremiah, head of the Coptic Orthodox Cultural Centre in Cairo, gave for resisting the insertion of non-Muslims into Article 3 is instructive. Such an insertion, he argued, would hurt both Muslims and Christians since "Christians would not be protected from the requests of Jehovah's Witnesses and other denominations that are not recognized by the churches."[156] The only way to ensure the interests of the nation, he argued, is to "tighten religious liberties."[157] This corresponds with the position of the Coptic Orthodox Church, which is that Jehovah's Witnesses are heretical.[158]

In Egypt, the constitutional commitment to Judaism and Christianity that was enshrined in the Constitutions of 2012 and 2014 indicates that the concept of the heavenly religions has become nationalized. The notion of judicial autonomy for non-Muslims has its origins in the legal pluralism of the premodern Islamic order and in the sharia. However, while it is tempting to see this judicial autonomy for Jews and Christians in terms of the reincarnation of sharia norms and therefore as Islamist, it has become a national cultural concept that is shared by multiple political parties. While Islamists and al-Azhar supported Article 3, the Copts, the military, and the secular elite also supported such a statement, showing that the concept of the divinely revealed religions has become central to the articulation of Egyptian nationalism. In fact, they took the commitment to the communal rights of Copts further. The concept of the divinely revealed religions is something that different groups could coalesce around and, in so doing, outdo the Islamists in their commitment to—and respect for—Christianity. It therefore aligned with the interests of a number of parties who wished to marginalize the Muslim Brotherhood. The fact that the particular hostility toward Baha'is dates to the 1960s and Gamal 'Abd al-Nasser shows how important the national unity between Muslims and Christians has been for Egyptian nation building. The move to restrict the recognition of Baha'is in the public sphere has coincided with the consolidation and centralization of the Egyptian state after 1952. The concept of the heavenly religions and the exclusion of the Baha'is continues on from premodern Islamic law and Ottoman forms, but takes on new forms in the context of Egyptian nation building.

While the exclusion of Baha'is is in part a product of what modern states do, as Mahmood has shown, the concept of the divinely revealed religions and the exclusion and inclusion that such a concept implies cannot solely be seen as a product of secular power. The question of official recognition, inclusion, and exclusion is a continuous one that operates in different historical contexts and operated at various moments in the Ottoman Empire. Here, it is again useful to think in terms of Emon's concept of the mutually reinforcing relationship between law and governance, by which certain ideas in the sharia gain traction at certain moments while others do not. It is the idea of unity between Christianity and Islam that has particular traction—in part because it has served a form of nationalism that has been used to exclude some Islamists—just as Islamic heterodoxy was so important in the later Ottoman period.

In addition, the concept of the heavenly religions cannot solely be linked to an increase in interreligious tension. It has resulted in exclusion for some and greater levels of state recognition and inclusion for others. The concept should therefore be seen as constituting the opening up of some opportunities and the closing off of others. Certainly, the codification of the right of Christians to have their own personal status law has formalized the boundaries between Muslims and Christians and other religious communities such as the Baha'is. Article 3 represents the state's commitment to the fact that some religious commitments are considered socially acceptable and others are not. It also represents the state's commitment to the idea that the divinely revealed religions is a concept that groups can rally around. Religious commitments that are considered acceptable have been brought into the fold of Egyptian national identity while those that are not considered acceptable have been excluded from the Egyptian national identity. While this has contributed to exclusion, it has also opened up the opportunity for Egyptian Christians to assert an increased, more formalized, and more exclusive level of judicial autonomy, albeit one that is centered on the church. As will be shown in chapter 7, the increased official recognition of Christianity through Article 3 has opened up the possibility for the Coptic Church and other Copts to assert greater communal autonomy.

To say that the concept of the divinely revealed religions is a key part of Egyptian nationalism today is not to deny that Copts are subject to levels of tension, discrimination, and violence. However, to say that unity between Christians and Muslims is a key part of Egyptian nationalism is to say that the concept, in terms of the national narratives that accompany it, serves a particular purpose now. The concept of the divinely revealed religions served the needs of the Egyptian nation state during the aborted revolutionary process.

CHAPTER 6

The Family Is the Basis of Society

In 2012 a columnist in the *Guardian* wrote, "Congratulations to all conservative male Muslims in Egypt. According to the draft constitution, you qualify as the model Egyptian 'citizen' and the state will be there for you all the way to uphold your rights and defend your freedoms."[1] This statement reflected a common occurrence in the debates about the 2012 Constitution, which is that it was accused of being deeply patriarchal, not only because of the constitutional clauses themselves but also due to the Islamist nature of the Constituent Assembly that drafted it.

The question of women's rights was used in the political disputes between the Islamists, the secular and liberal parties, and the military to delegitimize each other. How representative of Egyptian society the constitution was deemed to be was connected to the number and type of clauses it contained relating to women's rights. Article 10 of the 2012 Constitution, the first part of which stated that the "family is the basis of society" and that the foundations of the family "are religion, morality, and patriotism," was singled out for criticism. The article, it was argued, consigned women to the domestic sphere by emphasizing the family as the basis of Egyptian society. This article was portrayed as having the potential "for the establishment of morality police that would roam neighborhoods to enforce a traditional and hardline vision of society."[2]

Conversely, the dominant narrative about the Constitution of 2014 that was passed after the coup against the Egyptian president Muhammad Mursi in 2013 was that it represented a secular and inclusive Egypt, and supported women's rights. It was claimed that women's voices had been heard. There were numerous assertions that women enjoyed greater representation during the drafting process and that the constitution itself made a greater commitment to women's political rights.

One of the striking aspects of the debate about women and women's rights during the drafting of both constitutions was the moral outrage that accompanied criticism of the 2012 Constitution and the relative lack of criticism that accompanied coverage of the 2014 Constitution.[3] On one level, the stakes were not as great as they were portrayed to be, given that all constitutional articles are subject to their interpretation in case law. Catharine A. MacKinnon has shown that there is no direct relationship between the language about women's rights in constitutions and the enforcement of those rights. Yet a great deal of energy was invested in demonizing the 2012 Constitution and in praising the 2014 Constitution. While the rhetoric implied that the 2012 Constitution was a reflection of Islamist ideology and discontinuous with what went before, in fact both constitutions were drafted in an unsystematic manner that drew heavily on earlier constitutions.

Despite the rhetoric surrounding the drafting and the promulgation of the 2012 and 2014 Constitutions, both had considerable continuity with previous constitutions. In addition, there was considerable continuity between the Constitution of 2012 and the Constitution of 2014. This continuity was illustrated in the retention of a key article (Article 10), first established in Article 5 of the 1956 Constitution, confirming that the family is the basis of society. In continuing to emphasize the importance of the family for the national well-being, both the 2012 and 2014 Constitutions retained the state's right—first asserted in the 1956 Constitution—to manage and fashion women and the family as a symbol of national culture and religion.

This chapter explores the way in which the concept of the family has become entangled in modern constitutional debates about the religious or secular nature of the constitution. It investigates how women's rights and the family came to be used as a delegitimizing and legitimizing tool in debates about the Constitutions of 2012 and 2014. Constitutional debates continually asserted that any reference to the family was "Islamist." Yet, despite the rhetoric, the Constitution of 2012 had considerable continuity with previous constitutions since 1956 in this regard. The academic literature on Egypt has shown how the family has become a means by which national unity and, conversely, religious difference is articulated. The constitutional debates of 2012 and 2014 confirm this and illustrate the continuation of a particularly modern convergence between the family, religion, law, and culture.

The chapter contends that such constitutional debates demonstrate the fact that groups identified as secular or religious are debating within a very narrow range of possibilities and are much more similar than the discourse accounts for. This illustrates the unsustainability of the secular/religious binary that was so dominant in the debates. Drawing on the work of Tamir Moustafa, Malika Zeghal, and William Cavanaugh, the chapter advocates for the dispensation of such a binary and for thinking about tensions over the relationship between religion and state in Egypt in different terms. It argues that the constitutional debates show the ways that women and the family became a means by which different parties claimed a stake in the new post-revolutionary political reality.

In cutting across the secular/religious binary, this chapter demonstrates that there was something notable about the 2012 Constitution in relation to women's rights. The constitution illustrated that Islamists—like those deemed to be secular—shared a deep and pervasive understanding of the role of the state in society. It showed that the Muslim Brotherhood under-stands the role of the Islamic state in society as representing the interests of the governed in a way that moves far beyond the specific regulations of the sharia. Returning to Islamic political theory, it links the Muslim Brother-hood's understanding of family law with observations made in chapter 2 about the ways in which contemporary thinking about Islam has adopted the idea that the state is the locus of legal authority and has articulated a modern concept of siyasa shar'iyya.

The Authority of the Family

Talal Asad argues that one of the basic preconditions of secular modernity is the modern authority of the family. The concept of rights mediated by the private domain of the family, he argues, is integral to the process of governance and "to the normalization of social conduct in a modern, secu-lar state."[4] Marriage, for example, has become central to the governance of the modern state. It was not until the Protestant Reformation that marriage began to be managed and registered by the state in Europe. The Anglican commonwealth model of the sixteenth and seventeenth centuries saw mar-riage and the family as serving and symbolizing "the common good of the couple, the children, the church, and the state all at once."[5] The Marriage Act of 1753 in England required a marriage to have a formal ceremony that was registered with the state. The Matrimonial Causes Act of 1857 transferred all marriage and divorce jurisdiction from the church courts to the common law courts, so that the church courts no longer held formal legal authority over English marriage.[6]

In Islamic jurisprudence, however, Mounira Charrad illustrates that marriage is a private agreement between two families. Islamic legal texts do not necessitate that the marriage be registered with authorities. She points out that it is "a social and familial matter in which the state has no jurisdiction."[7] Charrad also show that, within the sharia, the conjugal bond is fragile. Instead, the sharia supports the cohesiveness of the extended patrilineal kin group.[8] The Shafi'i manual of jurisprudence, written by Ahmad Ibn Naqib al-Misri (d. 1368), reflects this. The manual mentions heirs (*waratha* and *warithuna*), unmarriageable kin (*maharim*), ancestors (*usul*), and descendants / children (*furu'*) and not the family as such. While it is clear that obligations to one's children and parents are prioritized, no neat separation between these obligations and others—as denoted by the nuclear family—is implied.[9] In addition, Islamic inheritance law, in which many members of an extended agnate kin group—and not the conjugal unit—are heirs to the deceased's estate, also shows the lack of centrality of the conjugal bond. Obligations to one's kin are conceived of in a broader sense than the nuclear family.

William Goode argues that the particular emphasis on the conjugal family, the nuclear family unit of parents and children, is partly the result of the forces of industrialization and urbanization.[10] The ideal of the conjugal family was also adopted in nineteenth-century Egypt, where, Kenneth Cuno shows, there was a move away from the extended family. Polygyny became less common among the upper classes. The Egyptian royal family adopted monogamy, which then became a model for other Egyptians. Cuno argues that this model was not antimodern but illustrated the way in which "a domestic sphere to serve as the married woman's domain" had been constructed "as part of the modernist project."[11]

Modernist intellectuals promoted the new family ideology during the last third of the nineteenth century. The acceptance of the conjugal family and companionate marriage among the educated elite meant that the question of the "emancipation of women" was utilized in colonial and nationalist counternarratives in the late nineteenth century.[12] Laura Bier has shown how Nasserists used state-sponsored feminism to transform Egyptian women into national symbols and make them representations of Egyptian cultural authenticity in the 1960s. Bier argues that, in the 1960s, Islamist and secular nationalist visions of women's roles shared a number of characteristics.

Within both, she argues, gender is a means by which Egyptians negotiate how modern or authentic Egyptian society is.[13]

Islamist discourse manifested a number of similarities with nationalist discourse. In 1930 Rashid Rida (1865–1935) saw modern Egypt as threatened by "women's revolution, the violation of marital vows, the disintegration of the family, and the bonds of kinship."[14] He felt national character and religious heritage were threatened. The preservation of religious heritage, traditions, values, the family—all backed up by a strong state—were central to this renewal project.[15] Ellen McLarney shows how Islamic revivalist writers "demonstrate an extraordinary investment in religiosity expressed through the family, reproduction, childrearing, and private sexuality."[16] The family, she argues, has become a means by which the concept of an Islamic ethics is expressed. Islamist writings envision mothers leading the Islamic family and forming the political community.[17]

Saba Mahmood argues that the family's entanglement with religion is one of the consequences of liberal secularism. She contends that, "even though religion is marginalized from the conduct of politics, it is simultaneously consecrated in the private sphere as a fundament of individual and collective identity in a liberal society."[18] Mahmood points out that the relegation of religion to the private sphere in turn politicizes religion and the family. Drawing on Marx, she contends that, "the secular liberal state does not simply *depoliticize* religion; it also embeds it within the social life of the polity by relegating it to the private sphere and civil society" (Mahmood's italics).[19] In a self-replicating process, religion becomes privatized and the more the family becomes associated with the private sphere, the more that sphere is associated with the family.

Yet, as was shown in chapter 2, the family—in a nonnuclear sense—was also an important means by which Christians distinguished themselves from Muslims in premodern Islamic history. Lev Weitz shows how family law was central for medieval Middle Eastern Christians in their articulation of difference from their Muslim counterparts. Marriage, with the development of its sacramental nature, and the family became central to the creation of an area of communal law for Christians.[20] Likewise, as will be shown in chapter 7, the autonomy of non-Muslims included—but was not limited to—family law which is why competition between the jurisdiction of non-Muslim communal courts and sharia courts occurred, among other things, around family law. While colonial intervention in support of the various privileges that the millet communities had in the late Ottoman period had the result of concentrating the idea that religious difference was based in the family, colonial intervention was using and building upon existing categories of identity. It is thus a continuation—and recalibration—of the importance of the family that became so evident in Egypt's constitutional debates.

The Family, Egypt's Constitutions, and National Culture

The conflation between culture and women and the idea that the well-being of culture is necessary for national survival manifested itself in constitutional debates about the role of women. Constitution writing has been historically engaged in by men and Egypt is no exception. Women's voices have been largely absent from official constituting processes and decisive interpretations until recently. Catharine A. MacKinnon argues that women have not, for the most part, written constitutions or decided on constitutional matters. Gendered language dominates constitutions, with the usage of the male singular pronoun for the bearers of rights. Citizenship, she argues, has been equated with maleness. While in recent times women have had some voice in constitutional decision making, they do not have the same influence as men.[21]

In Egypt, with the expansion of the state in the late nineteenth and early twentieth centuries, the category of the family and women emerged as an object to be constitutionally defined and managed. Such questions became inextricably intertwined with the nature of the religious identity of the state. In the 1882 Constitution, there was no reference to women, and while the 1923 Constitution was far more comprehensive, women's rights did not feature prominently and the question of the compatibility between women's rights and Islam was not raised. The 1923 Constitution made no reference to women and their role as members of the nation and its political system although it recognized the right of girls to education (Article 19). Article 3 of the 1923 Constitution mentioned equality before the law but excluded gender. This is despite the fact that women's rights were on the agenda of Egyptian nationalists. Women had played an important role in the 1919 revolution which lead to the limitation of British power in 1922.[22]

The 1956 Constitution, passed by the newly independent Egyptian state, however, reflected the emergence of the family as a concept in nation building and a greater concern with women's rights. This constitution reflected the expectation that women would play an increased role in the public sphere. For the first time, it stated that there would be no discrimination on the grounds of sex. Women were given the right to vote and to run for office although men were automatically registered to vote whereas women were given the choice to register themselves. Article 5 of the 1956 Constitution states that "the family is the basis of society and is founded on religion, morals, and nationalism."[23] This clause became a consistent feature of Egypt's constitutions.

Another clause linked the family and Egyptian society. Article 19 of the 1956 Constitution states that "the state makes it possible for women to balance (al-tawfiq) her work in society with her duties to the family."[24] This stipulation is particularly interesting on a number of accounts: it specifically associated women with the private sphere of the family; it voiced an expectation of women's increased role in public life; it put forward the assumption that state intervention was necessary to facilitate the role of women in public life; and it reflected the expectation of a possible conflict between the public and the private spheres. This section would be carried over into other constitutions in various forms.

This recognition of women as legal individuals with rights that had to be protected by the state was new and illustrates how, according to Laura Bier, feminist activism under Nasser was appropriated and monopolized by the state. Bier argues that the Nasser regime's attempts to "liberate" women "brought novel forms of state intervention into women's lives as well as new notions of equal rights—which were contingent upon gender-specific obligations that women were expected to meet as proper national subjects and citizens."[25] As such, Bier argues, "Egyptian secularism entailed the engineered inclusion of Islam within the political and legal system rather than its exclusion."[26]

With the 1971 Constitution, this focus on the family and associating women with domestic roles continued. However, Article 2 of the 1971 Constitution marked an important change. Article 2 stated that the principles of the Islamic sharia are the main source of legislation. In addition, the 1971 Constitution set up an additional dichotomy. It implied that a role for women in the public sphere was potentially opposed to the sharia. While the 1956 Constitution stated that the state should make it possible for women to balance their work in society with their duty to their families, it made no explicit mention of the sharia, although the reference to women's work in society being in agreement with her duty to the family could be taken as implying a potential conflict with religion. However, in the 1971 Constitution, this connection was made much more explicit when it emphasized that women were to have equal status with men and a role in the public sphere in a way that did not contravene the sharia:

The state shall ensure that it is possible for women to balance (al-tawfiq) their duties towards their family with their work in society—considering women's equal status with men in the political, social, cultural, and economic spheres—without contravening the laws of the Islamic sharia. (Article 11)[27]

The way the sharia was referred to in Article 11 differed from the way it was mentioned in Article 2. Article 2 relates to the principles of the Islamic sharia whereas Article 11 relates to its laws. While all laws are subject to interpretation, it does suggest that the court's latitude of interpretation would be narrower in relation to Article 11 than it would be in relation to Article 2. Thus, the area of women's rights was to be the area that would be most subject to limitation by the sharia.

Article 9 of the 1971 Constitution continued the commitment to the family although with a stronger statement of state intervention and management:

The family (al-usra) is the basis of society and is founded on religion (al-din), morality, and patriotism. The state will strive to preserve the genuine character of the Egyptian family and the values and traditions (qiyam wa taqalid) it personifies, while affirming and developing this character in the internal relations of Egyptian society.[28]

Thus, the family was seen as the embodiment of tradition, values, and, through the reference to the "genuine character of the Egyptian family," the family became the means of establishing a unitary culture.

The rhetoric of the Muslim Brotherhood leading up to the revolution of 2011 represents a continuation of these sentiments. For example, the Muslim Brotherhood's draft Party Platform of 2007 stated that "women are the balance of the family" and that

the role of women in the family is based upon the foundation that they are the ones who are primarily responsible for the education of the new generation. The role of women is also based on the fact that the family—in our Egyptian, Arab, and Islamic civilization—is the fundamental unit of society. The renaissance of our umma is based on the renaissance of the family as an essential structure. For this reason, we see the importance of realizing a balance in the roles that women undertake, and of bringing about their role in the family and in life in general without imposing demands upon them that would conflict with their nature and their role in the family.[29]

For the Muslim Brotherhood, like the Nasserists before them, the family constitutes an important mechanism by which a totalizing, unitary, and legible culture could be both promoted and managed. It is notable too that the Muslim Brotherhood considers the state as the primary mechanism for such a realization.

Snares and Ruses

Articles on women's rights were subject to claim and counterclaim during the events that unfolded after the revolution of 2011. The narrative in the Western and the non-Islamist Egyptian press was that women's rights were excluded from the 2012 Constitution and that women had been shut out of the constitution writing process. While the Constituent Assembly that emerged was consistent with the idea of popular sovereignty, of the Constituent Assembly's one hundred representatives, only six were women, three of whom had overtly Islamist sympathies. Discourse about the unrepresentative nature of the Constituent Assembly was related to general discourse about the unrepresentative nature of the constitution itself. Women's rights became a particular focal point for references to the constitution as a trick.

Hala Kamal, a women's rights activist and professor in the Department of English at Cairo University, voices some typical critiques. Kamal argued that "the brevity in the phrasing of its articles [on women] went against the modern methods of constitutional phrasing, where rights and duties are specified and elaborated in a manner that would ensure their realisation and states [sic] the consequences of their violation."[30] Such brief and imprecise phrasing, Kamal argues, could lead to women's rights being manipulated. Kamal also critiques the fact that women were mentioned only twice in the 2012 Constitution. She emphasizes that women were only referred to in the preamble and not in the main articles.[31]

Yet this brevity in the description of rights applies throughout Egypt's constitutions and is typical of Arab constitutions. It is interesting that Kamal downplays the importance of the preamble. Liav Orgad argues that the content of preambles can speak of historical narratives, goals, and abstract concepts and often explain the reasons for the constitution's enactment. She argues that, for Plato, preambles are "the soul of the laws" and a means by which the legislator "convinces the people to obey the law."[32] Orgad argues that preambles have played an important role in the making of law. While the preamble to the US Constitution generally does not enjoy binding legal status, this remains the exception rather than the rule. Orgad argues there has been a recent trend in comparative constitutional law that gives preambles "greater binding force—either independently . . . or as a guide for constitutional interpretation."[33] She argues that preambles can function to consolidate national identity, play a guiding role in statutory and constitutional interpretation, and serve as an independent source for constitutional rights.[34]

Preambles thus show the ways in which the writers of a constitution understand the common aspirations, national culture, and norms of the nation. The preamble to the 2012 Constitution makes a clear statement that women form an intrinsic part of the nation. It argues that women as well as men brought the 2011 revolution about: "We publicly declared our complete rights to 'bread, freedom, social justice, and human dignity' attended by the shedding of the blood of our martyrs, the pain of our wounded, the dreams of our children, and the struggle of our men and women."[35] The preamble declares adherence to a number of principles, one of which states that "the dignity of the individual is part of the dignity of the homeland. The homeland has no dignity if women in it do not have dignity. For women are the sisters of men and are their partners in national achievements and responsibilities."[36]

Despite the patriarchal reference to sisters, the preamble makes the first categorical commitment to equality between men and women. The preamble advocates "equality and equal opportunity for citizens, men and women, without discrimination or nepotism (wisata), and without favoritism in rights and duties."[37] The Constitution of 2012 was the first of all Egypt's constitutions to make such a statement. However, this particular clause was ignored or downplayed in discussions of the constitution and in references to its Islamist and unrepresentative nature.

According to Ellen McLarney, "The Morsi government's adaptation of the liberal language of women's rights represents the fruition of a long legacy of liberal language developed within the ranks of the Muslim Brotherhood."[38] Previous language on women from the Muslim Brotherhood has tended to be more patriarchal. Yet there has been a general trajectory toward elaborating on the subject of women's rights in Muslim Brotherhood writings. Whether this is by conviction or out of an attempt to convince others of its own moderation—or a mixture of both—is a matter for debate. Yet the distinction between public discourse and true intentions applies to all political parties seeking office. The former Muslim Brotherhood leader Muhammad al-Hudaybi (general guide 2002–4) argued that a woman has "the same rights as the man regarding participation in parliamentary, legislative and trade union elections. She also has the right to nomination and election at these councils" and he argued that she has the right to any public office, except—not insignificantly—the presidency.[39]

Muhammad Mursi's 2011 political manifesto, which was called the Renaissance Program, made a commitment to supporting women's greater role in society, in politics, and in other aspects of the country's national development. This springs, it states, "from our belief that woman is equal to man in terms of status and that she compliments him in his work and tasks."[40] The manifesto calls for removing those factors that hinder the participation of women in all fields of life, for protecting Egyptian women from being harassed in the streets and from discrimination when applying for jobs. It also advocates supporting women who want to set up and run their own businesses and private enterprises and for changing negative attitudes toward women's political participation.[41] There are two important points to note here: the fact that women are seen as necessary for society and national development, just as they were under Gamal 'Abd al-Nasser, and the fact that the Muslim Brotherhood speaks out about harassment and discrimination as a problem to be solved. The harassment of women in the public sphere is one of the pressing challenges facing women in Egypt.

Discussions of the 2012 Constitution's content and clauses included consideration of the clause in Article 11 of the 1971 Constitution that said the state should enable women to balance their duties toward their family with their work in society without contravening the laws of the Islamic sharia. The idea of transferring this clause from the 1971 Constitution and continuing it in the 2012 Constitution was discussed, with the provision being strongly promoted by Salafi members of the Constituent Assembly. However, it was removed after a public uproar. McLarney argues that "the removal of the clause speaks volumes about the liberal ambitions of the Morsi government."[42] The new government, she argues, clearly intended to show that women's equality is not incompatible with an Islamic society or with a Muslim Brotherhood president.[43]

Criticisms of the 2012 Constitution also focused on the fact that it did not list "sex" as one of the grounds for prohibiting discrimination, as no grounds are named.[44] Both Articles 9 and 33 state that citizens are equal before the law without discrimination, although they do not mention particular forms of discrimination. For Mirvat al-Tallawi, who was a member of the Committee of 50 that helped draft the 2014 Constitution, the fact that women are not specifically mentioned here constitutes a failure, although she does not mention the preamble. Read together with Article 10, the failure to specify discrimination on the grounds of gender becomes problematic, she argues.[45]

The most controversial clauses, however, were those that seemed to emphasize women's role in the home and link women with the family, domesticity, and religion. Articles 10 and 11 stated the following:

The family (al-usra) is the basis of society and is founded on religion (al-din), morality, and patriotism. The state and society desire to preserve the genuine character of the Egyptian family, its cohesion, stability, and to ensure that its moral values are firmly established and are protected. This is according to the law. The state provides mother-and-child services that are free of charge and pledges to reconcile the duties of women toward their families and their work in the public sphere. The state assumes responsibility for caring for and protecting female breadwinners, divorced women, and widows. (Article 10)

The state protects morality, decency, and public order, and a high level of education. It protects religious and national values, scientific truths, the Arabic culture and the historical and civilizational heritage of the people. All this is according to the law. (Article 11)[46]

Critics argued that these two articles would lead to the establishment of a morality police. Diana Serôdio states such clauses are more characteristic of what she calls "theocentric" states.[47] There was much debate about the phrase "genuine nature" in reference to the family. Secular groups protested against it with particular concern being expressed at the reference to society being responsible for its preservation, fearing that it would lead to the enactment of hisba, which refers to the right of an individual to bring a case against someone if that person sees the other person neglecting what is commanded and practicing what is forbidden within Islam.[48] Human Rights Watch argued against placing the "genuine nature of the family," morality, and public order before fundamental rights. For Human Rights Watch, the state's role should be confined to ensuring equality and nondiscrimination, without interfering with a woman's choices about her life, family, and profession.[49] Mirvat al-Tallawi lists the reference to balancing duties inside the home with those outside as one of the ways in which the 2012 Constitution failed to "recognize women as citizens with full equality in social, economic, and political rights."[50]

Article 10, however, was not new. The article was strikingly similar to those found in the 1971 Constitution. Zaid Al-Ali argues that "article 10 is copied almost verbatim from article 9 of the 1971 constitution."[51] Thus, rather than representing an attempt to "establish a Saudi-style religious state by stealth, article 10 is actually the product of offhand copying and pasting by a constituent assembly that was determined to meet a short deadline for completion."[52] The reference to the fact that it is the job of the state to facilitate the compatibility of work and family duties represented a continuation of the Nasserist expectation that the state must facilitate women's work in the public sphere.

In addition, in critiques of Article 10, very little attention was given to the significance of the second half of the article, in which the state undertakes to provide free services for mothers and children and to protect female breadwinners, divorced women, and widows. According to Nadia Sonneveld, for the first time in its history, the Egyptian government recognized female-only households, thereby exposing the myth that it is always the husband who provides.[53] This specifically acknowledged not only the economic vulnerability of divorced women and widows but also that Egyptian women are often the breadwinners of the family. Vast numbers of Egyptian women today take full responsibility for supporting their families.

In late 2013, after the removal of President Muhammad Mursi, a new constitution was drafted by the Committee of 10, made up of jurists and law experts, supported by the Committee of 50, which was to have an advisory role. While the Committee of 50 was overwhelmingly representative of state institutions, the committee tended to be lauded for its greater representation of Egyptian society in general and women in particular. While there were four women on the Committee of 50, and, therefore, the proportion of women was moderately higher, this committee was initially only advisory.[54] In addition, like most of the members of the committee, these women were representatives of state institutions, created and sponsored by the Egyptian state.

The 2014 Constitution was endorsed by such institutions as the Cairo Institute for Human Rights, which stated that it provided more safeguards for the protection of women; it "improved the status of women by explicitly stating that 'the state guarantees equality between men and women in political, social, and economic spheres.'"[55] The 2014 Constitution, it argues, also provides for affirmative action to encourage women's political participation.[56]

Indeed, the Constitution of 2014 was explicit on the question of women's political rights and, in that respect, surpassed the Constitution of 2012. Articles 10 and 11 stated the following:

The family (al-usra) is the basis of society and is founded on religion (al-din), morality, and patriotism. The state desires its cohesion and stability and to ensure that its values take root. (Article 10)

The state provides for equality between women and men in all civil, political, economic, social, and cultural rights in accordance with the provisions of the Constitution. The state will work to take responsible measures to guarantee the appropriate representation of women in the representative houses, as specified by law. The state provides for women the right to take up public positions and high administrative positions in the state, and to be nominated for judicial bodies and organizations without discrimination. The state undertakes to protect women against all forms of violence, and enable women to reconcile their duties toward their families with the requirements of work. The state undertakes to protect and make provision for motherhood and childhood, and for breadwinning and elderly women, and for women who are most in need. (Article 11)[57]

The part of Article 10 that referenced society as having a role in protecting the family was removed, and the state alone was allocated this role. Removed also was the part of Article 11 of the 2012 Constitution stating that "the state protects morality, decency, and public order, and a high level of education."[58]

Mirvat al-Tallawi argues that Article 11 of the 2014 Constitution rectifies the failure of the 2012 Constitution to mention women specifically in reference to the clause making discrimination illegal.[59] Article 53 outdid the preamble of the 2012 Constitution, stating:

Citizens are equal before the law. They are equal in rights, freedoms, and public duties. They are not to be discriminated against on the basis of religion, belief, sex, origin, race, color, language, disability, social class, political or geographical affiliation or for any other reason. Discrimination and incitement to hatred are crimes that are punishable by law. The state shall take all necessary measures to stop all forms of discrimination, and the law shall organize the creation of an independent commission for this purpose.[60]

However, references to the dignity of women in the preamble and to the uprising of January 25 in the 2012 Constitution were left out of the 2014 Constitution. The statement in the preamble to the 2012 Constitution that referenced "equality before the law and equal opportunities for all citizens, men and women, without discrimination or nepotism, especially in rights and duties" was also dropped.

Hala Kamal argues that, looking at the final draft of the 2014 Constitution, it becomes clear "that this time women's voices were heard."[61] She writes that, "aware of the importance of the Constitution in forging our present and future, we have engaged ourselves with the constitution-writing process and managed to convey our own vision of women's rights and to work together towards inserting them in the Constitution."[62] Reporting on the turnout to pass the Constitution of 2014 one reporter wrote: "Undeniably, Egyptian women were the stars of the show among the voters. They went down in full force. In Egypt where men and women normally queue separately and where women make up 48.5 percent of the electoral force, the women's queues were considerably longer than the men's. . . . Even more striking was their jubilation at the event. They did not queue to vote in silence; they chattered, sang, ululated and danced in joy."[63]

Despite differences, however, Articles 10 and 11 have a number of important similarities with the 2012 Constitution. Like the 2012 Constitution, Articles 10 and 11 of the 2014 Constitution ensure the state's obligation to reconcile the duties of a woman toward her family and her work requirements. While mention of the state's role in ensuring this compatibility was criticized in the 2012 Constitution, the clause, Mona Zulficar, a member of drafting committee of the 2014 Constitution, argued, has in fact facilitated a number of constitutional judgments by the Supreme Court to grant women privileges. It is a form of "positive discrimination," she argues, providing, for example, maternity leave, breastfeeding hours, and daycare facilities. So, Zulficar argued, "if we took that out because we wanted to be feminists . . . then we would lose lots of privileges for a lot of women who cannot afford to lose them."[64] Article 11 of the 2014 Constitution also continues the promise laid out in the 2012 Constitution to "protect and make provision for motherhood and childhood, and for breadwinning and elderly women, and for women who are most in need."[65]

In addition, if one looks at the discussions that took place in the committees drafting the constitutions, the continuities between the drafting processes are even greater. For example, the article that specifically mentioned gender in reference to discrimination was not easily passed. Mirvat al-Tallawi of the National Council for Women was instrumental in getting it through. While the Salafis objected to the clause and al-Azhar did not comment on it, she states that she was taken aback when she encountered opposition from members of the committee who are often identified as liberal. Mirvat al-Tallawi also states that Salafi members of the Committee of 10 wanted a special sharia provision on Article 11—that is, something along the lines of "without contravening the sharia" and that this was presented by the Committee of 10 and was only removed at the stage of consultation with the Committee of 50, following protest from her.[66] In addition, according to Mona Zulficar, many wanted the commitment to the proportional representation of women to be put into the section labeled "transitional provisions"—that is, provisions that would at some point be removed, since everyone was reluctant to accept that the state had this obligation. She fought for the measure to guarantee women's representation.[67] Significantly, most of Article 10 of the 2012 Constitution, which argued that family is the basis of society, founded on religion, morality and patriotism, was retained in the 2014 Constitution. This has been in every Egyptian constitution since 1956.

Dismantling the Secular/Religious Binary

The debates described in the previous section show that women's rights became hostage to the tensions that were so central to the 2012 and 2014 constitutional debates. These tensions were framed in terms of an opposition between religious and secular worldviews. Women's rights and the family were used as a tool to delegitimize and legitimize the 2012 and 2014 Constitutions respectively. Accompanied by considerable virtuous grandstanding and one-upmanship, the issue of women's rights was used by political actors to assert and deny authority. If constitutions create legibility for the state, the debate about women's rights involved considerable flag-waving.

The point, however, is not to argue that critiques of Islamism and its conservatism were necessarily wrong. In addition, to illustrate the continuities between the two constitutions and the misrepresentations of the 2012 Constitution is not to argue that women have nothing to fear from the social conservatism of a constitution that was written by a predominantly Islamist assembly. However, there were striking similarities between the constitutions in the way that women's rights were framed and understood. In addition, those constitutional statements would have to be put into law and the compatibility of those laws with the constitutional articles interpreted by the Egyptian judiciary. It also goes without saying that expunging the Muslim Brotherhood from the political scene has not outrooted social conservatism in Egypt.

Here, I would like to pick up on Gregory Starrett's point, which I discussed in chapter 1, that secularism cannot be a descriptive term but can only be treated as a normative one. In this vein, Malika Zeghal has argued that discourse about secularism and Islamism in Tunisia during the Arab Spring shows the way in which each camp in the debate reified the other.[68] In looking at contemporary Malaysia, Tamir Moustafa argues that "modern law plays a particularly important role in delineating the secular/religious dichotomy in the machinery of the modern state."[69] He argues that demarcating categories is central to what law does so that "law is an instrument that constructs the twin categories in opposition to one another."[70] Such a demarcation is particularly charged in times of considerable flux, such as a postrevolutionary context, when parties use the secular-religious binary to lay claim to new political realities and establish their own legitimacy. In the uncertainty of a postrevolutionary context, the parties involved are even more inclined to use such constructions to situate themselves vis-à-vis others and make claims on the new order.

The fact that the secular/religious binary was able to be utilized to the extent that it was and the fact that the similarities between Islamists and so-called secularists were so easily overlooked do tell us something important about secular constructions of politicized religion in general and about Islamism in particular. Such constructions of the Islamic and the secular show that these critiques fed on a particular temporal understanding of Islamism as somehow antithetical to modern values. Such understandings of Islamism have become internalized and naturalized so as to become an unquestioned tool in public debate. The fact that differences between the constitutions were enlarged to the extent of inspiring moral outrage in part stems from the myth of religious violence. William Cavanaugh argues that the assumption that religion is authoritarian, divisive, and predisposed to irrational violence is a myth that has its origins in the Wars of Religion, when the nascent nation state used the idea that religion is a source of conflict to justify the assertion of its power over the church. Since then, the myth of religious violence has, Cavanaugh argues, been used by state-making elites to marginalize discourse labeled as religious while promoting the idea that the unity of the nation state saves us from the divisiveness of religion.[71]

Cavanaugh argues that there would be a number of benefits to retiring the myth of religious violence from respectable discourse. It would liberate valuable empirical work and help us see that Western-style secularism is a contingent and local set of social arrangements and not a universal solution. He also contends that it would help the West understand the non-Western world, undermine a frequent pretext for military action, and mitigate the violence that feeds from such a binary.[72] Retiring the myth of religious violence might have militated against the nastiness that permeated the Egyptian public sphere.

Yet the binary between the religious and the secular is not simply a Western project that reinforces Western secular interests. It has also become entrenched in modern Islamic thought. The Muslim Brotherhood itself has used such a binary for its own legitimacy by accusing the 2014 Constitution of secularizing Egypt. Such discourse has in turn served to reinforce the differences between secularists and Islamists. In seeking to establish their own legitimacy, Islamists rail against secularism, although they are more circumspect about describing Egypt as a secular state on account of Article 2. Yet Egypt, including the Muslim Brotherhood, would benefit from eschewing a conceptual frame that defines the constitution and political actors as either secular or religious. In the case of the Egyptian constitution, eschewing the assumption that religion is necessarily more prone to forms of exclusion and discrimination than a situation in which religion is supposedly absent enables one to see the centrality of the concept of the family to Egyptian nationalism as a whole.

This is not to say that there were no differences between the two constitutions. There were differences on the question of women's political rights. This should not be dismissed, since it paved the way for a constitutional amendment in 2019 allocating 25 percent of parliamentary seats to women. Yet the emphasis on political rights is particularly interesting in light of the poor connection between political rights in the constitution and the political rights of Egyptians in reality, given how authoritarian the current military regime is. The discussion of women's political rights was also not connected to the question of class. The Constitution of 2012 pointed to Egypt's class divisions by stipulating that nepotism and favoritism were problems that should be tackled. Not situating the question of women's political rights within the context of political and socioeconomic rights for all suggests that it was partly used as a tool to triumph over the opposition.

What is most striking is the continuity that exists between the Constitution of 2012 and the Constitution of 2014 and between those two constitutions and the Constitutions of 1956 and 1971. The family—and, by association, women—and religion are framed as fundamental to the integrity of the Egyptian state and to Egyptian nationalism. In fact, the family and women are key to maintaining the true nature of Egyptian society. The implications of this are far-reaching. It continues to allow for state intervention in women's lives and in the family and the fashioning of the family as a symbol of religious and cultural authenticity.

Such an emphasis on the family is not specific to Islamist groups. Nor does the insistence on the family constitute some kind of reactionary revival of the sharia. This is not to say that the concept of the family is not a vitally important part of the Islamist reform program. Ellen McLarney has shown how it is. Nor is it to say that many Islamists do not have conservative notions about the family. Yet to point out how the family is not simply an Islamist construct shows that Islamists have responded to the contemporary importance of the concept of the family and used it as leverage in the same way that others have.

The Interests of the Governed

Dismantling the secular religious binary shows that there was a common underlying assumption held by both parties that the state was the appropriate vehicle for the management of women's rights. There were, of course, some differences. Those who identified themselves as secularists or liberals tended to emphasize that the state—as opposed to society—should save women from the forces of tradition. Such groups were more likely to express unease with the idea of giving society any role to advocate for the family. Society is often seen as a bastion of conservatism from which women need to be saved. This is why references to society's role in preserving the family were eventually removed from Article 10 of the 2014 Constitution. The Coptic churches were opposed to giving society a role to advocate for the family. This was shown in the attitude they took toward Article 10 of the Constitution of 2012. The Coptic churches, like the other members of both committees that drafted the constitutions, supported the commitment to family as the basis of society. Yet there was part of Article 10 of the 2012 Constitution that the Orthodox, Catholic, and Evangelical churches in Egypt objected to in discussions concerning the 2014 Constitution. They jointly issued a document expressing their concern and presented it to judge Mahmoud Mekki, who was then vice president of Egypt. The part of Article 10 they objected to stated that both "state and society" should "preserve the genuine character of the Egyptian family, its cohesion, stability," and "ensure that its moral values are firmly established and are protected."[73] The document called for deleting the word "community" from the clause that read "the state and the community are committed to preserve the genuine character of the Egyptian family." The reason for this objection, they said, is that it would allow the community, in addition to the state, to "intervene to defend the genuine character and ethical values of the family."[74] This, they argued, could lead to extremist groups acting like morality police in the name of "commanding good and forbidding wrong."[75] They argued that such groups make up rules and legislation and "use them to chase members of the community, judge them, and penalise them."[76] They insisted that this part of the clause constituted a "time-bomb."[77] As a result, the word "community" was deleted from the 2014 Constitution but the commitment to the state's policing and control of family law was maintained.

The Salafis were more supportive of putting a check on the state's ability to regulate women's rights through such clauses as "without contravening the laws of the sharia," which implies limits on the state's legal sovereignty. It was in the realm of women's rights that there was greater interest in placing more limits on how the sharia would be interpreted. While Article 219 of the 2012 Constitution had partly anchored the principles of the sharia to the four schools of law, this was softer than a more specific reference to "laws." Thus, the references to women's rights not contravening rules of the sharia represents something different from the broader idea of principles as expressed in Article 2. It expressed the idea that the state should be bounded in some way to the higher legal authority of the sharia in relation to the family. Thus, for those who advocated it, the family was to serve as the front line in limiting the state's sovereignty over law. Yet, while this clause existed in the 1971 Constitution, and was advocated by Salafis during the constitution drafting process, it was not insisted upon by the Muslim Brotherhood. In addition, it was also advocated by some—possibly Salafi—members of the Committee of 10 that consulted on the 2014 Constitution.

Beyond this, there was remarkable consistency in the desire for more specific articles that defined the role of state in intervening and regulating women and the family. That the Muslim Brotherhood agreed to omit the clause "without contravening the laws of the sharia" speaks to their acceptance that the locus of legal authority is the state. This is because it opens up or maintains the possibility that women's rights will not be determined by the sharia as represented by the ulama and the schools of law. This corresponds with the Muslim Brotherhood's general approach to the question of who has religious authority. As was seen in chapter 4, the Muslim Brotherhood has generally not supported giving Islamic legal authority to a body of religious scholars. While Article 219 of the 2012 Constitution partly anchored the principles of the sharia to the four schools of law, this was something that was insisted upon by the Salafis and not by the Muslim Brotherhood.

In addition, these constitutional articles show that the Muslim Brotherhood has a conception of the state's role over women and the family that is of considerable pervasiveness and depth. Here, I would like to return to the thinking of the Islamist lawyer and writer, Muhammad Salim al-ʿAwwa (b. 1942). In the decade or so leading up to the revolution, al-ʿAwwa had exerted considerable influence on the Muslim Brotherhood, particularly on its younger generation. Al-ʿAwwa also ran as a candidate in the presidential elections which ended up electing Muhammad Mursi. He is the former secretary-general of the International Union for Muslim Scholars, based in London, and head of the Egyptian Association for Culture and Dialogue.

In his seminal text, *On the Political System of the Islamic State*, al-ʿAwwa argues that the "objective of the government in the Islamic state" is to inculcate "submission to the teachings of Islam in all of its different aspects."[78] All government officials, he argues, must adhere to the teachings of Islam. In this respect, the government is to be bounded by the sharia. The state is obliged to achieve a definitive objective, he contends, and that objective is submission to the teachings of Islam. Yet his understanding of what constitutes submission to the teachings of Islam does not specifically refer to the teachings of Islamic jurisprudence as represented in the four schools of law. While he states that the government must adhere to the "provisions of Islam" and that the law the state applies must not contradict those provisions, he does not define the role of the state as limited to those provisions, but rather as enforcing something broader than that.[79]

Al-'Awwa argues that the role of the government in Islam is to manage and regulate the "interests of the governed." He states that, "while establishing religion is important" for the Islamic government, "the realization of the interests of the governed in the Islamic state—those of Muslims and non-Muslims—is no less important."[80] Establishing continuity between his idea of the interests of the governed and premodern Islamic jurisprudence, he argues that "the majority of jurists of the Islamic sharia agree that the provisions in their entirety and in their details are aimed at realizing the interests of people."[81] For al-'Awwa, the concept of siyasa shar'iyya was designed to facilitate the interests of the governed. Thus, he argues, "those in authority—rather Muslims in general—can adopt what is useful and appropriate from any place and take it by the best means to bring about the interests of Muslims."[82] Those in charge can adopt from non-Muslim nations and peoples.[83] He draws a further parallel between his concept of the interests of the people and the concept of public interest in Western secular states. He argues that what makes the Islamic state singular is that it is bounded by religion—and he says this in a generic sense—whereas the concept of the public interest in secular states is purely based on the whim of the people. Yet what is key here is that al-'Awwa does not see a difference between the two types of states in terms of the extent of the state's legal sovereignty over its people. This reflects the broader trend within Islamic revivalist thinking that the state should monopolize legal authority.[84] Al-'Awwa's argument is in line with that of the judge and writer Tariq al-Bishri, who argues that legislation should be made in the national interest. It is only broader principles, such as the idea that rights are not absolute but are restrained by the public interest, which should be taken from Islamic jurisprudence.[85]

Both Muhammad Salim al-'Awwa and Tariq al-Bishri exercised considerable influence over the formation of Muslim Brotherhood thinking in the decade or so leading up to the Arab Spring. The Muslim Brotherhood has also shown that it understands the role of an Islamic government in the sense of its role to represent the interests of the governed in a way that transcends the specific regulations of the sharia. This can be seen in Article 10 of the 2012 Constitution, which states that "the state will take care of and protect services for female breadwinners, divorced women, and widows. The state will protect morality, decency, and public order" (Article 10).[86] This article is notable in that it singles out divorced women, widows, and female breadwinners for specific mention in the constitution. The expressed intention to recognize and ameliorate the economic vulnerability of widows and divorced women is particularly interesting. It represents the Muslim Brotherhood's understanding that it is the role of the state to be a steward of women's lives. However, it also represents how the Muslim Brotherhood has adopted a deep and pervasive understanding of the role of the state by utilizing a modern form of siyasa shar'iyya.

The concept of siyasa shar'iyya allowed the ruler to assess public need and deal with areas about which Islamic literature gave little direction. At the same time, under the concept of siyasa shar'iyya, the sharia was a source of negative restrictions on the state's legislative power.[87] Ibn Taymiyya's (d. 1328) conception of siyasa shar'iyya was that a ruler's law was to be deemed legitimate if it was consistent with the sharia and if the ruler had cooperated with the jurists to ensure that the law did not command people to sin and advanced public welfare.[88] Mohammed Fadel asserts that ruling polities in the historical doctrines of Sunni law were "entitled to promulgate morally binding positive law" which went beyond "the pre-political rights and duties of the jurists' law."[89] He maintains that jurists held that administrative acts could compel an individual to perform or refrain from doing something that was neither disallowed or compulsory. Such acts had to be, he argued, related to the public good.[90] Thus, jurists were arguing for the legitimacy of state legislation from within the sharia.

Article 10, which undertakes to provide services for motherhood and to take care of economically vulnerable women, in some respects, represents a form of siyasa shar'iyya. It tries to offset some of the negative consequences of Islamic legal provisions for women and the family as they currently stand. Women, for example, continue to be economically disadvantaged in Islamic divorce law. Kenneth Cuno shows that the Hanafization of Egyptian law in the late nineteenth century had the effect of restricting the possibilities open to women: maintenance for married women became less secure. The Hanafi school held that unpaid maintenance could only be considered a debt that would be collected once the husband had acknowledged it or a judge prescribed it. The Hanafi school also severely restricted women's access to divorce and did not accept desertion or nonmaintenance as grounds.[91] The 1920 Personal Status Law, Egypt's first sharia-based codification of family law, partially reversed this by drawing on Maliki jurisprudence. While the Personal Status Laws of 1920 and 1929 introduced rules from the Maliki legal school, Hanafi law remained the legislative basis for judicial action on any new case that arose in the courts.[92] Personal Status Law No. 1 of 2000 affirmed the importance of Hanafi law although it shifted the emphasis to the opinion of the jurist Abu Hanifa himself. While this personal status code introduced *khulʿ* divorce law, thereby widening women's rights to petition for divorce, it remained contingent on women giving up their dowry and renouncing any financial claims.[93] Thus, in divorce law, women remain at a significant economic disadvantage. Women are also disadvantaged in Islamic inheritance law (see chapter 7), which mostly—although not exclusively—gives women half the legacy due the corresponding male heir. In addition, Islamic inheritance law does not privilege the spousal bond, but rather privileges offspring and the extended family. Such laws are based on the assumption that men—or the extended family—economically provide for their wives, mothers, and sisters.

The particular recognition that widows and divorced women are economically vulnerable and that it is the state's obligation to take care of them is therefore a striking acknowledgment of the limits of the way that codified sharia is applied as state-enforced personal status law in Egypt. The fact that the state undertakes to make up for those vulnerabilities has interesting implications for the sharia. The constitutional commitment to aiding widows and divorcées and to acknowledging female breadwinners does not contradict sharia provisions. However, it does supplement them—and point to their limitations—in a way that advances the interests of the people, as al-ʿAwwa calls for.

Muhammad Qasim Zaman argues that the concept of *maslaha*, the common good or public interest, "was a relatively minor part of the medieval legal tradition."[94] He argues that jurists had reservations since "considerations of maslaha were often seen as lacking explicit justification in the foundational texts."[95] While maslaha is an important and recognized concept in Islamic law, its application was subject to strict and complicated rules. Jurists from all schools of law used the concept. Al-Shafiʿi was more conservative "for he feared its encroachment upon the importance of the textual sources of the law."[96] Malik and Abu Hanifa used it only when texts and consensus could not provide an answer, and Ibn Hanbal allowed it as a subsidiary source of law and saw it as an extension of the goals of the sharia.[97]

Muhammad Qasim Zaman states that the concept of maslaha "has come to occupy a substantial space in modern Islamic discourses."[98] There has been increased interest in the concept of maslaha as legal reforms are sought "in order to meet the needs of the modern conditions of Islamic society."[99] Kerr argues that for Rashid Rida maslaha was a "basic source of legal interpretation in its own right and is no longer dependent upon the particular indications of textual sources."[100]

Muhammad al-Ghazali (1917–96), for example, contends that Islam grants the ruler the right to "restrict permissible actions (taqyid al-mubahat)" on the basis of general welfare or maslaha, and that "Islam gave the ruler the right to interfere with regard to permissible acts by forbidding them, if behind this interference was a sound purpose."[101] Al-Ghazali states that "the government— from a religious angle—has the right to suggest what solutions it wishes and to devise what system it wants to guarantee maslaha."[102] What is interesting about al-Ghazali's reference to the use of maslaha is not necessarily that it can be employed, which speaks of an inherent adaptability and flexibility in Islamic law, but that the state or government as opposed to the religious jurists have the right to define and employ maslaha. The implication is that religion should serve the state and be subordinate to it. It is interesting that al-Ghazali states that such a provision "guarantees that religion is for the government and not against it" although with the caveat that the government "is intent upon what is correct and strives for justice."[103]

Article 10 does not constitute a simple continuation from the concept of siyasa shar'iyya in premodern thinking. It was given the status of a constitutional commitment, which advances the clause as a form of state positive legislation that is less pliable than other forms of legislation. It thus goes beyond siyasa shar'iyya, which was designed to supplement and exist alongside the sharia. In making a commitment to take care of the economically vulnerable, the article has the potential to influence the way the sharia itself is interpreted. While the Tunisian Hanafi mufti Habib Belkhouja has contended that Qur'anic verses on inheritance are clear and are not subject to ijtihad, members of the Individual Freedoms and Equality Committee, established in Tunisia in 2016, have argued for equal inheritance for men and women. The committee, which includes a number of jurists, have appealed to the higher objectives of the sharia (maqasid al-shari'a) and have argued that inheritance constitutes the conduct of people among themselves (mu'amalat), which is subject to interpretation, as distinct from acts of worship (ibadat), which are not.[104] It is, of course, difficult to know if Article 10 expresses an intention to work around some of the existing negative consequences of sharia provisions or whether it has the potential to drive the interpretation of the sharia

in a particular direction. The relationship between this constitutional statement and the broader one about the principles of the sharia raise the questions of whether specific constitutional provisions can override a general
commitment to the sharia and how, precisely, they should work together.

Either way, the constitutional statement concerning caring for widows,
divorcées, and female breadwinners reflects an important intervention in the
question of what the state's role is vis-à-vis Islamic legal norms. It reflects
the assumption that the state is there to serve and reflect the interests of
the governed and supplement the sharia in terms of offsetting some of its
negative effects. The extent to which—and how—such commitments could
impact legislation remains to be seen although it is important to note that the
issue of inheritance law for women has received some attention of late. Since
2016 there has been an increase in initiatives to ensure that women actually
receive the inheritance they are entitled to by law. A seminar organized by
CARE International Egypt was run in Minya in 2016, in which Muslim and
Christian clerics, in addition to a number of local politicians, drew attention
to the problem of men depriving women of their inheritance rights.[105] The
National Council for Women has called for amending Law No. 77 of 1943
to criminalize the willful act of depriving women of their inheritance. The
organization has offered to represent women who want to bring lawsuits
pro bono.[106]

Such organizations are interested in making sure the existing inheritance
law is properly applied as opposed to revising the law itself. In addition, a constitutional commitment to offsetting the economic vulnerability of women
does not represent any kind of annulment of sharia rules contributing to that
vulnerability. Yet it has the potential to do what the Supreme Constitutional
Court has been doing since its foundation—directing the sharia to become
a relatively liberal form of modern Islamic state law that establishes the
absolute authority of state legislation, thus employing, but moving beyond,
siyasa shar'iyya.

Bruce Rutherford shows that the liberal constitutionalism of the Egyptian
Supreme Constitutional Court has a number of similar features to what he
defines as Islamic constitutionalism, the concept of Islamic democracy based
on a constitution and the balance of powers found in contemporary Islamic
thought. Both, he argues, advocate for a strong state and for the state's management of public morality. He demonstrates how the Supreme Constitutional Court has seen facilitating a balance between women's duty to the
family and her work in society as one of its constitutional obligations. The
Supreme Constitutional Court sees a strong state as necessary for the moral
character of society and for protecting the family. The need for a powerful

state that manages and intervenes in the family is one that Islamic constitutionalism and the liberal constitutionalism of the Supreme Constitutional Court share.[107] In making a constitutional commitment to female breadwinners, widows, and divorcées, it can be argued that the Muslim Brotherhood intended to continue to advance such an approach.

The rhetoric surrounding the drafting of the 2012 and 2014 Constitutions emphasized the ways in which the rights and role of women were used to highlight the differences between the two constitutions. This discourse emphasized that the 2012 Constitution was retrograde, Islamist, and patriarchal. Conversely, the Constitution of 2014 was framed as progressive and as a constitution in which women's voices were heard. Yet the Constitution of 2012 had considerable continuity with previous constitutions as the 2014 Constitution had with the 2012 Constitution. This is not to say that there were not important differences. Yet much was made of those differences and little of the similarities. In fact, the parallels are more striking than the differences. This was illustrated in the continuation of a key article (Article 10), first established in the 1956 Constitution, which confirmed that the family is the basis of society. In continuing to emphasize the importance of the family for national well-being, both the 2012 and 2014 Constitutions have retained the state's right—first asserted in the 1956 Constitution—to use women and the family as a symbol of national culture and religion.

The constitutional statement on the family as the basis of society should not be seen as specifically Islamist. Rather, it symbolizes the continuation and consolidation of the idea that the state is the vehicle for the regulation of the family, which started in the Nasserist period. It illustrates the continuation of a convergence between the family, women, and law which both secular and Islamist groups share.

For all Egyptians, gender and the family are a means by which they negotiate Egypt's national identity. Gender and the family have always been—and continue to be—used as a site for negotiating the meaning of what it is to be Egyptian. In seeing the religious and the secular as constructions, one can see how the family and women's rights became hostage to the intensity of the postrevolutionary context in which different parties tried to undermine one another and lay claim to the new political order.

The Muslim Brotherhood's sponsorship of making a constitutional commitment to supporting female breadwinners, divorcées, and widows illustrates that it had adopted the broader concept of the interests of the governed over and beyond the specific regulations of the sharia. In many respects, such an approach is in line with the premodern concept of siyasa shar'iyya since such a constitutional article did not override Islamic law provisions—it only supplemented them. Yet this use of siyasa shar'iyya is not entirely continuous with its premodern antecedents since making a constitutional commitment to widows and breadwinning women gives such an intention an elevated status that has the implication of shaping—as opposed to simply supplementing—the sharia. In making a constitutional commitment to female breadwinners, widows, and divorcées, it seems as if the Muslim Brotherhood intended to continue along the lines of the Supreme Constitutional Court in advocating a liberal approach to modern Islamic state law that is not necessarily tied to the sharia provisions of premodern schools of law.

CHAPTER 7

Judicial Autonomy and Inheritance

In 2011 Youssef Sidhom, editor of the Coptic newspaper *Watani*, wrote an article entitled "Eating Up a Woman's Inheritance." In it he stated that one of the "ugliest" issues faced by Egyptian women related to inheritance. Egyptian women, he asserted, face a double injustice. One injustice is that they are discriminated against in Islamic inheritance law, in which female heirs often receive half that of corresponding male heirs. The second injustice, Sidhom argues, is that many women are swindled out of the legacies that Islamic inheritance law gives them by male members of their family seeking to lessen the fragmentation of estates.[1] Since Islamic inheritance law in Egypt constitutes national law and is applied to Muslims and Christians, Sidhom calls for reopening the question of inheritance law and for Copts to be able to apply their own Christian inheritance law.

In Egypt, Islamic inheritance law constitutes national law. It is applicable for Muslims and has been applicable for Coptic Christians since the 1940s. The 1940s stipulation that Islamic inheritance law would apply to Copts was part of the new Egyptian state's efforts to create a single juridical jurisdiction. In so doing, it strengthened the new state's monopoly on legal authority and marked the encroachment of the sharia upon non-Muslim judicial autonomy.

In chapter 5, I argued that Article 3 of the 2012 and 2014 Constitutions illustrates that the concept of the divinely revealed religions has become nationalized. The concept of the heavenly religions has, on a legal and rhetorical level, created a stronger tie between Christianity and Islam in Egyptian nationalism. In this chapter, I argue that the promulgation of Article 3 has had, to use the words of Tamir Moustafa, a "radiating effect." It has opened up the possibility for renegotiating the nature and extent of the judicial autonomy of non-Muslims and therefore of revisiting the question of inheritance law. While Article 3 of the 2014 Constitution grants Jews and Christians the right to apply their own personal status law, what areas of law personal status law includes is not specified. In strengthening the grounds upon which Jews and Christians can be exempt from national law, Article 3 makes it possible for further negotiations to take place between Copts and the Egyptian state about the extent and nature of this exemption. Article 3 has empowered some Christians to seek to widen the area of personal status law over which they have jurisdiction to include inheritance.

Such a petition to widen the area over which non-Muslims have judicial autonomy might be seen as a revival of the millet system, as some have argued.[2] The nature and extent of the judicial autonomy of non-Muslims was always subject to negotiation between communities and the ruling polity. This happened in the Ottoman Empire, where the relationship between state law and the judicial autonomy of non-Muslim communities was fluid. The case of inheritance was particularly characterized by such changeability.

Yet, rather than seeing the petition to widen Christian personal status law as a reintroduction of the millet, I show the precise dynamics that are taking place in modern Egypt regarding the granting of judicial autonomy and legal pluralism to non-Muslims. Reaching back into Ottoman and pre-Ottoman history and comparing these periods with the ways in which Copts are petitioning for their personal status law to include inheritance law almost a decade on from the revolution of 2011, I show the continuities and discontinuities between premodern communal law and communal law in modern Egypt. I argue that the petitioning for personal status law to include inheritance does not constitute a revival of the millet system of governance under the Ottomans, although it does resonate with certain aspects of it.

In fact, the judicial autonomy of non-Muslims in contemporary Egypt involves a particular dynamic in which non-Muslims are free to apply their own law only by way of exemption from national law. The granting of an exemption is contingent on three conditions. First, an exemption from national law is predicated on the national recognition of the community that is being exempted. A community has to be officially recognized before it can be granted the exemption. In the case of Copts, such recognition is contingent on national unity narratives that emphasize the concept of the divinely revealed religions, which forms a key component of Egyptian nationalism.

Second, the granting of judicial autonomy is conditional on that area of law over which non-Muslims are to be given autonomy not contravening the public order. In Egypt, the judiciary's increasing concern with public order since the early twentieth century reflects the importance it attaches to a unitary public sphere. In Egyptian law, Islamic inheritance law for all Egyptians has been linked to public order and to the "feelings" of the Egyptian people. The granting of a separate inheritance law for Christians has the potential to produce further fractures in this aspired-for unitary public sphere.

Third, the granting of an exemption is contingent on defining the status—and its relationship with religion—of the act, law, or idea that is to be granted the exemption. This raises difficult questions about what a religious norm is, how essential that religious norm is, and whether that religious norm is important enough to be deemed worthy of an exemption. In the case of inheritance, negotiating a dispensation from national law involves Copts drawing on biblical texts and practices in the history of Coptic communal law to make the case that gender equality is an essential principle of Christianity. In so doing, Christianity in Egypt is being rearticulated and disciplined through modern conceptions of religion and gender.

To illustrate what is involved in the negotiation over the extent and nature of non-Muslim judicial autonomy in contemporary Egypt, I start by discussing the nature of this negotiation in premodern and Ottoman history. I proceed to address inheritance and how the question of its inclusion within personal status law for non-Muslims was subject to constant renegotiation. I then address how Islamic inheritance law became national law in modern Egypt and then illustrate the ways in which, since the revolution of 2011, Copts have asserted their right for a distinctly Christian inheritance law.

The Extent of Judicial Autonomy

The system of judicial autonomy for non-Muslims in premodern Islam refers to the right of non-Muslims to seek legal redress and mediation for their legal affairs in communal courts that were officially recognized when those cases were not interreligious and did not involve capital crimes. Discussions about such judicial autonomy have often emphasized the insular and self-contained nature of premodern non-Muslim communities. It has often been assumed that this is an area in which the ruling polity was not interested, where non-Muslims were simply left alone, and in which they had extensive judicial autonomy. Bernard Lewis argues that, for the most part, Jews of the Ottoman Empire were responsible for the conduct of their own internal affairs and were judged by their own courts, possessing a "whole apparatus of quasi autonomy."[3] Aryeh Shmuelevitz contends that the autonomy non-Muslims enjoyed was a continuation of the Byzantine and Sassanian practices. He points out that maintaining such autonomy logically coincided with the fact that the sharia was designed for Muslims, not for non-Muslims. The Ottomans, he writes, "consolidated the autonomous system of the non-Muslim communities under their rule into a well-organized and well-regulated administrative system."[4] Likewise, Amnon Cohen asserts that Jerusalem's Jewry in the sixteenth century had an independent legal system, "headed by rabbis who functioned within the framework of the Jewish community and in accordance with traditional Jewish legal tenets."[5]

However, others have disputed the argument that non-Muslims had extensive autonomy. Joseph Hacker argues that the Jewish community of the Ottoman Empire had no officially recognized and unlimited right to judicial autonomy even in matters of personal status. He maintains that dhimmi courts had no official standing in the Ottoman Empire, and that judging in accordance with Jewish law was often contingent on the agreement of the qadi. The law for all subjects of the Ottoman Empire was the sharia, although the sultan neither enforced the laws of the land upon the Jews nor compelled them to judge according to the sharia. This effectively enabled Jews to create their own legal systems.[6]

In looking at court records of late eighteenth- and nineteenth-century Damascus, Najwa al-Qattan argues that dhimmi communities used the sharia courts for the settlement of cases that related to numerous business and family law matters when their personal and financial interests were better served in so doing. Al-Qattan suggests that the extent to which dhimmis used the sharia courts raises questions about the extent of their own judicial autonomy. Pointing to the lack of documentary evidence to confirm the existence of the communal courts in Damascus, she contends that there are reasons to question the assumption that Ottomans had a policy of setting up and formally recognizing official courts for non-Muslim communities.[7]

In reconciling the polarity of these two positions, it is useful to think in terms of Anver Emon's concept of the relationship between law and governance and of the vast and varied areas over which the Ottoman Empire had control (mentioned in chapter 5). Given the variety of experiences that dhimmis had across the Ottoman Empire, it is fair to say that distinct communities did exist but that the level of institutional autonomy that those communities had and the extent of interaction between Muslims and non-Muslims varied. It is therefore likely that Jews and Christians had extensive interaction with the Muslim courts and moved between their own and other judicial systems. Amnon Cohen, for example, maintains that, in the sixteenth century, while

Jerusalem's Jews had an independent legal system, they also made extensive use of the sharia courts for the settlement of a number of issues partly
because the sharia courts could enforce its judgments.[8]

In thinking about the extent and nature of communal autonomy, it is
useful to think in terms of factors that shaped this autonomy. One of those
factors was whether the jurisdiction of the dhimmi courts was concurrent
or exclusive. In civil procedure, exclusive jurisdiction exists where one court
has the power to adjudicate a case to the exclusion of all other courts. Concurrent jurisdiction, however, means that more than one court may take
jurisdiction over the case. Pre-Ottoman and Ottoman non-Muslims would
have had an interest in preventing members of their communities from having recourse to the sharia courts, since this would be seen as threatening the
community's ability to keep itself culturally and religiously distinct.[9] Exclusive jurisdiction would mitigate against—although not entirely remove—
this possibility, whereas concurrent jurisdiction would restrict the means
by which non-Muslim leaders could prevent non-Muslims from using the
sharia courts.

For the most part, the Greek Orthodox Church in the Ottoman Empire
had exclusive jurisdiction, even though sometimes the Ottoman courts tried
cases that were under the control of the church.[10] This meant that all the
qadis and military governors had a duty to carry out the decisions of the
Greek Orthodox patriarch as far as they pertained to the Christians who were
under the patriarch's control.[11] The exclusive nature of its jurisdiction meant
that the church was able to inflict punishment on those who had recourse
to the sharia courts in the form of spiritual penances, including excommu-
nication. A number of agreements between the sultan and the patriarch
allowed the clergy to regulate matters according to their own law, but also
contained provisions prohibiting the Ottoman authorities from interfering.
While the qadi courts did sometimes officiate civil temporary marriage
agreements between Christians, the Greek Orthodox Church tried to limit
this by imposing spiritual penances and even requested the assistance of the
Ottoman authorities in prohibiting it. In 1819 a synodic bull referred to a
recent Ottoman decree that ordered imams and judges not to grant such
marriages to Christians.[12]

While some non-Muslim communities were granted exclusive jurisdiction, in many instances, dhimmis were only given concurrent as opposed to
exclusive rights to apply their own laws. This aligns with Islamic jurisprudence. The four schools of law stated that dhimmis were able to apply to
the sharia courts. However, the Shafi'i school of law preferred that the qadi
decline his jurisdiction when a dhimmi asked for it, and Imam Malik said the

qadi was able to abstain from passing a judgment. Abu Hanifa stated, however, that the qadi must pronounce judgment according to the sharia when sought by a dhimmi, except in cases relating to wine or pork, and emphasis was put on the voluntary decision of the dhimmis.[13]

There is a consistent pattern throughout the pre-Ottoman and Ottoman period of dhimmis applying to the Islamic courts. Tamer el-Leithy illustrates that, when the Mamluks established four judges from the schools of law in 1265, Copts had five legal options—their own communal courts and each of the four schools of law—and frequently sought out whichever courts would be most advantageous to their particular case.[14] Magdi Guirguis points out that occasionally Coptic families in the sixteenth century practiced polygamy and married in the sharia courts.[15] Al-Qattan shows that non-Muslims appealed to the sharia courts in eighteenth-century Damascus, and E. W. Lane reported that in 1830s Egypt, while the Coptic patriarch judged small disputes among Copts in Cairo and other clergy did the same in other areas, Copts were able to appeal to the qadi.[16] In many cases, the Ottoman authorities imposed one important restriction on the judicial autonomy of non-Muslims. In the case of the Jewish community, leaders could not prevent any of its members from resorting to the qadi. The penalty for a Jewish judge who tried to stop Jews from using the Islamic courts was suspension.[17]

The concurrent or exclusive nature of their jurisdiction was one factor that determined the experience of dhimmis. The second factor that shaped the possibilities of the lives of dhimmis was the level of formal recognition they had from the authorities. The more official the recognition a community received, the greater right they had to exclusive jurisdiction. Richard Clogg argues that the Greek Orthodox Church's expansive jurisdiction in civil and ecclesiastical matters was wider than that enjoyed in the Byzantine Empire and was a result of the system of official recognition that evolved into the millet system.[18] The exclusive nature of the jurisdiction of the Greek Orthodox Church meant that the Greek Orthodox community was able to increase the extent of its autonomy. Nikolaos Pantazopoulos maintains that, until the eighteenth century, the Ottomans limited the Greek Orthodox Church's authority to religious matters. By the end of the eighteenth century, the authority of the ecclesiastical courts had broadened and consolidated into a wide area of private law, including inheritance, debts, and many other aspects of Christian civil law.[19]

While the Greek Orthodox and Armenian churches had exclusive jurisdiction, the status of Jewish judicial activity was unstable since they did not have this level of official recognition.[20] Armenian Catholics, however, were not recognized as a separate millet until the nineteenth century. Thus, while they received some recognition and were spiritually governed by the Latin archbishop, they were governed in civil matters by a Muslim judge.[21] Similarly, when the Jewish community received more formal recognition with the establishment of the official rabbinate in 1835, their position improved. The Copts were not granted the status of a millet until 1883.

Another factor that shaped the possibilities of the lives of dhimmis was that state interference in the Ottoman Empire fluctuated with state control. Hacker argues that at the end of the sixteenth century, when the control of the Ottoman Empire was at its peak, qadis more frequently intervened in the appointment of non-Muslim community leaders.[22] The judicial autonomy of the non-Muslims was perhaps most concentrated—but at the same time more limited—in the nineteenth century, when the Ottoman Empire was becoming increasingly weak. One of the reasons for this was that Western powers lobbied for greater autonomy for the millets. One of the consequences of the Khatti Humayun Decree of 1856 was that it confirmed the exclusive jurisdiction of the Greek and Armenian patriarchs.[23]

In the following years, the privileges contained in this legislation were extended to other non-Muslim communities, although the extent to which this exclusive jurisdiction was upheld is unclear. According to Magdi Guirguis, in Egypt in 1868, a ministerial decree prohibited the sharia courts from hearing cases that were initiated by non-Muslims in matters of testamentary disposition, marriage, and divorce.[24] However, it appears that the exclusive nature of the jurisdiction of non-Muslims was not always upheld. B. L. Carter reports that the Copts of Egypt during the early part of the twentieth century were not bound by the communal court's decision and were able to take their cases to the sharia court.[25] Ron Shaham argues that, "practically speaking, the division of jurisdictions between the shari'a, the sectarian and the civil courts was not clear-cut and the different courts continuously competed for jurisdiction."[26]

While the overall effect of the Khatti Humayun Decree was to strengthen the exclusive jurisdiction of non-Muslims in the Ottoman Empire, it did reduce the area over which non-Muslims could exercise that jurisdiction. The religious communities ceded authority to the new secular state institutions in both legal and educational affairs. In 1886 the Ottoman Ministry of Justice issued a statement that the following matters would come under sharia court jurisdiction for Muslims and therefore communal court jurisdiction for non-Muslims: marriage, divorce, alimony, retaliation, bloodwite, wills, and inheritance.[27] This was the point at which the boundaries between personal status law and other areas of law began to take firmer shape. As a result, non-Muslim leaders lost the ability to prevent non-Muslim communities from applying to the sharia courts in other areas of law and in educational affairs. These new regulations carried over into twentieth-century Egypt so that, according to Shaham, Egyptian Jews had more—rather than less—room to move between the different types of courts.[28]

Inheritance

From the perspective of Islamic law, inheritance is one area that has a complex and comprehensive set of rules, many of which are explicitly stated in the Qur'an. Islamic inheritance law has a number of notable features. Perhaps the most well-known is that most female heirs, principally wives and daughters, inherit one-half of the share of the corresponding male relation. However, the laws are complex. There are circumstances in which male and female heirs of the same degree receive equal inheritance. For example, the mother and father of a deceased person who has left children behind inherit equal shares. Women also form the majority of the first set of heirs who receive a precise fractional share before lesser-degree heirs, although "the residue, usually the bulk of the inheritance reverts back to the male agnates."[29] Indeed, Islamic inheritance law can work to the detriment of all relatives on the maternal side, both male and female.[30] Another notable feature of Islamic inheritance law is that it limits—to a third of the estate—the individual's ability to bequeath property according to his or her wishes, although a larger portion can be left if there are no heirs. Legally designated heirs cannot also be beneficiaries of a bequest. These features reflect the partible nature of Islamic inheritance law. Partible systems tend to redistribute wealth at each generation and therefore hinder its accumulation. Islamic inheritance law denies any privileges to primogeniture. Inheritance law fragmented family fortunes although, as Pascale Ghazaleh shows, there were various mechanisms for mitigating this fragmentation.[31]

A look at Islamic history shows that inheritance is an area in which the ruling polity has been keenly interested. In the wake of the reign of Saladin (d. 1193), the Jews of Egypt complained about the interference of the authorities in an affair of inheritance. They presented their grievances to the sultan and argued that they were accustomed to relying on their religious authority for any matter that concerned them. Saladin consulted the Maliki and Shafi'i imams who replied that the Muslim judge could only exercise jurisdiction if all the parties in question were in agreement about appearing before him, and that even in this case the judge could decline his jurisdiction. If they did consent, the sharia had jurisdiction, but if they declined the jurisdiction of

the sharia, the qadi had to recuse himself and send them back to the authorities of their confession, which, of course, would apply their own law.[32]

There are indications that the Hanafi school of law became more assertive in applying Islamic law to non-Muslims. According to this school,
Islamic law governs the inheritance of the dhimmis in cases of intestacy.
If a non-Muslim dies without leaving any heirs or if the shares given to
legal heirs do not use up the entire estate, the remainder of his possessions
belongs to the treasury.[33] It is for this reason that the Ottomans were interested in getting involved in inheritance questions even when no one asked
the court to do so.[34]

Jews in the sixteenth century tried to stop the interference of the Ottoman authorities when there were no heirs, sometimes by producing ficti-
tious heirs.[35] Amnon Cohen reports that, in mid-1550s Jerusalem, the leaders
of the Jewish community complained to the Sublime Porte that the qadis in
Jerusalem were applying Islamic inheritance laws to the estates of deceased
Jews. In response, the shaykh al-Islam, Ebussuud Efendi (1490–1574), ruled
that the Jews should be allowed to behave in accordance with the laws of
their religion. As a result, the qadi of Jerusalem ruled that a Jew should follow his own law unless he explicitly requested the allocation of a legacy in
accordance with the sharia.[36] Yet Cohen reports that many Jews in Jerusalem
accepted the application of sharia laws.[37] While many non-Muslims were
able to apply their own religious law in matters of inheritance, this was less
so with regard to matters of intestate succession. From the sixteenth until
the nineteenth century, intestate succession was not treated the same as
other matters of communal law.[38]

Sometimes non-Muslims sought the Islamic court's involvement in matters of inheritance. Aryeh Shmuelevitz points out that, in the sixteenth century, Jewish daughters sometimes tried to claim part of their father's estate
according to the sharia.[39] Jewish inheritance law had developed to reflect
the needs of an agricultural society and mitigated against the fragmentation of estates by giving the eldest son the principal share. Women could
only inherit if there were no male heirs, in the absence of which women
got the entire estate.[40] Najwa al-Qattan illustrates that dhimmi communities
in eighteenth-century Damascus frequently resorted to the sharia courts to
resolve inheritance disputes.[41]

For the Greek Orthodox of the Ottoman Empire, inheritance appears
to have initially been regulated by Ottoman law. However, the church
had control over inheritances of the clergy when these inheritances were
bequeathed as donations. The church tried to extend its judicial jurisdiction
over the inheritance of the laity as well, and in many cases it succeeded,

using church laws, synodic rulings, and canonical edicts based on Byzantine law. By the late eighteenth century, the prelates of the Greek Orthodox Church were dealing with large areas of Christian civil law such as inheritances and debts.[42]

The extent to which Egypt's Coptic Christians had—or tried to exert—control over inheritance is not easy to ascertain. Fathy Ragheb Hanna argues that Egyptian Christians applied Christian rules and conditions to inheritance when Christianity came to Egypt in the first century.[43] Yet Maurits Berger suggests that Egyptian non-Muslims were formally subjected to Islamic succession law in cases of intestacy possibly from the eighth century when the Egyptian governor issued a decree to that effect. However, in cases of testate succession, Copts were allowed to apply their own law when the actual heirs were decided in accordance with the sharia and when all those heirs agreed on the application of the communal law of the community of the deceased.[44]

S. D. Goitein reports that, from the tenth until the beginning of the thirteenth century, many estates were "handled as though no outside interference was anticipated."[45] Non-Muslims were frequently banned by their own communities from applying to the sharia courts to improve their inheritance claims. However, in thirteenth-century Cairo, the authorities began to interfere in the estates of non-Muslims. They tried to lay claim to a portion of the estate, especially in cases in which there were female heirs, heirs who could not be found, or persons leaving their possessions for charitable purposes when they had no legal heirs.[46] Goitein reports that "the intervention of the qadi was dreaded so much because once he had laid his hands on an estate, it was difficult to get it away from him."[47]

A form of Coptic inheritance law does appear in the canons of Gabriel II (1131–45) and Cyril III (1235–43). The canons of Cyril III are to be found in the compilation of al-Safi Ibn al-'Assal (c. 1205–65) completed in 1238. Ibn al-'Assal's compendia formed the basis of ecclesiastical law for the Coptic Church of Egypt.[48] Despite a number of similarities between Islamic and Coptic inheritance law—its relatively partible nature and the recognition of the extended family—Ibn al-'Assal's regulations on inheritance law privilege the marital bond more than Islamic inheritance law does. They establish a much greater—but not complete—level of gender equity among heirs of the same degree, including, most notably, that male and female offspring and husband and wife inherit in equal measure. The laws still privilege the paternal side of the family.[49] Al-'Assal explains the fact that the husband and wife inherit from each other equally and have precedence in succession (although they cannot inherit more than their children) with reference to the nature of Christian marriage whereby men and women constitute "one flesh only as God has said."[50]

Tamer el-Leithy confirms that, in twelfth- and thirteenth-century Mamluk Egypt, Copts had their own inheritance law stipulating that sons and daughters would inherit equal shares of a deceased parent's estate, contributing to the perceived economic power of Coptic women. However, in 1354 the Mamluks issued a decree that if a non-Muslim chose to convert, his entire family had to convert. In addition, converts could not be stopped from inheriting from a non-Muslim relative, so that wealth could not stay within the non-Muslim community upon a community member's conversion to Islam. The decree also stipulated that a dhimmi's estate would revert to the treasury upon his or her death, unless the deceased's heirs presented proof of their claims, according to the sharia. The heirs would then receive their claims, with the rest of the estate reverting to the treasury. El-Leithy argues that the decree "served as an alibi for the Mamlūk state to insert itself within dhimmī communal affairs—most importantly, to extract wealth from these communities."[51] El-Leithy suggests that the dhimmis' use of the sharia, and the lack of segregation between religious communities resulted in the decline of Coptic law and the weakening of its legal autonomy.[52] It is possible that this happened with regard to inheritance.

Magdi Guirguis shows that, at the end of the Mamluk period (1517), the decree of appointment between the government and the Coptic pope stated that "he shall proceed according to what they profess, with regard to selling, breach of contract, inheritance, and marriage," although she concedes that decrees might not "correspond to reality on the ground."[53] In addition, Guirguis illustrates that, under the Ottoman sultanate, the Coptic patriarch was not granted the same kinds of privileges as the Greek Orthodox patriarch and a law, issued in 1525, removed legacies from the control of the Coptic patriarch.[54]

B. L. Carter states that the communal courts of the late nineteenth century and the first part of the twentieth century followed Islamic inheritance law unless the heirs privately agreed to a different division of the property.[55] This is supported by Samir Marcos who argues that the Coptic Orthodox Church did not have a position on inheritance and applied the sharia. This was because the Coptic Orthodox Church did not oppose any civil law as long as it did not interfere with the church's sacraments.[56] Yet Fathy Ragheb Hanna argues that the Ottoman decree in 1883, which was modified by a law in 1927 concerning the bylaws of the Coptic Orthodox general council, stipulated that Egyptian Christians were entitled to resort to their Christian doctrines in matters of inheritance.[57] It is possible that the greater autonomy granted in the second half of the nineteenth century enabled Copts to revive some of the practices that had been jettisoned in the fifteenth century. In any case, the lack of clarity regarding inheritance law is instructive as it speaks to the fluidity of the question of the extent and nature of personal status law in general and inheritance law in particular.

Inheritance, Personal Status Law, and National Culture

With the establishment of the modern Egyptian legal system, the nature and extent of the judicial autonomy of non-Muslims was handled differently. The judicial autonomy of non-Muslims was subject to the new state's need to unify Egypt's various juridical jurisdictions and unify and homogenize the law. In 1914 the millet system was continued when the Egyptian government agreed to recognize the existing privileges that non-Muslims already had. However, the area of law that was defined as the "personal status law" of non-Muslims became more exclusive and more restricted, since the state encroached on areas of personal status law which had not clearly been defined as religious. The relationship between this exclusivity and increasing restriction was filtered through the demands of national culture, legally referred to as the concept of public order. Public order, sometimes referred to as public policy, served to restrict the laws of non-Muslims that were seen as incompatible with the general mores and traditions of Egyptian society. At the same time, it was used to protect the rights of non-Muslims. This restriction meant that the nature and extent of non-Muslim personal status law was examined with reference to the essential beliefs of Christianity and the question of Christian personal status law's compatibility with the Islamic Egyptian public sphere.

Since the term "personal status" has no specific origins in the sharia and dates from the late nineteenth century, which areas it covered has been a matter of contention between civil and religious authorities. The Khatti Humayun Decree of 1856 and the ensuing negotiations ended up granting exclusive jurisdiction to the Greek Orthodox and Armenian patriarchs, including over matters of succession. In the following years, these concessions were extended to other non-Muslim communities in the Ottoman Empire.[58] For example, in 1868 a ministerial decree gave the communal courts in Egypt exclusive jurisdiction in matters of testate succession, marriage, and divorce and prohibited non-Muslims from bringing cases to the sharia courts.[59] However, in matters of intestate succession, the jurisdiction of the communal courts remained concurrent.[60]

In 1874 the Coptic community was reorganized and a Coptic Community Council (al-majlis al-milli) was established. The Coptic Orthodox community was given official recognition in the same year and this recognition was confirmed in 1883. The Sublime Porte empowered the Coptic Community Council to handle cases involving all matters of personal status according to Qadri Pasha's definition of personal status law, including wills, testate succession, endowments, and bequests.[61] With Egypt's separation from the Ottoman Empire in 1914, the authorities moved to recognize the privileges of the patriarchs presiding at that time. Law No. 8 of 1915 gave formal recognition to all extraordinary judicial authorities already established in Egypt and enabled those authorities to continue to exercise their rights and privileges based on Ottoman decrees.[62]

Yet this exclusive jurisdiction was not always adhered to in practice. It appears that it was not until the second half of the twentieth century that the Copts' right to exclusive jurisdiction was strictly upheld by the Egyptian Court of Cassation, Egypt's highest civil and criminal appellate court. In 1969 the court stated that, "as a matter of public policy, parties are not at liberty to opt for the family law of their choice."[63]

Inheritance and testaments were not regulated by the French civil codes of the nineteenth century, which provided that such "questions generally should be regulated by the law of personal status applicable to the deceased person."[64] In the Court of Cassation's definition of personal status in 1934, wills were included.[65] Carter suggests that the communal courts actually applied Islamic law for inheritance.[66] However, in the 1940s, the Egyptian state moved to limit the authority of the communal courts, starting with intestate succession and then proceeding to testate succession. Law No. 77 of 1943 codified Hanafi doctrine in the area of intestate succession and was deemed "applicable to all Egyptians irrespective of religion."[67] Law No. 25 of 1944 affirmed the application of the sharia in inheritance and stated that the laws of intestate succession (1943) and of testate succession are the state's laws. However, Law No. 25 also stated that if the deceased is not a Muslim, his estate can be divided up according to his communal law if all his heirs (in the eyes of the sharia) wish to do so. As a result, inheritance became a matter of concurrent rather than exclusive jurisdiction: the communal courts decided inheritance cases unless one of the heirs appealed to the sharia courts and to the laws of Islam. However, this changed in 1949 and Article 875 of the 1949 Civil Code declared Law No. 71 of 1946 on testate succession to be applicable to both Muslims and non-Muslims.[68]

The 1949 Civil Code contravened the Coptic Orthodox bylaws of 1938, published by the Coptic Community Council.[69] The bylaws of 1938 took a detailed position on inheritance. There are many similarities between the Coptic bylaws and Islamic inheritance law, such as the inclusion of multiple heirs of different degrees and some provision for discretionary legacies. Yet there are important distinctions. First, the husband and wife inherit from each other equally (a half if there are no children and a quarter if there are up to three children) although neither the husband nor the wife can exhaust the estate unless other heirs cannot be found (Articles 241 and 242). The guidelines do point to a system that is less partible than Islamic inheritance law. For example, the parents only inherit when the deceased has no children (Article 246) and the descendants of the deceased take precedence over all other relatives in inheritance. They take the entire estate or what remains of it after the spouse is given his or her share (Article 245). There is a greater emphasis on gender equality. The Coptic bylaws of 1938 state that if there are several descendants and they are all relatives of the same degree to the deceased, the estate is divided evenly among them, regardless of whether they are male or female (Article 245). Other clauses relating to other circumstances similarly imply that male and female descendants of the same degree to the deceased get an equal share (Articles 246 and 247). There is also no difference in the husband's and wife's right to inherit from one another (Article 242). There is an exception to this gender equity: when the deceased has no children, after the husband or wife inherits his or her share, the deceased's father inherits double that of the mother (Article 246).[70]

In 1956 Nasser nationalized the sharia and communal courts to make Egyptian law consistent and to strengthen the state's monopoly over law. Non-Muslims were, still, however, to be given a degree of judicial autonomy in matters relating to personal status law. Yet Law No. 462 of 1955 on the Abolition of the Sharia and Communal Courts did so by way of exemption. It stated:

> With regard to disputes connected to the personal status of non-Muslim Egyptians who are united in sect (al-ta'ifa) and rite (al-milla), and who at the time of passing of this law belong to organized communal judicial institutions, judgments will be passed—within the limits of public order (al-nizam al-'amm)—according to their law (tabqan li-shari'atihim).[71]

This altered the dynamic between non-Muslim communities and the state. It changed the basis upon which the state could grant non-Muslims the right to adjudicate according to their own law. Personal status law came to be governed by the sharia and non-Muslim law was only granted as an exemption.[72] The idea of an exemption from the application of national law made national recognition of the community that was to be given the dispensation more necessary, since it only applied to "organized sectarian judicial institutions" that had been formally recognized by the state. That dispensation was to be granted within the limits of public order—that is, it was contingent on being in the interests of the Egyptian state. In addition, it was implied that the exception should be compelling enough to be allowed.

The application of Islamic inheritance law on all Egyptians was confirmed in the 1960s by the Court of Cassation, which held that Islamic inheritance law applies to Muslims and non-Muslims.[73] In 1964 the Court of Cassation ruled that Islamic inheritance law was part of the Egyptian public order and was related to decorum (adab) because it is "connected to the legal and social order and has become firmly embedded in the conscience of society so that it would damage the general feelings [of society] if it were not applied."[74] Inheritance was not the only area of personal status law that was affected in this way. In the first part of the twentieth century, guardianship (1925, 1952), and family names, family ties, and legal capacity (1949) were removed from personal status law and classified as general law.[75]

Public order was a concept that ended up both restricting and enabling non-Muslim personal status law. This came about because non-Muslim personal status law was filtered through the concern that the public order should represent the essence or nature of the Egyptian nation. After 1955 the courts increasingly argued that non-Muslim family law could not violate public order—that is, the essential principles of the sharia. Thus, the extent of judicial autonomy was refracted through the necessity for the Egyptian state to formulate a unitary and homogenizing national culture. For example, forced Levirate marriage for Jews, in which the brother of a deceased man is obliged to marry his brother's widow, was ruled as a violation of Egyptian public order because it infringed upon the freedom to marry.[76] Public order, however, was also used to protect Christian law from encroachment by the state. Maurits Berger points out that the Egyptian courts have confirmed that, while Egypt's public policy codes do not embody the essential principles of non-Muslim law, Egyptian public policy is related to rules that are essential to Islamic law and that "the protection of the faiths of non-Muslims is an essential rule of Islamic law and hence of public policy."[77] For example, in 1979 the Egyptian Court of Cassation held that monogamous Christian marriage is considered one of the "essential principles (qawaʿid asliyya)" of the faith to which Christianity has adhered from its beginning.[78]

The concept of public order is of European origin, first appearing in the French Civil Code of 1804, and was introduced into the Egyptian legal system around the end of the nineteenth century. It appeared in Article 13 of the 1923 Constitution, which gave Egyptians the right to perform religious rituals "within the bounds of public order (al-nizam al-ʿamm) and decency (adab)."[79] In 1979 the Court of Cassation ruled that public order "includes rules that are aimed at securing the general public welfare of a country . . . . and surpasses the interests of individuals."[80] The court contended that while public order is based on a secular view and should not be connected with a particular law, sometimes, it asserted, public order "is related to religious belief when this belief is closely related to the legal and social system."[81] It contended that the rules of public order must apply "to all citizens, Muslims and non-Muslims regardless of their religion and public order cannot be divided. It is not possible to restrict some of the laws to Christians and make others unique to Muslims"[82] Berger shows how the concept of public order has been used to endorse Islamic rules, prevent the application of non-Muslim rules that violate Islamic law, and to protect the essential values of non-Muslim law and therefore the autonomy of nonreligious communities.[83]

It is the reference to an indivisible public order and its connection to the feelings of Egyptians that is so instructive for understanding what is at stake in petitions for a separate Christian inheritance law. While the new Egyptian state maintained the judicial autonomy of non-Muslims, this autonomy was predicated on its consistency with a unitary public sphere. This implies that the area of law in which non-Muslims are given legal independence has to be compelling enough for an exemption from national law to be granted. A compelling reason would be if the area of law for which the exemption is granted is related to something that is essential to Christianity. Some scholars defended limiting the jurisdiction of Egyptian non-Muslims to marriage and divorce, arguing that the legal independence of non-Muslims related to their religion and that only marriage and divorce were important enough to pertain to religious freedom.[84] This, of course, implies the case has to be made that any area of law given the exemption must be important and essential enough to the particular religious community to be granted the exemption.

Article 3 and Christian Law

The promulgation of Article 3 of the 2012 and 2014 Constitutions and its official recognition of the legal independence of non-Muslims opened up the possibility for Copts to renegotiate the nature and extent of this personal status law. In strengthening the grounds upon which Jews and Christians can be exempt from national law, Article 3 has made it possible for further negotiations about the extent and nature of this exemption to take place.

One consequence of Article 3 is that it has strengthened the grounds upon which Pope Shenouda restricted Copts' access to divorce and remarriage in 2008.[85] This has also led to a 2016 draft of new Coptic Orthodox bylaws, drafted under the papacy of Pope Tawadros II, who became pope in 2012. If they pass through parliament, these draft bylaws will further consolidate the church's position on divorce. These bylaws have laid the foundations for the draft of a unified Christian personal status law, the completion of which appears imminent in 2020. Copts have pushed for a unified personal status law since the 1970s, but the Egyptian state has, until the years succeeding the revolution of 2011, refused to accept one. Pursuant to the 1955 law, and upheld by the 2000 Egyptian Personal Status Law when non-Muslims are of a different sect and rite, the sharia, based on the sayings of Abu Hanifa, is applied to them.[86] Thus, a unified Christian personal status law would prevent Copts from being subject to sharia law when a divorce case, for example, involved individuals from different denominations.

Article 3 has also prompted a number of Christians to seek to widen the area of personal status law over which they have jurisdiction to include inheritance. This would involve receiving an exemption from Law No. 77 of 1943. The increase in the extent of judicial autonomy to include inheritance might well look like a continuation of the legal pluralism of the Ottoman Empire. However, the process by which certain exemptions from national law are given results in the judicial autonomy of non-Muslims being subject to a particular kind of dynamic. Thus, the application of the judicial independence of non-Muslims is not a simple holdover of the millet system. Rather, it is now subject to the fact that it is filtered through the concern about a unitary public sphere. In addition, an exemption can be given but this can only be done for communities that are nationally recognized and for which there are compelling reasons for the granting of the exemption.

The granting of exemptions by states is often done because it serves to further reinforce the cultural norms that bind a nation together. In the United States, exemptions in cases of religious freedom are given because the principle of freedom of religion is part of the mythology of the founding of the state. In Egypt, an exemption is given to the divinely revealed religions because the concept of the divinely revealed religions is an intrinsic part of Egyptian nationalism. Exemptions are also given because the sharia, with its principle of legal pluralism, is an important source of legislation in Egypt.

The granting of an exemption from national law has an important ramification. It can lead to more explicit boundaries between the communities that are exempt from the law and those for whom national law applies. In Mamluk Egypt (1250–1517), Sherman Jackson has shown that giving the schools of law exemptions so that the legal provisions of a school of law can be applied in turn reinforced the corporate status of the schools of law themselves. This contributed to greater formalization of the school of law and a consolidation of its internal control. Jackson writes that, in the thought of the Maliki jurist Shihab al-Din al-Qarafi (1228–85), each school could give a level of protection to its members. This meant that a Maliki living under a Shafi'i-dominated government—as was the case in Mamluk Egypt—would enjoy a level of exemption from rules on account of being a member of the Maliki school of law. Likewise, a ruling handed down by a Maliki judge would also be exempt on the condition that it reflected an opinion held by the school itself. In this capacity, Jackson argues, the school of law became a "constitutional unit that both defines and mediates the relationship between government and the community at large."[87] Granting an exemption thus has the potential to formalize the boundaries between the community that is to be given the exemption—in this case the Copts—and the rest of society, Egyptian Muslims.

The process of granting an exemption from national law also raises the question of the basis on which exemptions are to be given. Giving a religious exemption for personal status law requires establishing that there are compelling enough grounds to warrant an exemption from national law. For Coptic Christians this raises the question of what Christian law is, what Christian values are, who it is that belongs to this community, and who gets to define it.

In light of the promulgation of Article 3, there have been demands for inheritance to be included under the category of personal status law, and therefore under the category of law from which Christians and Jews can be exempt from national law. While inheritance was not talked about so frequently or publicly before the revolution of 2011, since then there has been an increase in expressions of dissatisfaction among Copts with inheritance law in Egypt.[88] First, there is dissatisfaction that Islamic inheritance law discriminates against the female offspring of the deceased.[89] Second, there is a problem with the enforcement of Islamic inheritance law. There are complaints that in areas like Upper Egypt—particularly when land is involved—women are deprived of their property and given less than they are legally entitled to under Islamic inheritance law. This is done in Muslim as well as Coptic communities.[90] Methods of depriving women of their inheritance have included the father conducting sham sales before his death, selling his property to his sons, and in turn depriving women of their share.[91]

Youssef Sidhom has long—and repeatedly—expressed his opposition to this situation. As editor of *Watani*, Sidhom argues that wounds over inheritance run deep, and most of the readers who write to him express their hope of recovering the equality that existed between men and women in Coptic history and establishing their equal rights in accordance with Christian doctrines.[92] This feeling of unfairness has led some Coptic families to redistribute the money equally within the family.[93] This only happens if all family members agree, and it is done after the state distributes the estate according to Islamic law. Youssef Sidhom calls upon the Coptic Church to seize the opportunity provided by Article 3 of the 2014 Constitution, and "revive Coptic legislation that treats men and women as equals regarding inheritance."[94] Sidhom says he hopes parliament "would possess the moral courage to defy the centuries-old male right to inherit double that of a female, and pass legislation to stipulate equal inheritance not only for Christian men and women but also for all Egyptians in general."[95]

Opposition to inheritance laws stretches across the secular-church divide. The Coptic thinker Kamal Zakhir is the founder of the Secular Copts Front, a group that is campaigning to reduce the church's official control over the lives of Copts. Yet Zakhir also affirmed that it is constitutional that *shari'a misihiyya*, "or Christian law," be applied in any matter relating to inheritance for Christians.[96] Nabil Ghibrial, a lawyer of the Supreme Administrative and Constitutional Courts, criticizes the prevalence—particularly in Upper Egypt—of what he refers to as "the male idea" (*al-fikr al-dhakuri*) that men are due twice what is due to women. He says that men there often think women lack intelligence so they think it is possible to dupe them and take their inheritance.[97]

Fathy Ragheb Hanna, a lawyer with the Constitutional Court and the Court of Cassation, asserts that the time has come, after the promulgation of Article 3 in 2012, for Christians in Egypt to demand the application of Christian rules of inheritance for Christian Egyptians. Syria issued Law No. 7 in 2011 to apply Christian rules of inheritance to members of the Greek Orthodox and Syriac Orthodox communities. Hanna contends that Christians in Egypt should have the same right.[98] Najib Ghibrial, a Coptic personal status law attorney and director of the Egyptian Union of Human Rights Organization (EUHRO), is often involved in inheritance disputes. He is a strong supporter of resisting any encroachment on the judicial autonomy of Copts and wants a separate law for inheritance.[99] He calls for punishing those who infringe upon the rights of women to inherit. He asserts that, while the Bible does not make a specific ruling on inheritance, equality between men and women is guaranteed in the New Testament.[100] Ghibrial adds that it is incumbent upon priests to convince men that their rights to inheritance are the same as those of women.[101] Monsef Soliman, a judge who was a member of the Coptic Community Council during Pope Shenouda's time, states that Article 3 allows for a family law for Christians to include regulations for inheritance, admitting that it is a major concern of families.[102]

It is often assumed that the Coptic Orthodox Church's control over the lives of Copts has resulted in the church's social conservatism being applied to Copts. This is indeed true, since the ability of Copts to divorce and remarry is more limited than it has been. Yet the church has also had an important role in bringing the question of gender equality in inheritance to light.[103] In cases where there is a problem of enforcement or women feel they have been unjustly treated by the courts over inheritance, Coptic women often appeal to the church to settle the problem.[104] This is shown in the case of three sisters who resorted to the church because their three brothers refused to give them their legal rights to the inheritance of their deceased father, who owned an estate comprising buildings and shops estimated at millions of pounds. The archbishop of the church intervened to solve the dispute, stating that each girl should get one hundred thousand pounds and an apartment. However, in this case the brothers refused to carry out the advice of the archbishop, leading to the sisters seeking legal redress.[105]

Bishop Thomas of the Diocese of al-Qussia in Upper Egypt argues that Islamic inheritance law goes against the Christian faith and the beliefs of the church. This in turn puts pressure on individual Christians to choose between their faith and the norms of society. It also puts pressure on the relationship between the church and individual Christians.[106] Father 'Abd al-Masih Basit, professor of defensive theology at the Coptic Orthodox Church, argues that, in matters of inheritance, Christians should be judged according to "their law" and that priests often try to intervene in such matters and advise Christians to treat men and women equally. However, he points out that priests cannot force families to treat men and women equally. He expressed his resentment that "in families in Upper Egypt daughters do not inherit a thing" and he states that "if the priest interferes he has succeeded if the daughter gets anything because that is better than nothing."[107]

Father Bakhumious Fu'ad, priest of the church of Marmarqis in Azbat al-Nakhl, affirmed the necessity for church leaders to resolutely pursue an inheritance issue that comes before the church on the basis of equality between men and women. He calls for priests to make the side determined on inflicting injustice upon women aware of God's displeasure. Father Bakhumious attributes the problems of inheritance in Christianity to upbringing and education and to people's lack of awareness about the Bible.[108]

The Protestant Church in Egypt has taken a particularly strong stance on this issue. Dr. Andrea Zaki Stephanous (b. 1960) is president of the Protestant

Community of Egypt and general director of the Coptic Evangelical Organization for Social Services. In recent negotiations over the unified Christian personal status law, he called for the endorsement of a clause that allows Copts to refer to their own canon code that provides for gender equality in inheritance.[109] The controversy over this question led to a delay in the law, and it was agreed that a consideration of this issue was "premature."[110]

Despite its position on inheritance, the Coptic Orthodox Church did not include inheritance provisions in the 2016 draft of the Coptic Orthodox bylaws which then formed the basis for negotiations concerning the unified Christian personal status law.[111] Sidhom argues that, when the church was drafting those bylaws, church members were in a hurry and concentrated on writing articles that regulated engagement, marriage, and divorce, but overlooked the issue of inheritance.[112] The Orthodox Church has not explained why it omitted inheritance regulations from the draft bylaws. There are a number of reasons why the church is reluctant to bring the issue before the Egyptian state. One reason might be because the current inheritance law suits patriarchal interests within parts of the Coptic community.[113] Explanations volunteered by prominent Coptic lawyers and other laymen claim that there were no specific inheritance rules cited in the Bible. They argue that it is difficult to invoke Christian canons on inheritance.[114] Others argue that the reason why a provision for inheritance was not included was because it would offend Egypt's Muslims if Christians were to apply different inheritance regulations.[115] Bishop Thomas argues that Christians are reluctant to push on this question because of the danger that the call for a Christian inheritance law would make it look as if Christians are attacking Islam.[116]

Bishop Thomas echoes how inheritance has been linked to the unitary public sphere and to the feelings of the Egyptian people. This implies that Christians can only reject Islamic legal norms when the grounds for such a rejection is connected to something that is mandated by their religion. Otherwise, it is seen as a renunciation of Islam as a whole with the potential to divide Egyptian society. Monsef Soliman stated that the matter "is mired in legal controversy" and that even though the bylaws of 1938 mentioned inheritance, none of the draft laws proposed by the church since 1979 have referenced inheritance.[117]

Clearly, there is much at stake in requesting that Copts have their own provisions for inheritance. First, Copts would have to make a case that inheritance provisions are essential enough to them to justify departing from Egypt's national law. Second, not applying Egypt's national law to Copts would have implications for Coptic-Muslim relations. National unity discourse is often contingent on expressing what unifies Copts and Muslims and how they are culturally the same. A separate Coptic inheritance law would serve to emphasize religious difference.

While many Copts appear to be calling for the widening of the personal status law to include inheritance, others argue that there should be a unified civil or national law for inheritance that applies to all individuals who have Egyptian nationality. The writer and journalist Karima Kamal also makes this argument. Strongly critical of the church's actions in limiting the access to divorce and remarriage, she calls for a civil unified personal status law for all Egyptians as necessary for a unified nation.[118] She has also spoken out on inheritance, arguing that "you should not implement the rules of one faith on people of another faith."[119]

Rather than rely on the church to mediate inheritance disputes, a number of Copts have been taking their cases to court. Some courts have been receptive to the claims. The plaintiffs are increasingly referring to the concept of shari'a misihiyya, arguing that Christian law establishes equality between men and women in matters of inheritance.[120] It is maintained that the application of Islamic inheritance law for Christians runs counter to the intent of the constitution since the constitution gives Christians freedom of personal status and there is a Christian law on inheritance. Ramses al-Najjar, a former legal adviser to the Coptic Church, said that the laws of inheritance for Christians are mentioned in the Coptic bylaws of 1938, thus Article 3 should allow Jews and Christians to be subject to their own laws. He points to the fact that the courts are beginning to apply stipulations particular to inheritance with regard to Christians according to their law, affirming that the Coptic laws do not distinguish between men and women who are heirs of the same degree.[121]

In November 2016 the Cairo Court of Appeals issued a ruling on a case in which a Coptic woman contested a lower court ruling that had granted her brother double her share of the inheritance of their sister's estate. The plaintiff demanded the equal division of the inheritance according to the 2014 Constitution and the principles of Christian doctrines. The court ruling invoked the Coptic bylaws of 1938. It stated that, "since the inheritors of the deceased are her brother . . . and her sister . . . therefore their inheritance shares should be equal according to Article 247 of the [1938] Coptic Orthodox bylaws. . . . According to their [Christian] doctrine there is no difference on that score between men and women."[122]

Another case involved a resident of Giza who appealed a judgment of 2016 from a first-level court, which restricted her inheritance from her late husband to a quarter of his legacy with the remaining two sisters taking two-thirds. She appealed on the grounds that existing laws contravene Article 3 of the 2014 Constitution.[123] Under the Coptic Orthodox bylaws of 1938, the wife would get half of her husband's estate if they have no children before the distribution to other heirs (Article 241).[124]

One case, mentioned earlier in this chapter, involved three sisters resorting to the church because their three brothers refused to give them their legal rights to the inheritance of their deceased father, whose estate consisted of buildings and shops estimated to be worth millions of Egyptian pounds. When the sisters took the case to court, "it was ruled that the share of the female is equal to the share of the male because both parties are Christians" and that the bylaws of the Orthodox Copts, which are legally enforced pursuant to Article 3, should be applied to them, considering the law that is particular to Christians is applied in a case when both claimants are of the same milla and ta'ifa.[125]

Most recently, in early 2019 the Cairo Court of Appeals ruled that Coptic Orthodox men and women are to inherit equal shares according to Article 3 of the Constitution and Article 247 of the Coptic Orthodox family bylaws of 1938. The ruling declared that, according to Article 247, if a person dies leaving no children or living parents, the spouse is given their share, and the remaining part of the estate is divided equally between the full brothers and sisters of the deceased.[126] Sidhom contends that, while this ruling might establish an important precedent, it "appears to have the effect of a stone cast in stagnant waters."[127] This is because the draft of the unified Christian personal status law before parliament does not include inheritance provisions.[128] If it does pass, this will weaken Coptic claims in the courts since the Coptic bylaws of 1938 would no longer be able to be invoked. Indeed, in July 2019 a court rejected an appeal by Huda Nasrallah, an Egyptian lawyer for the Egyptian Initiative for Personal Rights, against the ruling of the lower court. That court had applied sharia to her father's estate so that she received less than her brothers. At the time of writing, Nasrallah is challenging the rulings.[129]

Equality between Men and Women

One of the challenges Copts face regarding Article 3 and inheritance is articulating the grounds upon which this constitutes a Christian law or a part of the Christian faith. It requires establishing that matters of inheritance are religiously compelling enough to warrant the exemption from national law.[130] Shortly after the adoption of Law No. 462 of 1955 on the Abolition of the Sharia and Communal Courts, some courts interpreted "their law" as referring solely to the Gospels. However, in 1972 the Court of Cassation ruled that "their law" is a "general term the meaning of which is not limited to what is in the heavenly books alone, but also relates to everything that was applied in the communal legal councils before they were abolished, which are to be considered valid law."[131] There are obvious reasons why Copts who want to revise the inheritance law would want to address the question of when and how Copts had their own inheritance law in Islamic history. In addition, there are reasons why Copts would want to look at Christian texts regarding this matter.

The argument is emerging that an intrinsic part of Christian law is the principle of equality between men and women. The idea that men and women are equal is set up as a key difference between Islamic and Christian law. Bishop Marqus states that many people ask the church for advice about how they should distribute their inheritance and, he says, "we now respond from the Bible itself."[132] Coptic Orthodox Church members and writers articulate the principle of equality between men and women in the specific area of inheritance by appealing to the Bible. While the Bible is relatively silent on issues of inheritance specifically, for many, such as Father 'Abd al-Masih Basit, the verse of Paul's letter to the Galatians (Gal. 3:28)—"There is neither Jew nor Gentile, neither slave nor free, nor is there male and female, for you are all one in Christ Jesus"—affirms the necessity of applying equality between men and women in all rights and duties.[133]

Father Bakhumious Fu'ad goes further and argues that depriving daughters of their inheritance is a sin, the perpetrator of which could be prevented from entering the Kingdom of Heaven, because that is an irrevocable injustice. He argues that it is not possible for "those who are unjust to inherit the Kingdom of God."[134] Father Fu'ad also references Paul's Letter to the Galatians and goes on to reference the book of Numbers in the Old Testament, in which the daughters of Zelophehad petitioned Moses to secure a share of their father's inheritance, who had died without a son. God answered the daughters of Zelophehad and gave a direction concerning this: "Any man who dies and has no son shall transfer his property to his daughter" (Numbers 27:8).[135] Even though the verse only technically allows for females to inherit when there are no male heirs, for Father Fu'ad, it supports the Christian principle of equality between men and women in matters of inheritance.

Youssef Sidhom, likewise, is keen to assert that Christian doctrine is supportive of equal inheritance shares for men and women. He also cites the case of the daughters of Zelophehad in Numbers and the book of Joshua (Josh. 17:3–6), and Job 42:15—"And in all the land were no women found so fair as the daughters of Job: and their father gave them inheritance among their brethren."[136] Job had seven sons and three daughters. Giving his daughters an inheritance was exceptional and went against the Hebrew practice of inheritance; Job, having a plentiful estate, did this to oblige his daughters to settle and marry among their brethren.

For Sidhom, the concept of equality between men and women is not only rooted in the Christian texts but also in the history of the Coptic Church. He points out that, during the Coptic era, women had equal inheritance to that of men according to Christian-based legislation.[137] He also illustrates that Pope Kyrillos IV, the Coptic Orthodox pope from 1854 to 1861, resolved an inheritance dispute by arguing that because God does not reduce a person's reward in heaven on account of her being a woman, then inheritance in this world should follow God's example.[138]

For Sidhom, the metaphors of emasculation are used to express his disappointment at the status quo. He asserts that "men who have no qualms about seizing their mothers' or sisters' inheritance have lost their way to 'manliness' in the old sense of the word. . . . I intend to open this appalling file which seriously blemishes the gallantry of Egyptian men, even if equality between men and women regarding inheritance is legislated."[139]

Here, a distinction is made between the religion of Coptic Christians and the dominant culture. It is asserted that the culture of Copts in Egypt has been influenced by Islam and that people—including Copts who willingly seek to deprive women of inheritance—have become habituated to the idea that women do not deserve an equal share. Father 'Abd al-Masih Basit expresses his regret that Christians are more influenced by society than they are by the Bible, adding that "Christians adopting the customs and traditions of the middle ages meant that they were governed by Islamic law in matters of inheritance."[140]

Sidhom argues that among the excuses made for depriving women of their inheritance rights is that land should not be passed on to strangers. Even when the inheritance does not involve land, it is claimed that females are financially supported by males so should merit half their share.[141] Sidhom says these are all "lame excuses," since women today take full responsibility in supporting their families. Besides, he writes, "it is very common for those men who end up usurping their women relatives' legacies to contribute not the slightest effort or share towards supporting these women or their children. Traditional manly nobility has come to a sorry end."[142]

Such discourse does not reflect the opinion of all Copts. Many Coptic families do support Islamic inheritance law. Samir Marcos, a Coptic activist and intellectual, argues that many families accept giving men a greater share of inheritance.[143] Munir Fakhri ʿAbd al-Nur, former secretary-general of the Wafd party, points out that Copts accept the submission to the sharia because it is part of their overall cultural heritage and tradition and that there is "no such thing as Christian inheritance law."[144] Others, such as Ashraf Anis, the founder of Right to Life want Copts to be released from the Coptic Orthodox Church's control over personal status law and for the application of a civil personal status law.[145]

In addition, not all Muslims in Egypt agree with Islamic inheritance provisions. Indeed, in 2018 there were calls for reforming Egyptian Islamic inheritance law. This was in part precipitated by the announcement in the summer of 2018 by the Tunisian president that he intends to propose a new draft law which will make men and women equal in inheritance matters. The draft law however, has been postponed. Some, such as the media presenter Muhammad al-Baz are calling for such a change to happen in Egypt.[146] Dina ʿAbd al-Aziz, a member of the House of Representatives has also called for such a law. However, her request was rejected by other members of the House of Representatives and various faculty members at al-Azhar University on the grounds that it would violate the sharia.[147] Changing sharia provisions for inheritance would be challenging given that the provisions are clearly outlined in the Qurʾan and many argue they are not open to interpretation.

In this chapter, I have argued that discussions over the nature and extent of the judicial autonomy of non-Muslims in Egypt have taken on a distinct form in the modern context and since the 2011 revolution in particular. Discussions of personal status law in premodern Islamic history have often assumed that this is an area in which the ruling polity was not interested in asserting its authority. Such a position holds that non-Muslims were simply left alone to exercise their own autonomy. Yet dhimmis had a variety of experiences across the Ottoman Empire. While distinct non-Muslim communities did exist, the level of their institutionalization and their interaction with Muslims varied considerably. Such exchange was fluid and Jews and Christians often had extensive experience of the Muslim courts and moved between their own and other judicial systems. This was particularly so with regard to inheritance, where, in the case of Christians in particular, there were questions about the extent to which Christians felt that inheritance was covered by canon law. In addition, for financial reasons, the Ottoman state—and ruling polities before it—had tried to assert their control over inheritance, particularly in the area of intestate succession. At the same time, inheritance was also a means by which some non-Muslim communities asserted their judicial autonomy. The weakening of Ottoman control in the nineteenth century enabled non-Muslims to assert their right to exclusive jurisdiction. However, new conceptions of the role of the state in people's lives meant that the area over which non-Muslims had judicial control became increasingly restricted.

The modern Egyptian state was concerned with unifying Egyptian law and making it consistent as a way of strengthening the Egyptian nation. In 1940s Egypt, national law was used to restrict the personal status law of non-Muslims so that inheritance matters were governed by the sharia. Copts were effectively only given the right to judicial autonomy over marriage and divorce law. The concept of public order was used both to restrict and protect personal status law so the relationship between the judicial autonomy of non-Muslims and the state was recalibrated. While the Coptic bylaws of 1938, written by laymen, addressed the question of inheritance, the Coptic community generally did not oppose the imposition of Islamic inheritance law in the 1940s. Inheritance was effectively subsumed by the need for a unitary Islamic public sphere on the grounds that inheritance law was not part of the Christian canon.

However, Article 3 of the 2014 Constitution, which made a formal commitment to the right of Jews and Christians to have their own personal status law, has opened up the possibility for further negotiation about the nature and extent of the judicial autonomy of Christians. This has coincided with changing attitudes toward gender and the family. While it is tempting to see this negotiation as a relic of the Ottoman Empire's millet system—and, in some respects, it is—Article 3 does not constitute a mere reimposition of premodern norms governing the relationship between non-Muslims and the ruling polity. The issuance of Article 3 and the renegotiation over inheritance illustrate how the judicial autonomy of non-Muslims as emphasized in Article 3 has taken on distinct forms in modern Egypt.

Article 3 raises the question of when an exemption is warranted. Involved in this is the intractable question about what constitutes a religious norm and whether that religious norm is central enough to that religion to be deemed worthy of exemption. Copts who want to have their own inheritance law are having to make the case that gender equality in inheritance relates to an essential part of the Christian faith; they are employing biblical texts and referring to thirteenth-century approaches to inheritance to make such a case. Yet, while non-Muslim communities negotiated the extent and nature of their autonomy with Ottoman authorities, it did not involve the same kinds of questions about what the essential aspects of Christianity are.

The implications of granting non-Muslims greater judicial autonomy have also changed. Judicial autonomy was granted in the Ottoman Empire because it was a tactic that allowed the Ottoman area to govern vast and religiously diverse territories. The modern nation state, however, is predicated on the articulation of a national culture and the concept of the unitary public sphere. A request for a new exemption—even if Copts say that it would restore what had previously existed—implies drawing a line between Muslims and Christians, promoting the articulation of further differences between Muslims and Copts. This is in danger of fracturing the very unity for which the constitutional commitment to the divinely revealed religions is striving.

Conclusion

In December 2017, the head of the House of Representative's religious committee, 'Amr Hamrush, suggested proposing a bill to make atheism illegal. Hamrush emphasized "the necessity of criminalizing the phenomenon [of atheism] and of placing it in an article relating to the contempt of religion because atheists have no doctrine and try to insult the divinely revealed religions and do not recognize them."[1] Al-Azhar's Senior Scholars' Council supported the proposal to make atheism a crime, saying that Islam grants the ruler the right to demand that an apostate (al-mulhid) repent and, failing that, to execute the apostate in order to preserve Islamic society.[2]

This proposal received intense opposition and has yet to reach the form of a bill. Yet it is instructive. First, it illustrates one of the ironies of the revolution. The proposal is not entirely dissimilar to Article 44 of the 2012 Constitution, which stated that "insulting or opposing all messengers or prophets is forbidden." However, the December 2017 proposal goes much further than forbidding the public act of insulting religion to actually criminalizing a belief, along with stipulating that the penalty for such a crime should be death. The Muslim Brotherhood and other Islamists were criticized for Article 44, which did not appear in the 2014 Constitution. Criticisms of the 2012 Constitution helped facilitate a counterrevolution and the restoration of the status quo in 2013. 'Amr Hamrush's proposal makes one wonder whether Egypt has, in a number of respects, become more socially conservative even though the Muslim Brotherhood has been removed from the public sphere. The level of religious conservatism expressed in Hamrush's proposal raises questions about why the Muslim Brotherhood was demonized for its Islamism in the first place.

Al-Azhar paved the way for the discussion of this bill in the years before 2017 by issuing various statements denouncing atheism and warning of its growth in Egypt. Hamrush's proposal shows that, in the postrevolutionary environment, al-Azhar has emerged more definitively as the representative of Islam. While it had always been viewed as the guardian of Islam, since the 1960s its ability to do so had been questioned. It also had to face competing voices such as the Muslim Brotherhood and, since the 1990s, Islamist intellectuals associated with the organization's younger generation. One of these intellectuals is Muhammad Salim al-ʿAwwa, who maintains that there is no mention in the Qurʾan that punishment by death for apostasy should be enforced in this world and asserts that the death penalty contradicts the principle of "no compulsion in religion (2:256)."[3]

Now that the Muslim Brotherhood has been removed from the public sphere, al-Azhar does not have to face the Muslim Brotherhood's critique of it. Additionally, al-Azhar's right to speak for Islam is constitutionally enshrined. While the Constitution of 2014 affirmed the Supreme Constitutional Court's right to adjudicate on the constitutionality of legislation, the constitution also gave al-Azhar the means to assert itself more as the representative of Islam. There are indications that al-Azhar is doing just that. For example, in 2017, al-Azhar opposed suggestions made by President ʿAbd al-Fattah al-Sisi for an amendment to the personal status law requiring divorces to be registered with an authorized state official. This would have effectively made verbal divorce, which is allowed by the sharia, illegal. Al-Azhar's refusal to endorse the amendment illustrates that al-Azhar intends to guard its new constitutionally designated sphere.

Some contend that the constitutional commitment to al-Azhar's right to speak for Islam in a way that is not constitutionally binding returns al-Azhar to its historical role. Yet, in premodern Islamic systems, the sharia and state law were not so closely intertwined. In many respects, they were parallel and worked alongside one another. Yet a constitutional commitment to the sharia and to the role of al-Azhar has more specifically subordinated the sharia to modern Islamic state law. Al-Azhar currently finds itself in a precarious position balancing two inclinations: (1) to stand beyond politics and represent Islam from outside of the political process, drawing on premodern conceptions of the necessity for there to be distance between the scholar and the ruler, and (2) to shape modern Islamic state law in a way that adheres to its vision of Islam. These two potentially contradictory inclinations show the ways in which the relationship between the sharia and modern Islamic state law is deeply fraught and will likely be so for the foreseeable future.

'Amr Hamrush's proposal to criminalize atheism is also instructive because it implies that Judaism and Christianity can, like Islam, be blasphemed. It illustrates how the constitutional commitment to the heavenly religions has the potential to shape future legislation. The idea of the divinely revealed religions has become a national cultural concept and a key component of Egyptian nationalism. Christianity, represented by the Coptic Orthodox Church, has become more deeply intertwined with Islam in Egypt. Yet it is an Egyptian nationalism that is focused on religious communities as opposed to autonomous individuals. Article 3 and the concept of the divinely revealed religions have strengthened the authority of the church over the Coptic people. In the process, secular Copts who want to de-emphasize the leadership of the church and advance the principles of citizenship and legal equality have been sidelined. The concept of the divinely revealed religions has therefore created new forms of inclusion and exclusion by connecting Christianity and Islam and by excluding Baha'is and people of no religion in the process.

The constitutional commitment to the heavenly religions has thus resulted in a stronger alliance—at least for now—between the regime and the church than had existed under the Ottoman Empire. Coptic Orthodox Christianity, centered on the church, has, particularly since the coup against Muhammad Mursi in 2013, experienced more official and stronger forms of state recognition. This can be seen in the Egyptian government's hitherto absent support for church construction. This is not to deny the vulnerability of Copts with respect to the state itself and the Muslim majority, but it is to say that the church has achieved new levels of official, rhetorical, and legal recognition.

The introduction of Article 2 to the 1971 Constitution first raised this question: What are the precise ways in which the sharia and specific constitutional provisions work together? In the case of women and the family, the constitutional commitment to taking care of widows, divorcées, and breadwinning women, first seen in the Constitution of 2012, raises an important question about the relationship between the sharia and other constitutional commitments. A promise to provide for economically vulnerable women can be seen as a form of siyasa shar'iyya, whereby the state can supplement the sharia when it is in the public interest in a way that does not contradict the sharia. The concept of siyasa shar'iyya enabled the premodern Islamic polity to legislate in a way that did not go against the sharia. Yet the assumption is that the sharia and state law would work alongside one another and remain distinct. This constitutional commitment to the economic vulnerability of women did not annul the provisions of the sharia that contribute to this economic vulnerability. Yet it raised the question of how the commitment to the sharia could be balanced with other constitutional articles. Such balancing is subject to the interpretation of the Supreme Constitutional Court, which has generally rejected the idea that the sharia can override positive state legislation. The court has also taken a liberal and flexible approach to what constitutes the principles of the sharia. In making a constitutional commitment to female breadwinners, women, and divorcées, it looked as if Muslim Brotherhood intended to continue along the lines of the Supreme Constitutional Court's approach to modern Islamic state law. The constitutional commitment to economically vulnerable women showed that the organization embraces a broader sense of public interest that is not tied to the sharia provisions of the premodern schools of law. Rather than being reactionary, the Muslim Brotherhood actually represents a particularly modern convergence between family, religion, law, and culture.

The full ramifications of the constitutional articles discussed in this book have yet to be seen. One consequence, however, is already clear. The commitment to the personal status law of Christians in Article 3 has enabled the Copts to become more assertive over communal law. Some Copts are beginning to petition for an exemption from Islamic inheritance law in the name of gender equity. In so doing, they are rearticulating what Christianity in Egypt is. Thus, while the commitment to the concept of the divinely revealed religions has formed a basis upon which Christians and Muslims can unite, that same commitment has given leverage to Copts to emphasize religious difference. It might seem that Copts' petitioning for the widening of personal status law to include inheritance constitutes a revival of the judicial autonomy of non-Muslims under the Ottoman Empire and before. However, the question of judicial autonomy is now subject to a different set of requirements that have different ramifications for the Egyptian public sphere. Negotiating an exemption from national law involves making the case that the area that is to be exempt is compelling enough to be granted an exemption. Thus, Copts have to make the case that gender equality is an essential principle of Christianity. This, in turn, involves addressing whether the essential principles of Christianity should be measured by the Gospels or other texts from the Bible, or by Coptic customary law. Whether customary laws that have been allowed to lapse can be revived, and whether reviving them will contravene the Egyptian public order, including respecting the feelings of the Muslim majority, remains to be legally adjudicated.

In closely addressing the case studies of al-Azhar and religious authority, the concept of the divinely revealed religions, women's rights, and
judicial autonomy and inheritance, this book has shown how norms and
ideas, which are rooted in the sharia and in premodern Islamic history, are
constantly interacting with the evolving needs of the modern nation state.
When constitutional commitments are made to the sharia, the sharia is not
transformed but rather is recast. Modern Islamic state law therefore constitutes neither a break from—nor a continuation with—what went before.
Modern Islamic state law is the result of a reworking of legal norms derived
from the sharia. When Islamic legal norms are applied in constitutions, those
norms become recast because they are subject to the state's need to articulate a national culture and to speak in the name of the national will. It is
the state's need to delineate a national culture—through which it claims the
right to represent its citizens—that imposes particular demands on the populace. Constitutions are an expression of those demands which work on and
through law to produce particular outcomes.

This results in some aspects of the sharia being brought to bear on modern Islamic state law, while others are deemphasized. It is not possible to
say that the sharia determines the form that modern Islamic state law takes.
Nor is it possible to say that the sharia submits to the law of the state as the
artist of the mural with which I opened this book seems to advocate. The
sharia does not operate in a monolithic way. Rather, it is more accurate to
say that some aspects of the sharia influence the form that modern Islamic
state law takes while others are made subordinate to the needs of modern
Islamic state law.

In showing the particular forms that the sharia takes when it is applied
as modern Islamic state law, I do not imply that these forms are static and
unchanging. Quite the contrary. The relationship between the sharia and
modern Islamic state law is subject to constant negotiation. As the needs of
the modern Egyptian state change, other sharia-influenced laws, hitherto
perhaps dormant, may be worked into modern Islamic state law. The political and legal landscapes of contemporary Egypt have changed considerably
in the last decade. It is highly probable that they will continue to undergo
rapid change given Egypt's underlying political and economic instability.
The events described in this book show how brittle political systems can be.
The energy that was spent trying to capture what Egypt stands for in the
constitutional debates points to the deep divisions in Egyptian society. It is
quite possible that under different circumstances, other less palatable legacies of the sharia—such as al-Azhar's statement on apostasy—will be invoked
and referred to in constitutional and legal debates. These laws and attitudes

will no doubt serve the needs of those who are—at any given time—trying to shape the state. This does not mean that the sharia in itself needs to be feared so much as what individuals choose to do with it. So, when the needs of contemporary Egypt change—as they no doubt will—it is likely that modern Islamic state law will change as some aspects of the sharia are minimized while others are revived and invoked.

NOTES

Introduction

1. Wael B. Hallaq, *The Impossible State: Islam, Politics, and Modernity's Moral Predicament* (New York: Columbia University Press, 2013), 51.

2. Dustur jumhuriyyat misr al-ʿarabiyya (2012).

3. Ragab Saad and Moataz El Fegiery, "Citizenship in Post-Awakening Egypt: Power Shifts and Conflicting Perceptions," 1–2, *Democracy and Citizenship in North Africa after the Arab Awakening: Challenges for EU and US Foreign Policy* (Euspring: January 2014).

4. "Separating Law and Politics Challenges to the Independence of Judges and Prosecutors in Egypt," International Bar Association Human Rights Institute (IBAHRI), February 2014. Of course, this was not the only narrative that surrounded the promulgation of the Constitution of 2012. However, it was the dominant one—both in the Egyptian media and in the foreign press—and one that resulted in a considerable exercise of political power. For a very alternative narrative, see Amani Abu al-Fadl Faraj's book. Abu al-Fadl Faraj was a member of the Constituent Assembly that drafted the 2012 Constitution. She argues that there was a conflict on the committee between supporters of national sovereignty and the malignant agents of globalization, who wanted Egypt to enter into the "New World Order." Amani Abu al-Fadl Faraj, *Min kawalis al-dustur: siraʿ al-siyada al-wataniyya wa-l-irada al-dawliyya dakhil dustur misr* [From the scenes of the Constitution: The struggle between national sovereignty and the international will inside Egypt's Constitution] (Cairo: nahdat al-misr, 2013).

5. Dustur jumhuriyyat misr al-ʿarabiyya (2012).

6. Zaid Al-Ali, "Egypt's Draft Constitution: An Analysis," *Open Democracy*, November 8, 2012.

7. Zaid Al-Ali, "The New Egyptian Constitution: An Initial Assessment of Its Merits and Flaws," *Open Democracy*, December 26, 2012.

8. Brinkley Messick, *The Calligraphic State: Textual Domination and History in a Muslim Society* (Berkeley: University of California Press, 1993), 56.

9. Graeme Wood, "What Isis Really Wants," *Atlantic*, March 2015.

10. Hallaq, *Impossible State*; Hussein Ali Agrama, *Questioning Secularism: Islam, Sovereignty, and the Rule of Law in Modern Egypt* (Chicago: University of Chicago Press, 2012); Saba Mahmood, *Religious Difference in a Secular Age: A Minority Report* (Princeton, NJ: Princeton University Press, 2015).

11. Andrew March, "What Can the Islamic Past Teach Us about Secular Modernity?," *Political Theory* 43, no. 6 (2015): 848.

12. Khaled Fahmy, *In Quest of Justice: Islamic Law and Forensic Medicine in Modern Egypt* (Oakland: University of California Press, 2018), 179–226.

13. Mahmood, *Religious Difference in a Secular Age.*

14. Hallaq, *Impossible State,* 89, ix.

15. Nimer Sultany, *Law and Revolution: Legitimacy and Constitutionalism after the Arab Spring* (Oxford: Oxford University Press, 2017), xxx.

16. Talal Asad, *Formations of the Secular: Christianity, Islam, Modernity* (Stanford, CA: Stanford University Press, 2003), 25, 1–2.

17. Elizabeth Shakman Hurd, *The Politics of Secularism in International Relations* (Princeton, NJ: Princeton University Press, 2008).

18. Agrama, *Questioning Secularism,* 27–32.

19. Saba Mahmood, "Religious Freedom, the Minority Question, and Geopolitics in the Middle East," *Comparative Studies in Society and History* 54, no. 2 (2012): 419, 423–24; Humeira Iqtidar, "State Management of Religion in Pakistan and Dilemmas of Citizenship," *Citizenship Studies* 16, no. 8 (2012): 1014, 1022.

20. Tamir Moustafa, *Constituting Religion: Islam, Liberal Rights, and the Malaysian State* (Cambridge: Cambridge University Press, 2018), 4.

21. Nathalie Bernard-Maugiron, "Legal Reforms, the Rule of Law, and Consolidation of State Authoritarianism under Mubarak," in Arjomand and Brown, *Rule of Law, Islam, and Constitutional Politics,* 179–206; Nathan J. Brown, *Constitutions in a Nonconstitutional World: Arab Basic Laws and the Prospects for Accountable Government* (Albany: State University of New York Press, 2002); Mustafa Kamel Al-Sayyid, "Rule of Law, Ideology, and Human Rights in Egyptian Courts," in Arjomand and Brown, *Rule of Law, Islam, and Constitutional Politics,* 211–32.

22. Bruce K. Rutherford, *Egypt after Mubarak: Liberalism, Islam, and Democracy in the Arab World* (Princeton, NJ: Princeton University Press, 2008); Pietro Longo, *Theory and Practice in Islamic Constitutionalism: From Classical Fiqh to Modern Systems* (Piscataway, NJ: Gorgias Press, 2019).

23. Sultany, *Law and Revolution,* xxv.

24. Timothy Mitchell, *Colonizing Egypt* (Berkeley: University of California Press, 1991); James C. Scott, *Seeing Like a State: How Certain Schemes to Improve the Human Condition Have Failed* (New Haven, CT: Yale University Press, 1998).

25. Hanna Lerner, *Making Constitutions in Deeply Divided Societies* (Cambridge: Cambridge University Press, 2011), 4.

26. Moustafa, *Constituting Religion,* 2.

27. Moustafa, *Constituting Religion,* 3.

28. Winnifred Fallers Sullivan, *The Impossibility of Religious Freedom* (Princeton, NJ: Princeton University Press, 2005), 1.

1. Constitutions, National Culture, and Rethinking Islamism

1. Galal Amin, *Mihnat al-dunya wa-l-din fi misr* [The struggle between the world and religion in Egypt] (Cairo: dar al-shuruq, 2013), 10.

2. Amin, *Mihnat al-dunya wa-l-din fi misr,* 9.

3. Amin, *Mihnat al-dunya wa al-din fi misr,* 11–12.

4. Nathan J. Brown, *Constitutions in a Nonconstitutional World,* 9.

5. Lerner, *Making Constitutions in Deeply Divided Societies,* 16.

6. UK, Canada, New Zealand, Israel, and Saudi Arabia.

7. Brown, *Constitutions in a Nonconstitutional World,* xiii.

8. "'We Do Unreasonable Things Here': Torture and National Security in Al-Sisi's Egypt," Human Rights Watch, September, 2017.

9. Catharine A. MacKinnon, "Gender in Constitutions," in Rosenfeld and Sajó, *Oxford Handbook of Comparative Constitutional Law*, 401, 407.

10. Martin Krygier, "Rule of Law," in Rosenfeld and Sajó, *Oxford Handbook of Comparative Constitutional Law*, 242.

11. Lerner, *Making Constitutions in Deeply Divided Societies*, 16.

12. Krygier, "Rule of Law," 234.

13. Bernard-Maugiron, "Legal Reforms, the Rule of Law," 181, 200.

14. Brown, *Constitutions in a Nonconstitutional World*, 9, 98–99, 195.

15. Hannah Arendt, *Between Past and Future: Six Exercises in Political Thought* (New York: Viking Press, 1961), 120.

16. Arendt, *Between Past and Future*, 139.

17. Arendt, *Between Past and Future*, 140.

18. Arendt, *Between Past and Future*, 140–41.

19. Thomas C. Grey, "The Constitution as Scripture," *Stanford Law Review* 37, no. 1 (November 1984): 17.

20. Ulrich K. Preuss, "Constitutional Powermaking for the New Polity: Some Deliberations on the Relations between Constituent Power and the Constitution," in Rosenfeld, *Constitutionalism, Identity, Difference, and Legitimacy*, 143–45.

21. Mitchell, *Colonizing Egypt*, xiii.

22. Mitchell, *Colonizing Egypt*, xiii, 32–33.

23. Mitchell, *Colonizing Egypt*, 12.

24. Mitchell, *Colonizing Egypt*, 13, 33.

25. J. C. Scott, *Seeing Like a State*, 2.

26. J. C. Scott, *Seeing Like a State*, 32.

27. J. C. Scott, *Seeing Like a State*, 32, 55, 35.

28. J. C. Scott, *Seeing Like a State*, 32, 55, 78, 22.

29. J. C. Scott, *Seeing Like a State*, 91.

30. J. C. Scott, *Seeing Like a State*, 82.

31. Lerner, *Making Constitutions in Deeply Divided Societies*, 6.

32. Lerner, *Making Constitutions in Deeply Divided Societies*, 40, 62–63.

33. Brown, *Constitutions in a Nonconstitutional World*, 97.

34. Brown, *Constitutions in a Nonconstitutional World*, 11.

35. Saïd Amir Arjomand, "Constitutions and the Struggle for Political Order: A Study in the Modernization of Political Traditions," *European Journal of Sociology* 33, no. 1 (1992): 40.

36. Arjomand, "Constitutions and the Struggle for Political Order," 46.

37. Brown, *Constitutions in a Nonconstitutional World*, 11.

38. Hallaq, *Impossible State*, 45.

39. Hallaq, *Impossible State*, 96.

40. David Lloyd and Paul Thomas, *Culture and the State* (New York: Routledge, 1998), 10.

41. Lloyd and Thomas, *Culture and the State*, 3.

42. Lloyd and Thomas, *Culture and the State*, 1.

43. Lloyd and Thomas, *Culture and the State*, 1.

44. Hallaq, *Impossible State*, 38.

45. Raymond Williams, *Culture and Society, 1780–1850* (New York: Columbia University Press, 1983), xvi–xviii.

46. Tomoko Masuzawa, "Culture," in *Critical Terms for Religious Studies*, ed. Mark C. Taylor (Chicago: University of Chicago Press, 1998), 75–77.

47. Ayça Çubukçu, "It's the Will of the Turkish People, Erdogan Says. But Which People?," *Guardian*, July 26, 2016.

48. James McDougall, "This 'Will of the People' Talk Must Stop—We Need a Better Democracy Than That," *New Statesman*, February 7, 2017.

49. Tamir Moustafa, "Does Egypt Need a New Constitution?," *Foreign Policy*, February 10, 2011.

50. Talal Asad, "Thinking about Tradition, Religion, and Politics in Egypt Today," *Critical Inquiry* 42, no. 1 (Autumn 2015): 205–6. However, Asad argues that there is an inherent contradiction in the modern state's requirement of a homogeneous political identity. It becomes necessary for the modern state to emphasize "difference as significant in order to exercise the violence that is 'necessary' to its sovereignty," 195.

51. Asad, "Thinking about Tradition," 206.

52. Asad, "Thinking about Tradition," 195.

53. Dustur jumhuriyyat misr al-ʿarabiyya (2012).

54. Dustur jumhuriyyat misr al-ʿarabiyya (2014).

55. Dustur jumhuriyyat misr al-ʿarabiyya (2014).

56. "'Al-Ahram' yanshir mawad al-dustur, dustur li-kul al-misriyyin" [Al-Ahram publishes the articles of the constitution, a constitution for all Egyptians], *al-Ahram*, January 9, 2014.

57. Dustur jumhuriyyat misr al-ʿarabiyya (2014).

58. Dustur jumhuriyyat misr al-ʿarabiyya (2014).

59. Dustur jumhuriyyat misr al-ʿarabiyya (2014).

60. Peter Berger, *The Sacred Canopy: Elements of a Sociological Theory of Religion* (New York: Doubleday, 1967), 107.

61. Monica Duffy Toft, Daniel Philpott, and Timothy Samuel Shah, *God's Century: Resurgent Religion and Global Politics* (New York: W. W. Norton, 2011), 1.

62. Toft, Philpott, and Shah, *God's Century*, 79.

63. Hussein Ali Agrama, "Secularism, Sovereignty, Indeterminacy: Is Egypt a Secular or a Religious State?," *Comparative Studies in Society and History* 52, no. 3 (2010): 499.

64. Asad, *Formations of the Secular*, 25.

65. Asad, *Formations of the Secular*, 25.

66. Asad, *Formations of the Secular*, 2.

67. Agrama, *Questioning Secularism*, 21, 42–68.

68. As an example, see Sami Zubaida, *Law and Power in the Islamic World* (London: I. B. Tauris, 2005), 170.

69. Agrama, *Questioning Secularism*, 102.

70. Fahmy, *In Quest of Justice*, 183.

71. Ghazzālī [Ḥujjat al-Islām Abū Ḥāmid Muḥammad Ghazzālī Ṭūsī], *Al-Ghazzali on Enjoining Good and Forbidding Wrong*, trans. Muhammad Nur Abdus Salam (Chicago: Great Books of the Islamic World, 2002), 6.

72. Ahmad ibn Naqib al-Misri, *Reliance of the Traveller (Umdat al-Salik): A Classic Manual of Islamic Sacred Law* (Beltsville, MD: Amana, 1994), 716–17.

73. Agrama, "Secularism, Sovereignty, Indeterminacy," 503.

74. Agrama, "Secularism, Sovereignty, Indeterminacy," 502.

75. Also see Hurd, *Politics of Secularism.*

76. March, "What Can the Islamic Past Teach Us," 846.

77. March, "What Can the Islamic Past Teach Us," 847, quoting Agrama, *Questioning Secularism*, 33.

78. Gregory Starrett, "The Varieties of Secular Experience," *Comparative Studies in Society and History* 52, no. 3 (2010): 644–45.

79. Starrett, "Varieties of Secular Experience," 628.

80. Starrett, "Varieties of Secular Experience," 628, 648.

81. Malika Zeghal, "Competing Ways of Life: Islamism, Secularism, and Public Order in the Tunisian Transition," *Constellations* 20, no. 2 (2013): 265.

82. Zeghal, "Competing Ways of Life," 263.

83. Talal Asad, *Genealogies of Religion: Discipline and Reasons of Power in Christianity and Islam* (Baltimore: John Hopkins University Press, 1993), 18.

84. Yusuf al-Qaradawi, *Min fiqh al-dawla fi al-Islam* [On the jurisprudence of the state in Islam] (Cairo: dar al-shuruq, 1997), 89, 91.

85. Abdullahi Ahmed An-Naʿim, *Islam and the Secular State: Negotiating the Future of Shariʿa* (Cambridge, MA: Harvard University Press, 2008), 53–55.

86. Agrama, "Secularism, Sovereignty, Indeterminacy," 501.

87. Agrama, *Questioning Secularism*, 27.

88. Zeghal, "Competing Ways of Life," 258.

2. The Sharia as State Law

1. Hallaq, *Impossible State*, 156.

2. Sherman A. Jackson, *Islamic Law and the State: The Constitutional Jurisprudence of Shihāb al-Dīn al-Qarāfī* (Leiden: Brill, 1996), xiv.

3. Mohammed Fadel, "Islamic Law Reform: Between Reinterpretation and Democracy," *Yearbook of Islamic and Middle Eastern Law*, ed. Martin Lau and Faris Nasrallah, 18, no. 1 (2013–15): 44–45.

4. John Scott, "Judicial Reform in Egypt," *Journal of the Society of Comparative Legislation* 1, no. 2 (July 1899): 16.

5. Jackson, *Islamic Law and the State*, xv.

6. Hallaq, *Impossible State*, 10, 51.

7. Malcolm H. Kerr, *Islamic Reform: The Political and Legal Theories of Muḥammad ʿAbduh and Rashīd Riḍā* (Berkeley: University of California Press, 1966), 1.

8. Lawrence Rosen, *The Justice of Islam: Comparative Perspectives on Islamic Law and Society* (Oxford: Oxford University Press, 2000), 161–62, 182.

9. Shmuel Moreh, "Al-Jabarti's Attitude towards the ʿUlama' of His Time," in *Guardians of Faith in Modern Times: ʿUlama' in the Middle East*, ed. Meir Hatina (Leiden: Brill, 2008), 57.

10. Muhammad Qasim Zaman, *Religion and Politics under the Early ʿAbbāsids: The Emergence of the Proto-Sunnī Elite* (Leiden: Brill, 1997), 83–84.

11. Al-Mawardi, *The Ordinances of Government* [*Al-Aḥkām al-Sulṭāniyya w'al-Wilāyāt al-Dīniyya*], trans. Wafaa H. Wahba (London: Garnet, 1996), 16.

12. al-Misri, *Reliance of the Traveller*, 639, 646–7.

13. Asifa Quraishi, "The Separation of Powers in the Tradition of Muslim Governments," in Grote and Röder, *Constitutionalism in Islamic Countries*, 63, 72.

14. Zubaida, *Law and Power in the Islamic World*, 79.

15. Baber Johansen, *Contingency in a Sacred Law: Legal and Ethical Norms in the Muslim Fiqh* (Leiden: Brill, 1999), 69–70.

16. Kerr, *Islamic Reform*, 8.

17. Lawrence Rosen, *The Anthropology of Justice: Law and Culture in Islamic Society* (Cambridge: Cambridge University Press, 1989), 61.

18. Johansen, *Contingency in a Sacred Law*, 212–13.

19. Jackson, *Islamic Law and the State*, 192, 226, 213.

20. Fadel, "Islamic Law Reform, 79.

21. Zubaida, *Law and Power in the Islamic World*, 79, 51, 43.

22. Aharon Layish, "Islamic Law in the Modern World: Nationalization, Islamization, Reinstatement," *Islamic Law and Society* 21 (2014): 295.

23. Clark B. Lombardi, *State Law as Islamic Law in Modern Egypt: The Incorporation of the Sharī'a into Egyptian Constitutional Law* (Leiden: Brill, 2006), 49.

24. Imam Ibn Taymiyyah, *The Political Shariyah on Reforming the Ruler and the Ruled* (N.p.: dar ul fiqh, 2000), 244.

25. Lombardi, *State Law as Islamic Law*, 50.

26. Lombardi, *State Law as Islamic Law*, 50–53.

27. Quraishi, "Separation of Powers," 66–69.

28. Quraishi, "Separation of Powers," 70.

29. Quraishi, "Separation of Powers," 65, 70.

30. Sherman A. Jackson, "The Islamic Secular," *American Journal of Islamic Social Sciences* 34, no. 2 (2017): 1–38.

31. Fadel, "Islamic Law Reform," 50.

32. Fadel, "Islamic Law Reform," 49.

33. Lombardi, *State Law as Islamic Law*, 54.

34. Zubaida, *Law and Power in the Islamic World*, 104, 107, 111.

35. Ahmet T. Kuru, *Islam, Authoritarianism, and Underdevelopment: A Global and Historical Comparison* (Cambridge: Cambridge University Press, 2019); Zubaida, *Law and Power in the Islamic World*, 60, 103.

36. Zubaida, *Law and Power in the Islamic World*, 115.

37. Haim Gerber, *State, Society, and Law in Islam: Ottoman Law in Comparative Perspective* (Albany: State University of New York Press, 1994), 88–91.

38. Hallaq, however, emphasizes that the state's role in the Ottoman Empire remained "significantly marginal both as a legislator and as determinant of legal authority." Wael B. Hallaq, "Juristic Authority vs. State Power: The Legal Crises of Modern Islam," *Journal of Law and Religion* 19, no. 2 (2003–4): 255.

39. Rosen, *Anthropology of Justice*, 17, 60–61, 73–74.

40. Jackson, *Islamic Law and the State*, 96.

41. Jackson, *Islamic Law and the State*, xxx, 73, 76, 78, 108. Jackson also points out that, "contrary to the common assumption that *taqlīd* constitutes a decline to a more primitive stage of development, it is in this very process of legal scaffolding that a legal tradition reaches the height of innovative acumen." Jackson, *Islamic Law and the State*, 99.

42. al-Misri, *Reliance of the Traveller*, 22.

43. Khaled Abou El Fadl, "The Centrality of Sharīʿah to Government and Constitutionalism in Islam," in Grote and Röder, *Constitutionalism in Islamic Countries*, 57–61.

44. Zubaida, *Law and Power in the Islamic World*, 42–43.

45. Kenneth M. Cuno, *Modernizing Marriage: Family, Ideology, and Law in Nineteenth- and Early Twentieth-Century Egypt* (Syracuse, NY: Syracuse University Press, 2015), 125–26.

46. Jackson, *Islamic Law and the State*, xxv.

47. Jackson, *Islamic Law and the State*, xx.

48. Jackson, *Islamic Law and the State*, xx.

49. Jackson, *Islamic Law and the State*, 72.

50. Jackson, *Islamic Law and the State*, 72, xix.

51. Zubaida, *Law and Power in the Islamic World*, 64–65.

52. Cuno, *Modernizing Marriage*, 137, 123.

53. A. Chris Eccel, *Egypt, Islam and Social Change: Al-Azhar in Conflict and Accommodation* (Berlin: Klaus Schwarz Verlag, 1984), 133, 136–38.

54. Cuno, *Modernizing Marriage*, 146, 137.

55. Lombardi, *State Law as Islamic Law*, 15, 68–69.

56. Muhammad ʿAbduh, *The Theology of Unity: Risālat al-Tauḥīd*, trans. and ed. Isḥāq Musaʿad and Kenneth Cragg (Kuala Lumpur: Islamic Book Trust, 2004), 126.

57. ʿAbduh, "Theology of Unity," 127.

58. ʿAbduh, "Theology of Unity," 33–34.

59. Kerr, *Islamic Reform*, 165.

60. Simon A. Wood, *Christian Criticisms, Islamic Proofs: Rashid Rida's Modernist Defense of Islam* (Oxford: Oneworld, 2012), 203.

61. Anver M. Emon, "Shariʿa and the Modern State," in *Islamic Law and International Human Rights Law*, ed. Anver M. Emon, Mark S. Ellis, and Benjamin Glahn (Oxford: Oxford University Press, 2012), 61, 66.

62. Tariq al-Bishri, *Al-Wadʿ al-qanuni bayna al-shariʿa al-islamiyya wa-l-qanun al-wadʿi* [The legal foundation between the Islamic sharia and positive law] (Cairo: dar al-shuruq, 2005), 48.

63. al-Bishri, *Al-Wadʿ al-qanuni*, 48.

64. Benjamin Akzin, "Codification in a New State: A Case Study of Israel," *American Journal of Comparative Law* 5, no. 1 (Winter 1956): 50.

65. Zubaida, *Law and Power in the Islamic World*, 125.

66. Zubaida, *Law and Power in the Islamic World*, 123, 140.

67. Karen Barkey, *Empire of Difference: The Ottomans in Comparative Perspective* (Cambridge: Cambridge University Press, 2008), 292.

68. Messick, *Calligraphic State*, 56.

69. C. V. Findley, "Medjelle," in *The Encyclopaedia of Islam*, ed. P. Bearman et al., 2nd ed. (Leiden: Brill, 1991), 971–72.

70. Samy Ayoub, "The *Mecelle*, Sharia, and the Ottoman State: Fashioning and Refashioning of Islamic Law in the Nineteenth and Twentieth Centuries," *Journal of the Ottoman and Turkish Studies Association* 2, no. 1 (2015): 121–22.

71. Ayoub, "Mecelle," 122, 131.

72. Messick, *Calligraphic State*, 56.

73. Messick, *Calligraphic State*, 57.

74. Christina Jones-Pauly and Abir Dajani Tuqan, *Women under Islam: Gender, Justice and the Politics of Islamic Law* (London: I. B. Tauris, 2011), 111.

75. Agostino Cilardo, "Muhammad Qadri Pasha al-Hanafi," in *The Oxford International Encyclopedia of Legal History*, ed. Stanley N. Katz (Oxford: Oxford University Press, 2009), https://www.oxfordreference.com/view/10.1093/acref/9780195134056.001.0001/acref-9780195134056-e-561?print.

76. Cuno, *Modernizing Marriage*, 170–71.

77. Leonard Wood, *Islamic Legal Revival: Reception of European Law and Transformations in Islamic Legal Thought in Egypt, 1875–1952* (Oxford: Oxford University Press, 2016), 28.

78. Rudolph Peters, "Islamic and Secular Criminal Law in Nineteenth Century Egypt: The Role and Function of the Qadi," *Islamic Law and Society* 4, no. 1 (1997): 78.

79. Iza R. Hussin, *The Politics of Islamic Law: Local Elites, Colonial Authority, and the Making of the Muslim State* (Chicago: University of Chicago Press, 2016), 166.

80. Kenneth M. Cuno, "Disobedient Wives and Neglectful Husbands: Marital Relations in the First Phase of Family Law Reform in Egypt," in *Family, Gender and Law in a Globaliazing Middle East and South Asia*, ed. Kenneth M. Cuno and Manisha Desai (Syracuse, NY: Syracuse University Press, 2009), 4.

81. Nathan J. Brown, *The Rule of Law in the Arab World: Courts in Egypt and the Gulf* (Cambridge: Cambridge University Press, 1997), 8.

82. Brown, *Rule of Law in the Arab World*, 57.

83. L. Wood, *Islamic Legal Revival*, 4.

84. L. Wood, *Islamic Legal Revival*, 47, 29.

85. L. Wood, *Islamic Legal Revival*, 42.

86. Jones-Pauly and Tuqan, *Women under Islam*, 111.

87. Zubaida, *Law and Power in the Islamic World*, 133.

88. Cuno, *Modernizing Marriage*, 158.

89. Muhammad Rashid Rida, "Renewal, Renewing, and Renewers," in Kurzman, *Modernist Islam*, 82–83. However, Elgawhary argues that Rida did not support codification of the law but its consolidation. Tarek A. Elgawhary, "Restructuring Islamic Law: The Opinions of the *'Ulamā'* towards Codification of Personal Status Law in Egypt" (PhD diss., Princeton University, 2014), 133.

90. Brown, *Rule of Law in the Arab World*, 58.

91. Asad, *Formations of the Secular*, 215.

92. Brown, *Rule of Law in the Arab World*, 32–33.

93. Kerr, *Islamic Reform*, 16, 218.

94. Mohammad Fadel, "Judicial Institutions, the Legitimacy of Islamic State Law and Democractic Transition in Egypt: Can a Shift toward a Common Law Model of Adjudication Improve the Prospects of a Successful Democratic Transition?," *International Journal of Constitutional Law* 11, no. 3 (2013): 653.

95. Fadel, "Judicial Institutions," 652.

96. Hussin, *Politics of Islamic Law*, 153.

97. Lev E. Weitz, *Between Christ and Caliph: Law, Marriage, and Christian Community in Early Islam* (Philadelphia: University of Pennsylvania Press, 2018), 7.

98. Weitz, *Between Christ and Caliph*, 10.

99. Weitz, *Between Christ and Caliph*, 96–98.

100. Weitz, *Between Christ and Caliph*, 43.

101. Weitz, *Between Christ and Caliph*, 28.

102. Peter L. Strauss, ed., *The Fetha Nagast: The Law of Kings*, trans. Abba Paulos Tzadua (Durham, NC: Carolina Academic Press, 2009).

103. Niyazi Berkes, *The Development of Secularism in Turkey* (Montreal: McGill University Press, 1964), 95–96.

104. Berkes, *Development of Secularism in Turkey*, 97–98, 109, 132, 147.

105. Isaac S. Shiloh, "Marriage and Divorce in Israel," *Israel Law Review* 5, no. 4 (1970): 480; Zeina Ghandour, "Religious Law in a Secular State: The Jurisdiction of the Sharīʿa Courts of Palestine and Israel," *Arab Law Quarterly* 5, no. 1 (1990): 29–30.

106. Janet Halley and Kerry Rittich, "Critical Directions in Comparative Family Law: Genealogies and Contemporary Studies of Family Law Exceptionalism," *American Journal of Comparative Law* 58, no. 4 (Fall 2010): 755.

107. Findley, "Medjelle," 971–72; Berkes, *Development of Secularism in Turkey*, 169.

108. Berkes, *Development of Secularism in Turkey*, 170–71.

109. Jamal J. Nasir, *The Islamic Law of Personal Status* (The Hague: Kluwer Law International, 2002), 34.

110. Elgawhary, "Restructuring Islamic Law," 34.

111. Asad, *Formations of the Secular*, 211.

112. Cuno, *Modernizing Marriage*, 185–204.

113. Kerr, *Islamic Reform*, 216.

114. Elgawhary, "Restructuring Islamic Law," 38, 45, 80.

115. Muhammad ʿAbduh, "Laws Should Change in Accordance with the Conditions of Nations and the Theology of Unity," in Kurzman, *Modernist Islam*, 52–53.

116. ʿAbduh, "Laws Should Change," 52–53.

117. Elgawhary, "Restructuring Islamic Law," 166.

118. Elgawhary, "Restructuring Islamic Law," 217.

119. Cuno, *Modernizing Marriage*, 183.

120. Brown, *Rule of Law in the Arab World*, 62. Brown argues that Islamic modernists, along with liberals, nationalists, and socialists, did not object to the idea of bringing these personal status courts into a single unified legal structure (64).

121. Ron Shaham, "Jews and the Sharīʿa Courts in Modern Egypt," *Studia Islamica* 82 (1995): 121.

122. Nadav Safran, "The Abolition of Sharʿī Courts in Egypt," *Muslim World* 48 (1958): 21.

123. Safran, "Abolition of Sharʿī Courts in Egypt," 21–22.

124. Safran, "Abolition of Sharʿī Courts in Egypt," 21.

125. Hallaq, "Juristic Authority vs. State Power," 243.

126. L. Wood, *Islamic Legal Revival*, 5.

127. Fahmy, *In Quest of Justice*, 117–23.

128. L. Wood, *Islamic Legal Revival*, 48, 58, 5.

129. L. Wood, *Islamic Legal Revival*, 5.

130. L. Wood, *Islamic Legal Revival*, 47.

131. Kerr, *Islamic Reform*, 195–96.

132. Kerr, *Islamic Reform*, 185, 200.

133. Hussin, *Politics of Islamic Law*, 35.

134. Hussin, *Politics of Islamic Law*, 32–33.

135. Hussin, *Politics of Islamic Law*, 37.

136. al-Qaradawi, *Min fiqh al-dawla*, 13, 18.

137. al-Qaradawi, *Min fiqh al-dawla*, 19–20.

138. al-Qaradawi, *Min fiqh al-dawla*, 31.

139. al-Qaradawi, *Min fiqh al-dawla*, 51.

140. Armando Salvatore, "After the State: Islamic Reform and the 'Implosion' of *shari'a*," in *Muslim Traditions and Modern Techniques of Power*, ed. Armando Salvatore (Münster: Lit Verlag, 2001), 128.

141. Salvatore, "After the State," 128.

142. Salvatore, "After the State," 128.

143. Salvatore, "After the State," 123, 128, 130.

144. Salvatore, "After the State," 135n9.

145. Lombardi, *State Law as Islamic Law*, 60.

146. Salvatore, "After the State," 128.

147. An-Na'im, *Islam and the Secular State*, 7.

148. An-Na'im, *Islam and the Secular State*, 7.

149. An-Na'im, *Islam and the Secular State*, 1.

150. An-Na'im, *Islam and the Secular State*, 18.

151. Rutherford, *Egypt after Mubarak*, 106.

152. Tariq al-Bishri, *Bayn al-jami'a al-diniyya wa-l-jami'a al-wataniyya fi al-fikr al-siyasi* [Between the religious community and the national community in political thought] (Cairo: dar al-shuruq, 1998), 34.

153. Tariq al-Bishri, *Al-Muslimun wa-l-aqbat fi 'itar al-jama'a al-wataniyya* [Muslims and Copts in the framework of national community] (Cairo: dar al-shuruq, 1988), 681.

154. al-Bishri, *Al-Muslimun wa-l-aqbat*, 681, 706.

155. al-Bishri, *Bayn al-jami'a al-diniyya*, 35.

156. al-Bishri, *Al-Muslimun wa-l-aqbat*, 688, 705–6.

157. Tariq al-Bishri, interview by author, Cairo, 2003.

158. "Hizb al-hurriya wa-l-'adala: Hadha al-barnamij" [Freedom and Justice Party: This program], November 2011.

159. "Hizb al-hurriya wa-l-'adala."

160. Kuru, *Islam, Authoritarianism, and Underdevelopment*, 3–4.

3. Constitution Making in Egypt

1. Cited in Ziad Fahmy, *Ordinary Egyptians: Creating the Modern Nation through Popular Culture* (Stanford, CA: Stanford University Press, 2011), 134.

2. Ergun Özbudun, *The Constitutional System of Turkey: 1876 to the Present* (New York: Palgrave Macmillan, 2011), 3.

3. Article 1 of the Ottoman Constitution of 1876 asserted that the empire was indivisible. R. H. Davison, "Tanẓīmāt," in *The Encyclopaedia of Islam*, ed. P. Bearman et al. (Leiden: Brill, 2000), 208.

4. The Ottoman Constitution (1876).

5. The Ottoman Constitution (1876).

6. Al-Dustur al-masri li-sanat 1882.

7. Brown, *Constitutions in a Nonconstitutional World*, 31–32.

8. Such a perspective holds that the Khedive Muhammad 'Ali (1769–1849) played a key role in the development of Egyptian nationalism. It argues that Muhammad 'Ali

founded a dynasty that was to rule Egypt until 1952 and started a process of modern-
ization that laid the foundations for the development of the modern Egyptian state.
Afaf Lutfi Al-Sayyid Marsot, *A Short History of Modern Egypt* (Cambridge: Cambridge
University Press, 1994), 53.

9. Khaled Fahmy, *All the Pasha's Men: Mehmed Ali, His Army and the Making of
Modern Egypt* (Cairo: American University in Cairo Press, 2002).

10. Will Hanley, *Identifying with Nationality: Europeans, Ottomans, and Egyptians in
Alexandria* (New York: Columbia University Press, 2017), 238–40.

11. Nathan J. Brown, "Islam in Egypt's Cacophonous Constitutional Order," in
Arjomand and Brown, *Rule of Law, Islam, and Constitutional Politics*, 236.

12. Brown, *Constitutions in a Nonconstitutional World*, 32–33. This was partly
because European powers encouraged enhancing the power of the state rather than
limiting it (62).

13. Hanley, *Identifying with Nationality*, 294.

14. Mervat F. Hatem, "The Pitfalls of the Nationalist Discourses on Citizenship,"
in *Gender and Citizenship in the Middle East*, ed. Suad Joseph (Syracuse, NY: Syracuse
University Press, 2000), 33.

15. Hatem, "Pitfalls of the Nationalist Discourses on Citizenship," 38.

16. Hasan al-Banna, "Risalat al-mu'tamar al-khamis" [Message of the fifth confer-
ence], in *Wikibidia al-ikhwan al muslimin* (ikhwanwiki.com, 1939).

17. al-Banna, "Risalat al-mu'tamar al-khamis."

18. Hasan al-Banna, *Majmu'at rasa'il al-imam al-shahid Hasan al-Banna* [The collection of tracts of the martyr Imam Hasan al-Banna] (Alexandria: dar al-da'wa li-l-tabi'
wa-l-nashr wa-l-tawzi', 2002), 188–90.

19. B. L. Carter, *The Copts in Egyptian Politics* (London: Croom Helm, 1986),
130–31.

20. Dustur misr li-sanat 1923.

21. Brown, *Constitutions in a Nonconstitutional World*, 180–81.

22. Brown, "Islam in Egypt's Cacophonous Constitutional Order," 236.

23. al-Banna, *Majmu'at rasa'il al-imam al-shahid Hasan al-Banna*, 188–89.

24. Samir Marcos, *Al-Akhar . . . al-hiwar . . . al-muwatana* [The other . . . dialogue . . .
citizenship] (Cairo: maktabat al-shuruq al-dawliyya, 2005), 166.

25. Carter, *Copts in Egyptian Politics*, 290, 299.

26. Paul Sedra, "Copts and the Millet Partnership: The Intra-Communal Dynamics behind Egyptian Sectarianism," *Journal of Law and Religion* 29, no. 3 (2014): 496–97.

27. Carter, *Copts in Egyptian Politics*, 303.

28. Carter, *Copts in Egyptian Politics*, 131.

29. Dustur jumhurriyat misr (1956).

30. Dustur jumhurriyat misr (1956).

31. Hatem, "Pitfalls of the Nationalist Discourses on Citizenship," 48.

32. Brown, *Constitutions in a Nonconstitutional World*, 79.

33. Brown, *Rule of Law in the Arab World*, 76.

34. Hatem, "Pitfalls of the Nationalist Discourses on Citizenship," 48.

35. Dustur jumhurriyat misr (1956).

36. Dustur jumhurriyat misr (1956).

37. Hatem, "Pitfalls of the Nationalist Discourses on Citizenship," 48.

38. Hatem, "Pitfalls of the Nationalist Discourses on Citizenship," 48.

39. Hatem, "Pitfalls of the Nationalist Discourses on Citizenship," 53.

40. Brown, *Constitutions in a Nonconstitutional World*, 80.

41. Dustur jumhurriyat misr al-ʿarabiyya li-sanat 1971.

42. Dawood I. Ahmed and Tom Ginsburg, "Constitutional Islamization and Human Rights: The Surprising Origin and Spread of Islamic Supremacy in Constitutions," *Virginia Journal of International Law* 54, no. 3 (2013): 59–60, University of Chicago Public Law Working Paper No. 477.

43. Brown, *Constitutions in a Nonconstitutional World*, 82.

44. Dustur jumhuriyyat misr al-ʿarabiyya li-sanat 1971.

45. Dustur jumhuriyyat misr al-ʿarabiyya li-sanat 1971.

46. Nathan J. Brown, "The Transition: From Mubarak's Fall to the 2014 Presidential Election," in Hokayem, *Egypt after the Spring*, 18.

47. Brown, "Transition," 20.

48. "'We Do Unreasonable Things Here': Torture and National Security in Al-Sisi's Egypt."

49. Preuss, "Constitutional Powermaking," 148, 160.

50. After the suspension of the 1971 Constitution, there was also a protracted initial debate about whether it should be amended. In March 2011, the Supreme Council of Armed Forces held a constitutional referendum about amending some articles of the 1971 Constitution. While the referendum was passed with 77 percent of the votes, with Islamists supporting it, opponents insisted that the revolution had ousted not only Mubarak but also the constitution itself and that the constitution had helped facilitate his authoritarian rule. Less than two weeks after the referendum, the Supreme Council of the Armed Forces announced a Constitutional Declaration of sixty-three articles which effectively superseded the 1971 Constitution. The Constitutional Declaration laid out the constitutional framework that would govern Egypt until a new constitution was declared. Kristen Stilt, "The End of 'One Hand': The Egyptian Constitutional Declaration and the Rift between the 'People' and the Supreme Council of Armed Forces," *Yearbook of Islamic and Middle Eastern Law* 16 (2010–11): 46–48.

51. Stilt, "End of 'One Hand,'" 46.

52. Amina Shafiq, "We Need the Constitution First," *Al-Ahram Weekly*, no. 1055, July 7–13, 2011.

53. Shafiq, "We Need the Constitution First."

54. Maged Amani, "Whose Principles?," *Al-Ahram Weekly*, no. 1061, August 18–24, 2011.

55. Amani, "Whose Principles?"

56. "Musawwada ʿilan al-mabadi' al-asasiyya li-dustur al-dawla al-misriyya al-haditha" [Draft of the declaration of fundamental principles for the constitution of the modern Egyptian state), November 1, 2011.

57. "Musawwada ʿilan al-mabadi' al-asasiyya."

58. "Musawwada ʿilan al-mabadi' al-asasiyya."

59. According to Rowe, eight Copts were elected to the People's Assembly in 2012, all representing liberal opposition, several of whom were put on the Constituent Assembly. He argues that "Coptic participation in the legislature contributed to a sense of optimism, in spite of the general suspicion that ordinary Copts felt for the Islamist movements." Paul S. Rowe, "Church-State Relations in the 'New Egypt,'" in *Decentering Discussions on Religion and State: Emerging Narratives, Challenging*

Perspectives, ed. Sargon George Donabed and Autumn Quezada-Grant (Lanham, MD: Lexington Books, 2015), 223.

60. Al-Ali, "New Egyptian Constitution."

61. Sultany, *Law and Revolution*, 313.

62. "Egypt: New Constitution Mixed on Support of Rights," Human Rights Watch, November 30, 2012.

63. Saad and El Fegiery, "Citizenship in Post-Awakening Egypt," 5–6.

64. Layish, "Islamic Law in the Modern World," 298.

65. Yasser El-Shimy, "The Muslim Brotherhood," in Hokayem, *Egypt after the Spring*, 76.

66. "Hilary Clinton Email Archive" (WikiLeaks, 2012), Doc no. C05796154, November 26, 2012.

67. "Hilary Clinton Email Archive" (WikiLeaks, 2012), Doc no. C05796437, November 28, 2012.

68. The Coptic intellectual Samir Marcos also resigned his post as assistant to the president. Rowe, "Church-State Relations in the 'New Egypt,'" 224–25.

69. "Egypt Churches Withdraw from Morsi's National Dialogue," *ahramonline*, January 24, 2013.

70. El-Shimy, "Muslim Brotherhood," 90.

71. Patrick Kingsley, "How Mohamed Morsi, Egypt's First Elected President, Ended Up on Death Row," *Guardian*, June 1, 2015.

72. Sarah Childress, "The Deep State: How Egypt's Shadow State Won Out," *PBS*, September 17, 2013.

73. Kingsley, "How Mohamed Morsi."

74. El-Shimy, "Muslim Brotherhood," 91.

75. Brown, "Transition," 22–23.

76. Sultany, *Law and Revolution*, xxvii.

77. Al-Ali, "New Egyptian Constitution."

78. Masooda Bano, "At the Tipping Point? Al-Azhar's Growing Crisis of Moral Authority," *International Journal of Middle East Studies* 50, no. 4 (2018): 722, 715.

79. Fathiyya al-Dukhakhni, "Al-Ri'asa: Lajnat al-50 satadim murashshahin islamiyyin wa wahidan li-l-jaysh wa 3 li-l-kanisa wa 3 li-l-Azhar" [The leadership: The committee of 50 will include Islamist candidates, one for the army, 3 for the church and 3 for al-Azhar], *al-Masri al-yawm*, August 7, 2013.

80. Sultany, *Law and Revolution*, 251.

81. Zeinab Abul-Magd, "The Military," in Hokayem, *Egypt after the Spring*, 65–66.

82. Brown, "Transition," 28.

83. Dustur jumhurriyat misr al-'arabiyya li-sanat 1971.

84. Sayyid Qutb, *Fi zilal al-Qur'an* [In the shade of the Qur'an] (Beirut: dar al-shuruq, 2001), 2:828–29.

85. Qutb, *Fi zilal al-Qur'an*, 1:562.

86. Sayyid Qutb, *Hadha al-din* (Kuwait: maktabat al-faysal, 1989), 18–19.

87. Qutb, *Hadha al-din*, 19.

88. Ahmed and Ginsburg, "Constitutional Islamization and Human Rights," 18.

89. Ahmed and Ginsburg, "Constitutional Islamization and Human Rights," 22, 61–63.

90. Brown, "Islam in Egypt's Cacophonous Constitutional Order," 237–38.

91. Adel Omar Sherif, "The Relationship between the Constitution and the Sharī'ah in Egypt," in Grote and Röder, *Constitutionalism in Islamic Countries*, 126.

92. Sherif, "Relationship between the Constitution and the Sharī'ah in Egypt," 126.

93. Sherif, "Relationship between the Constitution and the Sharī'ah in Egypt," 126, 133.

94. Brown, *Rule of Law in the Arab World*, 98n9.

95. Brown, *Rule of Law in the Arab World*, 125–26.

96. Brown, *Constitutions in a Nonconstitutional World*, 148–49.

97. Lombardi, *State Law as Islamic Law*, 183.

98. Tamir Moustafa, *The Struggle for Constitutional Power: Law, Politics and Economic Development in Egypt* (Cambridge: Cambridge University Press, 2007), 107.

99. Adel Omar Sherif, "Commentary: Shari'a as Rule of Law," in *Islamic Law and International Human Rights Law*, ed. Anver M. Emon, Mark S. Ellis, and Benjamin Glahn (Oxford: Oxford University Press, 2012), 116.

100. Lombardi, *State Law as Islamic Law*, 141. By the early 1990s, Tamir Moustafa argues, the Supreme Constitutional Court become an important institution and worked to overturn economic policies from the Nasser era, strengthen property rights, curtail executive power, and protect civil society groups. Moustafa, *Struggle for Constitutional Power*, 118, 93, 17.

101. Moustafa, *Struggle for Constitutional Power*, 108–10.

102. Lombardi, *State Law as Islamic Law*, 158.

103. Lombardi, *State Law as Islamic Law*, 5–6. Bruce Rutherford argues that, while the Egyptian judiciary has advocated for liberal reform and liberal constitutionalism, it is "more comfortable with a powerful and invasive state than classical liberals." Rutherford, *Egypt after Mubarak*, 55.

104. Lombardi, *State Law as Islamic Law*, 179.

105. Lombardi, *State Law as Islamic Law*, 188, 199–200, 205.

106. Nathan J. Brown and Clark B. Lomdardi, "Contesting Islamic Constitutionalism after the Arab Spring: Islam in Egypt's Post-Mubarak Constitutions," in Grote and Röder, *Constitutionalism, Human Rights and Islam*, 258.

107. Fadel, "Judicial Institutions," 657, 664.

108. Lombardi, *State Law as Islamic Law*, 49.

109. Sherif, "Commentary: Shari'a as Rule of Law," 116–17.

4. The Ulama, Religious Authority, and the State

1. Muhammad al-Ghazali, *Al-Islam wa-l-awda' al-iqtisadiyya* [Islam and the economic conditions] (Cairo: dar al-kitab al-'arabi bi misr, 1952), 15.

2. Muhammad al-Ghazali, *Min huna na'lam . . . !* [From here we learn] (Cairo: nahdat misr, 2006), 100.

3. al-Ghazali, *Al-Islam wa-l-awda' al-iqtisadiyya*, 127.

4. Taqi ad-Din Ibn Taymiyyah, *Ibn Taymiyyah Expounds on Islam: Selected Writings of Shaykh al-Islam Taqi ad-Din Ibn Taymiyyah on Islamic Faith, Life, and Society*, trans. Muhammad Abdul-Haqq Ansari (Riyadh: Imam Muhammad Ibn Saud University, 2000), 509, 516–17.

5. Kuru, *Islam, Authoritarianism, and Underdevelopment*, 4.

6. Daniel Crecelius, "Nonideological Responses of the Egyptian Ulama to Modernization," in *Scholars, Saints, and Sufis: Muslim Religious Institutions since 1500*, ed. Nikki R. Keddie (Berkeley: University of California Press, 1978), 183.

7. "Qanun raqm 103 li-sanat 1961 bi-sha'n i'adat tanthim al-Azhar wa-l-hay'at allati yashmilha" [Law no. 103 of year 1961 on the issue of the reorganization of al-Azhar and the institutions that are included with it], *al-Jarida al-rasmiyya*, no. 153, July 10, 1961.

8. Tamir Moustafa, "Conflict and Cooperation between the State and Religious Institutions in Contemporary Egypt," *International Journal of Middle East Studies* 32, no. 1 (2000): 5.

9. Hasan Al-Banna', *Six Tracts of Hasan Al-Bana': A Selection from the Majmū'at Rasā'il al-Imām al-Shahīd Hasan al-Bannā'*. (Accra, Ghana: Africaw, 2006), 142.

10. 'Abd al-Mun'im Abu al-Futuh, interview by author, Cairo, 2008.

11. Fahmi Huwaydi, interview by author, Cairo, 2007.

12. Muhammad Shahat al-Gindi, interview by author, Cairo, 2008.

13. Jonathan P. Berkey, "Madrasas Medieval and Modern: Politics, Education, and the Problem of Muslim Identity," in Hefner and Zaman, *Schooling Islam*, 55–56; Muhammad Qasim Zaman, *The Ulama in Contemporary Islam: Custodians of Change* (Princeton, NJ: Princeton University Press, 2002), 2.

14. Malika Zeghal, "Religion and Politics in Egypt: The Ulema of Al-Azhar, Radical Islam, and the State (1952–94)," *International Journal of Middle East Studies* 31, no. 3 (1999): 372, 388.

15. Malika Zeghal, "The 'Recentering' of Religious Knowledge and Discourse: The Case of al-Azhar in Twentieth-Century Egypt," in Hefner and Zaman, *Schooling Islam*, 108.

16. Moustafa, "Conflict and Cooperation," 3.

17. Nathan J. Brown, "Post-Revolutionary Al-Azhar," in *The Carnegie Papers* (Washington DC: Carnegie Endowment for International Peace, 2011), 7–8.

18. Ibrahim Najm, interview by author, Cairo, 2008; 'Abd al-Mu'ti al-Bayyumi, interview by author, Cairo, 2008; Ahmed al-Tayyib, interview by author, Cairo, 2008.

19. Brown and Lombardi, "Contesting Islamic Constitutionalism," 255.

20. The Muslim Brotherhood, "Barnamij al-Hizb" [Party program] (Cairo, 2007): 10–11.

21. Layish, "Islamic Law in the Modern World, 298.

22. 'Abd al-Hamid al-Ghazali, interview by author, Cairo, 2008; 'Issam al-'Aryan, interview by author, Cairo, 2008.

23. 'Abd al-Mun'im Abu al-Futuh, interview by author, Cairo, 2008.

24. Ahmed al-Tayyib, "Wathiqat al-Azhar bi sha'n mustaqbal misr" [The document of al-Azhar on the future of Egypt], June 6, 2011.

25. al-Tayyib, "Wathiqat al-Azhar."

26. al-Tayyib, "Wathiqat al-Azhar."

27. al-Tayyib, "Wathiqat al-Azhar."

28. al-Tayyib, "Wathiqat al-Azhar." The Senior Scholars' Council was established in 1911 and then abolished in the early 1960s. The organization was reestablished in 2012.

29. Assem Hefny, "Religious Authorities and Constitutional Reform: The Case of al-Azhar in Egypt," in Grote and Röder, *Constitutionalism, Human Rights and Islam*, 102.

30. al-Tayyib, "Wathiqat al-Azhar."

31. Brown, "Post-Revolutionary Al-Azhar," 13.

32. "Al-Majlis al-'ala li-l-quwat al-musallaha marsum bi-qanun raqm 13 li-sanat 2012" [The Supreme Council of Armed Forces Decree no. 13 of the year 2012], *al-Jarida al-rasmiyya* 3, January 19, 2012.

33. "Al-Majlis al-'ala li-l-quwat al-musallaha."

34. "Al-Majlis al-'ala li-l-quwat al-musallaha."

35. "Al-Majlis al-'ala li-l-quwat al-musallaha."

36. "Qirar ra'is majlis al-wuzara' raqm 501 li-sanat 2013" [Decision of the prime minister no. 501 of 2013], *al-Jarida al-rasmiyya*, May 21, 2013.

37. Michael Wahid Hanna, "Egypt's Non-Islamist Parties," in Hokayem, *Egypt after the Spring*, 107, 113.

38. Faraj, *Min kawalis al-dustur*, 212; Carrie Rosefsky Wickham, *The Muslim Brotherhood: Evolution of an Islamist Movement* (Princeton, NJ: Princeton University Press, 2013), 271.

39. Dustur jumhuriyyat misr al-'arabiyya (2012).

40. David Kirkpatrick, *Into the Hands of the Soldiers: Freedom and Chaos in Egypt and the Middle East* (New York: Penguin, 2018), 181.

41. Fadel, "Judicial Institutions," 664.

42. Dustur jumhuriyyat misr al-'arabiyya (2012).

43. Dustur jumhuriyyat misr al-'arabiyya (2012).

44. Hasan al-Shafi'i, interview by author, Cairo, 2013.

45. Hasan al-Shafi'i, interview by author.

46. Wickham, *Muslim Brotherhood*, 271.

47. "Hizb al-hurriya wa-l-'adala: Hadha al-barnamij" [Freedom and Justice Party: This program], November, 2011.

48. "Hizb al-hurriya wa-l-'adala."

49. "Hizb al-hurriya wa-l-'adala."

50. Dustur jumhuriyyat misr al-'arabiyya (2012).

51. Dustur jumhuriyyat misr al-'arabiyya (2012).

52. The law was submitted to the Shura Council because the Supreme Council of Armed Forces had dissolved the People's Assembly in June 2012.

53. "'Al-Buhuth al-islamiyya' yafrid mushru' 'al-sukuk al-islamiyya' li-'khaturathi 'ala siyada al-dawla' ['The Islamic Research Academy' rejects the 'law of the Islamic sukuk' because it 'endangers the state']," *al-Masri al-yawm*, January 1, 2013.

54. "Tusa'id al-khilafat hawla qanun al-sukuk al-islamiyya fi misr [Disagreement mounts over the law of Islamic sukuk in Egypt], *Akhir al-akhbar*, January 20, 2013.

55. 'Issam al-'Aryan, "Al-'Aryan: Al-Barlaman huwa sahib al-tashri' wa-l-Azhar haya mustaqila" [al-'Aryan: Parliament is the responsible for legislation and al-Azhar is an independent organization], YouTube, February 10, 2013.

56. Rafiq Habib, "Al-Azhar wa-l-ikhwan: Al-sira'a al-muftarad 'ala al-marji'iyya" [Al-Azhar and the brotherhood: The struggle over the frame of reference], in *Tahawwulat al-dawla wa-l-mujtama'a ba'ad al-rabi'a al-'arabi* [Transformations of the state and society after the Arab Spring], April 2013, https://rafikhabib.blogspot.com/2013/04/blog-post_28.html?m=0, 5.

57. Maher 'Abd al-Wahid, "Jibhat al-difa' 'an al-Azhar taltaqi bi-'al-Tayyib' al-yawm" [The front for the defense of al-Azhar meets with al-Tayyib today], *al-Yawm al-sabi'*, January 16, 2013.

58. "Jibhat al-difa' 'an al-Azhar min aswan: Al-jibhat hiyya ihda khatwat inqadh misr" [The front for the defense of al-Azhar in Aswan: The front is one of the steps for saving Egypt], *al-Dustur*, May 17, 2013.

59. Habib, "Al-Azhar wa-l-ikhwan," 7.

60. "Sukuk Law in State of Flux until Al-Azhar Review," *Egypt Independent*, April 4, 2013.

61. Habib, "Al-Azhar wa-l-ikhwan," 1–12.

62. Habib, "Al-Azhar wa-l-ikhwan," 8, 11.

63. "Mursi yuqi' qanun al-sukuk li-inqadh iqtisad misr al-muta'athir [Mursi brings about the sukuk law to save the ailing Egyptian economy], *al-'Arabiyya*, May 9, 2013.

64. Mansour, 'Adly, "'Ilan dusturi" [Constitutional declaration], *al-Jarida al-rasmiyya*, No. 27, July 8, 2013.

65. Jayson Casper, "Safwat al-Bayādī: Negotiating Religion in the Constitutional Committee," *Arab-West Report*, December 27, 2013.

66. Dustur jumhuriyyat misr al-'arabiyya (2014).

67. Dustur jumhuriyyat misr al-'arabiyya (2014).

68. Ahmed al-Tayyib, interview by author, Cairo, 2008.

69. Agrama, *Questioning Secularism*, 35, 131–44.

70. Agrama, *Questioning Secularism*, 144.

71. Agrama, *Questioning Secularism*, 35.

72. Agrama, *Questioning Secularism*, 120.

73. Agrama, *Questioning Secularism*, 142.

74. Hallaq, "Juristic Authority vs. State Power," 250.

75. al-Ghazali, *Min huna na'lam . . . !*, 103.

76. Indira Falk Gesink, *Islamic Reform and Conservatism: Al-Azhar and the Evolution of Modern Sunni Islam* (London: I. B. Tauris, 2009), 9.

77. Zubaida, *Law and Power in the Islamic World*, 102. Ibn Taymiyyah accuses many people—by implication, the ulama—of being dominated solely by "din (religion)" and of turning away from the very affairs of the world which help establish that "din." Ibn Taymiyyah, *Political Shariyah*, 256.

78. While the Fatwa Council is not free from the authority of the state, it is not an institution associated with state power and law in the way that the personal status courts are even though Agrama states that both "are products of modern reforms and both are institutions under the state and "both are based in the Shari'a." Agrama, *Questioning Secularism*, 90. One important feature of the Fatwa Council is that the muftis there combined all four schools of law, "not only in the traditional Azhari sense that all four of them were taught alongside and recognized one another, but also to the extent that the *madhāhib* were cooperating and actually giving fatwas and making decisions jointly." Jakob Skovgaard-Petersen, *Defining Islam for the Egyptian State: Muftis and Fatwas of the Dār al-Iftā* (Leiden: Brill, 1997), 154. Thus, the Fatwa Council has a stronger connection with the tradition of the four schools of law than the Personal Status Courts do.

79. Kuru, *Islam, Authoritarianism, and Underdevelopment*, 3.

80. Bruce K. Rutherford, "Surviving under Rule by Law: Explaining Ideological Change in Egypt's Muslim Brotherhood during the Mubarak Era," in Arjomand and Brown, *Rule of Law, Islam, and Constitutional Politics*, 255.

81. ʿAbd al-Khaliq al-Sharif, interview by author, Cairo, 2013.

82. ʿAbd al-Khaliq al-Sharif, interview by author.

83. Rowe, "Church-State Relations in the 'New Egypt,'" 225.

84. Habib, "Al-Azhar wa-l-ikhwan," 5, 11.

85. Habib, "Al-Azhar wa-l-ikhwan," 11–12.

86. Habib, "Al-Azhar wa-l-ikhwan," 4.

87. Habib, "Al-Azhar wa-l-ikhwan," 4.

88. Muhammad Salim al-ʿAwwa, *Azmat al-muʾassasa al-diniyya* (The crisis of the religious establishment] (Cairo: dar al-shuruq, 2003), 8.

89. al-ʿAwwa, *Azmat al-muʾassasa al-diniyya*, 22, 29–30.

90. Rutherford, *Egypt after Mubarak*, 112.

91. Muhammad Salim al-ʿAwwa, *Al-Haqq fi al-taʿbir* [The right of expression] (Cairo: dar al-shuruq, 1998), 35.

92. al-ʿAwwa, *Al-Haqq fi al-taʿbir*, 35.

93. Hasan al-Shafiʿi, interview by author, Cairo, 2013.

94. Hasan al-Shafiʿi, interview by author.

95. Hasan al-Shafiʿi, interview by author.

96. Muhammad ʿAbd al-Fadil al-Qusi and al-Qasabi Mahmud Zalat, interview by author, Cairo, 2013.

97. al-Qusi and Zalat, interview by author.

98. Muhammad ʿAbd al-Fadil al-Qusi, *Ruʾiyya islamiyya fi qadaya al-ʿasr* [An Islamic perspective on the issues of the time] (Cairo: dar al-Islam, 2012), 102–3, 151.

99. al-Qusi, *Ruʾiyya islamiyya*, 151.

100. al-Qusi, *Ruʾiyya islamiyya*, 152.

101. Nathan J. Brown and Michele Dunne, "Egypt's Draft Constitution Rewards the Military and Judiciary," *Carnegie Endowment for International Peace*, December 4, 2013.

102. Gesink, *Islamic Reform and Conservatism*, 49. For most of the Ottoman period, the Shafiʿi school was dominant, followed by the Maliki, and then the Hanafi. The Hanbali school was given a small representation. Bayard Dodge, *Al-Azhar: A Millennium of Muslim Learning* (Washington, DC: Middle East Institute, 1961), 116.

103. Ahmed al-Tayyib, interview by author, Cairo, 2008.

104. By the 1860s, more Azhari students were registering as Hanafis than had previously been the case. Gesink, *Islamic Reform and Conservatism*, 52. By 1902 the Hanafi school of law had come to roughly equal that of the Maliki school in terms of professorial representation, although the Shafiʿi school was still dominant. Dodge, *Al-Azhar*, 137. In 1911 the institution of the Senior Scholars' Council and the Islamic Research Academy were established. In both, all four schools were represented, but the Hanafi school was given the greater representation. Dodge, *Al-Azhar*, 142; Eccel, *Egypt, Islam and Social Change*, 202.

105. In the 1930s, the shaykh of al-Azhar, Muhammad al-Zawahiri, lamented the lack of studies that compared all the schools of law, and in 1950 the shaykh of al-Azhar established a committee for the rapprochement between the schools of law. Eccel, *Egypt, Islam and Social Change*, 151, 452, 271, 438.

106. "Al-Majlis al-'ala li-l-quwat al-musallaha."

107. Habib, "Al-Azhar wa-l-ikhwan," 11.

108. Ibrahim El-Houdaiby, "The Identity of Al-Azhar and Its Doctrine," *Jadaliyya*, July 29, 2012.

109. I. El-Houdaiby, "Identity of Al-Azhar."

110. I. El-Houdaiby, "Identity of Al-Azhar."

111. Rosen, *Anthropology of Justice*, 63.

112. Jackson, "Islamic Secular," 1–38.

113. John Locke, *Two Treatises of Government and a Letter concerning Toleration*, ed. Ian Shapiro (New Haven, CT: Yale University Press, 2003), 215.

114. Locke, *Two Treatises of Government*, 218.

115. Locke, *Two Treatises of Government*, 218.

116. Winnifred Fallers Sullivan, *The Impossibility of Religious Freedom* (Princeton, NJ: Princeton University Press, 2005), 138.

117. "Sukuk law in state of flux until al-Azhar review."

118. Mohamed Salah, "Sukuk Law to Be Deliberated by Shura Council, Wednesday," *Daily News Egypt*, February 19, 2013.

119. Gamal 'Abd al-Sattar, interview by author, Cairo, 2013.

120. Gamal 'Abd al-Sattar, interview by author.

121. 'Abd al-Hamid al-Ghazali, interview by author, Cairo, 2008.

122. 'Abd al-Hamid al-Ghazali, interview by author.

123. 'Abd al-Mu'ti al-Bayyumi, interview by author, Cairo, 2008.

124. Ibrahim Najm, interview by author, Cairo, 2008.

5. The "Divinely Revealed Religions"

1. Dustur jumhuriyyat misr al-'arabiyya (2014).

2. Dustur jumhuriyyat misr al-'arabiyya (2012).

3. Mahmood, *Religious Difference in a Secular Age*, 2.

4. Mahmood, *Religious Difference in a Secular Age*, 1–2, 15.

5. Mahmood, *Religious Difference in a Secular Age*, 4.

6. Mahmood, *Religious Difference in a Secular Age*, 22.

7. Anver M. Emon, *Religious Pluralism and Islamic Law: Dhimmīs and Others in the Empire of Law* (Oxford: Oxford University Press, 2012), 3.

8. Emon, *Religious Pluralism and Islamic Law*, 7, 18.

9. The introduction of the term "millet" in the nineteenth century projected this level of systematization back onto Ottoman history. The Ottomans argued that the three officially sanctioned millets had been the tradition since the second reign of Mehmed II (1451–81). Bernard Lewis, *The Jews of Islam* (Princeton, NJ: Princeton University Press, 1984), 126.

10. Benjamin Braude, "Foundation Myths of the *Millet* System," in Braude and Lewis, *Christians and Jews*, 1:74.

11. Barkey, *Empire of Difference*, 116.

12. Kemal Karpat, "*Millets* and Nationality: The Roots of the Incongruity of Nation and State in the Post-Ottoman Era," in Braude and Lewis, *Christians and Jews*, 141–42.

13. Barkey, *Empire of Difference*, 115.

14. N. J. Pantazopoulos, *Church and Law in the Balkan Peninsula during the Ottoman Rule* (Thessaloniki: Institute for Balkan Studies, 1967), 92:24–25.

15. Barkey, *Empire of Difference*, 151, 137, 141.

16. Lewis, *The Jews of Islam*, 125–27.

17. Avigdor Levy, introduction to Levy, *Jews of the Ottoman Empire*, 106.

18. Avigdor Levy, "*Millet* Politics: The Appointment of a Chief Rabbi in 1835," in Levy, *Jews of the Ottoman Empire*, 434.

19. Bruce Masters, *Christians and Jews in the Ottoman Arab World: The Roots of Sectarianism* (Cambridge: Cambridge University Press, 2001), 108.

20. Davison, "Tanẓīmāt," 203.

21. A. H. Hourani, *Minorities in the Arab World* (London: Oxford University Press, 1947), 21.

22. Masters, *Christians and Jews in the Ottoman Arab World*, 61–62.

23. Magdi Guirguis, "The Organization of the Coptic Community in the Ottoman Period," in Hanna and Abbas, *Society and Economy in Egypt and the Eastern Mediterranean*, 201.

24. Magdi Guirguis and Nelly van Doorn-Harder, *The Emergence of the Modern Coptic Papacy: The Egyptian Church and Its Leadership from the Ottoman Period to the Present* (Cairo: American University in Cairo Press, 2011), 9; Febe Armanios, *Coptic Christianity in Ottoman Egypt* (Oxford: Oxford University Press, 2011), 23.

25. Barkey, *Empire of Difference*, 110.

26. Amnon Cohen, "On the Realities of the *Millet* System: Jerusalem in the Sixteenth Century," in Braude and Lewis, *Christians and Jews*, 2:14–15.

27. Aaron W. Hughes, *Abrahamic Religions: On the Uses and Abuses of History* (New York: Oxford University Press, 2012), 3.

28. Davison, "Tanẓīmāt," 204.

29. "Rescript of Reform—Islahat Fermani" (Istanbul: Boğaziçi University, Atatürk Institute of Modern Turkish History, 1856).

30. Davison, "Tanẓīmāt," 202, 204.

31. Davison, "Tanẓīmāt," 202. For example, the first lay Jewish community in Alexandria was established in 1840. Jacob M. Landau, *Jews in Nineteenth-Century Egypt* (New York: New York University Press, 1969), 52.

32. Davison, "Tanẓīmāt," 202. The loss of control over education was opposed by the *millets*. Berkes, *Development of Secularism in Turkey*, 108.

33. Shaham, "Jews and the Sharīʿa Courts in Modern Egypt," 118.

34. Berkes, *Development of Secularism in Turkey*, 95–96.

35. "Rescript of Reform—Islahat Fermani."

36. Berkes, *Development of Secularism in Turkey*, 152.

37. Karpat, "*Millets* and Nationality," 164.

38. "Rescript of Reform—Islahat Fermani."

39. "Rescript of Reform—Islahat Fermani."

40. Karpat, "*Millets* and Nationality," 163, 144.

41. Maurits Berger, "Public Policy and Islamic Law: The Modern *Dhimmī* in Contemporary Egyptian Family Law," *Islamic Law and Society* 8, no. 1 (2001): 92.

42. George N. Sfeir, "The Abolition of Confessional Jurisdiction in Egypt: The Non-Muslim Courts," *Middle East Journal* 10, no. 3 (1956): 250n2.

43. Shaham, "Jews and the Sharīʿa Courts in Modern Egypt," 119.

44. Hourani, *Minorities in the Arab World*, 41.

45. Carter, *Copts in Egyptian Politics*, 231.

46. From the early twentieth century on, the state attempted to control and restrict religious authority. During the 1930s, the Egyptian government sometimes required each community to codify and publish the procedural and substantive rules that it applied. The Rabbinate courts of Alexandria and Damanhur and the Karaite court in Cairo did not do this and lost state authorization. Shaham, "Jews and the Sharī'a Courts in Modern Egypt," 121–12.

47. Emon, *Religious Pluralism and Islamic Law*, 5.

48. Mahmood, *Religious Difference in a Secular Age*, 153.

49. Mahmood, *Religious Difference in a Secular Age*, 153.

50. Mahmood, *Religious Difference in a Secular Age*, 7n14.

51. Yaron Friedman, "Ibn Taymiyya's Fatāwā against the Nuṣayrī-'Alawī Sect," *Der Islam: Journal of the History and Culture of the Middle East* 82, no. 2 (2005): 349–63.

52. Hourani, *Minorities in the Arab World*, 20.

53. Barkey, *Empire of Difference*, 163.

54. Nabil Al-Tikriti, "Ibn-i Kemal's Confessionalism and the Construction of an Ottoman Islam," in *Living in the Ottoman Realm: Empire and Identity, 13th to 20th Centuries*, ed. Christine Isom-Verhaaren and Kent. F. Schull (Bloomington: Indiana University Press, 2016), 102–3.

55. Necati Alkan, "Fighting for the Nuṣayrī Soul: State, Protestant Missionaries and the 'Alawīs in the Late Ottoman Empire," *Die Welt des Islams* 52 (2012): 25–26.

56. Under the British mandate, the legal authorities extended the legal nonexistence of the Druze by declining to define them as a religious community. In 1957 the Israeli government recognized the Druze as forming a religious community. Ghandour, "Religious Law in a Secular State," 37–39.

57. Necati Alkan, *Dissent and Heterodoxy in the Late Ottoman Empire: Reformers, Babis and Bahai'is* (Piscataway, NJ: Gorgias Press, 2009), 44.

58. Alkan, "Fighting for the Nuṣayrī Soul," 27.

59. Alkan, "Fighting for the Nuṣayrī Soul," 32–33.

60. Alkan, "Fighting for the Nuṣayrī Soul," 31.

61. Zubaida, *Law and Power in the Islamic World*, 139.

62. Alkan "Fighting for the Nuṣayrī Soul," 43.

63. Emon, *Religious Pluralism and Islamic Law*, 19.

64. Michel Rosenfeld, "Modern Constitutionalism as Interplay between Identity and Diversity," in Rosenfeld, *Constitutionalism, Identity, Difference, and Legitimacy*, 28.

65. Hatem, "Pitfalls of the Nationalist Discourses on Citizenship," 35–36.

66. Hatem, "Pitfalls of the Nationalist Discourses on Citizenship," 36.

67. S. S. Hasan, *Christians versus Muslims in Modern Egypt: The Century-Long Struggle for Coptic Equality* (New York: Oxford University Press, 2003), 260–61.

68. Salvatore, "After the State," 135.

69. Hatem, "Pitfalls of the Nationalist Discourses on Citizenship," 37.

70. Sebastian Elsässer, *The Coptic Question in the Mubarak Era* (Oxford: Oxford University Press, 2014), 33.

71. Elsässer, *Coptic Question*, 33.

72. Milak Tamir Mikha'il, *Al-Qada' al-milli wa-l-ahwal al-shakhsiyya 'ind al-aqbat al-misriyyin* [The milli judge and personal status law for Coptic Egyptians] (Giza: dar fikra li-l-nashr wa al-tawzi'a, 2019), 6, 14.

73. Nabil Luqa Bibawi, *'Adam dusturiyyat qanun al-ahwal al-shakhsiyya al-mutabbiq 'ala al-misihiyyin* [The personal status laws for Christians are unconstitutional] (Cairo: dar al-bibawi li-l-nashr, 2004), 23–35.

74. Nushin Atmaca, "Article II in the Debate about Constitutional Amendments in 2007," in *The Sharia as the Main Source of Legislation? The Egyptian Debate on Article II of the Egyptian Constitution*, ed. Cornelis Hulsman (Marburg: Tectum Verlag, 2012), 188, 192–93.

75. Atmaca, "Article II," 197.

76. Atmaca, "Article II," 196–7.

77. Atmaca, "Article II," 197.

78. Rachel M. Scott, "Islamic law, Unitary State law, and Communal Law: Divorce and Remarriage in Egypt's Coptic Community," *Exchange: Journal of Contemporary Christianity in Context* 4, no. 4 (2020), 215–236.

79. Dustur jumhuriyyat misr al-'arabiyya (2012).

80. Dustur jumhuriyyat misr al-'arabiyya (2012).

81. Dustur jumhuriyyat misr al-'arabiyya li-sanat 1971.

82. Supreme Administrative Court, December 16, 2006, No. 16834/18971, Year 52. However, in 2008 an Administrative Court ruling gave Baha'is a small concession and allowed them to leave the religion box on their identity cards empty or to put a dash in it.

83. Paul Sedra, "Copts and the Power over Personal Status," *Jadaliyya*, December 3, 2012.

84. Nader Shukry, "Churches Applaud Second Article," *Watani*, July 13, 2012. Initially, the clauses had been proposed to form part of Article 2.

85. Mariz Tadros, "Vicissitudes in the Entente between the Coptic Orthodox Chruch and the State in Egypt (1952–2007)," *International Journal of Middle East Studies* 41 (2009): 271.

86. Sedra, "Copts and the Millet Partnership, 491.

87. Samir Marcos, interview by author, Cairo, 2007.

88. Samir Marcos and Vivian Fouad, "Our Experience Dialogue Based on Citizenship," in *Al-Akhar . . . al-hiwar . . . al-muwatana* [The other . . . dialogue . . . citizenship], by Samir Marcos (Cairo: maktabat al-shuruq al-dawliyya, 2005), 156.

89. Marcos and Fouad, "Our Experience Dialogue Based on Citizenship," 161.

90. Mariz Tadros, *Copts at the Crossroads: The Challenges of Building Inclusive Democracy in Contemporary Egypt* (Cairo: American University in Cairo Press, 2013), 119.

91. Angie Heo, *The Political Lives of Saints: Christian-Muslim Mediation in Egypt* (Oakland: University of California Press, 2018), 12.

92. Nathalie Bernard-Maugiron, "Divorce and Remarriage of Orthodox Copts in Egypt: The 2008 State Council Ruling and the Amendment of the 1938 Personal Status Regulations," *Islamic Law and Society* 18 (2011).

93. Ishak Ibrahim, "Personal Affairs Law for Christians: The Responsibility of the Church, the State, and Individuals," *Eshhad*, October 6, 2015.

94. Paul S. Rowe, "Christian-Muslim Relations in Egypt in the Wake of the Arab Spring," *Digest of Middle East Studies* 22, no. 2 (Fall 2013): 264.

95. Youssef Sidhom, "Why Say 'Yes' to the Constitution," *Watani*, December 14, 2013.

96. al-Ghazali, *Min huna na'lam . . . !*, 119–21; Muhammad 'Imara, *Samahat al-Islam* [The tolerance of Islam] (Cairo: al-falah, 2002), 32; Muhammad Salim al-'Awwa, *Fi al-nitham al-siyasi li-l-dawla a-islamiyya* [On the political system of the Islamic state] (Cairo: dar al-shuruq, 1989), 249.

97. Muhammad M. Al-Hudaibi, *The Principles of Politics in Islam* (Cairo: Islamic Inc., 2000), 28–30.

98. "Hizb al-hurriya wa-l-'adala: Hadha al-barnamij."

99. "Hizb al-hurriya wa-l-'adala: Hadha al-barnamij."

100. Juan Cole, "Rashid Rida and the Baha'i Faith—a Utilitarian Theory of the Spread of Religions," *Arab Studies Quarterly* 5, no. 3 (Summer 1983): 280.

101. Johanna Pink, "A Post-Qur'anic Religion between Apostasy and Public Order: Egyptian Muftis and Courts on the Legal Status of the Bahā'ī Faith," *Islamic Law and Society* 10, no. 3 (2003): 409.

102. Pink, "Post-Qur'anic Religion," 418.

103. Cole, "Rashid Rida and the Baha'i Faith," 281–82, 289.

104. Pink, "Post-Qur'anic Religion," 428, 432.

105. Jadd al-Haqq 'Ali Jadd al-Haqq, "Zawaj al-baha'i min al-muslima batil" [The marriage of a Baha'i and a Muslim woman is invalid], *al-Fatawa al-islamiyya min dar al-ifta' al-misriyya* 8, no. 23 (1982): 2999.

106. al-Haqq, "Zawaj al-Baha'i min al-muslima batil," 2999–3002.

107. al-Haqq, "Zawaj al-Baha'i min al-muslima batil," 2999.

108. Pink, "Post-Qur'anic Religion," 428, 432.

109. Muhammad Habib, interview by author, Cairo, 2007.

110. Shoghi Effendi, *God Passes By* (Haifa: Bahá'í Reference Library, 1944), 191.

111. Effendi, *God Passes By*, 192.

112. Effendi, *God Passes By*, 192.

113. "News of Other Lands—Egypt," *Bahá'í News*, no. 175, June 1945.

114. Noha El-Hennawy, "The Fourth Faith?," *Egypt Today*, September 2006.

115. "News of Other Lands—Egypt," *Bahá'í News*, no. 181, March 1946.

116. Effendi, *God Passes By*, 193.

117. "Messages from the Guardian," *Bahá'í News*, no. 160, February 1943.

118. Effendi, *God Passes By*, 192.

119. "Fifteenth Annual Convention of Bahá'ís of Egypt," *Bahá'í News*, no. 134, March 1940.

120. Effendi, *God Passes By*, 192.

121. Effendi, *God Passes By*, 193.

122. "News of Other Lands—Egypt," *Bahá'í News*, no, 173, February 1945.

123. "News of Other Lands—Egypt," *Bahá'í News*, no. 175, June 1945.

124. There were reports of anti-Bahá'í sentiment which made Bahá'ís reluctant to go out of doors. "Persecutions in Egypt," *Bahá'í News*, no. 104, December 1936. And an important Baha'i book was banned in 1942. "From Haifa News Letter," *Bahá'í News*, no. 151, February 1942. Also see "News of Other Lands—Egypt," *Bahá'í News*, no. 178, December 1945.

125. N. El-Hennawy, "Fourth Faith?"

126. Pink, "Post-Qur'anic Religion," 422–23.

127. Karima Kamal, *Talaq al-aqbat* [Divorce of the Copts] (Cairo: dar al-mirit, 2006), 165.

128. Court of Cassation, January 17, 1979, No. 26/16, Year 48

129. Pink, "Post-Qur'ānic Religion," 423.

130. Pink, "Post-Qur'ānic Religion," 428.

131. Al-Sayyid, "Rule of Law, Ideology, and Human Rights," 217.

132. El-Hennawy, "Fourth Faith?"

133. El-Hennawy, "Fourth Faith?"

134. Dustur jumhurriyat misr al-ʿarabiyya li-sanat 1971.

135. Supreme Administrative Court, December 16, 2006, No. 16834/18971, Year 52.

136. The concept of the divinely revealed religions did not figure prominently in how the Ottoman Empire distinguished among its religious minorities in the Constitution of 1876.

137. Tadros, *Copts at the Crossroads*, 120.

138. Amani Maged, "Whose Principles?," *Al-Ahram Weekly*, August 18–24, 2011.

139. al-Tayyib, "Wathiqat al-Azhar."

140. Youssef Sidhom, "A Snare of a Constitution," *Watani*, January 30, 2013.

141. Sidhom, "Snare of a Constitution."

142. Mansour, "'Ilan dusturi."

143. Cornelis Hulsman and Diana Serôdio, "Interview with Human Rights Lawyer Mona Zulficar about the Constitution," *Arab-West Report*, August 5, 2014.

144. Hulsman and Serôdio, "Interview with Human Rights Lawyer Mona Zulficar."

145. Yosra El-Gendi, "What Do the Copts Want in the Constitution?," *Arab-West Report*, October 1, 2013.

146. Yosra El-Gendi, "Bishop Bola: Church Does Not Wish to Amend Article 3," *Arab-West Report*, September 29, 2013; El-Gendi, "What Do the Copts Want in the Constitution?"

147. Jayson Casper, "Safwat al-Bayādī: Negotiating Religion in the Constitutional Committee," *Arab-West Report*, December 27, 2013.

148. Nader Shukry, "The Nuances of Writing a Constitution," *Watani*, December 14, 2013.

149. Sabri ʿAbd al-Hafiz, "Al-Islamiyyin: Mada bi-l-dustur tabih zawaj al-mithliyyin wa ʿibadat al-shaytan" [The Islamists: An Article of the Constitution Would Allow the Marriage of Homosexuals and Satan Worshippers], *Elaph*, September 25, 2013.

150. Hulsman and Serôdio, "Interview with Human Rights Lawyer Mona Zulficar."

151. Dustur jumhuriyyat misr al-ʿarabiyya (2014).

152. Dustur jumhuriyyat misr al-ʿarabiyya (2014).

153. Dustur jumhuriyyat misr al-ʿarabiyya (2014).

154. Moustafa Rahuma, "Mudhakkirat al-kanisa li-ʿAmr Moussa" (The church's memorandum to ʿAmr Moussa), *al-Watan*, November 10, 2013.

155. Sedra, "Copts and the Power over Personal Status."

156. El-Gendi, "What Do the Copts Want in the Constitution?"

157. El-Gendi, "What Do the Copts Want in the Constitution?"

158. H. H. Pope Shenouda III, *The Heresy of Jehovah's Witnesses* (Baramous: Monastery Press, 1997).

6. The Family Is the Basis of Society

1. Khaled Diab, "Egypt's Draft Constitution Leans towards Conservative Islam," *Guardian*, October 23, 2012.

2. Al-Ali, "New Egyptian Constitution."

3. While the entire media and press did not voice these positions, the non-Islamist press, which in Egypt represents the majority of the press, voiced these narratives. It is the views of the non-Islamist press that have the most influence on media in the West.

4. Asad, *Formations of the Secular*, 227.

5. John Witte Jr., *From Sacrament to Contract: Marriage, Religion, and Law in the Western Tradition* (Louisville, KY: Westminster John Knox Press, 2012), 9.

6. Witte, *From Sacrament to Contract*, 310.

7. Mounira M. Charrad, *States and Women's Rights: The Making of Postcolonial Tunisia, Algeria, and Morocco* (Berkeley: University of California Press, 2001), 32.

8. Charrad, *States and Women's Rights*, 28–29.

9. al-Misri, *Reliance of the Traveller*, books L and M.

10. William J. Goode, *World Revolution and Family Patterns* (London: Collier-Macmillan, 1963), 2, 7.

11. Cuno, *Modernizing Marriage*, 11–12, 39, 207. Leslie Pierce suggests that, in sixteenth-century Ottoman-controlled Aintab, polygamy was not widespread. Leslie Pierce, *Morality Tales: Law and Gender in the Ottoman Court of Aintab* (Berkeley: University of California Press, 2003), 229.

12. Leila Ahmed, *Women and Gender in Islam: Historical Roots of a Modern Debate*. New Haven, CT: Yale University Press, 1992.

13. Laura Bier, *Revolutionary Womanhood: Feminisms, Modernity, and the State in Nasser's Egypt* (Stanford, CA: Stanford University Press, 2011), 42.

14. Muhammad Rashid Rida, "Renewal, Renewing, and Renewers," in Kurzman, *Modernist Islam*, 78.

15. Rida, "Renewal, Renewing, and Renewers," 78.

16. Ellen Anne McLarney, *Soft Force: Women in Egypt's Islamic Awakening* (Princeton, NJ: Princeton University Press, 2015), 7.

17. McLarney, *Soft Force*, 12.

18. Mahmood, *Religious Difference in a Secular Age*, 14.

19. Mahmood, *Religious Difference in a Secular Age*, 21.

20. Weitz, *Between Christ and Caliph*, 7, 43.

21. MacKinnon, "Gender in Constitutions," 397–98, 409.

22. Hala Kamal, "Inserting Women's Rights in the Egyptian Constitution: Personal Reflections," *Journal for Cultural Research* 19, no. 2 (2015): 152.

23. Dustur jumhurriyat misr (1956).

24. Dustur jumhurriyat misr (1956)

25. Bier, *Revolutionary Womanhood*, 6.

26. Bier, *Revolutionary Womanhood*, 104.

27. Dustur jumhurriyat misr al-'arabiyya li-sanat 1971.

28. Dustur jumhurriyat misr al-'arabiyya li-sanat 1971.

29. The Muslim Brotherhood, "Barnamij al-hizb" [Party program], (Cairo, 2007), 66.

30. H. Kamal, "Inserting Women's Rights in the Egyptian Constitution," 156.

31. H. Kamal, "Inserting Women's Rights in the Egyptian Constitution," 156.

32. Liav Orgad, "The Preamble in Constitutional Interpretation," *International Journal of Constitutional Law* 8, no. 4 (2010): 717, 738.

33. Orgad, "Preamble," 715.

34. Orgad, "Preamble," 715.

35. Dustur jumhuriyyat misr al-'arabiyya (2012).

36. Dustur jumhuriyyat misr al-'arabiyya (2012).

37. Dustur jumhuriyyat misr al-'arabiyya (2012).

38. Ellen McLarney, "Women's Rights in the Egyptian Constitution: (Neo)Liberalism's Family Values," *Jadaliyya*, May 22, 2013.

39. Muhammad M. Al-Hudaibi, *The Principles of Politics in Islam* (Cairo: Islamic Inc., 2000), 32.

40. Mohammed Mursi, "Dr. Morsi's Electoral Program—General Features of Nahda (Renaissance Project)," *Ikhwan Web*, April 28, 2012.

41. Mursi, "Dr. Morsi's Electoral Program."

42. McLarney, "Women's Rights in the Egyptian Constitution."

43. McLarney, "Women's Rights in the Egyptian Constitution."

44. "Egypt: New Constitution Mixed on Support of Rights," Human Rights Watch, November 30, 2012.

45. Jayson Casper, "Mirvat al-Tallāwī: Women's Rights in the Constitution," *Arab-West Report*, January 26, 2014.

46. Dustur jumhuriyyat misr al-'arabiyya (2012).

47. Omar Ali, "June Forum Meeting: A Comparative Analysis of the 2012 & 2014 Egyptian Constitutions by Diana Serôdio," *Arab-West Report*, July 9, 2014.

48. Faraj, *Min kawalis al-dustur*, 175.

49. "Egypt: New Constitution Mixed on Support of Rights."

50. Casper, "Mirvat al-Tallāwī."

51. Al-Ali, "New Egyptian Constitution."

52. Al-Ali, "New Egyptian Constitution."

53. Nadia Sonneveld, "Introduction: *Shari'a* in Revolution? A Comparative Overview of Pre- and Post-Revolutionary Developments in *Shari'a*-Based Family Law Legislation in Egypt, Indonesia, Iran, and Tunisia," *New Middle Eastern Studies* 5 (2015): 9.

54. Mirvat al-Tallawi from the National Council for Women; 'Izzat Muhammad Sa'id al-'Ashmawi from the National Council for Motherhood and Childhood; Mona Zulficar, a human rights lawyer, from the National Council for Human Rights; and Hoda al-Sada.

55. Saad and El Fegiery, "Citizenship in Post-Awakening Egypt," 14.

56. Saad and El Fegiery, "Citizenship in Post-Awakening Egypt," 14.

57. Dustur jumhuriyyat misr al-'arabiyya (2014).

58. Dustur jumhuriyyat misr al-'arabiyya (2012).

59. Casper, "Mirvat al-Tallāwī."

60. Dustur jumhuriyyat misr al-'arabiyya (2014).

61. H. Kamal, "Inserting Women's Rights in the Egyptian Constitution," 159.

62. H. Kamal, "Inserting Women's Rights in the Egyptian Constitution," 159.

63. Mervat Ayoub, "The Turnout for the Referendum on the New Constitution Comes," *Watani*, January 24, 2014.

64. Cornelis Hulsman and Diana Serôdio, "Interview with Human Rights Lawyer Mona Zulficar."

65. Dustur jumhuriyyat misr al-ʿarabiyya (2012).

66. Casper, "Mirvat al-Tallāwī."

67. Hulsman and Serôdio, "Interview with Human Rights Lawyer Mona Zulficar."

68. Zeghal, "Competing Ways of Life," 265.

69. Moustafa, *Constituting Religion*, 14.

70. Moustafa, *Constituting Religion*, 14.

71. William T. Cavanaugh, *The Myth of Religious Violence: Secular Ideology and the Roots of Modern Conflict* (New York: Oxford University Press, 2009).

72. Cavanaugh, *Myth of Religious Violence*, 227.

73. Dustur jumhuriyyat misr al-ʿarabiyya (2012).

74. Youssef Sidhom, "Fixing the Constitution," *Watani*, January 19, 2013.

75. Sidhom, "Fixing the Constitution."

76. Sidhom, "Fixing the Constitution."

77. Sidhom, "Fixing the Constitution."

78. al-ʿAwwa, *Fi al-nitham al-siyasi*, 136.

79. al-ʿAwwa, *Fi al-nitham al-siyasi*, 137.

80. al-ʿAwwa, *Fi al-nitham al-siyasi*, 138.

81. al-ʿAwwa, *Fi al-nitham al-siyasi*, 139.

82. al-ʿAwwa, *Fi al-nitham al-siyasi*, 141.

83. al-ʿAwwa, *Fi al-nitham al-siyasi*, 141.

84. al-ʿAwwa, *Fi al-nitham al-siyasi*, 141–42.

85. al-Bishri, *Al-Wadʿ al-qanuni*, 48.

86. Dustur jumhuriyyat misr al-ʿarabiyya (2012).

87. Lombardi, *State Law as Islamic Law*, 53.

88. Lombardi, *State Law as Islamic Law*, 49.

89. Fadel, "Islamic Law Reform," 50.

90. Fadel, "Islamic Law Reform," 79, 81.

91. Cuno, *Modernizing Marriage*, 123–25.

92. Cuno, "Disobedient Wives and Neglectful Husbands," 17–18.

93. "Qanun raqm 1 li-sanat 2000 bi-isdar qanun tanthim baʿd awdaʿ wa ijraʾat al-taqadi fi masaʾil al-ahwal al-shakhsiyya" [Law no. 1 of the year 2000 promulgating the organization of the conventions and procedures for the litigation of matters of personal status], https://egypt.gov.eg/arabic/laws/personal/introduction.aspx, accessed June 16, 2020.

94. Muhammad Qasim Zaman, *Modern Islamic Thought in a Radical Age: Religious Authority and Internal Criticism* (New York: Cambridge University Press, 2012), 108.

95. Zaman, *Modern Islamic Thought in a Radical Age*, 109.

96. Deina Abdelkader, "Modernity, the Principles of Public Welfare (*maṣlaḥa*) and the End Goals of Sharīʿa (*maqāṣid*) in Muslim Legal Thought," *Islam and Christian-Muslim Relations* 14, no. 2 (2003): 170.

97. Abdelkader, "Modernity, the Principles of Public Welfare," 171–72.

98. Zaman, *Modern Islamic Thought in a Radical Age*, 108.

99. Majid Khadduri, "Maslaha," in *Encyclopaedia of Islam*, ed. P. Bearman et al., 2nd ed. (Leiden: Brill, 1991), 739.

100. Kerr, *Islamic Reform*, 196.

101. Muhammad al-Ghazali, *Al-Islam al-muftara ʿalayhi bayn al-shuyuʿyyin wa-l-ra'smaliyyin* [Islam between its communist and capitalist enemies] (Cairo: nahdat misr, 2006), 109.

102. al-Ghazali, *Al-Islam wa-l-awdaʿ al-iqtisadiyya*, 117.

103. al-Ghazali, *Al-Islam wa-l-awdaʿ al-iqtisadiyya*, 117.

104. Sari Hanafi and Azzam Tomeh, "Gender Equality in the Inheritance Debate in Tunisia and the Formation of Non-Authoritarian Reasoning," *Journal of Islamic Ethics* 3, nos. 1–2 (2019): 210, 216–17.

105. Muhammad Kafafi, "Nadwa bil-Saʿid" [A conference in Upper Egypt), *Misr al-ʿarabiyya*, May 18, 2016.

106. "Al-Qawmi li-l-mar'a" [The National Council for Women), *al-Bawaba News*, January 10, 2016; Muhammad Sharqawi, "Al-Qawmi li-l-mar'a" (The National Council for Women), *al-Yawm al-sabiʿa*, January 2, 2018.

107. Rutherford, *Egypt after Mubarak*, 57–58, 190–93.

7. Judicial Autonomy and Inheritance

1. Youssef Sidhom, "Eating Up a Woman's Inheritance," *Watani*, December 15, 2011.

2. Paul S. Rowe, "Neo-Millet Systems and Transnational Religious Movements: The *Humayun* Decrees and Church Construction in Egypt," *Journal of Church and State* 49, no. 2 (2007): 331; Fiona McCallum, "The Coptic Orthodox Church," in *Eastern Christianity and Politics in the Twentieth Century*, ed. Lucian N. Leustean (London, New York: Routledge, 2014), 521–541.

3. Lewis, *Jews of Islam*, 105–6.

4. Aryeh Shmuelevitz, *The Jews of the Ottoman Empire in the Late Fifteenth and the Sixteenth Centuries: Administrative, Economic, Legal and Social Relations as Reflected in the Responsa* (Leiden: Brill, 1984), 15–16.

5. Amnon Cohen, *Jewish Life under Islam: Jerusalem in the Sixteenth Century* (Cambridge, MA: Harvard University Press, 1984), 110.

6. Joseph R. Hacker, "Jewish Autonomy in the Ottoman Empire: Its Scope and Limits; Jewish Courts from the Sixteenth to the Eighteenth Centuries," in Levy, *Jews of the Ottoman Empire*, 160–73, 165–66.

7. Najwa al-Qattan, "*Dhimmis* in the Muslim Court: Documenting Justice in Ottoman Damascus, 1775–1860" (PhD diss., Harvard University, 1996), 150, 154–55, 163, 204, 347–48. Jennings also suggests that the frequency of *dhimmi* cases in the sharia courts in Kaysera, Central Anatolia, suggests that "they had no internal judicial apparatus of their own, or at least a very weak one." Ronald C. Jennings, "Zimmis (Non-Muslims) in Early 17th Century Ottoman Judicial Records: The Sharia Court of Anatolian Kayseri," *Journal of the Economic and Social History of the Orient* 21, no. 3 (1978): 271. It is not impossible, he argues, that Kayseri dhimmis "generally followed Islamic law in family matters, or that their traditional family law closely resembled that of the Muslims" (274).

8. Cohen, *Jewish Life under Islam*, 110, 126–27.

9. Shaham, "Jews and the Sharī'a Courts in Modern Egypt," 113.

10. Pantazopoulos, *Church and Law in the Balkan Peninsula*, 92:24, 54.

11. M. A. Ubicini, *Letters on Turkey: An Account of the Religious, Political, Social, and Commercial Condition of the Ottoman Empire*, trans. Lady Easthope (New York: Arno Press, 1973), 2:36.

12. Pantazopoulos, *Church and Law in the Balkan Peninsula*, 54, 93–99.

13. Antoine Fattal, *Le statut légal des non-musulmans en pays d'Islam* (Beirut: Imprimerie Catholique, 1958), 353–55.

14. Tamer el-Leithy, "Coptic Culture and Conversion in Medieval Cairo, 1293–1524 A.D." (PhD diss., Princeton University, 2005), 418.

15. Guirguis and van Doorn-Harder, *Emergence of the Modern Coptic Papacy*, 19.

16. Al-Qattan, "*Dhimmis* in the Muslim Court," 347; E. W. Lane, *Manners and Customs of the Modern Egyptians* (New York: Cosimo, 2005), 130–31.

17. Shmuelevitz, *Jews of the Ottoman Empire*, 43–44. Nevertheless, non-Muslim communities tried to stop their members from having recourse to the sharia courts. Shmuelevitz, *Jews of the Ottoman Empire*, 67. The Coptic pope Gabriel VII (1525–68) opposed Copts practicing polygamy by ordering the community to shun offenders. Guirguis and van Doorn-Harder, *Emergence of the Modern Coptic Papacy*, 19.

18. Richard Clogg, "The Greek *Millet* in the Ottoman Empire," in Braude and Lewis, *Christians and Jews*, 1:186–87.

19. Pantazopoulos, *Church and Law in the Balkan Peninsula*, 6, 19, 43–45, 56–57; Clogg, "Greek *Millet*," 186–87.

20. Hacker, "Jewish Autonomy in the Ottoman Empire," 183.

21. Ubicini, *Letters on Turkey*, 319.

22. Hacker, "Jewish Autonomy in the Ottoman Empire," 176–77.

23. Initially, the reform made this jurisdiction concurrent in Article 17 of the Khatti Humayun Decree of 1856. However, this shift from exclusive to concurrent jurisdiction encountered heated opposition from the heads of the religious minorities. As a result, the Ottoman authorities retreated and issued several decrees which restored to non-Muslim courts exclusive jurisdiction in most personal status affairs, including marriage, maintenance, divorce, and testate succession. Shaham, "Jews and the Sharī'a Courts in Modern Egypt," 118–19. This exclusive jurisdiction was formalized in the two *hautes circulaires* issued by the Sublime Porte in 1891 which rendered the jurisdiction of the Greek Orthodox and Armenian patriarchs compulsory and exclusive. Sfeir, "Abolition of Confessional Jurisdiction in Egypt," 249–50.

24. Magdi Guirguis, *Al-Qada' al-qibti fi misr: Dirasa ta'rikhiyya* [The Coptic judge in Egypt: A historical study] (Cairo: mirit, 1999), 58.

25. Carter, *Copts in Egyptian Politics*, 231.

26. Ron Shaham, "Shopping for Legal Forums: Christians and Family Law in Modern Egypt," in *Dispensing Justice in Islam: Qadis and Their Judgments*, ed. Muhammad Khalid Masud, Rudolph Peters, and David S. Powers (Leiden: Brill, 2005), 454.

27. Berkes, *Development of Secularism in Turkey*, 170.

28. Shaham, "Jews and the Sharī'a Courts in Modern Egypt," 131–32.

29. John L. Esposito, *Women in Muslim Family Law* (Syracuse, NY: Syracuse University Press, 1982), 41.

30. Judith E. Tucker, *Women, Family, and Gender in Islamic Law* (Cambridge: Cambridge University Press, 2008), 138.

31. These included endogamy, religious endowments, gifts, and debts as a way of directing wealth to favored heirs. When heirs were counted among the deceased's creditors, these debts had to be paid out of the estate before the distribution of the estate. Pascale Ghazaleh, "Heirs and Debtors: Blood Relatives, Qur'anic Heirs, and Business Associates in Cairo, 1800–50," in Hanna and Abbas, *Society and Economy in Egypt and the Eastern Mediterranean*, 146–52.

32. Fattal, *Le statut légal des non-musulmans en pays d'Islam*, 358, 140.

33. Fattal, *Le statut légal des non-musulmans en pays d'Islam*, 140–41.

34. Ottomans also confiscated inheritance of government employees when there was misuse of office, Fatma Müge Göçek, "Toward a Theory of Westernization and Social Change: Eighteenth and Nineteenth Century Ottoman Society" (PhD diss., Princeton University, 1988), 208n23.

35. Shmuelevitz, *Jews of the Ottoman Empire*, 77.

36. Cohen, *Jewish Life under Islam*, 62.

37. Cohen, *Jewish Life under Islam*, 133.

38. Shaham, "Jews and the Sharīʿa Courts in Modern Egypt," 117. Cohen argues that, while Jews in Jerusalem accepted the sharia laws for intestacy, circumventing the application of the sharia was contingent on a will. Cohen, *Jewish Life under Islam*, 133.

39. Shmuelevitz, *Jews of the Ottoman Empire*, 66.

40. However, according to Goitein, the situation was more egalitarian for Jews in Cairo between the tenth and the thirteenth centuries. Daughters receiving equal shares with sons was also common. S. D. Goitein, *A Mediterranean Society: The Jewish Communiites of the Arab World as Portrayed in the Documents of the Cairo Geniza*, vol. 3, *The Family* (Berkeley: University of California Press, 1978), 281, 287.

41. al-Qattan, "*Dhimmis* in the Muslim Court," 185.

42. Pantazopoulos, *Church and Law in the Balkan Peninsula*, 45, 56, 91–92.

43. Fathi Ragheb Hanna, "Ahkam wa qawaʿid al-mawarith wa-l-wasiya wafqan li-ahkam al-shariʿa al-misihiyya wa ahkam al-shariʿa al-islamiyya" [Rules and regulations of inheritance and testamentary disposition according to the rules of the Christian sharia and the Islamic sharia] (Bishop of Central Cairo Churches, 2015), 3; Youssef Sidhom, "Needed: Inheritance Law for Christians," *Watani*, February 7, 2015.

44. M. Berger, "Public Policy and Islamic Law," 95n24–25.

45. Goitein, *Mediterranean Society*, 3:280.

46. Goitein, *Mediterranean Society*, 3:277–78, 280–81.

47. Goitein, *Mediterranean Society*, 3:286.

48. Khalil Samir, "Al-Ṣafī Ibn Al-ʿAssāl," in *The Coptic Encyclopedia*, ed. Aziz S. Atiya (New York: Macmillan, 1991), 2076.

49. Peter L. Strauss, ed., *The Fetha Nagast: The Law of Kings*, trans. Abba Paulos Tzadua (Durham, NC: Carolina Academic Press 2009), 236–39. In Ethiopia, it is called the *Fetha Nagast*. The *Fetha Nagast* is a translation of al-ʿAssal's nomocanon via Geʿez Ethiopian Manuscripts.

50. Strauss, *Fetha Nagast*, 237.

51. El-Leithy, "Coptic Culture and Conversion in Medieval Cairo," 95–96.

52. El-Leithy, "Coptic Culture and Conversion in Medieval Cairo," 456. Youssef Sidhom, in a personal interview in 2007, stated that there is only evidence as far back

as the fourteenth and fifteenth centuries that the church dealt directly with inheritance. He states that Copts used Islamic inheritance law because they had not come up with an alternative, although it is more likely that Coptic inheritance law became increasingly influenced by Islamic inheritance law. Youssef Sidhom, interview by author, Cairo, 2007.

53. Guirguis and van Doorn-Harder, *Emergence of the Modern Coptic Papacy*, 8.

54. Guirguis and van Doorn-Harder, *Emergence of the Modern Coptic Papacy*, 8–9.

55. Carter, *Copts in Egyptian Politics*, 253.

56. Marcos and Fouad, "Our Experience Dialogue Based on Citizenship," 177.

57. F. Hanna, "Ahkam wa qawa'id al-mawarith," 3.

58. Sfeir, "Abolition of Confessional Jurisdiction in Egypt," 250.

59. Maurits S. Berger, "Secularizing Interreligious Law in Egypt," *Islamic Law and Society* 12, no. 3 (2005): 401.

60. Shaham, "Jews and the Sharī'a Courts in Modern Egypt," 118–19.

61. Sfeir, "Abolition of Confessional Jurisdiction in Egypt," 250. Sfeir's list mentions succession and wills but does not distinguish between testate and intestate succession; Shaham gives more details and makes it clear that the two were split with intestate succession being made a matter of concurrent jurisdiction. Shaham, "Jews and the Sharī'a Courts in Modern Egypt," 119.

62. Shaham, "Jews and the Sharī'a Courts in Modern Egypt," 118–19.

63. M. Berger, "Secularizing Interreligious Law in Egypt," 404.

64. Richard A. Debs, *Islamic Law and Civil Code: The Law of Property in Egypt* (New York: Columbia University Press, 2010), 90.

65. Nasir, *Islamic Law of Personal Status*, 35.

66. Carter, *Copts in Egyptian Politics*, 253.

67. Shaham, "Jews and the Sharī'a Courts in Modern Egypt," 120.

68. Shaham, "Jews and the Sharī'a Courts in Modern Egypt," 120–21.

69. This is even though in a 2000 ruling, the Supreme Constitutional Court stated that the 1938 bylaws were binding legal rules that were subject to constitutional control by the Supreme Constitutional Court. Supreme Constitutional Court, June 3, 2000, No. 151, Year 50.

70. "Nusus la'ihat al-ahwal al-shakhsiyya al-sadira 'an al-majlis al-milli al-'amm li-l-aqbat al-urthuduks" [The texts of the bylaws of the personal status law issued by the Coptic Orthodox Communal Council], in *Talaq al-aqbat* [Divorce of the Copts], by Karima Kamal (Cairo: dar al-mirit, 2006), 207–62.

71. Karima Kamal, *Talaq al-aqbat* [Divorce of the Copts] (Cairo: dar al-mirit, 2006), 165.

72. Court of Cassation, January 17, 1979, No. 26/16, Year 48.

73. Court of Cassation, June 19, 1963, No 40, Year 29.

74. Court of Cassation, May 27, 1964, No 17, Year 32.

75. M. Berger, "Public Policy and Islamic Law," 94–95.

76. M. Berger, "Secularizing Interreligious Law in Egypt," 406, 411, 413.

77. M. Berger, "Public Policy and Islamic Law," 119.

78. Court of Cassation, January 17, 1979, No. 26/16/, Year 48.

79. Dustur misr li-sanat 1923.

80. Court of Cassation, January 17, 1979, No. 26/16, Year 48.

81. Court of Cassation, January 17, 1979, No. 26/16, Year 48.

82. Court of Cassation, January 17, 1979, No. 26/16, Year 48.

83. M. Berger, "Public Policy and Islamic Law," 126, 129–30.

84. M. Berger, "Public Policy and Islamic Law," 128.

85. R. M. Scott, "Islamic Law, State Law, and Communal Autonomy."

86. "Qanun raqm 1 li-sanat 2000."

87. Jackson, *Islamic Law and the State*, 72.

88. Cornelius Hulsman, interview by author, Cairo, 2007.

89. Vivian Fu'ad, interview by author, Cairo, 2007.

90. Sidhom, "Needed: Inheritance Law for Christians."

91. There are similarities between this and Judith Tucker's description of the nineteenth century, where, she argues, Egyptian women were prevented from inheriting land. Judith E. Tucker, *Women in Nineteenth-Century Egypt* (Cambridge: Cambridge University Press, 1985), 47–49.

92. Youssef Sidhom, "Inheritance as Seen in the Bible," *Watani*, April 10, 2016.

93. Youssef Sidhom, interview by author, Cairo, 2007; Munir Fakhri 'Abd al-Nur, interview by author, Cairo, 2007.

94. Youssef Sidhom, "Towards Gender Equality in Inheritance: Tunisia Leads, Coptic Church Stands Still," *Watani*, September 17, 2017.

95. Sidhom, "Needed: Inheritance Law for Christians."

96. Marilyn 'Abd al-Malik, "Mirath al-aqbat: Al-dai' bayn al-shari'a wa-l-qanun" [The inheritance of Copts: Getting lost between the sharia and law], *al-Bawaba*, May 1, 2017.

97. 'Abd al-Malik, "Mirath al-aqbat."

98. F. Hanna, "Ahkam wa qawa'id al-mawarith," 4–5.

99. Najib Ghibrial, interview by author, Cairo, 2007.

100. Fadi Habashi, "Christians Claim Equality between Men and Women concerning Inheritance," *Arab-West Report (al-Fajr)*, April 10, 2006.

101. 'Abd al-Malik, "Mirath al-aqbat."

102. Youssef Sidhom, "Inheritance Rules Revisited," *Watani*, March 27, 2016.

103. F. Hanna, "Ahkam wa qawa'id al-mawarith," 1.

104. Bishop Thomas, interview by author, Anafora, 2007.

105. 'Abd al-Malik, "Mirath al-aqbat."

106. Bishop Thomas, interview by author, Anafora, 2007.

107. 'Abd al-Malik, "Mirath al-aqbat."

108. 'Abd al-Malik, "Mirath al-aqbat."

109. Guirguis Safwat, "Masadir kanisiyya: Hala jadaliyya jadida bi-sha'n qanun al-ahwal al-shakhsiyya" [Church sources: A new dispute over the question of personal status law], *al-Dustur*, July 23, 2018; Peter Majdi and Marina Milad, "Interview with the head of the Coptic Evangelical Church," *al-Tahrir*, May 21, 2016.

110. Guirguis Safwat, "Ba'd tawaqquf 6 ashhur . . . tafasil 'awdat harakat milaff al-ahwal al-shakhsiyya" [After a pause of six months . . . details on the return of the enterprise "the personal status file"], *al-Dustur*, June 19, 2018.

111. "Al-Nass al-kamil li-mashru' qanun al-ahwal al-shakhsiyya li-l-aqbat 2016 wa-l-la'iha al-dakhiliyya li-l-majlis al-iklirki" [The complete text of the 2016 draft of the personal status law for Copts and the internal bylaws for the Clerical Council]," ed. Faith Protectors Association-Rabitat Hamlat al-'Iman (Cairo, 2016), http://protectors-faith.com/?p=4532.

112. Youssef Sidhom, "Kudos for Tunisia," *Watani*, July 3, 2016.

113. Vivian Fuʿad, interview by author, Cairo, 2007; Youssef Sidhom, interview by author, Cairo, 2007.

114. Sidhom, "Inheritance Rules Revisited"; Munir Fakhri ʿAbd al-Nur, interview by author, Cairo, 2007.

115. Sidhom, "Inheritance as Seen in the Bible."

116. Bishop Thomas, interview by author, Anafora, 2007.

117. Sidhom, "Inheritance Rules Revisited."

118. K. Kamal, *Talaq al-aqbat*, 108; Karima Kamal, *Al-Ahwal al-shakhsiyya li-l-aqbat* [Coptic personal status law] (Cairo: dar nahdat misr, 2012), 8–9.

119. "Egyptian Woman Fights Unequal Islamic Inheritance Law," *al-Jazeera*, November 15, 2019.

120. ʿAbd al-Malik, "Mirath al-aqbat."

121. ʿAbd al-Malik, "Mirath al-aqbat."

122. Youssef Sidhom, "Secure Coptic Woman's Fair Share of Inheritance," *Coptic Solidarity*, January 15, 2017.

123. ʿAbd al-Malik, "Mirath al-aqbat."

124. "Nusus la'ihat al-ahwal al-shakhsiyya al-sadira."

125. ʿAbd al-Malik, "Mirath al-Aqbat."

126. "Nusus la'ihat al-ahwal al-shakhsiyya al-sadira."

127. Youssef Sidhom, "Court Ruling: Equal Inheritance for Men and Women," *Watani*, June 2, 2019.

128. "Mashruʿ qanun al-ahwal al-shakhsiyya al-mawahhid li-ʿamm 2018," in Mikha'il, *Al-Qada' al-milli*, 323–44.

129. "Egyptian Woman Fights Unequal Islamic Inheritance Law."

130. In the United States, when statutes and constitutional principles, such as the First Amendment (1791) to the Bill of Rights and the Religious Freedom Restoration Act of 1993, give special treatment to a religious action or organization, courts must be able to say what is religious. Winnifred Fallers Sullivan argues that, when the law has to make decisions about religion, lines must be drawn between what is religious and what is not. Addressing this is fraught with problems. Sullivan argues that the free exercise and disestablishment clauses overpromise what they cannot deliver, Winnifred Fallers Sullivan, *The Impossibility of Religious Freedom* (Princeton, NJ: Princeton University Press, 2005), 148.

131. Court of Cassation, May 10, 1972, No. 18 Year 39.

132. Bishop Marqus, interview by author, Cairo, 2007.

133. ʿAbd al-Malik, "Mirath al-aqbat."

134. ʿAbd al-Malik, "Mirath al-aqbat."

135. ʿAbd al-Malik, "Mirath al-aqbat."

136. Sidhom, "Inheritance as Seen in the Bible."

137. Sidhom, "Eating Up a Woman's Inheritance"; Sidhom, "Towards Gender Equality in Inheritance: Tunisia Leads, Coptic Church Stands Still."

138. Youssef Sidhom, "Constitution and Law Secure: Coptic Woman's Fair Share of Inheritance," *Watani*, January 15, 2017.

139. Youssef Sidhom, "Inheritance in Family Law for Christians," *Watani*, November 13, 2016.

140. ʿAbd al-Malik, "Mirath al-aqbat."

141. Youssef Sidhom, "A Woman's Inheritance," *Watani*, July 25, 2010.

142. Sidhom, "A Woman's Inheritance."

143. Samir Marcos, interview by author, Cairo, 2007.

144. Munir Fakhri ʿAbd Al-Nur, interview by author, Cairo, 2007.

145. Mustafa Rahuma, "'Al-Haqq fi al-hayat': Mashruʿ qanun al-injiliyyin li-l-ahwal al-shakhsiyya mukhalif li-l-dustur" [The right to life: The plan of the evangelicals for the law of personal state violates the constitution], *al-Watan*, January 21, 2017.

146. Yusam Ramadan, "Al-Baz: Ma al-maniʿ ʿan yakun li-dunya qanun yusawi bayn al-rajl wa-l-marʾa fi al-mirath?" [Al-Baz: What is preventing us from having a law that makes men and women equal in inheritance?], *al-Masri al-yawm*, August 13, 2018.

147. Mahmood ʿAbd al-Hamid, "Intifada barlamaniyya did daʿwat al-musawa fi al-mirath" [A parliamentary intifada against calls for equality in inheritance], *Ahl misr*, October 19, 2018.

Conclusion

1. Muhammad Bakr Iman al-Sanhuri, "'Hamrush': Mashruʿa qanun li-thahirat al-ilhad" [Hamrush: A proposal for a bill for the phenomenon of atheism], *al-Bawaba*, December 24, 2017.

2. Hanan Tawfiq, "Hayat kibar al-ʿulamaʾ: Al-Islam yuʿti al-haqq li-l-hakim fi iʿdam al-mulhid" [The Senior Scholars' Council: Islam gives the ruler the right to execute apostates], *Sada al-balad*, January 28, 2018.

3. Mohamed S. El-Awa (Muhammad Salim al-ʿAwwa), *Punishment in Islamic Law* (Indianapolis: American Trust, 1982), 50–51.

BIBLIOGRAPHY

Abdelkader, Deina. "Modernity, the Principles of Public Welfare (*maṣlaḥa*) and the End Goals of Sharīʿa (*maqāṣid*) in Muslim Legal Thought." *Islam and Christian-Muslim Relations* 14, no. 2 (2003): 163–74.

ʿAbduh, Muhammad. "Laws Should Change in Accordance with the Conditions of Nations *and* the Theology of Unity." In Kurzman, *Modernist Islam*, 50–60.

——. *The Theology of Unity: Risālat al-Tauḥīd*. Translated and edited by Isḥāq Musaʿad and Kenneth Cragg. Kuala Lumpur: Islamic Book Trust, 2004.

Abou El Fadl, Khaled. "The Centrality of Sharīʿah to Government and Constitutionalism in Islam." In Grote and Röder, *Constitutionalism in Islamic Countries*, 35–61.

Abul-Magd, Zeinab. "The Military." In Hokayem, *Egypt after the Spring*, 53–74.

Agrama, Hussein Ali. *Questioning Secularism: Islam, Sovereignty, and the Rule of Law in Modern Egypt*. Chicago Studies in Practices of Meaning. Chicago: University of Chicago Press, 2012.

——. "Secularism, Sovereignty, Indeterminacy: Is Egypt a Secular or a Religious State?" *Comparative Studies in Society and History* 52, no. 3 (2010): 495–523. https://doi.org/10.1017/S0010417510000289.

Ahmed, Dawood I., and Tom Ginsburg. "Constitutional Islamization and Human Rights: The Surprising Origin and Spread of Islamic Supremacy in Constitutions." *Virginia Journal of International Law* 54, no. 3 (2013): 1–82; University of Chicago Public Law Working Paper No. 477.

Ahmed, Leila. *Women and Gender in Islam: Historical Roots of a Modern Debate*. New Haven, CT: Yale University Press, 1992.

Akzin, Benjamin. "Codification in a New State: A Case Study of Israel." *American Journal of Comparative Law* 5, no. 1 (Winter 1956): 44–77. http://www.jstor.org/stable/838139.

Ali, Omar. "June Forum Meeting: A Comparative Analysis of the 2012 & 2014 Egyptian Constitutions by Diana Serôdio." *Arab-West Report*, July 9, 2014.

Al-Ali, Zaid. "Egypt's Draft Constitution: An Analysis." *Open Democracy*, November 8, 2012.

——. "The New Egyptian Constitution: An Initial Assessment of Its Merits and Flaws." *Open Democracy*, December 26, 2012.

Alkan, Necati. *Dissent and Heterodoxy in the Late Ottoman Empire: Reformers, Babis and Bahai's*. Analecta Isisiani: Ottoman and Turkish Studies. Piscataway, NJ: Gorgias Press, 2009.

——. "Fighting for the Nuṣayrī Soul: State, Protestant Missionaries and the ʿAlawīs in the Late Ottoman Empire." *Die Welt des Islams* 52 (2012): 23–50. https://doi.org/10.1163/157006012X627896.

"Al-Majlis al-ʿala li-l-quwat al-musallaha marsum bi-qanun raqm 13 li-sanat 2012" [The Supreme Council of Armed Forces Decree no. 13 of the year 2012], *al-Jarida al-rasmiyya* 3, January 19, 2012.

"Al-Nass al-kamil li-mashruʿ qanun al-ahwal al-shakhsiyya li-l-aqbat 2016 wa-l-la'iha al-dakhiliyya li-l-majlis al-iklirki" [The complete text of the 2016 draft of the personal status law for Copts and the internal bylaws for the Clerical Council], edited by Faith Protectors Association-Rabitat Hamlat al-'Iman (Cairo, 2016), http://protectors-faith.com/?p=4532.

Amin, Galal. *Mihnat al-dunya wa-l-din fi misr* [The struggle between the world and religion in Egypt]. Cairo: dar al-shuruq, 2013.

An-Naʿim, Abdullahi Ahmed. *Islam and the Secular State: Negotiating the Future of Shariʿa.* Cambridge, MA: Harvard University Press, 2008.

Arendt, Hannah. *Between Past and Future: Six Exercises in Political Thought.* New York: Viking Press, 1961.

Arjomand, Saïd Amir. "Constitutions and the Struggle for Political Order: A Study in the Modernization of Political Traditions." *European Journal of Sociology* 33, no. 1 (1992): 39–82. https://www.jstor.org/stable/23999501.

——, eds. *The Rule of Law, Islam, and Constitutional Politics in Egypt and Iran.* Albany: State University of New York Press, 2013.

Armanios, Febe. *Coptic Christianity in Ottoman Egypt.* New York: Oxford University Press, 2011.

al-ʿAryan, ʿIssam. "Al-ʿAryan: al-barlaman huwa sahib al-tashriʿ wa-l-azhar haya mus-taqila" [Al-ʿAryan: Parliament is responsible for legislation and al-Azhar is an independent organization]. *YouTube,* February 10, 2013.

Asad, Talal. *Formations of the Secular: Christianity, Islam, Modernity.* Stanford, CA: Stanford University Press, 2003.

——. *Genealogies of Religion: Discipline and Reasons of Power in Christianity and Islam.* Baltimore: John Hopkins University Press, 1993.

——. "Thinking about Tradition, Religion, and Politics in Egypt Today." *Critical Inquiry* 42, no. 1 (Autumn 2015): 166–214. https://doi.org/0093-1896/15/4201-0007.

Atmaca, Nushin. "Article II in the Debate about Constitutional Amendments in 2007." In *The Sharia as the Main Source of Legislation? The Egyptian Debate on Article II of the Egyptian Constitution,* edited by Cornelis Hulsman, 179–206. Marburg: Tectum Verlag, 2012.

al-ʿAwwa, Muhammad Salim. *Al-Haqq fi al-taʿbir* [The right of expression]. Cairo: dar al-shuruq, 1998.

——. *Azmat al-muʾassasa al-diniyya* [The crisis of the religious establishment]. Cairo: dar al-shuruq, 2003.

——. *Fi al-nitham al-siyasi li-l-dawla al-islamiyya* [On the political system of the Islamic state]. Cairo: dar al-shuruq, 1989.

El-Awa, Mohamed S., *Punishment in Islamic Law.* Indianapolis: American Trust, 1982).

Ayoub, Samy. "The *Mecelle,* Sharia, and the Ottoman State: Fashioning and Refash-ioning of Islamic Law in the Nineteenth and Twentieth Centuries." *Journal of the Ottoman and Turkish Studies Association* 2, no. 1 (2015): 121–46.

al-Banna, Hasan. *Majmuʿat rasaʾil al-imam al-shahid Hasan al-Banna* [The collection of tracts of the martyr Imam Hasan al-Banna]. Alexandria: dar al-daʿwa li-l-tabiʿ wa-l-nashr wa-l-tawziʿ, 2002.

——. "Risalat al-mu'tamar al-khamis" [The Message of the 5th Conference]. In *Wiki-bidia al-ikhwan al-muslimin*, 1939. https://www.ikhwanwiki.com/index.php?title=%D8%B1%D8%B3%D8%A7%D9%84%D8%A9_%D8%A7%D9%84%D9%85%D8%A4%D8%AA%D9%85%D8%B1_%D8%A7%D9%84%D8%AE%D8%A7%D9%85%D8%B3.

——. *Six Tracts of Hasan Al-Bana': A Selection from the Majmū'at Rasā'il al-Imām al-Shahīd Hasan al-Bannā'* Accra, Ghana: Africaw, 2006.

Bano, Masooda. "At the Tipping Point? Al-Azhar's Growing Crisis of Moral Author-ity." *International Journal of Middle East Studies* 50, no. 4 (2018): 715–34. https://doi.org/10.1017/S0020743818000867.

Barkey, Karen. *Empire of Difference: The Ottomans in Comparative Perspective.* Cam-bridge: Cambridge University Press, 2008.

Berger, Maurits S. "Apostasy and Public Policy in Contemporary Egypt: An Evalua-tion of Recent Cases from Egypt's Highest Courts." *Human Rights Quarterly* 25 (2003): 720–40. https://www.jstor.org/stable/20069684.

——. "Public Policy and Islamic Law: The Modern *Dhimmī* in Contemporary Egyp-tian Family Law." *Islamic Law and Society* 8, no. 1 (2001): 88–136. https://www.jstor.org/stable/3399487.

——. "Secularizing Interreligious Law in Egypt." *Islamic Law and Society* 12, no. 3 (2005): 394–418. http://www.jstor.org/stable/3399407.

Berger, Peter. *The Sacred Canopy: Elements of a Sociological Theory of Religion.* New York: Doubleday, 1967.

Berkes, Niyazi. *The Development of Secularism in Turkey.* Montreal: McGill University Press, 1964.

Berkey, Jonathan P. "Madrasas Medieval and Modern: Politics, Education, and the Problem of Muslim Identity." In Hefner and Zaman, *Schooling Islam*, 40–60.

Bernard-Maugiron, Nathalie. "Divorce and Remarriage of Orthodox Copts in Egypt: The 2008 State Council Ruling and the Amendment of the 1938 Personal Status Regulations." *Islamic Law and Society* 18 (2011): 356–86. https://doi.org/10.1163/156851910X537829.

——. "Legal Reforms, the Rule of Law, and Consolidation of State Authoritarianism under Mubarak." In Arjomand and Brown, *Rule of Law, Islam, and Constitu-tional Politics*, 179–206.

Bibawi, Nabil Luqa. *'Adam dusturiyyat qanun al-ahwal al-shakhsiyya al-mutabbiq 'ala al-misihiyyin* [The personal status laws for Christians are unconstitutional]. Cairo: dar al-bibawi li-l-nashr, 2004.

Bier, Laura. *Revolutionary Womanhood: Feminisms, Modernity, and the State in Nasser's Egypt.* Stanford, CA: Stanford University Press, 2011.

al-Bishri, Tariq. *Al-Muslimun wa-l-aqbat fi itar al-jama'a al-wataniyya* [Muslims and Copts in the framework of national community]. Cairo: dar al-shuruq, 1988.

——. *Al-Wad' al-qanuni bayna al-shari'a al-islamiyya wa-l-qanun al-wad'i* [The legal foun-dation between the Islamic sharia and positive law]. Cairo: dar al-shuruq, 2005.

——. *Bayn al-jami'a al-diniyya wa-l-jami'a al-wataniyya fi al-fikr al-siyasi* [Between the religious community and the national community in political thought]. Cairo: dar al-shuruq, 1998.

Braude, Benjamin. "Foundation Myths of the *Millet* System." In Braude and Lewis, *Christians and Jews*, 1:69–88.

Braude, Benjamin, and Bernard Lewis, eds. *Christians and Jews in the Ottoman Empire: The Functioning of a Plural Society*. Vol. 1: *The Central Lands*. Vol. 2: *The Arabic-Speaking Lands*. New York: Holmes and Meier, 1982.

Brown, Nathan J. *Constitutions in a Nonconstitutional World: Arab Basic Laws and the Prospects for Accountable Government*. Albany: State University of New York Press, 2002.

——. "Islam in Egypt's Cacophonous Constitutional Order." In Arjomand and Brown, *Rule of Law, Islam, and Constitutional Politics*, 233–48.

——. "Post-Revolutionary Al-Azhar." In *The Carnegie Papers*, 1–24. Washington, DC: Carnegie Endowment for International Peace, September 2011.

——. *The Rule of Law in the Arab World: Courts in Egypt and the Gulf*. Cambridge Middle East Studies, 6. Cambridge: Cambridge University Press, 1997.

——. "The Transition: From Mubarak's Fall to the 2014 Presidential Election." In Hokayem, *Egypt after the Spring*, 15–32.

Brown, Nathan J., and Michele Dunne. "Egypt's Draft Constitution Rewards the Military and Judiciary." *Carnegie Endowment for International Peace*, December 4, 2013.

Brown, Nathan J., and Clark B. Lombardi. "Contesting Islamic Constitutionalism after the Arab Spring: Islam in Egypt's Post-Mubarak Constitutions." In Grote and Röder, *Constitutionalism, Human Rights and Islam*, 245–60.

Carter, B. L. *The Copts in Egyptian Politics*. London: Croom Helm, 1986.

Casper, Jayson. "Mirvat al-Tallāwī: Women's Rights in the Constitution." *Arab-West Report*, January 26, 2014.

——. "Safwat al-Bayādī: Negotiating Religion in the Constitutional Committee." *Arab-West Report*, December 27, 2013.

Cavanaugh, William T. *The Myth of Religious Violence: Secular Ideology and the Roots of Modern Conflict*. New York: Oxford University Press, 2009.

Charrad, Mounira M. *States and Women's Rights: The Making of Postcolonial Tunisia, Algeria, and Morocco*. Berkeley: University of California Press, 2001.

Childress, Sarah. "The Deep State: How Egypt's Shadow State Won Out." *PBS*, September 17, 2013.

Cilardo, Agostino. "Muhammad Qadri Pasha al-Hanafi." In *The Oxford International Encyclopedia of Legal History*, edited by Stanley N. Katz, 195–96. Oxford: Oxford University Press, 2009.

Clogg, Richard. "The Greek *Millet* in the Ottoman Empire." In Braude and Lewis, *Christians and Jews*, 1:185–207.

Cohen, Amnon. *Jewish Life under Islam: Jerusalem in the Sixteenth Century*. Cambridge, MA: Harvard University Press, 1984.

——. "On the Realities of the *Millet* System: Jerusalem in the Sixteenth Century." In Braude and Lewis, *Christians and Jews*, 2:8–18.

Cole, Juan. "Rashid Rida on the Baha'i Faith—a Utilitarian Theory of the Spread of Religions." *Arab Studies Quarterly* 5, no. 3 (Summer 1983): 276–91.

Court of Cassation, January 17, 1979, No. 26/16, Year 48.

Court of Cassation, June 19, 1963, No. 40, Year 29.

Court of Cassation, May 10, 1972, No. 18, Year 39.

Court of Cassation, May 27, 1964, No. 17, Year 32.

Crecelius, Daniel. "Nonideological Responses of the Egyptian Ulama to Modernization." In *Scholars, Saints, and Sufis: Muslim Religious Institutions since 1500*, edited by Nikki R. Keddie, 167–209. Berkeley: University of California Press, 1978.

Cuno, Kenneth M. "Disobedient Wives and Neglectful Husbands: Marital Relations in the First Phase of Family Law Reform in Egypt." In *Family, Gender, and Law in a Globalizing Middle East and South Asia*, edited by Kenneth M. Cuno and Manisha Desai, 3–28. Syracuse, NY: Syracuse University Press, 2009.

——. *Modernizing Marriage: Family, Ideology, and Law in Nineteenth- and Early Twentieth-Century Egypt*. Syracuse, NY: Syracuse University Press, 2015.

Davison, R. H. "Tanẓīmāt." In *The Encyclopaedia of Islam*, edited by P. Bearman, Th. Bianquis, C. E. Bosworth, E. van Donzel, and W. P. Heinrichs, 201–9. 2nd ed. Leiden: Brill, 2000.

Debs, Richard A. *Islamic Law and Civil Code: The Law of Property in Egypt*. New York: Columbia University Press, 2010.

Dodge, Bayard. *Al-Azhar: A Millenium of Muslim Learning*. Washington, DC: Middle East Institute, 1961.

Eccel, A. Chris. *Egypt, Islam and Social Change: Al-Azhar in Conflict and Accommodation*. Berlin: Klaus Schwarz Verlag, 1984.

Effendi, Shoghi. *God Passes By*. Haifa: The Bahá'í Reference Library, 1944.

"Egypt: New Constitution Mixed on Support of Rights." Human Rights Watch, November 30, 2012.

Elgawhary, Tarek A. "Restructuring Islamic Law: The Opinions of the *'Ulamā'* towards Codification of Personal Status Law in Egypt." PhD diss., Princeton University, 2014.

El-Gendi, Yosra. "Bishop Bola: Church Does Not Wish to Amend Article 3." *Arab-West Report*, September 29, 2013.

——. "What Do the Copts Want in the Constitution?" *Arab-West Report*, October 1, 2013.

El-Hennawy, Noha. "The Fourth Faith?" *Egypt Today*, September 2006.

El-Houdaiby, Ibrahim. "The Identity of Al-Azhar and Its Doctrine." *Jadaliyya*, July 29, 2012.

El-Leithy, Tamer. "Coptic Culture and Conversion in Medieval Cairo, 1293–1524 A.D." PhD diss., Princeton University, 2005.

Elsässer, Sebastian. *The Coptic Question in the Mubarak Era*. Oxford: Oxford University Press, 2014.

El-Shimy, Yasser. "The Muslim Brotherhood." In Hokayem, *Egypt after the Spring*, 75–103.

Emon, Anver M. *Religious Pluralism and Islamic Law: Dhimmīs and Others in the Empire of Law*. Oxford Islamic Legal Studies. Oxford: Oxford University Press, 2012.

——. "Shari'a and the Modern State." In *Islamic Law and International Human Rights Law*, edited by Anver M. Emon, Mark S. Ellis, and Benjamin Glahn, 52–81. Oxford: Oxford University Press, 2012.

Esposito, John L. *Women in Muslim Family Law*. Contemporary Issues in the Middle East. Syracuse, NY: Syracuse University Press, 1982.

Fadel, Mohammad. "Islamic Law Reform: Between Reinterpretation and Democracy." *Yearbook of Islamic and Middle Eastern Law*, edited by Martin Lau and Faris Nasrallah, 18, no. 1 (2013–15): 44–90.

——. "Judicial Institutions, the Legitimacy of Islamic State Law and Democratic Transition in Egypt: Can a Shift toward a Common Law Model of Adjudication Improve the Prospects of a Successful Democratic Transition?" *International Journal of Constitutional Law* 11, no. 3 (2013): 646–65. https://doi.org/10.1093/icon/mot022.

Fahmy, Khaled. *All the Pasha's Men: Mehmed Ali, His Army and the Making of Modern Egypt*. Cairo: American University in Cairo Press, 2002.

——. *In Quest of Justice: Islamic Law and Forensic Medicine in Modern Egypt*. Oakland: University of California Press, 2018.

Fahmy, Ziad. *Ordinary Egyptians: Creating the Modern Nation through Popular Culture*. Stanford, CA: Stanford University Press, 2011.

Faraj, Amani Abu al-Fadl. *Min kawalis al-dustur: sira' al-siyada al-wataniyya wa-l-irada al-dawliyya dakhil dustur misr* [From the scenes of the constitution: The struggle between national sovereignty and the international will inside Egypt's constitution]. Cairo: nahdat al-misr, 2013.

Fattal, Antoine. *Le statut légal des non-musulmans en pays d'Islam*. Vol. 10. Recherches publiées sous la direction de l'Institute de lettres orientales de Beyrouth. Beirut: Imprimerie Catholique, 1958.

"Fifteenth Annual Convention of *Bahá'ís* of Egypt." *Bahá'í News*, no. 134, March 1940.

Findley, C. V. "Medjelle." In *The Encyclopaedia of Islam*, edited by P. Bearman, Th. Bianquis, C. E. Bosworth, E. van Donzel, and W. P. Henrichs, 971–72. 2nd ed. Leiden: Brill, 1991.

Friedman, Yaron. "Ibn Taymiyya's Fatāwā against the Nuṣayrī-'Alawī Sect." *Der Islam: Journal of the History and Culture of the Middle East* 82, no. 2 (2005): 349–63.

"From Haifa News Letter." *Bahá'í News*, no. 151, February 1942.

Gerber, Haim. *State, Society, and Law in Islam: Ottoman Law in Comparative Perspective*. Albany: State University of New York Press, 1994.

Gesink, Indira Falk. *Islamic Reform and Conservatism: Al-Azhar and the Evolution of Modern Sunni Islam*. London: I. B. Tauris, 2009.

Ghandour, Zeina. "Religious Law in a Secular State: The Jurisdiction of the Sharī'a Courts of Palestine and Israel." *Arab Law Quarterly* 5, no. 1 (1990): 25–48. http://www.jstor.org/stable/3381561.

Ghazaleh, Pascale. "Heirs and Debtors: Blood Relatives, Qur'anic Heirs, and Business Associates in Cairo, 1800–50." In Hanna and Abbas, *Society and Economy in Egypt and the Eastern Mediterranean*, 143–58.

al-Ghazali, Muhammad. *Al-Islam al-muftara 'alayhi bayn al-shuyu'yyin wa-l-ra'smaliyyin* [Islam between its communist and capitalist enemies]. Cairo: nahdat misr, 2006.

——. *Al-Islam wa-l-awda' al-iqtisadiyya* [Islam and the economic conditions]. Cairo: dar al-kitab al-'arabi bi-misr, 1952.

——. *Min huna na'lam . . . !* [From here we learn]. Cairo: nahdat misr, 2006.

Ghazzālī [Ḥujjat al-Islām Abū Ḥāmid Muḥammad Ghazzālī Ṭūsī]. *Al-Ghazzali on Enjoining Good and Forbidding Wrong*. Translated by Muhammad Nur Abdus Salam. Chicago: Great Books of the Islamic World, 2002.

Göçek, Fatma Müge. "Toward a Theory of Westernization and Social Change: Eighteenth and Nineteenth Century Ottoman Society." PhD diss., Princeton University, 1988.

Goitein, S. D. *A Mediterranean Society: The Jewish Communities of the Arab World as Portrayed in the Documents of the Cairo Geniza*. Vol. 3, *The Family*. Berkeley: University of California Press, 1978.

Goode, William J. *World Revolution and Family Patterns*. London: Collier-Macmillan, 1963.

Grey, Thomas C. "The Constitution as Scripture." *Stanford Law Review* 37, no. 1 (November 1984): 1–25. http://www.jstor.org/stable/1228651.

Grote, Rainer, and Tilman J. Röder, eds. *Constitutionalism, Human Rights and Islam after the Arab Spring*. Oxford: Oxford University Press, 2016.

——, eds. *Constitutionalism in Islamic Countries: Between Upheaval and Continuity*. New York: Oxford University Press, 2012.

Guirguis, Magdi. *Al-Qada' al-qibti fi misr: dirasa ta'rikhiyya* [The Coptic judge in Egypt: A historical study]. Cairo: mirit, 1999.

——. "The Organization of the Coptic Community in the Ottoman Period." In Hanna and Abbas, *Society and Economy in Egypt and the Eastern Mediterranean*, 201–16.

Guirguis, Magdi, and Nelly van Doorn-Harder. *The Emergence of the Modern Coptic Papacy: The Egyptian Church and Its Leadership from the Ottoman Period to the Present*. Cairo: American University in Cairo Press, 2011.

Habashi, Fadi. "Christians Claim Equality between Men and Women concerning Inheritance." *Arab-West Report (al-Fajr)*, April 10, 2006.

Habib, Rafiq. "Al-Azhar wa-l-ikhwan: al-sira'a al-muftarad 'ala al-marji'iyya" [Al-Azhar and the brotherhood: The struggle over the frame of reference]. *Tahawwulat al-dawla wa-l-mujtama'a ba'ad al-rabi'a al-'arabi* [Transformations of the state and society after the Arab Spring]. April 2013. https://rafikhabib.blogspot.com/2013/04/blog-post_28.html?m=0.

Hacker, Joseph R. "Jewish Autonomy in the Ottoman Empire: Its Scope and Limits; Jewish Courts from the Sixteenth to the Eighteenth Centuries." In Levy, *Jews of the Ottoman Empire*, 153–202.

Hallaq, Wael B. *The Impossible State: Islam, Politics, and Modernity's Moral Predicament*. New York: Columbia University Press, 2013.

——. "Juristic Authority vs. State Power: The Legal Crises of Modern Islam." *Journal of Law and Religion* 19, no. 2 (2003–4): 243–58. https://www.jstor.org/stable/3649176.

Halley, Janet, and Kerry Rittich. "Critical Directions in Comparative Family Law: Genealogies and Contemporary Studies of Family Law Exceptionalism." *American Journal of Comparative Law* 58, no. 4 (Fall 2010): 753–75. https://doi.org/10.5131/ajcl.2010.0001.

Hanafi, Sari, and Tomeh, Azzam. "Gender Equality in the Inheritance Debate in Tunisia and the Formation of Non-Authoritarian Reasoning." *Journal of Islamic Ethics* 3, no. 1–2 (2019): 207–32. https://doi.org/10.1163/24685542-12340026.

Hanley, Will. *Identifying with Nationality: Europeans, Ottomans, and Egyptians in Alexandria*. New York: Columbia University Press, 2017.

Hanna, Fathi Ragheb. "Ahkam wa qawa'id al-mawarith wa-l-wasiya wafqan li-ahkam al-shari'a al-misihiyya wa ahkam al-shari'a al-islamiyya" [Rules and regulations of inheritance and testamentary disposition according to the rules of the Christian sharia and the Islamic sharia]. Bishop of Central Cairo Churches, 2015.

Hanna, Michael Wahid. "Egypt's Non-Islamist Parties." In Hokayem, *Egypt after the Spring*, 105–30.

Hanna, Nelly, and Raouf Abbas, eds. *Society and Economy in Egypt and the Eastern Mediterranean 1600–1900: Essays in Honor of André Raymond*. Cairo: American University in Cairo Press, 2005.

al-Haqq, Jadd al-Haqq 'Ali Jadd. "Zawaj al-baha'i min al-muslima batil" [The marriage of a Baha'i and a Muslim woman is invalid]. *al-Fatawa al-islamiyya min dar al-ifta' al-misriyya* 8, no. 23 (1982): 2999–3002.

Hasan, S. S. *Christians versus Muslims in Modern Egypt: The Century-Long Struggle for Coptic Equality*. New York: Oxford University Press, 2003.

Hatem, Mervat F. "The Pitfalls of the Nationalist Discourses on Citizenship." In *Gender and Citizenship in the Middle East*, edited by Suad Joseph, 33–57. Contemporary Issues in the Middle East. Syracuse, NY: Syracuse University Press, 2000.

Hefner, Robert, and Muhammad Qasim Zaman, eds. *Schooling Islam: The Culture and Politics of Modern Muslim Education*. Princeton, NJ: Princeton University Press, 2007.

Hefny, Assem. "Religious Authorities and Constitutional Reform: The Case of al-Azhar in Egypt." In Grote and Röder, *Constitutionalism, Human Rights and Islam*, 89–122.

Heo, Angie. *The Political Lives of Saints: Christian-Muslim Mediation in Egypt*. Oakland: University of California Press, 2018.

"Hilary Clinton Email Archive." WikiLeaks, 2012.

"Hizb al-hurriya wa-l-'adala: Hadha al-barnamij" [Freedom and Justice Party: This program]. November 2011.

Hokayem, Emile, ed. *Egypt after the Spring: Revolt and Reaction*. With Hebatalla Taha. London: Routledge for the International Institute for Strategic Studies, 2006.

Hourani, A. H. *Minorities in the Arab World*. London: Oxford University Press, 1947.

Al-Hudaibi, Muhammad M. *The Principles of Politics in Islam*. Cairo: Islamic Inc., 2000.

Hughes, Aaron W. *Abrahamic Religions: On the Uses and Abuses of History*. New York: Oxford University Press, 2012.

Hulsman, Cornelis, and Diana Serôdio. "Interview with Human Rights Lawyer Mona Zulficar about the Constitution." *Arab-West Report*, August 5, 2014.

Hurd, Elizabeth Shakman. *The Politics of Secularism in International Relations*. Princeton Studies in International History and Politics. Princeton, NJ: Princeton University Press, 2008.

Hussin, Iza R. *The Politics of Islamic Law: Local Elites, Colonial Authority, and the Making of the Muslim State*. Chicago: University of Chicago Press, 2016.

Ibn Taymiyyah, Taqi ad-Din. *Ibn Taymiyya Expounds on Islam: Selected Writings of Shaykh al-Islam Taqi ad-Din Ibn Taymiyyah on Islamic Faith, Life, and Society*. Translated by Muhammad Abdul-Haqq Ansari. Riyadh: Imam Muhammad Ibn Saud University, 2000.

——. *The Political Shariyah on Reforming the Ruler and the Ruled*. N.p.: dar ul fiqh, 2000.

Ibrahim, Ishak. "Personal Affairs Law for Christians: The Responsibility of the Church, the State, and Individuals." *Eshhad*, October 6, 2015.

'Imara, Muhammad. *Samahat al-Islam* [The tolerance of Islam]. Cairo: al-falah, 2002.

Iqtidar, Humeira. "State Management of Religion in Pakistan and Dilemmas of Citizenship." *Citizenship Studies* 16, no. 8 (2012): 1013–28. https://doi.org/10.1080/13621025.2012.735026.

Jackson, Sherman A. *Islamic Law and the State: The Constitutional Jurisprudence of Shihāb al-Dīn al-Qarāfī*. Leiden: Brill, 1996.

——. "The Islamic Secular." *American Journal of Islamic Social Sciences* 34, no. 2 (2017): 1–38.

Jennings, Ronald C. "Zimmis (Non-Muslims) in Early 17th Century Ottoman Judicial Records: The Sharia Court of Anatolian Kayseri." *Journal of the Economic and Social History of the Orient* 21, no. 3 (October 1978): 225–93.

Johansen, Baber. *Contingency in a Sacred Law: Legal and Ethical Norms in the Muslim Fiqh*. Leiden: Brill, 1999.

Jones-Pauly, Christina, and Abir Dajani Tuqan. *Women under Islam: Gender, Justice and the Politics of Islamic Law*. London: I. B. Tauris, 2011.

Kamal, Hala. "Inserting Women's Rights in the Egyptian Constitution: Personal Reflections." *Journal for Cultural Research* 19, no. 2 (2015): 150–61.

Kamal, Karima. *Al-Ahwal al-shakhsiyya li-l-aqbat* [Coptic personal status law]. Cairo: dar nahdat misr, 2012.

——. *Talaq al-aqbat* [Divorce of the Copts]. Cairo: dar al-mirit, 2006.

Karpat, Kemal H. "*Millets* and Nationality: The Roots of the Incongruity of Nation and State in the Post-Ottoman Era." In Braude and Lewis, *Christians and Jews*, 1:141–70.

Kerr, Malcolm H. *Islamic Reform: The Political and Legal Theories of Muḥammad 'Abduh and Rashīd Riḍā*. Berkeley: University of California Press, 1966.

Khadduri, Majid. "Maslaha." *Encyclopaedia of Islam*, edited by P. Bearman, Th. Bianquis, C. E. Bosworth, E. van Donzel, and W. P. Henrichs, 738–40. 2nd ed. Leiden: Brill, 1991.

Kirkpatrick, David. *Into the Hands of the Soldiers: Freedom and Chaos in Egypt and the Middle East*. New York: Penguin, 2018.

Krygier, Martin. "Rule of Law." In Rosenfeld and Sajó, *Oxford Handbook of Comparative Constitutional Law*, 233–49.

Kuru, Ahmet T. *Islam, Authoritarianism, and Underdevelopment: A Global and Historical Comparison*. Cambridge: Cambridge University Press, 2019.

Kurzman, Charles, ed. *Modernist Islam, 1840–1940: A Sourcebook*. New York: Oxford University Press, 2002.

Landau, Jacob M. *Jews in Nineteenth-Century Egypt*. New York: New York University Press, 1969.

Lane, E. W. *Manners and Customs of the Modern Egyptians*. New York: Cosimo, 2005.

Layish, Aharon. "Islamic Law in the Modern World: Nationalization, Islamization, Reinstatement." *Islamic Law and Society* 21 (2014): 276–307. https://doi.org/10.1163/15685195-00213PO4.

Lerner, Hanna. *Making Constitutions in Deeply Divided Societies*. Cambridge: Cambridge University Press, 2011.

Levy, Avigdor. Introduction to Levy, *Jews of the Ottoman Empire*, 1–123.

——, ed. *The Jews of the Ottoman Empire*. Princeton, NJ: Darwin Press, 1994.

——. "*Millet* Politics: The Appointment of a Chief Rabbi in 1835." In Levy, *Jews of the Ottoman Empire*, 425–38.

Lewis, Bernard. *The Jews of Islam*. Princeton, NJ: Princeton University Press, 1984.

Lloyd, David, and Paul Thomas. *Culture and the State*. New York: Routledge, 1998.

Locke, John. *Two Treatises of Government and a Letter concerning Toleration*. Edited by Ian Shapiro. New Haven, CT: Yale University Press, 2003.

Lombardi, Clark B. *State Law as Islamic Law in Modern Egypt: The Incorporation of the Shari'a into Egyptian Constitutional Law*. Studies in Islamic Law and Society. Leiden: Brill, 2006.

Longo, Pietro. *Theory and Practice in Islamic Constitutionalism: From Classical* Fiqh *to Modern Systems*. The Modern Muslim World, 5. Piscataway, NJ: Gorgias Press, 2019.

MacKinnon, Catharine A. "Gender in Constitutions." In Rosenfeld and Sajó, *Oxford Handbook of Comparative Constitutional Law*, 397–416.

Mahmood, Saba. *Religious Difference in a Secular Age: A Minority Report*. Princeton, NJ: Princeton University Press, 2015.

——. "Religious Freedom, the Minority Question, and Geopolitics in the Middle East." *Comparative Studies in Society and History* 54, no. 2 (2012): 418–46. https://doi.org/10.1017/S0010417512000096.

Majdi, Peter, and Marina Milad. "Interview with Dr. Rev. Andre Zaki." *Arab-West Report*, May 21, 2016.

Mansour, 'Adly. "'Ilan dusturi" [Constitutional Declaration]. *al-Jarida al-rasmiyya*, 27, July 8, 2013.

March, Andrew. "What Can the Islamic Past Teach Us about Secular Modernity?" *Political Theory* 43, no. 6 (2015): 838–49. https://www.jstor.org/stable/24571698.

Marcos, Samir. *Al-Akhar . . . al-hiwar . . . al-muwatana* [The other . . . dialogue . . . citizenship]. Cairo: maktabat al-shuruq al-dawliyya, 2005.

Marcos, Samir, and Vivian Fouad. "Our Experience Dialogue Based on Citizenship." In *Al-Akhar . . . al-hiwar . . . al-muwatana* [The other . . . dialogue . . . citizenship], by Samir Marcos, 150–202Cairo: maktabat al-shuruq al-dawliyya, 2005.

Marsot, Afaf Lutfi Al-Sayyid. *A Short History of Modern Egypt*. Cambridge: Cambridge University Press, 1994.

Masters, Bruce. *Christians and Jews in the Ottoman Arab World: The Roots of Sectarianism*. Cambridge Studies in Islamic Civilization. Cambridge: Cambridge University Press, 2001.

Masuzawa, Tomoko. "Culture." In *Critical Terms for Religious Studies*, edited by Mark C. Taylor, 70–93. Chicago: University of Chicago Press, 1998.

Al-Māwardī. *The Ordinances of Government [Al-Aḥkām al-Sulṭāniyya w'al-Wilāyāt al-Dīniyya]*. Translated by Wafaa H. Wahba. Great Books of Islamic Civilization. London: Garnet, 1996.

McCallum, Fiona. "The Coptic Orthodox Church." In *Eastern Christianity and Politics in the Twentieth Century*, ed. Lucian N. Leustean, 521–41. London, New York: Routledge, 2014.

McLarney, Ellen Anne. *Soft Force: Women in Egypt's Islamic Awakening*. Princeton Studies in Muslim Politics. Princeton, NJ: Princeton University Press, 2015.

——. "Women's Rights in the Egyptian Constitution: (Neo)Liberalism's Family Values." *Jadaliyya*, May 22, 2013.

"Messages from the Guardian." *Bahá'í News*, no. 160, February 1943.

Messick, Brinkley. *The Calligraphic State: Textual Domination and History in a Muslim Society*. Berkeley: University of California Press, 1993.

Mikha'il, Milak Tamir. *Al-Qada' al-milli wa-l-ahwal al-shakhsiyya 'ind al-aqbat al-misriyyin* [The milli judge and personal status law for Coptic Egyptians]. Giza: dar fikra li-l-nashr wa-l-tawzi'a, 2019.

al-Misri, Ahmad ibn Naqib. *Reliance of the Traveller (Umdat al-Salik): A Classic Manual of Islamic Sacred Law*. Beltsville, MD: Amana, 1994.

Mitchell, Timothy. *Colonizing Egypt*. Berkeley: University of California Press, 1991.

Moreh, Shmuel. "Al-Jabarti's Attitude towards the 'Ulama' of His Time." In *Guardians of Faith in Modern Times: 'Ulama' in the Middle East*, edited by Meir Hatina, 47–63. Leiden: Brill, 2008.

Moustafa, Tamir. "Conflict and Cooperation between the State and Religious Institutions in Contemporary Egypt." *International Journal of Middle East Studies* 32, no. 1 (2000): 3–22. https://www.jstor.org/stable/259533.

——. *Constituting Religion: Islam, Liberal Rights, and the Malaysian State*. Cambridge Studies in Law and Society. Cambridge: Cambridge University Press, 2018.

——. "Does Egypt Need a New Constitution?" *Foreign Policy*, February 10, 2011.

——. *The Struggle for Constitutional Power: Law, Politics and Economic Development in Egypt*. New York: Cambridge University Press, 2007.

Mursi, Mohammed. "Dr. Morsi's Electoral Program—General Features of Nahda (Renaissance Project)." *Ikhwan Web*, April 28, 2012.

"Musawwada 'ilan al-mabadi' al-'asasiyya li-dustur al-dawla al-misriyya al-haditha" [Draft of the declaration of fundamental principles for the constitution of the modern Egyptian state]. November 1, 2011.

Muslim Brotherhood. "Barnamij al-hizb" [Party program]. Cairo, 2007.

Nasir, Jamal J. *The Islamic Law of Personal Status*. The Hague: Kluwer Law International, 2002.

"News of Other Lands—Egypt." *Bahá'í News*, no. 173, February 1945.

"News of Other Lands—Egypt." *Bahá'í News*, no. 175, June 1945.

"News of Other Lands—Egypt." *Bahá'í News*, no. 178, December 1945.

"News of Other Lands—Egypt." *Bahá'í News*, no. 181, March 1946.

"Nusus la'ihat al-ahwal al-shakhsiyya al-sadira 'an al-majlis al-milli al-'amm li-l-aqbat al-urthuduks" [The texts of the bylaws of the personal status law issued by the Coptic Orthodox communal council]. In *Talaq al-aqbat* [Divorce of the Copts], edited by Karima Kamal, 207–62. Cairo: dar al-mirit, 2006.

Orgad, Liav. "The Preamble in Constitutional Interpretation." *International Journal of Constitutional Law* 8, no. 4 (2010): 714–38. https://doi.org/10.1093/icon/mor010.

Osman, Ahmed Zaki. "The Baha'i Case as an Ordeal of Citizenship and Freedom of Belief in Egypt." *Cairo Institute for Human Rights Studies*, January 16, 2007.

"The Ottoman Constitution." 1876.

Özbudun, Ergun. *The Constitutional System of Turkey: 1876 to the Present*. New York: Palgrave Macmillan, 2011.

Pantazopoulos, N. J. *Church and Law in the Balkan Peninsula during the Ottoman Rule*. Vol. 92. Thessaloniki: Institute for Balkan Studies, 1967.

"Persecutions in Egypt." *Bahá'í News*, no. 104, December 1936.

Peters, Rudolph. "Islamic and Secular Criminal Law in Nineteenth Century Egypt: The Role and Function of the Qadi." *Islamic Law and Society* 4, no. 1 (1997): 70–90.

Pierce, Leslie. *Morality Tales: Law and Gender in the Ottoman Court of Aintab.* Berkeley: University of California Press, 2003.

Pink, Johanna. "A Post-Qur'ānic Religion between Apostasy and Public Order: Egyptian Muftis and Courts on the Legal Status of the Bahā'ī Faith." *Islamic Law and Society* 10, no. 3 (2003): 409–34. http://www.jstor.org/stable/3399425.

Preuss, Ulrich K. "Constitutional Powermaking for the New Polity: Some Deliberations on the Relations between Constituent Power and the Constitution." In Rosenfeld, *Constitutionalism, Identity, Difference, and Legitimacy,* 143–64.

"Qanun raqm 1 li-sanat 2000 bi-isdar qanun tanthim ba'd awda' wa ijra'at al-taqadi fi masa'il al-ahwal al-shakhsiyya" [Law no 1 of the Year 2000 promulgating the organization of the conventions and procedures for the litigation of matters of personal status]. https://egypt.gov.eg/arabic/laws/personal/introduction.aspx, accessed June 16, 2020.

"Qanun raqm 103 li-sanat 1961 bi-sha'n i'adat tanthim al-Azhar wa-l-hay'at allati yas-hmilha" [Law no. 103 of year 1961 on the issue of the reorganization of al-Azhar and the institutions that are included with it]. *al-Jarida al-rasmiyya* 153 (July 10, 1961).

al-Qaradawi, Yusuf. *Min fiqh al-dawla fi al-Islam* [On the jurisprudence of the state in Islam]. Cairo: dar al-shuruq, 1997.

al-Qattan, Najwa. "*Dhimmis* in the Muslim Court: Documenting Justice in Ottoman Damascus, 1775–1860." PhD diss., Harvard University, 1996.

"Qirar ra'is majlis al-wuzara' raqm 501 li-sanat 2013" [Decision of the prime minister no. 501 of 2013]. *Al-Jarida al-rasmiyya* 21, May 23, 2013.

Quraishi, Asifa. "The Separation of Powers in the Tradition of Muslim Governments." In Grote and Röder, *Constitutionalism in Islamic Countries,* 63–73.

al-Qusi, Muhammad 'Abd al-Fadil. *Ru'iyya islamiyya fi qadaya al-'asr* [An Islamic perspective on the issues of the time]. Cairo: dar al-Islam, 2012.

Qutb, Sayyid. *Fi zilal al-Qur'an* [In the shade of the Qur'an]. 6 volumes. Beirut: dar al-shuruq, 2001.

——. *Hadha al-din.* Kuwait: maktabat al-faysal, 1989.

"Rescript of Reform—Islahat Fermani." Istanbul: Boğaziçi University, Atatürk Institute of Modern Turkish History, 1856.

Rida, Muhammad Rashid. "Renewal, Renewing, and Renewers." In Kurzman, *Modernist Islam,* 77–85.

Rosen, Lawrence. *The Anthropology of Justice: Law and Culture in Islamic Society.* Cambridge: Cambridge University Press, 1989.

——. *The Justice of Islam: Comparative Perspectives on Islamic Law and Society.* Oxford: Oxford University Press, 2000.

Rosenfeld, Michel, ed. *Constitutionalism, Identity, Difference, and Legitimacy: Theoretical Perspectives.* Durham, NC: Duke University Press, 1995.

——. "Modern Constitutionalism as Interplay between Identity and Diversity." In Rosenfeld, *Constitutionalism, Identity, Difference, and Legitimacy,* 3–35.

Rosenfeld, Michel, and András Sajó. *The Oxford Handbook of Comparative Constitutional Law.* Oxford: Oxford University Press, 2013.

Rowe, Paul S. "Christian-Muslim Relations in Egypt in the Wake of the Arab Spring." *Digest of Middle East Studies* 22, no. 2 (Fall 2013): 262–75. https://doi.org/10.1111/dome.12034.

——. "Church-State Relations in the 'New Egypt.'" In *Decentering Discussions on Religion and State: Emerging Narratives, Challenging Perspectives*, edited by Sargon George Donabed and Autumn Quezada-Grant, 213–29. Lanham, MD: Lexington Books, 2015.

——. "Neo-Millet Systems and Transnational Religious Movements: The *Humayun* Decrees and Church Construction in Egypt." *Journal of Church and State* 49, no. 2 (2007): 329–50. http://www.jstor.org/stable/23922410.

Rutherford, Bruce K. *Egypt after Mubarak: Liberalism, Islam, and Democracy in the Arab World*. Princeton Studies in Muslim Politics. Princeton, NJ: Princeton University Press, 2008.

——. "Surviving under Rule by Law: Explaining Ideological Change in Egypt's Muslim Brotherhood during the Mubarak Era." In Arjomand and Brown, *Rule of Law, Islam, and Constitutional Politics*, 249–78.

Saad, Ragab, and Moataz El Fegiery. "Citizenship in Post-Awakening Egypt: Power Shifts and Conflicting Perceptions," 1–15. "Democracy and Citizenship in North Africa after the Arab Awakening: Challenges for EU and US Foreign Policy." Euspring, January 2014.

Safran, Nadav. "The Abolition of Shar'i Courts in Egypt." *Muslim World* 48 (1958): 20–28.

Salvatore, Armando. "After the State: Islamic Reform and the 'Implosion' of *shari'a*." In *Muslim Traditions and Modern Techniques of Power*, Yearbook of the Sociology of Islam, edited by Armando Salvatore, 123–40. Münster: Lit Verlag, 2001.

Samir, Khalil. "Al-Ṣafī Ibn Al-'Assāl." In *The Coptic Encyclopedia*, edited by Aziz S. Atiya, 2075–79. New York: Macmillan, 1991.

Al-Sayyid, Mustafa Kamel. "Rule of Law, Ideology, and Human Rights in Egyptian Courts." In Arjomand and Brown, *Rule of Law, Islam, and Constitutional Politics*, 211–32.

Scott, James C. *Seeing Like a State: How Certain Schemes to Improve the Human Condition Have Failed*. New Haven, CT: Yale University Press, 1998.

Scott, John. "Judicial Reform in Egypt." *Journal of the Society of Comparative Legislation* 1, no. 2 (July 1899): 240–52. http://www.jstor.org/stable/752198.

Scott, Rachel M. "Islamic law, Unitary State law, and Communal Law: Divorce and Remarriage in Egypt's Coptic Community," *Exchange: Journal of Contemporary Christianity in Context* 4, no. 4 (2020), 215–236.

——. "Copts and the Millet Partnership: The Intra-Communal Dynamics behind Egyptian Sectarianism." *Journal of Law and Religion* 29, no. 3 (2014): 491–509. https://doi.org/10.1017/jlr.2014.26.

——. "Copts and the Power over Personal Status." *Jadaliyya*, December 3, 2012.

"Separating Law and Politics Challenges to the Independence of Judges and Prosecutors in Egypt." International Bar Association Human Rights Institute (IBAHRI), February 2014.

Sfeir, George N. "The Abolition of Confessional Jurisdiction in Egypt: The Non-Muslim Courts." *Middle East Journal* 10, no. 3 (Summer 1956): 248–56. http://www.jstor.org/stable/4322823.

Shaham, Ron. "Jews and the Sharīʿa Courts in Modern Egypt." *Studia Islamica* 82 (1995): 113–36.

——. "Shopping for Legal Forums: Christians and Family Law in Modern Egypt." In *Dispensing Justice in Islam: Qadis and Their Judgments*, edited by Muhammad Khalid Masud, Rudolph Peters, and David S. Powers, 451–69. Studies in Islamic Law and Society. Leiden: Brill, 2005.

Shenouda, H. H. Pope, III. *The Heresy of Jehovah's Witnesses*. Baramous: Monastery Press, 1997.

Sherif, Adel Omar. "Commentary: Shariʿa as Rule of Law." In *Islamic Law and International Human Rights Law*, edited by Anver M. Emon, Mark S. Ellis, and Benjamin Glahn, 115–20. Oxford: Oxford University Press, 2012.

——. "The Relationship between the Constitution and the Sharīʿah in Egypt." In Grote and Röder, *Constitutionalism in Islamic Countries*, 121–33.

Shiloh, Isaac S. "Marriage and Divorce in Israel." *Israel Law Review* 5, no. 4 (October 1970): 479–98.

Shmuelevitz, Aryeh. *The Jews of the Ottoman Empire in the Late Fifteenth and the Sixteenth Centuries: Administrative, Economic, Legal and Social Relations as Reflected in the Responsa*. Leiden: Brill, 1984.

Sidhom Youssef. "Secure Coptic Woman's Fair Share of Inheritance." *Coptic Solidarity*, January 15, 2017.

Skovgaard-Petersen, Jakob. *Defining Islam for the Egyptian State: Muftis and Fatwas of the Dār al-Iftā*. Leiden: Brill, 1997.

Sonneveld, Nadia. "Introduction: *Shariʿa* in Revolution? A Comparative Overview of Pre- and Post-Revolutionary Developments in *Shariʿa*-Based Family Law Legislation in Egypt, Indonesia, Iran, and Tunisia." *New Middle Eastern Studies* 5 (2015): 1–11. http://www.brismes.ac.uk/nmes/archives/1407.

Starrett, Gregory. "The Varieties of Secular Experience." *Comparative Studies in Society and History* 52, no. 3 (2010): 626–51. https://doi.org/10.1017/S00 10417510000332.

Stilt, Kristen. "The End of 'One Hand': The Egyptian Constitutional Declaration and the Rift between the 'People' and the Supreme Council of Armed Forces." *Yearbook of Islamic and Middle Eastern Law* 16 (2010–11): 43–52.

Strauss, Peter L., ed. *The Fetha Nagast: The Law of Kings*. Translated by Abba Paulos Tzadua. Durham, NC: Carolina Academic Press, 2009.

Sullivan, Winnifred Fallers. *The Impossibility of Religious Freedom*. Princeton, NJ: Princeton University Press, 2005.

Sultany, Nimer. *Law and Revolution: Legitimacy and Constitutionalism after the Arab Spring*. Oxford Constitutional Theory. Oxford: Oxford University Press, 2017.

Supreme Administrative Court, December 16, 2006, No. 16834/18971, Year 52.

Supreme Constitutional Court, June 3, 2000, No. 151, Year 50.

Tadros, Mariz. *Copts at the Crossroads: The Challenges of Building Inclusive Democracy in Contemporary Egypt*. Cairo: American University in Cairo Press, 2013.

——. "Vicissitudes in the Entente between the Coptic Orthodox Church and the State in Egypt (1952–2007)." *International Journal of Middle East Studies* 41 (2009): 269–87. https://doi.org/10.1017/S0020743809090667.

al-Tayyib, Ahmed. "Wathiqat al-Azhar bi-sha'n mustaqbal misr" [The document of al-Azhar on the future of Egypt]. June 6, 2011.

Al-Tikriti, Nabil. "Ibn-i Kemal's Confessionalism and the Construction of an Otto-man Islam." In *Living in the Ottoman Realm: Empire and Identity, 13th to 20th Centuries*, edited by Christine Isom-Verhaaren and Kent. F. Schull, 95–107. Bloomington: Indiana University Press, 2016.

Toft, Monica Duffy, Daniel Philpott, and Timothy Samuel Shah, *God's Century: Resurgent Religion and Global Politics*. New York: W. W. Norton, 2011.

Tucker, Judith E. *Women, Family, and Gender in Islamic Law*. Themes in Islamic Law, 3. Cambridge: Cambridge University Press, 2008.

——. *Women in Nineteenth-Century Egypt*. Cambridge Middle East Library. Cambridge: Cambridge University Press, 1985.

Ubicini, M. A. *Letters on Turkey: An Account of the Religious, Political, Social, and Commercial Condition of the Ottoman Empire*. Translated by Lady Easthope. 2 vols. New York: Arno Press, 1973.

"'We Do Unreasonable Things Here': Torture and National Security in Al-Sisi's Egypt." Human Rights Watch, September 5, 2017.

Weitz, Lev E. *Between Christ and Caliph: Law, Marriage, and Christian Community in Early Islam*. Philadelphia: University of Pennsylvania Press, 2018.

Wickham, Carrie Rosefsky. *The Muslim Brotherhood: Evolution of an Islamist Movement*. Princeton, NJ: Princeton University Press, 2013.

Williams, Raymond. *Culture and Society, 1780–1850*. New York: Columbia University Press, 1983.

Witte, John, Jr. *From Sacrament to Contract: Marriage, Religion, and Law in the Western Tradition*. Louisville, KY: Westminster John Knox Press, 2012.

Wood, Graeme. "What ISIS Really Wants." *Atlantic*, March 2015.

Wood, Leonard. *Islamic Legal Revival: Reception of European Law and Transformations in Islamic Legal Thought in Egypt, 1875–1952*. Oxford: Oxford University Press, 2016.

Wood, Simon A. *Christian Criticisms, Islamic Proofs: Rashid Rida's Modernist Defense of Islam*. Oxford: Oneworld, 2012.

Zaman, Muhammad Qasim. *Modern Islamic Thought in a Radical Age: Religious Authority and Internal Criticism*. New York: Cambridge University Press, 2012.

——. *Religion and Politics under the Early ʿAbbāsids: The Emergence of the Proto-Sunnī Elite*. Leiden, Brill, 1997.

——. *The Ulama in Contemporary Islam: Custodians of Change*. Princeton Studies in Muslim Politics. Princeton, NJ: Princeton University Press, 2002.

Zeghal, Malika. "Competing Ways of Life: Islamism, Secularism, and Public Order in the Tunisian Transition." *Constellations* 20, no. 2 (2013): 254–74. https://doi.org/10.1111/cons.12038.

——. "The 'Recentering' of Religious Knowledge and Discourse: The Case of al-Azhar in Twentieth-Century Egypt." In Hefner and Zaman, *Schooling Islam*, 107–30.

——. "Religion and Politics in Egypt: The Ulema of Al-Azhar, Radical Islam, and the State (1952–94)." *International Journal of Middle East Studies* 31, no. 3 (1999): 371–99. http://links.jstor.org/sici?sici=0020-7438%281999908%2931%3A3%3C371%3ARAPIET%3E2.0.CO%3B2-T.

Zubaida, Sami. *Law and Power in the Islamic World*. London: I. B. Tauris, 2005.

INDEX

Names and terms beginning with "al-" or "el-" are indexed under the first major section; thus Yasser El-Shimy will be found in the S's.